The RoutledgeFalmer Reader in Language and Literacy

D0796698

In this essential collection of readings, Teresa Grainger provides carefully chosen journal articles and chapters that offer significant and serious insights into the changing face of literacy. The twenty-five contributors all adopt a broad conception of literacy and contemporary literacy practices and recognise that the world of language and literacy is in a constant state of transition and transformation.

Together, the chosen contributors examine the past, the present and the future of literacy and celebrate the interests and expertise of the learners. They acknowledge that the textual environments of today are complex and fluid, shaped by the rapid emergence of new technologies and the influential nature of popular culture. Children's engagement with multiple forms of text is also highlighted, including the oral, the visual, the electronic and the written. In addition, issues of pedagogy are explored, through the voices of teachers, parents and children. Many chapters offer particular perspectives based on classroom experience, reflection and research.

The contributors here perceive a common and urgent need to acknowledge the diverse forms of living literacy and to redesign the curriculum accordingly. With an inspiring introduction and postscript by the editor, this Reader will be an invaluable and accessible companion for all students of literacy.

Teresa Grainger is immediate past president of the United Kingdom Reading Association, editor of the journal *Reading Literacy and Language*, and is a Reader in Education at Canterbury Christ Church University College.

Readers in Education

The RoutledgeFalmer Reader in Higher Education
Edited by Malcolm Tight

The RoutledgeFalmer Reader in Inclusion
Edited by Keith Topping and Sheelagh Maloney

The RoutledgeFalmer Reader in Language and Literacy
Edited by Teresa Grainger

The RoutledgeFalmer Reader in Multicultural Education
Edited by David Gillborn and Gloria Ladson-Billings

The RoutledgeFalmer Reader in Psychology of Education
Edited by Harry Daniels and Anne Edwards

The RoutledgeFalmer Reader in Science Education
Edited by John Gilbert

The RoutledgeFalmer Reader in Sociology of Education
Edited by Stephen J. Ball

The RoutledgeFalmer Reader in Teaching and Learning
Edited by Ted Wragg

The RoutledgeFalmer Reader in Language and Literacy

Edited by
Teresa Grainger

RoutledgeFalmer
Taylor & Francis Group

LONDON AND NEW YORK

First published 2004 by RoutledgeFalmer
11 New Fetter Lane, London EC4P 4EE

Simultaneously published in the USA and Canada
by RoutledgeFalmer
29 West 35th Street, New York, NY 10001

RoutledgeFalmer is an imprint of the Taylor & Francis Group

© 2004 Teresa Grainger for editorial matter and selection

Typeset in Sabon by
Florence Production Ltd, Stoodleigh, Devon
Printed and bound in Great Britain by
TJ International, Padstow, Cornwall

British Library Cataloguing in Publication Data
A catalogue record for this book is available from
the British Library

Library of Congress Cataloging in Publication Data
A catalog record for this book has been requested

ISBN 0–415–32766–0 (hbk)
ISBN 0–415–32767–9 (pbk)

CONTENTS

ACKNOWLEDGEMENTS

Chapter 5, *Where are the Childhoods in Childhood Literacy? An Exploration in Outer (School) Space* by Anne Haas Dyson is reproduced from *Journal of Early Childhood Literacy* (2001), 1, 1 with kind permission of Sage Publications Ltd.

Chapter 6, *Learning as Puzzle Solving* by Peter Geekie, Brian Cambourne and Phil Fitzsimmons is reproduced from *Understanding Literacy Development* (1999) with the kind permission of Trentham Books Ltd.

Chapter 8, *Group Work: Learning Through Talk* by Roy Corden is reproduced from *Literacy and Learning Through Talk: Strategies for the Primary Classroom* (2002) with the kind permission of Open University Press.

Chapter 13, *Television and Film* by Jackie Marsh and Elaine Millard is reproduced from *Literacy and Popular Culture: Using Children's Culture in the Classroom* (2000) with the kind permission of Sage Publications Ltd.

Chapter 16, *The Reader in the Writer* by Myra Barrs is reproduced from *Reading Literacy and Language* (2000), 34, 2, with the kind permission of Blackwell Publishing.

All other chapters are reproduced with kind permission of Taylor & Francis Books Ltd.

INTRODUCTION

Travelling across the terrain

Teresa Grainger

The window looked strange in the dazzling air of the desert, giving on to the deep-shaded bush, a square of thick vegetation hanging in the air like a painting. The Gallivespians wanted to look at it, and were astounded to see how it was just not there from the back, and how it only sprang into being when you came round from the side.

'I'll have to close it when we're through' Will said.

Lyra tried to pinch the edges together, but her fingers couldn't find it at all; nor could the spies, despite the fineness of their hands. Only Will could feel exactly where the edges were, and he did it cleanly and quickly.

'How many worlds can you enter with the knife?' said Tialys.

'As many as there are out there' said Will. 'No one would ever have time to find out'.

(*The Amber Spyglass*, Pullman, 2000: 182)

In *The Amber Spyglass*, the last of Philip Pullman's trilogy, *His Dark Materials*, Lyra and Will travel through many worlds searching first for Roger and later for their beloved daemons. On their travels they meet old friends, like Iorek Byrnison, the armoured bear, and make new ones, such as the dragonfly Gallivespians and the mulefa, wheeled creatures with the power to see dust. These allies widen their vision, help them see the world more clearly and challenge their previous knowledge and understanding.

Similarly, in this book, the reader may become a traveller, traversing different domains as they search for meaning in the complex and challenging world of language and literacy. The research, conceptual understanding and scholarship of the expedition guides may affirm or extend the understanding of those who travel alongside. Much will depend upon the resources in the backpacks of the itinerant readers, their openness to new terrain, and their ability to develop a dialogue with the team. Philip Pullman himself reflects that a good way of working is to 'read like a butterfly and write like a bee'.

Let yourself be beguiled by a pretty shape or be blown sideways by a wayward breeze, and flit from book to book, subject to subject, idea to idea, place to place, picking up whatever nectar you can find.

(Pullman, 2002: 23)

I invite the interested reader to take flight as a butterfly, to be beguiled and settle wherever they will. In selecting articles for this RoutledgeFalmer Reader, I have flitted from book to book, from journal to journal and from theme to theme, re-reading avidly, regularly altering the eighteen permissible chapters, and restructuring sections in response to the emerging themes and my colleagues' views. This preparation for the expedition has been a fascinating challenge: choosing guides to lead others forward and to support the genuine enquiry of fellow travellers. I am acutely conscious of the absence of many talented explorers and of certain issues, but inevitably choices have had to be made. I believe, however, that all the guides present offer the earnest traveller significant and serious insights into the world of literacy in the early twenty-first century. Much of their work is based upon substantial research projects, encompassing a variety of research methods and spanning several years, other guides offer their particular perspective based upon experience, reflection and informed study. Many include the voices of young people, their teachers, parents and friends, and honour their views, reflecting the diversity and particularity of their lives and literacy practices.

All our guides recognise that we live in a world in which technological innovations are driving rapid social and economic change, and are aware of the attendant increase in forms of meaning making and communication. As Bearne and Kress observe in response to this reality 'our existing theories of literacy will not do' (2001: 93). Yet, despite the changing face of communication and the shifting nature and existence of multiple literacies, governments continue to profile narrow and prescribed curricula, accountability and control. These purportedly final vocabularies restrain both teachers and children alike and exert considerable pressure on the system. Teachers of language and literacy are buffeted on all sides, not only by the winds of change in literacy and communication, but also by directive education systems over which they feel they have little control. The guides in this book are all researching, working and writing in such directive systems, albeit in different countries and locales. So, in order for the travellers intent upon joining the expedition to recognise these pressures and understand their impact, the challenges of the current context are outlined prior to departure.

The pressure on the curriculum

Current curricula for literacy and the language arts are both prescriptive and comprehensive and in these circumstances, coverage can come to dominate teachers' concerns. This is particularly evident when high stakes assessment is intertwined with lengthy specifications such as the National Literacy Strategy (NLS) in the UK. In such a culture, with closely monitored and inspected teaching and the requirement to provide comprehensive plans to demonstrate coverage, it is almost inevitable that teachers will feel expected to deliver the curriculum and not take the time to develop it in interaction with their learners. Arguably, the pressure of time to achieve set targets and prepare for tests has resulted in a narrowing of learning experiences, so that emotional engagement, full participation, experiential and inquiry based learning as well as spontaneity and creativity have been pushed to the margin. Such practices may be viewed as optional extras and briefly attended to if there is time or even squeezed out altogether (Frater, 2000; Leavers, 2000). Concerns about the demise of creativity in the curriculum, for example, have been widely voiced (Puttnam, 1998; Craft, 2000; Sedgwick, 2001). As the Design Council (DfEE 1999a: 83) state: 'The more prescriptive the curriculum, the greater the need to be explicit about creativity and not leave it to chance'.

The core curriculum and, in particular, literacy and numeracy in the UK have been profiled at the expense of the arts and the humanities, and fragmented experiences in different subject domains are all too common. Another consequence of this prescription is that the gap between schooled literacy and the literacies of everyday life widens: many children are operating in a multi-modal textual environment in their homes and communities, yet their teachers are expected to operate in a print bound frame in school (Marsh and Thompson, 2001; Marsh, 2003). There is an evident tension between the relatively narrow curriculum and the ever widening range of textual forms which children encounter. The world of popular, media and consumer texts interest and involve children, influencing the texts they read and write and the activities they choose to engage in, moreover they influence their developing sense of self and identity. Despite the lack of recognition of these texts in the curriculum, the audiovisual texts of television, film, video and computer generated images are undoubtedly shaping what it means to be literate in the twenty-first century (Hilton, 1998; Kress and van Leeuwen, 1996). Some schools, however, have been confident enough to innovate and adapt their practice, drawing on the breadth of literacy practices engaged in by children outside school, making connections and adopting more coherent and holistic approaches to learning, even in the context of high stakes assessment.

The backwash of high stakes assessment

The publication of results, whether district by district, as in Ohio for example, or school by school as in England, has inevitably resulted in teaching to the test and increased pressure on teachers (Messenheimer and Packwood, 2002). Teachers take from the test criteria what they need to ensure success for their children (Madaus, 1994; Dann, 2001). The force of this very public pressure has even prompted teachers to 'cheat' on behalf of their students, since results are often perceived as a personal comment on their competence as individual teachers (Hoff, 2000). Performance related pay in the UK is only likely to exacerbate this stressful situation while, in contrast, in the US, increasing numbers of educators are evaluated for merit pay, based on peer observations of their effectiveness (Archer and Blair, 2001).

Classroom practice has arguably become visibly shaped by assessment criteria leading to an instrumental approach to literacy teaching, and impacting upon teachers' understandings of the nature of literacy development. A surface approach to literacy is likely to profile forms and features of texts at the expense of meaning and purpose, so that from a child's perspective, naming and knowing may appear to be given precedence over using and understanding language in meaningful contexts. In such an assessment oriented climate, the experience of literacy may simply become the analysis of language as an abstract object (Frater, 2000). A recent survey of 65 UK teachers, indicated that their understanding of quality writing was very closely aligned to national test criteria (Grainger *et al.*, 2002). No mention was made of the engagement of the reader, the content of the writing, the writer's style or authorial voice. Rather, writing seemed to have been redefined for these teachers and only encompassed easily observable and testable features. Has the strong arm of accountability de-skilled members of the profession?

The pressure to profile teaching not learning

Another consequence of the specification of the curriculum and the culture of accountability, is that knowledge becomes reified and teachers feel pressured to concentrate on achieving set targets, not on developing children's learning. The recent focus on the acquisition of knowledge about language and the 'training' of teachers to deliver nationally produced materials, has arguably sidelined teachers' and student teachers' understanding of learning. This has been borne out by research in the UK indicating that the detail of the NLS and the Initial Teacher Training National Curriculum has so overwhelmed student teachers, that they fail to comprehend the frameworks which underpin them (Twiselton, 2000). In this study, Twiselton found that most of the final year education students fell into a 'curriculum deliverers' group, while few could be defined as 'concept builders', able to offer a rationale for the learning planned or show how this related to other literacy concepts and skills. Such a bias disables the potential practitioner, who can only become a classroom operative, parcelling out their curriculum content knowledge in regularised chunks. Are we in danger of producing teachers who are simply bricklayers, competent just to secure the bricks with mortar? (Mortimore, 1999). Other research has also suggested that teachers have a limited understanding of the pedagogical principles underpinning the NLS (Fisher, 2001), and in a study by English *et al.* (2002) teachers expressed the view that they were obliged to short-change their pedagogical principles, in their anxiety to implement national strategies and be accountable to parents: 'In an educational climate dominated by monitoring, inspection and test results, teaching for understanding was regarded as an optional extra, permissible once the learning objectives had been met' (English *et al.*, 2002: 22).

The pressure created by the imposition of knowledge based objectives and public target setting creates dilemmas for teachers, especially when placed alongside demands for 'interactive teaching' which is 'well paced with a sense of urgency' (DfEE, 1998). However, a rapid pace of interaction, does not per se engender learning and may severely reduce opportunities for extended interaction and tentativeness (Mercer, 1995; Alexander, 2000; English *et al.*, 2002). The discourse of the literacy hour, in relation to whole class teaching, remains asymmetrical with the teacher dominating the patterns of interaction as Mroz *et al.* (2000) have shown. Their work confirms earlier findings that in the context of whole class teaching, the majority of questions used by teachers are closed or factual (Hardman and Williamson, 1998; Galton *et al.*, 1999). Teachers may understand the role of dialogue in learning, but the application of such pedagogical knowledge appears to be compromised in the current climate. As the second year evaluation of the NLS acknowledges, we need to 'increase the number of teachers who are expert – teachers who are learning about learning' (Earl *et al.*, 2001).

The challenge to professionalism

The demand for curriculum coverage, the degree of surveillance through inspection, and the backwash of assessment into the curriculum, act as restrictions on the profession and are likely to reduce the self-confidence of teachers and their use of innovative teaching approaches. The emphasis on teaching structures and control may turn teachers into 'trained technicians with little opportunity to create productive interchanges of knowledge or work with their pupils' prior knowledge base' (Millard, 2003: 4). If this situation continues, teachers, positioned partly as puppets in an externally evaluated and imposed system, may become de-motivated and disengaged from the act of teaching. In England, it has been argued that in recent years the professional self-confidence of teachers has been drained and their love of language and literature has been suppressed (Anderson *et al.*, 2000; Frater, 2000). In the last decade or so 'schooling' has become 'official', concerned only with statistics and measurement, not children and learning (Sedgwick, 2001). Education, by contrast, as Sedgwick asserts, is almost never official.

> Education is present when teachers learn from the children that they teach and from each other as they research their teaching together. If teachers ever learn again the importance of this collaborative activity, they will regain some control over their work with children. They will lift themselves, . . . from the shameful status of hired hands to which they have been relegated.
>
> (Sedgwick, 2001: 5)

Concerned to cover the national requirements and to prepare children for official assessments, many teachers have appeared tentative and insecure in recent years, asking 'Are we allowed?' Permission to employ their professional knowledge and make their own decisions has been sought by many experienced teachers. In this increasingly controlled and assessed system, teachers' professionalism has clearly been both reduced and re-described, 'curbing aspirations to autonomy and self regulation' (Burgess *et al.*, 2002). It has never been more important for the profession to re-establish its autonomy, its creative capacity, and for teachers to assert their corporate experience of teaching and learning and their intuitive knowledge base (Claxton, 2000). We need to remind ourselves that teaching is an art form, an imaginatively engaging and creative endeavour, an act of exploration and investigation.

Our corporate professionalism must continue to acknowledge, celebrate and debate the complexity of language and literacy learning, using insights gained from our own contexts in order to question, consider and discuss the issues raised by others. As responsible professionals, we must constantly seek out new knowledge and different perspectives that enable us to grasp more fully the challenge ahead. It is to such perspectives that we now turn in travelling across the landscape of literacy in this period of unprecedented change.

Part I: mapping the landscape of literacy

Our first guides examine the nature of the literacy landscape and seek to provide a sense of the past, the present and the future as they acknowledge the significance of culture, community and difference. Initially, Peter Hannon reflects upon five millennia of written language and shows how the history of literacy is much more than the story of various writing systems and their attendant technologies. He examines the constructed nature of school literacy through a historical lens and highlights the socio-political nature of educational change. Current curricula and conceptions of schooled literacy arguably conform to what Street (1984) has labelled as an autonomous model of literacy, which tends to conceive of literacy as little more than a set of unidirectional cognitive skills. Such limited models are 'based on a re-affirmation of a standard written national language transmitted largely through a print based linear pedagogy' (Millard, 2003: 4). Other writers and theorists have also challenged the unitary view of literacy, arguing rather for the existence of many literacies, different sets of social practices associated with written language in a culture (e.g. Lankshear, 1987; Barton, 1994; Barton and Hamilton, 1998; Gee, 1996). Peter, in showing how literacy is historically situated, also observes how the nature of literacy is frequently redefined as a result of technological changes in a culture and comments pertinently: 'If the past is any guide to the future, we should expect information technology to transform literacy rather than eradicate it' (Hannon, 2002: 23).

In exploring this ongoing transformation, Peter highlights examples such as the relative absence of linearity in hypertext and the role of graphics in production and communication. In examining the future of reading and writing, he obliges us to reconsider our assumptions and face the provisional nature of literacy and its development. Posing more questions than answers, Peter closes by challenging the profession to prepare learners for the literacy landscape of today and tomorrow.

As Peter and all our guides show, literacy is never static, it changes and is changed by those who use it. Individuals use different literacies associated with different domains of their life e.g. home, school, work. Such domains are structured contexts in which literacy is used and learned, supported by various institutions, e.g. family, religion, education (Barton and Hamilton, 1998). Children's lived experience is highly specific, therefore, and not able to be assumed, since prior to school the language and culture at home, structures and shapes their meaning making (Brice Heath, 1983). In a chapter describing and analysing the literacy practices of residents in the East End of London, Eve Gregory and Ann Williams provide detailed evidence of such diversity and difference. Their writing draws on a longitudinal study (1992–99) that aimed to uncover the literacy practices of past and present generations of families with close links to two schools, one in Spitalfields and one just over the border in the City of London. Eve and Ann used a range of ethnographic methods in collecting evidence about the literacy practices of monolingual English families and Bangladeshi-British families.

Through the voices of parents, grandparents and children, historical records and observations, the nature of the 'unofficial literacies' in which the families engage is revealed. The London Bangladeshi children's ability to blend and use strategies learned in their Bengali and Arabic classes and their mainstream English school is considerable, resulting in what Eve terms 'syncretic literacy' (Gregory, 1998). For the monolingual children, there exists a clear distinction between the literature enjoyed at home, the 'emergent tradition' associated with popular culture and the literature they experienced at school, the 'residual tradition' (Luke, 1992). Eve and Ann's work shows the interplay between dominant and vernacular literacies; between those that originate in the dominant institutions of society and those that have their roots in everyday life, and they question the narrow definition of literacy currently in opera-tion. As many researchers have shown, when mismatches occur in the way literacy is defined at home and school, then the chances for school success are compromised (Brice Heath, 1983; Au, 1993; Gee, 1996). It is clear, therefore, that teachers need to acknowledge difference, to build on the cultural knowledge, wide linguistic competence and contrasting literacy practices of the people they teach. In addition, they need to recognise that learners, particularly learners with a different home language to that of school, actively draw upon home and school learning. Eve and Ann's research demonstrates clearly that: 'Literacy cannot be taken as a given, a known technology from context to context. Literacy practices remain to be discovered, investigated, researched' (Baynam, 1995).

Building on the needs, interests and competencies of today's children should be a pre-emi-nent feature of curriculum design, argue Allan Luke and Victoria Carrington as they guide our travels in the next chapter. They describe how the impact of cultural differences, new economies and globalisation in Harlow, Queensland, were read by the teachers as signs of student 'deficit' and they voice concern that these Australian teachers, who were committed and involved professionals, were offering a disconnected, skills based programme. This was not only pre-digital and anti-popular culture, but was also 'irrelevant' in its approach to teaching literacy. As Allan and Victoria comment, for all their assiduous intentions, these teachers were unaware of what counted as literacy in the lives of the children and their families and were also unaware of the literacy demands of the twenty-first century. As a result, they operated a recovery model and leant upon packages and programmes to deliver knowledge and skills. The authors, while acknowledging the evident tensions for these professionals, argue persuasively that teachers need to recognise that education, literacy practices and the nature of childhood are in the process of significant change and transition. They suggest we need to re-envision the landscape of literacy and encompass a broader understanding of critical literacy in both curriculum design and everyday practice.

Part II: exploring literacy and learning

The predominant model of learning in western societies Wells (1992) argues, has been one of information transfer, in which children, seen as empty vessels, are deemed to be passive learners receiving information from their teacher. This transmission model involves the teacher determining the order and content of what is to be learnt, demonstrating these skills in action and ensuring they are mastered through repeated practice. While more interactive models have gained credence in theory and in practice, more limited models are likely to be revis-ited in prescribed teaching cultures which tend to ignore the domestic curriculum of the child and deem irrelevant the child's existing body of knowledge. In pressured contexts, teachers may be drawn back to such chalk and talk delivery models (Hilton, 1998).

In response to this situation and the prevailing pressures of our times, I have selected three guides who adopt alternative models of learning. All three recognise the active role of the learner and their existing knowledge, experience and interests and explore various ways of analysing children's meaning making practices. They also challenge the assumption that teaching and learning are primarily cognitive processes, and acknowledge that learning is an emotional, aesthetic and ethical act (Kreehevsky and Stork, 2002). Initially, Gunther Kress articulates a theory of meaning making from the child's point of view. He demonstrates forcibly the transformative nature of meaning making and the role of interest, affect, experience and cultural factors in this process. He argues that learners' journey on different paths to cultur-ally similar outcomes, yet still retain a sense of their own individuality, even within a socialised and acculturated system. Gunther also insists that children do not copy, but reshape and transform their understanding as they construct meaning in action and interaction. Throughout the chapter he uses examples of children acting multi-modally, in the things they use, the objects they make and the engagement of their bodies. The role of the body in the gener-ation of ideas (Johnson, 1987) and in literacy learning altogether deserves greater attention, particularly in relation to our understanding of multi-modal literacy (this is an issue returned to by Margaret Mackey in Chapter 14). In exploring the effects of multi-modality, Gunther faces the reader with the new worlds of representation and communication and warns against nostalgia and ignorance. He argues that the brain's capacity to move across media 'mentally' – synaesthesia – is not currently being encouraged, and that the power of the imagination to help children step across boundaries and make interconnections between modes needs to be recognised and nurtured more explicitly.

Anne Haas Dyson, our guide in the following chapter, provides rich evidence of this inter-connectivity at work in some fascinating transcripts of children composing. She examines key events in particular children's case histories, gathered from a year-long ethnographic project in an urban primary school in the US. Her research affirms the shifting nature of the literacy landscape outlined by earlier guides, and provides closely observed and documented evidence of these young learners' playful engagement in literacy learning. As they compose, the chil-dren make extensive use of the materials they deem relevant to the enterprise; whether these have been encountered on TV, radio, through conversation, or experience of church, school or other community practices. Anne perceptively reveals how the process of transporting cultural material across social boundaries, underpins these children's pathways into school literacy. The markedly different symbolic and communicative experiences which learners bring to school, and the transformative process of 'semiotic recycling' which they undertake, is the key, Anne argues, to understanding childhood literacy. In working to re-imagine developmental trajec-tories, her research explores literacy learning as a process of text appropriation and recontextualisation, and highlights the youngsters' remarkable flexibility and ability to adapt their cultural resources. In her acknowledgement of the children's 'textual unruliness', I was reminded of the recent work of Pahl (2001), who also describes the apparent messiness of young children's transformative meaning making. Anne, like Gunther challenges us to recog-nise the visual, literate, oral and physical modes of communication which children employ and highlights the playful nature of their textual encounters.

In perceiving learning as puzzle solving, Peter Geekie, Brian Cambourne and Phil Fitzsimmons, three Australian researchers, celebrate the active engagement of the child and provide a detailed description of one three-year-old, Liam, in order to show how he learns through 'shared thinking' with his mother. They also observe five-year-olds becoming confi-dent and independent during their first year at school, and reflect upon the reasons for their success. Drawing on the work of Vygotsky, Bruner and others, these guides highlight some principles underpinning learning, proposing that effective teaching is scaffolded by emergent learning and works towards an eventual state of independence. In adopting Wood's (1988) explanation that effective instruction leads by following, Peter and his colleagues make it clear that instruction must be responsive not directive, and should involve the full participation of both teacher and learner. Teachers' knowledge of children's emergent expertise and interests is critical in being able to anticipate areas of ripening understanding for particular individ-uals, as the work of Ruddell (1997), Browne (1996), Corden (2000) and many others has shown. Another principle they identify is that learning depends on the negotiation of meaning and is a transformation of participation, with the learners gradually assuming more responsi-bility for their learning and the adults gradually passing control to the children. In particular, they emphasise the adults' role in supporting and guiding thinking, rather than prompting and organising it. Their work leads us into considering more closely the role of the spoken word in literacy learning and seeking other guides to help us explore texts which are predominantly oral.

Part III: exploring oral texts

Spoken language is an integral dimension of literacy, since all societies are fundamentally oral (Meek, 1991) and our understanding of literacy must encompass and recognise such orality. Recent national curricula in the UK (e.g. DfEE, 1995; DfEE, 1999b) have recognised talk as a language mode, but tend to emphasise effective speech and adopt a somewhat vocational orientation towards developing adequate communication skills (Doddington, 1998). Learners also need opportunities to use language as a tool for enquiry, reflection and knowledge creation. In England, the influential NLS failed to identify speaking and listening objectives in the primary *Framework for Teaching* (DfEE, 1998), so this mode is seen as somewhat of a 'sleeping partner in the business of literacy' (Haworth, 2001). This situation is exacerbated through the pressures already acknowledged, such as assessment, target setting and curriculum coverage which tend to widen the gap between the rhetoric and the reality of classroom practice. The profile of oracy can be raised however, through developing knowledge about talk and enabling teachers to understand more fully how children learn to use language for collective and individual thinking.

Focusing on this issue from a socio-cultural perspective, Neil Mercer guides us in an exploration of the process of children's 'guided participation' into the intellectual life of the community (Rogoff, 1995). The notion of children recycling the language they hear is revisited, with Neil proposing that this may be a significant way in which children assimilate the collective ways of thinking in their community. He also examines the deliberate guidance strategies which teachers use and the role of observation and joint activity in the 'intermental development zone'. In this zone, an adaptation of Vygotsky's zone of proximal development, Neil describes the teacher and learner negotiating their way through an activity together. The quality of the teaching and learning he proposes, is thus a product of the process of interthinking.

To develop children's use of language as a tool for thinking collectively, Neil and his colleagues, Lyn Dawes, Rupert Wegerif and Karen Littleton investigated the use of teacher-led classroom activities. He reports on their research findings here, and demonstrates the advantages of raising children's awareness of both how they talk together and how language can be used for reasoning and problem solving. The high quality of the target children's talk, Neil argues, relates to the presence of exploratory talk, the constructively challenging kind of talk in which reasoning is made visible, alternatives are offered and agreement is sought. The development of such talk, he perceives, depends upon the introduction of ground rules for exploratory talk, the effectiveness of teacher talk and the creation of communities of enquiry in the classroom. The most successful teachers in a Mexican research study he undertook with Sylvia Rojas-Drummond treated learning as a social communicative process, used questions to guide the development of understanding and taught not just subject content, but also ways of solving problems and making sense. They explained the meaning and purpose of activities to the children, encouraged them to voice their views and helped them make explicit their own thought processes. This concurs with the findings of the Effective Teachers of Literacy Project which also found that effective educators in the primary phase involved children in their learning and explained to them the meaning and purpose of all activities (Medwell *et al.*, 1998).

The learning potential of co-operative group work, in which problem solving and exploratory talk may take place, is the focus of our next guide's chapter. Roy Corden also adopts the view that successful group work depends on children having a joint conception of what they are trying to achieve and a shared understanding of the purpose of the task. He persuasively argues that learners need to recognise their individual and collective responsibilities, and then explores in some detail various examples of children agreeing ground rules for group work. As Roy acknowledges, group work will also be determined by the nature of the task, the roles adopted by the learners, the stages in group discussion and the particular learning context. He thoughtfully demonstrates the cognitive demands and social skills required to undertake activities collaboratively, and highlights the need to organise groups flexibly and in response to children's needs, interests, background knowledge and experience. Roy's work in the National Oracy Project (1987–93) is used to good effect here with revealing transcripts from classrooms, which show the value of talk in helping children grasp new ideas, understand concepts and clarify their thinking. He also offers a valuable theoretical framework for learning, which adopts a more enquiry-based, investigative approach than the current orthodoxy of explicit instruction implies.

From a focus on learning through talk, our exploration moves on to examine the spoken word as an object in itself. Ron Carter's recent work on the grammar of spoken English (Carter, 2003) is contributing to the creation of new insights and innovative language awareness practices in twenty-first century classrooms. In this chapter, set in the context of English as a second/foreign language, Ron celebrates the remarkably creative and playful nature of everyday conversation. Drawing on the five million word CANCODE corpus (Cambridge and Nottingham Corpus of Discourse of English), held at Nottingham University, he reflects critically on the overemphasis in recent years on transactional uses of language at the expense of interactive and creative uses. Through a wealth of appealing and accessible examples, Ron shows how our so-called ordinary discourse is often patterned inventively in the context of, for example, jokes, adverts and journalism. He also demonstrates how, in casual conversation, some language may draw attention to itself, and argues that such verbal play is underscored by almost literary qualities. Creativity in conversation, he claims, plays a significant part in interpersonal relations, even if it does rely on specific cultural knowledge for a full appreciation of its layers of meanings. Ron argues that increased language awareness can open a door to enriched literary competence and in profiling the creative and literary nature of patterned representational language, he demonstrates that pleasure and verbal play are a part of everyday discourse which deserve recognition and attention.

In related work, Cameron (2002: 19) suggests that some oral texts need to be recognised as art forms, and that learners should both study and practise using a range of spoken genres, experiencing a variety of subject matters, purposes, types of audience and levels of formality. In this way children would hear, discuss and try for themselves a variety of oral genres, including the rhetorical and performance genres used by politicians, preachers, comedians, TV talk show hosts, rappers and storytellers. Through retelling tales for example, they can develop their verbal artistry, their ability to use language to create effects, and employ pause, pace, intonation, gesture and feeling in the process. Providing children with such opportunities can enrich their creative potential, enable them to hear their own tunes, refine their skills and develop their communicative competence (Fox, 1993; Rosen, 1993; Zipes, 1995; Grainger, 2002). The implications for the environment and culture of the classroom are clear: adults need to be open to the kind of creative and poetic language use that Ron profiles. Teachers as well as other professionals can model storytelling, and employ a variety of media to access examples of performance genres. Teachers can also notice the poetic and the playful in children's speech and provide opportunities for developing children's language awareness, pleasure and verbal play through engaging them in a variety of verbal art forms.

Another art form that makes extensive use of the spoken word is drama. Although, as Helen Nicholson reminds the interested traveller, drama includes the languages of movement, sound, music and image as well as the spoken word. In her chapter, she explores how these different languages combine and develop a range of literacies too often ignored in a curriculum dominated by the primacy of the written word. Dramatic texts are self evidently multi-modal, involving the adoption of multiple perspectives and a thought provoking oscillation between engagement and reflection. In drama, teachers deliberately leave doors open to ascertain areas of interest or desire and find themselves 'raising possibilities rather than confirming probabilities' (Taylor, 1995), making the situation more complex and uncertain. Helen considers that the real challenge for teachers working in drama is to create the kind of cooperative classroom culture that is conducive to such creative exploration. But in a similar vein to both Neil and Roy, she acknowledges that students sometimes lack the social skills and oral strategies to work together to create effective drama. She perceives questions, challenges, alternative perspectives and interpretations are critical in seeking to create a community of learners, and recognises diversity and difference are integral to this multitextual art form. Helen also wisely observes that 'learning to live with ambiguity is both part of the process of working collaboratively and the process of making art'. Yet, there appears to be little space for ambiguity and uncertainty in the current climate. In literacy, accuracy in written construction and referential responses to text, foreground much practice. Secure frameworks of staged progression, commonly used pedagogies and explicit assessment criteria are aspects of the certainty offered to teachers and learners, such certainty may limit their ways of seeing, thinking and learning and fail to recognise the complexity of current multi-modal texts.

Part IV: exploring visual texts

> Children currently in school have been born into a mesmerising and kaleidoscopic world of representation, where sound, image and print are constantly refracted by each other, presenting endless possibilities for transformative play.
>
> (Millard, 2003: 3)

Recent changes to the ways in which children communicate with one another and their increasing exposure to electronically and digitally produced texts have considerable implications for both schooling and literacy. The multi-modal texts they encounter require different reading patterns and their familiarity with these new forms means they are 'thinking differently from those adults who were brought up in a more print-dominated world' (Bearne, 2003). Yet, many literacy teachers have not been trained to use the new media, nor encouraged to develop imaginative ways to employ them in classroom contexts. The young, who are rapidly becoming multi-modally literate, deserve to have their competencies recognised, enriched and developed in order to become critically literate (Lankshear and Bigum, 1999). So in this section of the book, I have selected guides that are well travelled in the domain of new media and visual texts.

Evelyn Arizpe and Morag Styles lead our first foray forwards, sharing insights from their recent research project into how visual texts are read by children. In exploring the potential of visual literacy and the skills children need to deal with picture books, Evelyn and Morag were joined by Helen Bromley, Kathy Coulthard, Janet Campbell and Kate Rabey. The team used open ended group discussions, individual interviews and drawing, in response to picture books by Anthony Browne and Satashi Kitamura, and encouraged the children to become involved in the texts, both privately and collaboratively. They reflect upon the complexity of the children's aesthetic, cognitive and affective responses, which the authors argue, enabled the young people to step back and observe themselves as readers, speculating, hypothesising, shaping and confirming their ideas. There was evidence of the children's use of modal verbs, tentative exploratory talk and collective inter-thinking in the transcripts which highlight the role of teachers' questions, particularly in fostering children's 'visible thinking' and development in understanding. The interviews, conducted some months after the initial discussions, allowed the children to revisit the texts. Their insightful comments at this stage powerfully demonstrate the importance of what Britton (1982) refers to as 'the incubatory period of literature'. Finding the time for re-reading, revisiting and reflection certainly deserves more attention. The study's conclusions with regard to ethnicity, gender and popular culture also have ramifications for the classroom, relating to teacher expectations and the need to develop children's confidence in expressing their emotions and discussing their values. It is clear that when young learners are taught to look and look more closely, and are prompted to share their insights in communal and supported contexts, they become both more creatively engaged and more visually literate in the process.

David Lewis, our guide in the following chapter, offers another close examination of visual texts. He explains some of the key features of the visual image, including: line, colour, action and movement, size and location and symbolism, and draws attention to the subtle ways in which these features are employed and the inter-animation of them in various picture books. In this process, he reveals the range of remarkably complex choices made by artists in making meaning and allows the voices of youngsters to show how rapidly they interpret the visuals and make decisions about what they mean. Through analysing and commenting upon pictures from children's fiction texts, David examines the structural organisation that a picture may possess and offers a valuable introduction to the grammar of visual design (Kress and van Leeuwen, 1996). He demonstrates how both the grammar of the image and Halliday's (1985) functional grammar are rooted in a concern with meaning and the use to which words or images are put. David acknowledges that our comprehension of visual structures will be combined with other kinds of knowledge in reading picture books, and realises such readings are always contextualised literacy events, but also shows us that the grammar of visual design can focus our looking and make a real contribution to our understanding of how the pictures may contribute to the story.

Moving images, perhaps even more than still ones, play a central part in children's cultural lives, through TV, film and video. Our next guides, Jackie Marsh and Elaine Millard recognise this and, using research evidence, they challenge the constant arguments levelled in this area, including those relating to passive viewing, the influence of violent scenes, reductions in book reading and the purportedly addictive nature of the medium. Their overview highlights both the similarities and differences in reading print and televisual texts and demonstrates the rich interplay possible between these media. As Jackie and Elaine observe, children are highly motivated to read media texts and the intertextuality of films and books can promote rather than inhibit reading. Children are immersed in a world of popular culture, and their particular pleasure and interest in both TV and film and the need to engage them critically, suggests that work in media literacy needs our focused attention. Our guides also note that since TV is a medium that all children share, regardless of their socio-economic, cultural or linguistic background, it can provide rich opportunities to build shared discourses in the classroom and enhance work in reading and writing. A variety of practical suggestions and examples are offered to engage children, including making their own animated films, video diaries and weather reports and teachers are urged not to underestimate children's sophisticated, if implicit understanding of media codes and conventions. The potential of soap operas, quiz shows and media diaries is also explored. As Jackie and Elaine assert, children need to be supported in developing their ability to understand, analyse and produce moving images as part of the literacy curriculum.

In the following chapter, Margaret Mackey, draws together the findings from her research and reflects upon the remarkable assurance that young people show in moving through the complex textual environment. The Canadian students in this study accepted their textual mobility, knew how to process some kinds of texts and fully expected to meet new forms which would both challenge and interest them, and which they felt confident they would learn to handle. Other studies have also shown that children engage with ease in a semiotic world in which texts in various modes are linked (Dyson, 1997; Browne, 1999; Marsh, 2003). Margaret's research involved making a close-up record of the ways in which, over an 18-month period, young people aged 10–14 years, explored texts in print, video, computer game, electronic book, DVD, CD-ROM encyclopaedia and CD-ROM story book. Audio and video recordings, field notes and student diaries were used to investigate what happens during the activity of reading, viewing or playing of a text. The recordings allowed Margaret to pay attention to both the person and the text, she also observed students engage with texts, in whatever medium, with their hands and bodies as well as their minds.

Margaret uses the metaphor of playing the text to describe the interpretative elements which were common across many media and examines playing as: pretending, performing, engaging with the rules, strategising, orchestrating, fooling around and not working. Taking this 'playing' argument into the classroom, she profiles the term and suggests emphasising the performance element of silent reading or video watching, making allowances for the bodily requirements of playing the text and recognising the need for autonomy and the nego- tiation of meaning. The implications of her ecology of attention in relation to young people's sense of agency and autonomy are complex; what is clear is their ease of movement in a fluid textual universe. Our need as professionals to create curriculum frameworks in literacy and language that recognise children's out of school lives and the complexity of young people's meaning making practices is also evident.

Part V: exploring written texts

As our exploration moves to texts which are more predominantly written in orientation, issues of autonomy and young people's rights are revisited. Eve Bearne and Gabrielle Cliff Hodges examine readers' rights and responsibilities, drawing on Daniel Pennac's (1994) powerful list of such rights in his book *Reads Like a Novel*. Our guides wisely focus on the role of moti- vation and the desire to know, arguing that success, personal satisfaction and the role of the teacher are crucial in this process. They also observe with concern, the relative lack of atten- tion afforded to fairly fluent readers and the real challenge of gathering information about the breadth and diversity of their encounters with text. Eve and Gabrielle also reflect upon the complexity of gender issues and pose possible ways forward, including the involvement of more teachers in action research. This is a critical strategy, for if we are to move forward as a profession then teachers need to develop their knowledge, beliefs and understanding through reading, reflection and their own research (Medwell *et al.*, 1998). Through response to text activities (e.g. reading journals, reading groups and autobiographies), teachers can, our guides suggest, not only learn what it is that motivates their youngsters to continue reading, but also about the very act of reading itself. Voices from the classroom confirm this position, with examples of children offering pertinent advice to reading partners and their teachers. In the process, the young people reveal their not inconsiderable metalinguistic know- ledge and their own insights and understanding about the nature of reading. Eve and Gabrielle consider that the recent priority given to assessing knowledge about language, text structures and comprehension has shortchanged the essential skills of developing preferences and opin- ions, making informed choices and increasing children's independence. As Martin (2003) observes, there is a real difference between a child's minimum reading entitlement, enshrined by nationally set targets, and their maximum entitlement to become a reflective and critical reader for life.

Our next guide, Myra Barrs, discusses the role of reading in the development of writing. Her argument is based upon research undertaken at the Centre for Language in Primary Education, which explored the influence of children's reading of literature on their writing. Myra highlights the intimacy involved in hearing the writer's voice and also draws on the work of Daniel Pennac in asserting the significance of voice in marking the tunes and patterns, rhythm and flow of written text. In this research, undertaken with five classes of 9–10-year-olds, literary texts by Kevin Crossley Holland and Henrietta Branford were explored in some detail. The resultant writing was subjected to close analysis to establish whether the texts made a specific impact on the writing and to examine whether any of the pedagogical practices employed were particularly effective in supporting the young writers. One striking finding concerned the effect of the stance, position and perspective of the writer. The children, engaged in living through the drama (Bolton, 1998), explored the text from the 'inside out' prior to writing in role from the point of view of one of the characters. The motivating and emotive nature of the drama enabled them to investigate and experience the themes of the text, and this clearly influenced the quality of their writing. Through the adoption of multiple role perspectives and alternative viewpoints, drama can shape new insights and enable children to imaginatively project themselves into others' shoes. The power of empathy seemed to enable them to 'feel the tug of life as someone else feels it' (Cremin, 1998) and this was powerfully conveyed in their writing. As Myra observes, the children became part of a dialogue with the text and the author, taking on a narrator's voice and role. The role of response partners was also drawn out, which helped to develop children's awareness of the impact their writing had on a reader. The research also demonstrated the significance of reading aloud; this seemed to foreground the tunes and rhythms of the text in a way that subsequently influenced the children's writing. In the project classrooms, authors' voices were brought to life by skilful and sensitive teachers, who also read their children's work back to them, ensuring their own patterns could be heard. As Chambers (1993) comments, 'only through listening to words in print being spoken, does one discover their colour, their life, their movement'.

Taking a broader view, Mary Bailey, our next guide in this terrain, argues that in order to raise standards in writing, national policies should reflect more explicitly the findings from research. Such connections, she believes, would increase teacher confidence about what constitutes effective writing development and the principles that underpin it. In taking the UK National Literacy Strategy as a focused example, Mary shows how some elements are thoroughly grounded in the research literature while, disconcertingly, others are not. She supports Hilton's (2001) position, that the NLS is somewhat unsupported by research evidence in relation to teaching writing in the primary phase. She also reviews the survey work of Frater (2000), who examined work in 32 primary schools (1999/2000). He found that in the schools in which writing was least effective, assiduous teachers tended to interpret the NLS literally, giving priority to discrete word, sentence and text level practice, which eroded the time spent on written composition. As Mary notes, such practice is all the more likely to occur when teachers lack confidence and/or have a limited understanding of literacy development, and when national or state policies lack secure links to research evidence. She examines a range of research discourses in the field of composition studies, including cognitive process models of writing, genre theory and socio-cognitive models of composition. Two themes are identified which connect these different perspectives, namely scaffolding an understanding of written communication and scaffolding the writing process. In arguing for a readjustment in our understanding, Mary asserts that teachers need principles, not merely routines, to which I would add, teachers need education not training. Mary revisits Flower's (1994) socio-cognitive claims about literacy, which profile the process of meaning making and focus on thinking and learning. Without such principles based upon research, criteria for teaching and assessing writing may continue to reflect only discrete and assessable skills.

Carole King, our last guide, also begins from the premise that writing development is not simply related to a growing command of its codes and conventions. In revisiting Britton's (1993) continuum of language development, Carole focuses mainly on poetry and story writing within the poetic mode. As she observes, the predominance of genre theory has led to a concentration on transactional forms and the neglect of language in the spectator role as a way of making meaning. Carole perceptively examines examples of young writers crafting personal and emotive communications, and shows how writing in the spectator role can enable children to construct and convey their own voices. The significance of choice and autonomy in developing voice and verve in writing has also been affirmed by recent research into the use of writing journals in the classroom. This shows that such journals can effect a bridge between home and school practices, allowing the learners to explore their own worlds and imagined worlds (Graham, 2001, 2003). Carole also refers to the Effective Teachers of Literacy Project and reminds us again of the need to teach skills in meaningful contexts and to prioritise meaning (Medwell *et al.*, 1998). Work in the US has also shown that exemplary professionals profile the meaningful components in any literacy learning process (Block, 2001). In addition, Carole demands that teachers respond as readers first and teachers second, in line with D'Arcy's (1999) two layers of response: engagement and appreciation. As writers and spectators of their own experience, the teachers she worked with were able to forge new understandings about themselves, about writing and their role as teachers of writing. Such enriching professional development opportunities, enabling teachers to research their classroom practice should be offered more widely to teachers to widen their knowledge and understanding. To support such enquiries, teachers can also journey through this text, raising questions for discussion and areas for further exploration as they travel.

References

Alexander, R. (2000) *Culture and Pedagogy*. Oxford: Blackwell.

Anderson, H. *et al.* (2000) Hourwatch: monitoring the inception of the NLS. *Reading* 34: 3 pp. 113–118.

Archer, J. and Blair, J. (2001) Performance testing being readied for Ohio teachers. *Education Week* 20: 19 pp. 14.

Au, K. (1993) *Literacy Instruction in Multicultural Settings*. Fort Worth: Harcourt Brace Jovanovich.

Barton, D. (1994) *Literacy: An Introduction to the Ecology of Written Language*. Oxford: Blackwell.

Barton, D. and Hamilton, M. (1998) *Local Literacies: Reading and Writing in One Community*. London: Routledge.

Baynham, M. (1995) *Literacy Practices: Investigation, Literacy in a Social Context*. London: Longman.

Bearne, E. (2003) Rethinking literacy: communication representation and text. *Reading Literacy and Language* 37: 3.

Bearne, E., and Kress, G. (2001) Editorial. *Reading Literacy and Language* 35: 3 pp. 89–93.

Black, C., Oak, M. and Hurt, N. (2002) 'The expertise of literacy teachers: a continuum from preschool to grade 5', *Reading Research Quarterly* 37: 2 pp. 178–206.

Bolton, G. (1998) *Acting in Classroom Drama: A Critical Analysis*, Stoke-on-Trent: Trentham Books.

Bordieu, P. (1977) *Outline of a Theory of Practice*. Cambridge: Cambridge University Press.

Brice-Heath, S. (1983) *Ways with Words: Language, Life and Work in Communities and Classrooms*. Cambridge: Cambridge University Press.

Britton, J. (1982) *From Prospect to Retrospect*. London: Heinemann.

Britton, J. (1993) *Literature in its Place*, London: Cassell.

Browne, A. (1996) *Developing Language and Literacy, 3–8*, London: Sage.

Browne, A. (1999) *Young Children's Literacy Development and the Role of Televisual Texts*. London: Falmer.

Burgess, T. *et al.* (2002) *When the Hurly Burly's Done: What's Worth Fighting for in English in Education*. Sheffield: NATE.

Cairney, T. H. (2000) Beyond the classroom walls: the rediscovery of the family and community as partners in education. *Educational Review* 52: 2 pp. 163–174.

Cameron, D. (2002) Schooling spoken language: beyond communication, in *New Perspectives on Spoken English in the Classroom*, Conference Papers, 27 June 2002. London: QCA.

Carter, R. (2003) *The Grammar of Spoken English*, paper presented at UKRA conference, 28 February 2003, Croydon.

Carter, R., Hughes, R. and McCarthy, M. (2000) *Exploring Grammar in Context*. Cambridge: Cambridge University Press.

Chambers, A. (1993) *Tell Me: Children Reading and Talk*. Stroud: Thimble Press.

Claxton, G. (2000) The anatomy of intuition, in Atkinson, T. and Claxton, G. (eds) *The Intuitive Practitioner: On the Value of Not Always Knowing What One is Doing*. Buckingham: Open University Press.

Corden, R. (2000) *Literacy and Learning through Talk*. Milton Keynes: Open University Press.

Craft, A. (2000) *Creativity across the Primary Curriculum: Framing and Developing Practice*. London: Routledge.

Cremin, M. (1998) The imagination and originality in English and classroom drama. *English in Education* 32: 2 NATE.

Dann, R. (2001) *Assessment as Learning.* London: RoutledgeFalmer.

D'Arcy, P. (1999) *Two Contrasting Paradigms from the Teaching and the Assessment of Writing,* Leicester: NAAE, NAPE and NATE.

DfEE (1995) *English in the National Curriculum,* London: DfEE.

DfEE (1998) *The National Literacy Strategy Framework for Teaching.* London: DfEE.

DfEE (1999a) *All Our Futures: Creativity, Culture and Education.* Report of the National Advisory Committee on Creative and Cultural Education. London: DfEE.

DfEE (1999b) *English in the National Curriculum for England and Wales,* London: DfEE.

Doddington, C. (1998) Significant Speech, in Bearne, E. (ed.) *Use of Language across the Primary Curriculum.* London: Routledge.

Dyson, A. H. (1997) *Writing Superheroes: Contemporary Childhood, Pop Culture and Classroom Literacy.* New York: Teachers' College Press.

Earl, L. Levin, B., Leithwood, K., Fullan, M. and Watson, N. (2001) *Watching and Learning II.* Ontario: Institute for Studies in Education/UT Evaluation of the Implementation of the NL and NS strategies. Toronto: OISE.

English, E., Hargreaves, L., Hislam, J. (2002) Pedagogical dilemmas in the national literacy strategy: primary teachers' perceptions, reflections and classroom behaviour. *Cambridge Journal of Education* 32: 1 pp. 9–26.

Fisher, R. (2001) *Inside the Literacy Hour: Learning from Classroom Experience.* London: Routledge.

Flower, L. (1994) *The Construction of Negotiated Meaning: A Social Cognitive Theory of Writing.* Carbondale: Southern Illinois University Press.

Fox, C. (1993) *At the Very Edge of the Forest: The Influence of Literature by Storytelling on Children,* London: Cassell.

Frater, G. (2000) Observed in practice: English in the National Literacy Strategy: *Some Reflections, Reading Literacy and Language* 34: 3, pp. 107–112.

Frater, G. (2002) *Effective Practice at KS2: Essential Extras.* London: The Basic Skills Agency.

Galton, M., Hargreaves, L., Comber, C., Wall, D. and Pell, A. (1999) *Inside the Primary Classroom: 20 Years On.* London: Routledge.

Gee, P. (1996) *Social Linguistics and Literacies: Ideology in Discourse* 2nd edn, London: Taylor & Francis.

Graham, L. (2001) From Tyrannosaurus to Pokemon: autonomy in the teaching of writing. *Reading Literacy and Language* 35: 1 pp. 18–26.

Graham, L. (2003) Research in progress: writing journals: an investigation. *Reading Literacy and Language* 37: 1 pp. 40–43.

Grainger, T. (2002) Storytelling: the missing link in storywriting, in Ellis, S. and Mills, C. *Connecting, Creating: New Issues in the Teaching of Writing.* Cambridge: UKRA.

Grainger, T., Goouch, K. and Lambirth, A. (2002) The voice of the child: 'We're Writers' Project. *Reading Literacy and Language.* 36: 3 pp. 135–140.

Gregory, E. (1998) Siblings as mediators of literacy in linguistic minority communities. *Language and Education: An International Journal* 12: 1 pp. 33–55.

Halliday, M. A. K. (1985) *An Introduction to Functional Grammar.* London: Edward Arnold.

Hannon, P. (2002) *Reflecting on Literacy in Education.* London: Routledge.

Hardman, F. and Williamson, J. (1998) The discourse of post-16 English teaching. *Educational Review* 50: 1 pp. 5–14.

Hardy, B. (1977) Towards a poetics of fiction: an approach through narrative, in Meek, M. *et al.* (eds) *The Cool Web.* London: Bodley Head.

Haworth, A. (2001) The re-positioning of oracy: a millennium project. *Cambridge Journal of Education* 31: 1 pp. 11–23.

Hilton, M. (1998) Raising literacy standards: the true story. *English in Education* 32: 3 pp. 4–46.

Hilton, M. (2001) Writing process and progress: where do we go from here? *English in Education* 35: 1 pp. 4–12.

Hoff, D. J. (2000) As stakes rise, definition of cheating blurs. *Education Week* 19: 41 pp. 14–16.

Johnson, M. (1987) *The Body in the Mind: The Bodily Basis of Meaning Imagination and Reason,* Chicago: University of Chicago Press.

Krechevsky, M. and Stork, J. (2000) 'Challenging educational assumptions: lessons from an Italian-American collaboration', *Cambridge Journal of Education* 30: 1: pp. 57–73.

Kress, G. and van Leeuwen, T. (1996) *Reacting Images: The Grammar of Visual Design.* London: Routledge.

Lankshear, C. (1987) *Changing Literacies.* Buckingham: Open University Press.

Lankshear, C. and Bigum, C. (1999) Literacies and new technologies in school settings. *Curriculum Studies* 7: 3 pp. 445–464.

Leavers, F. (2000) Forward to basics! deep learning and the experiential approach. *Early Years* 20: 2 pp. 20–29.

Luke, A. (1992) The social construction of literacy in the primary school, in Unsworth, L. (ed.) *Literacy, learning and Teaching: Language as a Social Practice in the Classroom*. Melbourne: Macmillan.

Luke, A. and Luke, C. (2001) Adolescence lost/childhood regained: on early intervention and the emergence of the techno-subject. *Journal of Early Childhood Literacy* 1: 1 pp. 91–120.

Madaus, G. (1994) in Gipps, C. *Beyond Testing*. Lewes: Falmer.

Marsh, J. (2001) 'It's taboo isn't it?' *Popular Culture and the Literacy Curriculum*. Paper presented at the British Educational Research Association Annual Conference, Leeds, Sept. 2001.

Marsh, J. (2003) Contemporary models of communicative practice: shaky foundations in the foundation stage. *English in Education* 37: 1 pp. 38–46.

Marsh, J. and Thompson, P. (2001) 'Parental involvement in literacy development using media texts', *Journal of Research in Reading* 24: 3 pp. 233–268.

Martin, T. (2003) Minimum and maximum entitlements: literature at key stage 2. *Reading Literacy and Language* 37: 1.

Medwell, J., Wray, D., Poulson, L. and Fox, R. (1998) *The Effective Teachers of Literacy Project*. Exeter: University of Exeter.

Meek, M. (1991) *On Being Literate*. London: The Bodley Head.

Mercer, N. (1995) *The Guided Construction of Knowledge Talk among Teachers and Learners*. Clevedon: Multilingual Matters.

Messenheimer, T. and Packwood, A. (2002) Writing: the state of the state vs the state of the art in English and American schools. *Reading Literacy and Language* 36: 1 pp. 11–16.

Millard, E. (2003) Towards a literacy of fusion: new times, new teaching and learning? *Reading, Literacy and Language* 37: 1 pp. 3–8.

Mortimore, P. (ed.) (1999) *Understanding Pedagogy and Its Impact on Learning*. London: Paul Chapman.

Mroz, M., Smith, F. and Hardman, F. (2000). The discourse of the literacy hour. *Cambridge Journal of Education* 30: 3 pp. 380–389.

Pahl, K. (2001) Texts as artefacts crossing sites: map making at home and at school. *Reading Literacy and Language* 35: 3.

Pahl, K. (2002) Habitus and the home: texts and practices in families. *Ways of Knowing* 2: 1.

Pennac, D. (1994) *Reads Like a Novel*. London: Quartet.

Prentice, R. (2000) Creativity: a reaffirmation of its place in early childhood education. *The Curriculum Journal* 11: 2 pp. 145–158.

Pullman, P. (2000) *The Amber Spyglass*. London: Scholastic.

Pullman, P. (2002) *Perverse, all Monstrous, all Prodigious Things. Perspectives on English Teaching 2*. Loughborough: NATE.

Puttnam, D. (1998) Puttnam fears for the arts. *The Independent* 10 April.

Rogoff, B. (1995) Observing sociocultural activity on three planes: participatory appropriation, guided participation and apprenticeship, in Wertsch, J. *et al.* (eds) *Sociocultural Studies of Mind*. Cambridge: Cambridge University Press.

Rosen, B. (1991) *Shapers and Polishers: Teachers as Storytellers*. London: Mary Glasgow.

Rosen, B. (1993) *And None of it was Nonsense*, London: Mary Glasgow.

Sedgwick, F. (2001) *Teaching Literacy: A Creative Approach*. London: Continuum.

Street, B. (1984) *Literacy in Theory and Practice*. Cambridge: Cambridge University Press.

Street, B. (1993) *Cross-cultural Approaches to Literacy*. Cambridge: Cambridge University Press.

Street, B. (1997) The implications of the new literacy studies for evaluation. *English in Education* 31: 3 pp. 45–59.

Taylor, P. (1995) *Pre Text and Story Drama: The Artistry of Cecily O'Neill and David Booth*, Research Monograph Series, Australia: NADIE.

Twiselton, S. (2000) 'Seeing the wood for the trees, the NLS and ITE; pedagogical intent knowledge and structure of subjects', *Cambridge Journal of Education* 30: 3 pp. 391–403.

Wells, G. (1992) The Centrality of Talk in Education, in Norman, K. (ed.) *Thinking Voices: The Work of the NOP*. London: Hodder & Stoughton.

Wood, D. (1988) *How Children Think and Learn*, Oxford: Blackwell.

Wray, D., Medwell, J. and Poulson, L. (2001) *Teaching Literacy Effectively in the Primary School*. London: Routledge.

Zipes, J. (1996) *Creative Storytelling: Building Communities, Changing Lives*, London: Routledge.

PART I

MAPPING THE LANDSCAPE
OF LITERACY

CHAPTER 1

THE HISTORY AND FUTURE OF LITERACY

Peter Hannon

Reflecting on Literacy in Education, London: RoutledgeFalmer, 2000, pp. 14–29

Introduction

It is easy to think of the literacy which is taught in education today as the only kind of literacy there could be. Yet the literacy we see now is only one point in a line of development with a long past and an unknown future. The aim of this chapter is to reflect upon some aspects of the history of literacy and to imagine possibilities for its future. An historical perspective enables us to see taken-for-granted features of written language in a new light. It enables us to examine the claims often heard that literacy brings about economic progress, a higher level of cultural development or political change. Although it is hard to discern how literacy in education may change in the future, it is necessary to be open to the inevitability of there being changes of some kind.

Five millennia of written language

Studying the history of literacy is both important and difficult. It is important because an understanding of how our ancestors created and used writing systems can give us a clearer appreciation of literacy today. It is difficult because it involves trying to puzzle out what happened in the past when many pieces of evidence are missing. It is hard enough to analyse the nature of present day literacy and how it is used in our society. How much harder it is to draw conclusions about ancient societies when all we have are those archaeological fragments which happen to have survived. Yet without an historical perspective it is easy to overlook certain features of present day literacy or fall into the trap of thinking that other features are 'natural' or 'inevitable'.

As far as can be inferred from the archaeological record, the earliest writing systems from which ours evolved can be traced back to around 3300 BC in Mesopotamia and perhaps around the same time in Egypt. There were comparable developments in subsequent millennia in China and in the Americas. Of course, much earlier than 5,000 years ago there were the precursors of writing in cave drawings and carvings and it is an interesting issue to judge at what point such representations can be considered writing. Pictures can tell a story. Also there were mark making systems for counting objects and the passage of time, or identifying possessions. What distinguishes the early writing systems as such is the use of stylised, conventional marks which can be combined in different ways to make different meanings.

The marks in early writing systems were initially pictograms, that is marks with some obvious similarity to whatever they represented but, over time, they became abbreviated or stylised. Others were ideograms, representing ideas or concepts which cannot so easily be pictured. Chinese writing, described as ideographic or logographic, is a present day example of a system where such origins are still visible.

In the earliest writing systems marks represented the world rather in the way that a picture represents an object or a scene. A development of major importance in our system of writing was the use of marks to represent oral language. Like other developments this was probably quite gradual – extending the use of a mark which represented one thing (because it looked like it) to also represent the word for something else (perhaps because the word for the second thing sounded like the word for the first).

From a psychological point of view this development was momentous. It meant that writing became a 'second order symbolic system' in which marks did not represent the world directly but something else – language – which in turn represented the world. Using marks in this way presupposes a certain awareness of language, for example seeing it as consisting of words. It could even be argued that the concept of a 'word' is a result of a culture having a system of writing. Another implication is that anyone learning to read has to grasp the fact that writing is not like pictures. Literacy learners can find this difficult. Vygotsky suggested that learning written language 'must be as much harder than oral speech for the child as algebra is harder than arithmetic' (Vygotsky, 1962: 99).

Individual language users have vocabularies of thousands of words, language communities many more. In order to avoid having to learn a specific writing mark for each word, some systems developed marks to represent sounds within words. As words are made up of combinations of a limited number of sounds within a language it is possible to represent words by combinations of marks. This is the principle which underlies alphabetic writing systems such as English. The idea was first developed around 3,000 years ago by the Phoenicians and has reached us via the Greeks and Romans. Alphabetic systems have advantages over logographic systems (e.g. fewer characters to learn) but some disadvantages too (e.g. initial learning may be more difficult).

In human history the development of written language must have meant a change of the same order as the earlier evolution of spoken language. Not only did writing facilitate within-group communication and recording for our ancestors, but also it greatly accelerated the process whereby one generation could build upon the accumulated knowledge of previous generations.

There is undoubtedly an association between economic development and literacy. More industrialised societies have a wider spread of literacy in the population. It is sometimes suggested that increases in literacy are actually the cause of economic development but, as Graff (1979, 1987) has shown from historical studies of particular communities, this is too simple a view. Literacy may *follow* economic growth. This should not be surprising since successful economic activity can obviously create a need for record keeping and communication.

Among the earliest surviving examples of writing are agricultural accounts, followed by texts relating to religious and governmental practices (Jean, 1992). The use of written language to express and to explore human experience came later. At first this was in written versions of spoken forms such as stories, myths, songs, poetry or drama – written probably to aid memory. Subsequently, writing became more important in the development of these forms so that the written versions preceded the spoken ones. In many narrative genres (most obviously the novel) the written form stands alone. Children and adults who are able to read such material therefore have access to a vast and intricately depicted range of human experience and reflection stored in the literature of the world. For those who are illiterate in this sense, that door is closed.

The history of literacy is also the history of writing technology. A very wide range of tools (styluses, brushes, pens, typewriters, keyboards) have been used to make marks on a very wide range of surfaces (wood, clay tablets, papyrus, bamboo strips, fabric, stone, parchment, paper, video screens). Technological changes have affected how much can be written, how quickly, and how long the writing lasts. Often what follows is change in the uses for written language, not just more efficient ways of doing the same thing. In Western culture the printing press is celebrated as an invention which transformed literacy by increasing access to written materials, but in the history of written language it has to take its place towards the end of a line of other 'inventions' such as clay tablets, ink, paper, quill pens, or book binding. In any case, technological innovation does not act autonomously upon culture. Elisabeth Eisenstein (1982), in a book titled *The Printing Press as an Agent of Change*, makes this point nicely. She rejects a simple cause and effect analysis of how printing changed literacy and society in the fifteenth century and instead shows how it arose from cultural need and how its effects were shaped by culture.

The history of literacy is more than the story of writing systems and technologies. It is also the history of the *uses* to which these have been put. The earliest examples of writing which survive from ancient societies often concern trade, administrative/legal matters and religious uses. More personally expressive uses such as letters, narrative or story are found later.

Literacy and intellectual history

Some commentators have argued that literacy enables societies to reach a higher level of intellectual achievement. In one sense this is obviously true for it is hard to see how scientific and cultural thinking could get very far at all unless each generation is able to build upon the discoveries of previous ones. But some claims have gone further than this. Much has been made of the distinction between 'oral societies' and 'literate societies'. One eighteenth-century historian wrote, 'The use of letters is the principal circumstance that distinguishes a civilized people from a herd of savages, incapable of knowledge or reflection' (Gibbon, 1776/1896: 218). Subsequent writers have made the same point more gently.

> The civilization created by the Greeks and Romans was the first on the earth's surface which was founded upon the activity of the common reader; the first to be equipped with the means of adequate expression in the inscribed word; the first to be able to place the inscribed word in general circulation; the first, in short, to become literate in the full meaning of that term, and to transmit its literacy to us.
>
> (Havelock, 1982: 40)

The claim here is that there is a great divide between literate and other societies. David Barton (1994), in his book *Literacy: An Introduction to the Ecology of Written Language*, sets it out as follows.

> An important aspect of the great divide proposal is the notion that modern literate societies are fundamentally different in many aspects of social organisation

from earlier, simpler societies, and that these differences are ultimately attributable to literacy. Aspects of modern societies that are said to hinge upon the existence of literacy include the development of democracy, certain forms of political organization and the possibility for technological advance.

(Barton, 1994: 117)

Barton goes on to criticise this claim as grossly oversimplified and lacking in evidence. For example, one version, which he terms the 'Greek' argument, makes much of the simultaneous emergence in Greece of an alphabetic writing system, new forms of logic and forms of democracy. Yet historical research has established that the first two developed much earlier than the third, both in Greece and in other societies.

A more sophisticated view of the intellectual consequences of literacy in society has been put forward by David Olson (1994). He argues that literacy has had profound intellectual consequences but his argument rests on a point made earlier in this chapter, that writing is a way of representing language. Hence being literate means having a certain sort of awareness of language (e.g. that it consists of words, sounds). Writing has proved to be a very effective way of representing what people say but one of its weaknesses is that it is hard to capture in writing *how* people say things. Olson gives the example of the statement, 'Dinner is at eight'. Our writing system is perfectly adequate for indicating what was said but it is poor at indicating whether the words should be taken as a prediction, a statement, an invitation, or a promise. Yet in real life if we heard someone say, 'Dinner is at eight', we would probably have no difficulty in using non-verbal cues to tell which of these possibilities was meant. Something gets left out in the writing (something which philosophers term the 'illocutionary force' of a speech act). Olson suggests, that in order to overcome this weakness, users of written language were forced to create a vocabulary and conceptual system to describe how people meant words to be taken – their mental states/feelings/intentions and so on – and that this created an enhanced awareness of individual psychology.

> The history of literacy, in other words, is the struggle to recover what was lost in simple transcription. The solution is to turn non-lexical properties of speech such as stress and intonation into lexical ones; one announces that the proposition expressed is to be taken as an assumption or an inference and whether it is to be taken metaphorically or literally. But in making those structures explicit, that is representing them as concepts, and marking them in a public language, those structures themselves become objects of reflection.
>
> (Olson, 1994: 111)

In his book, *The World on Paper*, Olson (1994) speculates further about how literacy changed awareness of language as a tool of scientific enquiry in the seventeenth and eighteenth centuries, thereby paving the way for the achievements of modern science. The issues are complex, but Olson offers an intriguing and stimulating argument that is likely to fuel debates in this field for some time to come. He concludes his book thus,

> there seems little doubt that writing and reading played a critical role in producing the shift from thinking about things to thinking about representations of those things, that is, thinking about thought. Our modern conception of the world and our modern conception of ourselves are, we may say, by-products of the invention of a world on paper.
>
> (Olson, 1994: 282)

The spread of literacy within societies

For most of its history written language has been the preserve of the powerful in society and the way in which it has been used has reflected their interests. Only in modern times have the least powerful been expected to acquire literacy and even then the kind of literacy thought appropriate for them may differ from that exercised by the powerful.

In nineteenth-century Britain for example, working class political aspirations included a concern with literacy as a part of universal education and universal suffrage. One of the leading Chartists, William Lovett, in 1841 made detailed proposals for a method of teaching reading and writing. It was intended to replace learning 'by rote, without understanding' with a 'closer connection of words and things', with meaningful learning. Crucially, however, this was coupled with a political vision of education for the working classes which went beyond 'the mere teaching of "reading, writing, and arithmetic"' and which sought to remove 'the obstacles to their liberty and impediments to their happiness which ignorance still presents'. Lovett wanted to develop literacy because he believed it would enable the oppressed to understand what was being done to them.

> The fact of an insignificant portion of the people arrogating to themselves the political rights and powers of the whole, and persisting in making and enforcing such laws as are favourable to their own 'order', and inimical to the interests of the many, affords a strong argument in proof of the ignorance of those who submit to such injustice.
>
> (Lovett, 1841, quoted in Simon, 1972: 245)

The problematic, even contentious, nature of current school literacy is often hidden and it is hard to imagine alternative conceptions of it. However, one way to appreciate the *constructed* nature of school literacy is to take an historical perspective. In the past, there certainly were different conceptions of school literacy. An interesting issue has been the teaching of writing – particularly for working class children. For example, in the 1790s, Hannah More, an influential figure in the establishment of Sunday schools for working class children, is quoted by Brian Simon as insisting that they should not be taught to write at all. 'I allow of no writing for the poor. My object is not to make them fanatics, but to train up the lower classes in habits of industry and piety' (quoted in Simon, 1960: 133).

Simon also quotes Andrew Bell, who became superintendent of the 'National Society' which promoted church schools for the poor. In 1805 Bell argued that children should be taught to read (the Bible) but he felt differently about writing. 'It is not proposed that the children of the poor be educated in an expensive manner, or even taught to write and to cypher' (quoted in Simon, 1960: 133).

Later in the century, the state became involved in funding mass education for the working classes. In 1862 this led to the notorious 'Revised Code' which stipulated what level of attainment was required of children for a school to be funded. There were six levels or 'standards'. From a twenty-first century perspective these were not very ambitious but one striking feature from a late twentieth-century perspective is the fact that reading was seen as *oral reading*. Also, writing was conceived of as *writing from dictation*. The idea of pupils writing something of their own does not appear to have been valued. In fact it was many years before 'composition' was considered appropriate in the elementary school curriculum, and then at first only for older pupils (Birchenough, 1914).

Now, several generations on, there is again a national curriculum in England. It seems obvious that the current version is not as restrictive as the last one at the end of the nineteenth century. But who can say how it will be regarded from a vantage point at the end of the twenty-first century? Even now a struggle is taking place between those who wish children taught phonic skills more explicitly and at an earlier age and those who would rather emphasise meaning and engagement in the early school years; between those who want older children to learn to appreciate certain texts in a national 'literary heritage' and those who prefer a wider choice. The only certain things about any changes which are made is that they will be decided politically and that they will not be permanent. The point is that what counts as school literacy at any particular time is not a given but the result of social processes.

The future of literacy

Now to something which does not exist – at least something which does not exist yet – literacy in the future. We are living in a period when literacy is changing particularly rapidly and no one can be certain what will happen next. This part of the chapter therefore depends more than the rest on the interests, prejudices and particular limitations of the author. The aim is to share some reflections about current trends and some speculations about the future in order to increase awareness that literacy really is changing in front of our eyes, and to pose the question, 'Where is it leading?'

We can begin by reflecting on changes which have occurred in the recent past – in our own lifetimes – and then confront the question, 'Is this the end of literacy?' The end may not be nigh but profound changes are underway in reading, in writing and in the uses of written language.

Changes in our lifetimes

There is a temptation for every generation to believe that its particular historical period is momentous in one way or another but there are strong reasons for believing that the period of the second half of the twentieth century and the dawn of the twenty-first has been, and will continue to be, truly dramatic for literacy. Think back to the time when you first learned to read and write. Compare the literacy technology and resources available to you then to what you use now, and to what is available for literacy learners today. Think what has changed.

In my case I have been struck by the extent of technological changes. I started school in England in the 1950s when writing involved steel nib pens, inkwells and blotting paper. A time traveller from the sixteenth century, familiar with quill pens and the then-new material of paper, would have been entirely comfortable with this technology for mark making. True, pencils were used in reception and infant classes but by older pupils only for 'rough' work. Ball-point pens were still expensive and frowned upon in school on the grounds that they encouraged sloppy handwriting. Only a few children acquired fountain pens from home before the end of primary school. Consequently, the activity of writing for children was often laborious and the results could be unsightly. Contrast that with the experience of children today who have much more convenient writing implements – including not just ball-point pens but fibre-tipped ones too, in many colours – and plentiful supplies of different kinds of paper. Fountain pens have come and gone and are now novelty items. Even more dramatic, some children's earliest writing experiences today are with computers, using keyboards and making marks on screen with all the power of word processing software for amending text and printing out perfect hard copy. Today, even the smallest schools in Britain have computers, printers and photocopiers whereas in the 1950s, at best, they had manual typewriters and duplicating machines.

In reading too there has been an enormous change. In the 1950s the amount of material for young readers in classrooms was very limited and I cannot remember anyone being excited by the content. Today, advances in printing technology have meant that there are many more books for children and they are better written, illustrated and produced than ever before. The revolution in children's publishing in the 1970s and 1980s meant new markets, the emergence of new authors committed to engaging young readers, and new genres integrating text with colour illustrations and graphics. This revealed the poverty of traditional reading schemes and prompted many teachers of young children to rethink their entire approach to teaching reading by basing it more on so-called 'real books'. There have also been changes in children's out of school reading which, for many families, may be more dramatic than those affecting in-school reading. Some families are able to buy the new books for children but even in poorer families children are now growing up in a world saturated with environmental print on advertisements, notices, packaging, junk mail and television.

Even in recent years as an adult, I have experienced rapid change in the technology of literacy. Most of what I now write and read has been produced, processed, stored or transmitted by methods such as photocopying, word processing, laser printing, fax, computer networks or electronic mail – methods which have become routine in my workplace since the late 1980s. Carbon paper, duplicating machines, card indexes and telegrams have slipped into history. Manual typewriters are at the point of extinction even for domestic use. Staff and students in higher education have to keep up with almost monthly developments in information technology (e.g. in libraries, computer networks, CD-ROM, the internet) which affect both teaching and research.

Does literacy have a future?

It is sometimes suggested that reading and writing will not be very important in the future, particularly as the full impact of information technology is felt. It is certainly true that there are certain contexts in which many of us now have less use for written language than did our parents' generation (or perhaps even than we did ourselves in the 1970s). For example, one can think of the way in which the increased use of the telephone (and the availability of mobile phones, message and voice-mail facilities) has meant a decline in the writing of all kinds of letters or the way in which television and video viewing has replaced the reading of books. Yet we have to be careful about concluding that this means less writing and reading. The telephone has also led to the fax machine which reinstates written language. Television has also provided new reasons for reading (e.g. programme listings), new genres (mini-reviews of films, print in advertisements), new ways of reading (teletext), and has stimulated new appetites for books (e.g. classic novels, cookery books). It is safer to conclude that literacy use is *different* rather than less than it was formerly.

Computer based information technology will continue to change the uses and necessity for written language but, again, it is likely that it will decrease some uses while at the same time stimulating others. For example, written language has recently taken on a new importance as a method of human–machine communication – usually in inputting instructions or data through a computer keyboard (i.e. writing) and in reading from a screen. This may eventually be superseded by other methods based on graphic displays and direct voice input/output but for reasons of speed and efficiency these will almost certainly still require literacy at least in being able to read messages on screen. The idea that advances in information technology reduce the need for literacy ignores the fact that a great deal of this technology is devoted to the storage, organisation, and processing of text. On-line help systems are often heavily text dependent. Also, information technology appears to generate a huge amount of ancillary printed material in the form of user manuals, specialist magazines and other documentation.

David Reinking (1994) has suggested that there are four fundamental differences between printed and electronic texts. First, he points out that while it has often been suggested that readers interact with text in a metaphorical sense, in the case of electronic text this can be literally true, for example in the way readers can respond to some text by switching to other texts via 'hot links'. Second, it is possible for electronic texts to guide or restrict the reading path according to educational or other criteria, e.g. requiring re-reading of passages if comprehension questions are not answered correctly. Third, the structure of electronic text can be radically different in 'hypertext' (to be discussed in a later section). Fourth, electronic texts often employ new symbolic elements – not just illustrations but video clips and other graphics, including text 'navigation' aids. One can argue about whether or not these features of electronic literacy are desirable but that they have arrived and that they represent a radical shift seems beyond argument.

Advances in the technology of visual media – films, videos – may at first sight appear to diminish the importance of conventional literacy but, as Colin MacCabe (1998) has argued, this is to ignore the complex interplay between writing and visual media – in both production and reception.

> The interdependence between print and image is much more than a simple reliance on books as source material for films. At every stage of film-making, the written work is central to the production process. Our culture encourages this promiscuity of media, and the computer mixes image and print in ever more complex ways.
>
> (MacCabe, 1998: 14)

In her study of differences in the literacy of boys and girls, Elaine Millard (1997) tells how she came to rethink both the nature of literacy and the connection between print literacy and electronic literacy.

> Literacy was a process that I associated only with immersion in books. As the enquiry progressed I changed my opinion of the computer's distracting influence, and even modified my view of the role of computer games, as negative competitors with literacy activities. This was because I found that working with personal computers not only often involved on-screen reading activities, but that it also engaged young players in a secondary reading of complex texts in order to update their hardware or to progress onto higher levels of difficult games.
>
> (Millard, 1997: 153)

The nature of literacy in a culture is repeatedly redefined as the result of technological changes. Throughout history the introduction of new materials (stone tablets, skins, papyrus, paper) and new mark making methods (scratching, chiselling, ink, the printing press, typewriters, ball-points, laser printers, and so on) has meant both new users and new uses for written language. The consequences of such changes can be very complex – not just in terms of more literacy but different literacy (Eisenstein,

1982). Technology begins by making it easier to do familiar things; then it creates opportunities to do new things. Our literacy today is consequently very different from that of medieval England not just because the printing press is more efficient than having scribes copy manuscripts in monasteries but also because printing and other technologies have stimulated entirely new uses for written language (e.g. tax forms, novels, postcards, advertisements) unimagined by medieval society. If the past is any guide to the future, we should expect information technology to transform literacy rather than eradicate it. To get some idea of the transformations which may be on the way, let us consider in turn the futures of writing and reading.

The future of writing

There are two main changes to consider in writing. The first concerns how text is produced and processed; the second, how it is transmitted to others. Both may have far reaching consequences.

Regarding the first change, I am writing this chapter on a standard 1990s word processing package which allows me to do things which a few years ago would have been regarded as quite magical but which are now taken for granted. I can write as fast as I can type. I can delete text and it vanishes – completely – leaving no trace. I can insert extra text anywhere and the computer moves other text to accommodate it. I can move text from one point in a document to another. A spelling check can eliminate many of my mistakes. I have an enormous choice of page layouts, print fonts and sizes, paragraph and line formats. The screen display is graphical (showing text proportionally spaced and characters in different fonts). It is easy to insert other graphics. There are endless possibilities for editing and polishing. It is almost easier to tinker with the text than leave it alone. When I have done as much as I wish, a touch of a virtual button produces a printed paper copy (or multiple copies if I wish) of a quality which only professional print shops could produce a few years ago.

I see this page on screen virtually as readers see it now in its printed paper version (as wysiwyg – 'what you see is what you get'). However, unlike all previous mark making systems in the history of writing I am not really making marks on anything at all. Until it is printed out, this text exists only in electronic form.

> The bits of text are simply not on a human scale. Electronic technology removes or abstracts the writer and reader from the text. If you hold a magnetic or optical disc up to the light, you will not see text at all. . . . In the electronic medium several layers of sophisticated technology must intervene between the writer or reader and the coded text. There are so many levels of deferral that the reader or writer is hard put to identify the text at all: is it on the screen, in the transistor memory, or on disk?
>
> (Bolter, 1990: 42–3)

The technology is powerful because software plus computer and video screen make it look as if the writing is onto paper but all that exists is virtual writing. The capacity of information technology to mimic conventional forms of communication can be taken further in virtual books or (as in some university courses these days) 'virtual seminars'.

The implications of this power for writing in the future include the following.

Word processing obviously makes it easier to revise and edit writing. For those who wish to write better – whether they are striving to be more effective, more economical, more persuasive, or whatever – the possibility of being able to try a version of a text and to amend it without significant physical labour is obviously going to make it easier to accomplish their goals. Optimists will see word processing as, on the whole, likely to lead to more writers and to better writing in the future but it can also make life easier for those who write carelessly.

Being able to create and insert non-text graphics in a document could have far-reaching consequences. We have grown up with a very text-bound concept of writing because the production of graphics (illustrations, diagrams, embellishments) has hitherto been so difficult for ordinary writers. Yet graphics has become very important – even dominant – in newspapers, magazines, advertisements, packaging, notices and so on. Perhaps everyone will be 'writing' with images in this way in the future and the nature of writing itself will change.

The fact that it is easier to print superb quality documents using standard word processing packages (never mind desktop publishing systems) means a certain demo-cratisation of literacy. Anyone can be a publisher – well, almost a publisher (mass production and distribution still matter) – and to that extent the authority of the printed text is no longer the preserve of the few.

Thus far it has been assumed that writing in the future involves getting text on to paper but of course that is now a limited conception of writing. The second major change in writing is how it is transmitted. If writing is encoded electronically it can be transmitted that way from one output device (terminal, computer, screen, printer) to another.

This morning, working at my desk in the university, I replied to messages from three work colleagues using email (electronic mail). One of them works in the same building as me but the other two work in universities in the United States and South Africa. The procedure was identical in each case. I read their message on my computer screen, clicked on an icon to reply, typed my reply and then clicked on another icon to send the message. My colleague at Sheffield would have been able to read my reply within seconds; it would probably not take much longer for the overseas messages to reach their destinations too. Not only is this kind of 'letter' astonish-ingly quick, but also it is entirely paperless. No time is spent hunting for notepaper, writing the message, making a copy, folding it, placing it in an envelope, stamping it, and remembering to post it. Eliminating these stages not only speeds up the process of writing letters but also, like earlier technological developments in literacy, changes the uses for written language. It encourages a casual, immediate style of communi-cation and it becomes possible, for example, to sustain a research collaboration with people thousands of miles away.

The use of email is part of a wider set of possibilities for reading, writing and communicating via interrelated networks of computers across the world which is the internet. It means that those with access to the technology can search distant data-bases and 'bulletin boards' serving specialist interests. Already, more than 100 million people worldwide use the internet to read documents, journal articles or books which will never be published in paper form and many of them publish to the world through their websites.

The future of reading

In reading the main change to be considered is in the nature of text itself. We have grown up with some taken-for-granted assumptions about text which now need to be changed.

It is perfectly possible to read a document – this book, for example – on a computer much as one would read it on paper. The screen image can look quite like the printed version, pressing the PageUp and PageDown keys is akin to turning real pages, and one can 'turn' to specified page numbers. However, the computer permits other reading possibilities. Some of the simplest, available within most current word processing software, are jumping to points in the text where a specific word or phrase is used or viewing two widely separated sections of a document simultaneously, in adjacent 'windows'. There are no exact parallels to these strategies in reading printed text. More advanced software, now routinely available, allows one to go further. For example, the readers can point to certain words or symbols (with a cursor or 'mouse') and immediately gain access to another text. This is useful if they wish to consult a footnote or read another document which has been cited. It is possible to repeat the procedure with the second text to access a third, and so on. Imagine being able to do this with all the readings and references for a university course. As readers progress through a document in the order which suits them best, with digressions into other documents, they are in effect creating their own version of the document. The technology can allow them to save their particular pathway for future reference with any notes they may wish to add (without affecting the original versions which remain available too).

It no longer seems adequate to refer to what is being read as 'text' in the conventional sense. Instead the term hypertext (as opposed to print text) has gained currency. Tuman (1992) also distinguishes between what he calls print literacy and on-line literacy to distinguish the ways of reading and writing associated with print and computer-based uses of written language. In hypertext readers' pathways through a text need not be linear – they can take sections in whatever order they choose and integrate several different texts. There may be no order other than the ones created by the readers.

The linearity of print text can certainly be a problem for writers struggling to work out the best order in which to set out interconnected ideas and trying to avoid referring to ideas which have not already been introduced to the reader or wanting to define several terms simultaneously. It is a considerable challenge to linearise a set of concepts which are interlinked as a structure in thinking. A 70,000 word book is essentially a thin string of typing up to a mile in length – the fact that it is arranged in 6-inch segments (i.e. lines), 30 or so to a page, disguises this linear quality. A good writer can make it easy for readers to follow the string, picking up needed information and ideas in the easiest possible order. Also, if the writer provides 'signposts' (a preface, a list of contents, chapter headings, subheadings, clear paragraph structure, and so on) readers do not have to follow the string closely but can skip bits and revisit earlier segments if they wish. However, writers of print texts cannot usually rely on such jumping back and forth to make the text readable – they have to provide at least one clear, 'recommended' route through the text.

One may ask, 'Does hypertext eliminate the need for linearity in writing?' Some enthusiasts would answer, 'yes' and see it as a virtue of hypertext that it frees the reader from the control of the writer because there is no single reading or meaning of a text. One example, quoted by Tuman (1992: 55), is Nelson (1987) who argues the case thus:

> Imagine a new libertarian literature with alternative explanations so anyone can choose the pathway or approach that bests suits him or her; with ideas accessible

and interesting to everyone, so that a new richness and freedom can come to the human experience; imagine a rebirth of literacy.

(Nelson, 1987: 1/4)

One could take the contrary view, however. Even in hypertext some processes must operate to select certain texts and not others; to facilitate certain paths and not others. Also, the absence of linearity might be a loss as well as a gain. Without the discipline of linearity, writers may not be forced to develop clear concepts or to iron out contradictions within their arguments. Readers may consequently find it more difficult, not less, to grasp the writer's meaning. This could be particularly problematic in teaching situations.

Implications for understanding literacy today

Many of the future possibilities discussed in this chapter are either in an early stage of development or confined to relatively privileged groups. For example in education, developments have gone further in universities than in adult basic education or primary schools; many people have access to personal computers but not all have CD-ROM facilities and internet connections. Change may be on the way but until it arrives is there any point in bothering about it? There is – for the following reasons.

All our literacy students will end up using written language tomorrow in ways very different from those we can teach them today. This applies to adult students – even older ones who may, for example, be taught to write using conventional pen and paper technology but who may go on to use internet facilities at a local library. It applies much more strongly to younger students and children who, if development proceeds in the next fifty years as it has in the past fifty, will use written language in ways which we cannot even imagine. What matters in this context is that we teach what is important about written language – those essentials which can be expected to endure in future contexts. These could include the ideas that the value of written language depends on what we want to do with it, that all texts can be read critically, that there are many genres, that literacy has a potential for liberation, that writing can aid thinking, that reading can be enjoyable, that public writing is for readers not writers, and so on.

Almost all pronouncements about literacy – its nature, use, development, and how it should be taught – have now to be considered as provisional and temporary. Whatever we think or say about literacy is bound to be a reflection of our particular historical period with its technology and uses for written language. To see how this might be so consider how someone in the sixteenth century might have seen the arrival of printed books. Marshall McLuhan (1962) speculated that the reaction could have been as follows.

> Could a portable, private instrument like the new book take the place of the book one made by hand and memorized as one made it? Could a book which could be read quickly and even silently take the place of book read slowly aloud? Could students trained by such printed books measure up to the skilled orators and disputants produced by manuscript means?
>
> (McLuhan, 1962: 145)

The point is that our own view of literacy today could be just as much shaped by our conceptions of the uses we have for written language.

A major research task is to elucidate the real nature of the changes which we are now encountering and which are likely to get more pronounced in the twenty-first century. What, in fact, are the new demands for using written language in the workplace or the school? How will it affect processes of learning and teaching? What are the political implications?

How is information technology exacerbating or reducing social inequalities in literacy? In the 1980s, Hannon and Wooler expressed these concerns.

> There is every reason to believe that the gulf between children of different social classes will widen. Access to IT devices in school could be reasonably equal for all children (although our experience of the distribution of other educational resources may give grounds for doubt) but there are bound to be huge differences in home use of computers and computer-based equipment like video disks and database terminals. Entire 'curricula' are likely to be marketed by software houses or large publishing corporations. The result will be fatal to the opportunities of many working class children who will be disadvantaged in terms of the sheer amount of time they will be able to spend learning via computers. Economic differences between families are likely to be translated even more directly into educational differences.
>
> (Hannon and Wooler, 1985: 93)

Much of this had indeed come to pass. What these authors did not foresee, however, was expansion of the internet which – arguably – has some potential for equalising access to electronically stored knowledge if families can pass the threshold of computer internet connection. Even then, it must be admitted that differences in terms of computer skills, adult support and cultural know-how may be too great for some children ever to overcome.

Landow (1992) points out that 'almost all authors on hypertext who touch upon the political implications of hypertext assume that the technology is essentially democratizing and that it therefore supports some sort of decentralized, liberated existence' (Landow, 1992: 33). On the other hand, Michael Apple (1986) has suggestedthat

> computers involve ways of thinking that are primarily technical. The more the new technology transforms the classroom in its own image, the more a technical logic will replace critical political and ethical understanding.
>
> (Apple, 1986: 171)

Those involved in teaching literacy – in any capacity – need to think about how they are preparing learners for literacy in the future. What assumptions are made about the future? Are there specific aspects of literacy which deserve more emphasis? How would it be possible to provide this?

Determining the actual, as opposed to the possible, impact of the new technology on literacy could be one of the most interesting research challenges in this field in the twenty-first century.

References

Apple, M.W. (1986) *Teachers and Texts: A Political Economy of Class and Gender Relations in Education*, New York: Routledge and Kegan Paul.

Barton, D. (1994) *Literacy: An Introduction to the Ecology of Written Language*, Oxford: Blackwell.

Birchenough, C. (1914) *History of Elementary Education in England and Wales*, London: University Tutorial Press.

Bolter, J.D. (1990) *Writing Space*, Hillsdale, NJ: Lawrence Erlbaum.

Eisenstein, E.L. (1982) *The Printing Press as an Agent of Change: Communications and Cultural Transformations in Early-Modern Europe*, Cambridge: Cambridge University Press.

Gibbon, E. (1896) *The History of the Decline and Fall of the Roman Empire*, London: Methuen (original work published 1776).

Graff, H. (1979) *The Literacy Myth: Cultural Integration and Social Structure in the Nineteenth Century*, New Brunswick, NJ: Transaction.

Graff, H. (1987) *The Labyrinths of Literacy*, Lewes: Falmer Press.

Hannon, P. and Wooler, S. (1985) 'Psychology and educational computing', in Wellington, J.J. (Ed.) *Children, Computers and the Curriculum*, London: Croom Helm.

Havelock, E. (1982) *The Literate Revolution in Greece and its Cultural Consequences*, Princeton, NJ: Princeton University Press.

Jean, G. (1992) *Writing: The Story of Alphabets and Scripts*, London: Thames and Hudson.

Landow, G.P. (1992) *Hypertext: The Convergence of Contemporary Critical Theory and Technology*, Baltimore, MD: Johns Hopkins University Press.

MaCabe, C. (1998) 'End of the word?', *Guardian*, Screen, 10 July, p. 14.

McLuhan, H.M. (1962) *Gutenberg Galaxy: the Making of Typographic Man*, Toronto: University of Toronto Press.

Millard, E. (1997) *Differently Literate: Boys, Girls and the Schooling of Literacy*, London: Falmer Press.

Nelson, T. (1987) *Literary Machines*, edition 87.1. [Quoted and cited in Tuman, 1992, p. 55.]

Olson, D. (1994) *The World on Paper*, Cambridge: Cambridge University Press.

Reinking, D. (1994) *Electronic Literacy: Perspectives in Reading Research No. 4*, Universities of Georgia and Maryland: National Reading Research Center.

Simon, B. (1960) *Studies in the History of Education, 1780–1870*, London: Lawrence and Wishart.

Simon, B. (Ed.) (1972) *The Radical Tradition in Education in Britain*, London: Lawrence and Wishart.

Tuman, M. (1992) *Word Perfect: Literacy in the Computer Age*, London: Falmer Press.

Vygotsky, L.S. (1962) *Thought and Language*, Cambridge, MA: MIT Press.

CHAPTER 2

LIVING LITERACIES IN HOMES AND COMMUNITIES

Eve Gregory and Ann Williams

City Literacies, London: Routledge, 2000, pp. 158–79

Introduction

> The differences that children bring to classrooms, therefore, are not simply individual differences or idiosyncrasies ... They are the products and constructions of the complex and diverse social learning from the cultures where children grow, live and interact ... These, too, are dynamic and hybrid: mixing, matching and blending traditional values and beliefs, child-rearing practices and literacy events with those of new, post-modern, popular cultures.
>
> (Luke and Kale, 1997: 16)

This chapter focuses upon the new generation of Spitalfields residents, the children who with their families and teachers took part in the Family Literacy History project in the mid-1990s. This study was carried out at a time of grave concern over standards in education and in particular over reading standards. Three Inner London boroughs had recently been the focus of a special investigation (Ofsted, 1996), which demonstrated that children in these inner-city areas performed less well in literacy tests than their counterparts elsewhere. Although many factors, including poverty, poorly resourced schools and large numbers of children for whom English is an additional language, must account to some extent for the disappointing results, parents' own skills were also considered to play a crucial role in their children's performance.

Home literacy practices have long been seen as a contributory factor in a child's success or failure in school. Research by ALBSU (1993) suggested that parents' level of education was the strongest predictor of a child's success. Large-scale studies by scholars such as Wells (1985) found correlations between home story reading and early proficiency in school reading. Snow and Ninio went further, stating that home story reading was essential to provide children with the 'skills which they have to learn if they are to participate successfully in book reading interactions' (1986: 136). Government reports also encouraged parental involvement. The Bullock Report (DES, 1975) stated that a major priority was to 'help parents recognise the value of sharing the experience of books with their children'; the Cox Report (DES, 1988) exhorted parents to 'share books with their children from their earliest days and read aloud to them and talk about stories they (had) enjoyed together'. The School Curriculum and Assessment Authority Report on Desirable Outcomes for Children's Learning in Nurseries (SCAA, 1996) urged parents to 'support learning opportunities at home through reading and sharing books'. This was followed up by a government green paper proposing that parents should be obliged to read with their children on a daily basis.

> Parents will be asked to sign an undertaking to read with their children at home for at least 20 minutes per day under government proposals for improving literacy published yesterday ... Stephen Byers, the schools minister, said he was fighting back against the dumbing down of British culture as exemplified by the Teletubbies and declining standards on Radio 4.
>
> (Guardian, 1997)

It is clear then, that home story reading both to and with children is considered to be a pivotal factor in the successful acquisition of literacy, and there would appear to exist in both education and government circles a set of beliefs concerning good practice. It is assumed:

- that story reading, as it is practised in Western homes is the most valuable preparation for literacy development;
- that the same home-reading practices are suitable for all children whether their home language is English or another language;
- that parents need to perform activities approved by the school and that successful practices are transferred from school to home;
- that it is parents rather than other family members who should carry out the literacy activities with the children;
- that very little literacy besides that taken from the school goes on in the homes.

While the government initiatives are admirable and clearly reflect a political will to improve standards for all children, they nevertheless focus on a very narrow definition of literacy; that is, that which is variously described as 'mainstream' by Heath (1983), 'schooled' by Street and Street (1995) or 'official' by Dyson (1997). Little account appears to be taken of what happens in non-Western homes nor of the unofficial literacy practices in which people engage. Yet the people of Spitalfields have a long tradition of 'alternative' literacies, ranging from studying the Talmud to publishing working-class poetry. One aim of our project was to uncover the 'unofficial literacies' in which people engage and to examine the part they can play in supporting children's school learning. We begin by looking at the reading experiences of the mothers who took part in the project and who were aged between 23 and 40 when the project was carried out.

Reading at home

The monolingual mothers

> My dad was a reader. He read anything and everything from the newspapers. That's why Simon could read the newspaper; he could pick all the horses out. He was four and a half when he came here [to school] and he was reading the newspaper. He still does, the back page. At the time he could see what horses were running, what the prizes were, what colours they had, who the jockey was ... the lot, he still does ...
>
> (Mrs Radford)

As we can see from the above quotation, the route to becoming literate for some of our participants did not necessarily depend on reading from approved texts, nor was it school based. The six monolingual mothers who took part in the project provided surprisingly homogeneous accounts of their formal literacy experiences in Inner London primary and comprehensive schools of the 1970s and 1980s. For the most part, their 'schooled' or 'official' reading experiences had been painful and disappointing. All felt dissatisfied with their own schooling and wanted their children to have the educational opportunities they felt they themselves had missed. Four of the women had truanted regularly from both their primary and secondary schools, afraid to go to school because of bullying or encouraged to stay at home by parents. One was dyslexic, one fell behind in her work because of her frequent absences and another left before taking any examinations because of the bullying she suffered. The feeling expressed by some of the mothers was that the 'significant adults' in the process, the teachers, had been uninterested in them and had not encouraged them to work hard nor to strive for success in school. Memories of learning to read in the formal context of school therefore were painful:

> I was never really that good in school. I was partially dyslexic as well and still am with writing. They used to leave me in a corner with a picture book.
>
> (Mrs Turner)

> I was slow at reading. I was behind for a long time. My mum used to let me have a lot of time off and then once you fall behind in your work you don't want to go back any more, do you?
>
> (Mrs White)

In contrast, true learning and reading with real enjoyment took place at home. Thus, Mrs Radford who left school with no qualifications, when asked about how she learned to read, responded, 'I've always been able to read. My dad was a reader'. Mrs Turner, who was dyslexic, stated,

> Whatever I learned was down to my mum and dad. They were good in that department because my mum's dyslexic. On Saturday morning, we used to get comics through the door. I used to sit there for hours. I used to get all of them – *Buster, Beano, Dandy* . . . my mum used to read them as well.

Mrs Taylor who had been an indifferent student in school, and who 'just used to walk out of school a lot of the time', nevertheless 'used to love going to the library ''cos [she] used to go behind the counter and sort the tickets out' and had some 'beautiful books' at home, which she bought with her dad at W.H. Smith at Elephant and Castle. All the mothers spoke with evident pleasure of the books and comics they had read at home as children. Enid Blyton was cited by all as a favourite author, along with classics such as *Black Beauty* and *Treasure Island*.

For these women, then, it was the home rather than the school literacy practices that had shaped their learning, and in almost every case there was an interested and caring adult in the home, a literacy broker or a 'guiding light' (Padmore, 1994) who encouraged them and provided books and materials. In the case of Mrs Radford it was her father who 'was a reader'; Mrs Turner's parents coped with her dyslexia by providing comics; and Mrs Taylor's father took her shopping for books.

Interestingly, the love of reading, which they remembered so vividly from their childhoods, has remained with them and the five mothers now read regularly for pleasure. Mrs White, who missed about two years of schooling, reads 'a lot now, mainly biography and horror'. Mrs Radford, who left school with no formal qualifications, is now a parent governor, chair of her local residents' association and still an avid reader, sharing and discussing books with a circle of friends. Mrs Turner, once dyslexic, now reads mainly 'on a night' and on Sundays when she 'sits on the settee all day with a book' and 'doesn't move'. Mrs Anderson, the youngest mother at 23, who left school before completing her education, says of her husband, 'He's not really a reader. I'm the reader'. Interestingly, there was no suggestion in the interviews that their reading should be educational or 'improving' in any sense. Nor was there any mention of 'good books'. For these women, reading is a purely pleasurable occupation and the authors such as Catherine Cookson, Harry Bowling, Virginia Andrew, Ruth Rendell, and Agatha Christie, whose works they read so avidly, would be considered writers of 'popular fiction'.

In this way, the monolingual mothers differed from both the Bangladeshi-British mothers and from the two mainstream schoolteachers. For the latter group, there had been no 'pain–pleasure' dichotomy attached to learning to read as children and they had happy memories of both school and home reading, remembering authors such as Enid Blyton, Noel Streatfield and Eleanor Brent-Dyer. Unlike the children's mothers, however, they felt that they now had no time to read, except in school holidays, and even then, it was suggested by one teacher, it was preferable to try to read 'good' books. The 'reading for pleasure' dimension that had been such an enjoyable part of their childhood reading patterns has now disappeared from their lives.

The children

As might be expected, the monolingual mothers viewed the reading, writing and other literacy practices in which the children engaged at home largely as activities to be enjoyed, and there was a wide variety, ranging from playing schools to attending drama classes, with the boys enjoying computer games and drawing, and the girls preferring reading, writing and playing schools, along with the usual television and video viewing. Playing schools, which involved writing registers, 'correcting' work and writing on the blackboard, was the preferred pastime of all the girls, even if they had to play alone.

AW: What do you like doing at home?
Nadia: At home I like playing teachers because I've got a board and I can write on it. It's not a board, it's like ... you know a folder, it's a folder with all paper in and I've got pens to write with and I say a few names that's in my class but some I don't know.
AW: And do you play by yourself?
Nadia: Yes.
AW: When do you read all these books?
Sarah: Sometimes when I'm playing teachers. Sometimes I play it with Amy, sometimes with Nadia and sometimes on my own.

Writing can also be an absorbing occupation for a solitary child. Nadia and Sophie both enjoyed writing:

she'll sit in her room and she'll fold her legs and she'll write.

(Mrs Taylor)

I do stories sometimes. I've got a little diary with Minnie Mouse on it and I write in there. Not every day ... sometimes.

(Nadia)

I like to write stories and I like to do my handwriting and I like to do pictures and cards and give them to everybody. I made a Valentine's card. It had hearts and Sellotape over and then I stuck them with glue.

(Sophie)

Unlike the girls, the boys did not enjoy solitary occupations but actively sought out other children to play with. As well as playing imaginative games with toys such as Batman, the Power Rangers and Ninja Turtles, they played computer games, which require two players:

AW: What do you do when your mum says he's not allowed in?
Ricky: I just let him in and then we look to see if anyone is sitting in the chair near the door and then we creep into the bedroom.
AW: And what do you do in there?
Ricky: Play. We play on the computer and sometimes we play Sonic, Sonic 2 and Street Fighter.

Although such games involve reading instructions and typing in names, they are not literacy-based activities in the same way as playing schools, writing or reading books, the preferred occupations of the girls.

All the children talked about books they read at home, however. The girls in particular enjoyed both reading and collecting books:

AW: What do you think would be your best book?
Sophie: I think it would be my Mr Men books.
AW: Have you got all of them?
Sophie: Nearly. I've got twenty-one more to collect.
AW: What about the Little Miss books?
Sophie: I'm not collecting them yet.

I've got thousands of books. I've got loads ... I have to have two shelfs [sic] for them. I've got a collection of dinosaur books. My grandad buys all the dinosaur books and I've got ninety-nine so when I go today [to visit him] I'll have a hundred.

(Sarah)

Family size, position in the family and family circumstances also had an effect on the children's play. Two girls were 'only children' and the two others were the youngest child in the family by several years and therefore obliged to entertain themselves much of the time. All were used to playing alone, and reading, of course, is an ideal activity for a solitary child:

There are times when we want to relax and be quiet, and she'll be gone for an hour and she'll be down here reading on her own.

(Mrs Anderson, mother of Sophie)

I just read some books to myself in my bedroom . . . but I've read them so many times, I'm fed up with them.

(Sarah)

Although only 6 years old, the children already possessed many books:

AW: If somebody gave you a present what would you choose?
Sophie: I'd choose a bookcase 'cos I've got so many books I have to have a toybox to put them all in and I have them on a shelf and all the rest on the landing. I can't fit them anywhere.

Their tastes in books were wide ranging and diverse but much of their reading matter would not necessarily meet with approval from teachers, nor would it be found in school bookshelves. Luke (1992) identifies two main strands in children's literature: the 'residual' tradition, exemplified in fairytales and works by approved authors; and the 'emergent', alternate tradition, which is closely associated with popular culture. Materials which fall into the latter category are rarely approved in schools as 'official' literature. At home, however, these 'unofficial' texts formed a substantial part of the children's reading, creating 'a pattern of mutually reinforcing intertextual references', with characters who appeared on television, in films, in comics, in books, and as toys (Luke, 1992: 39). Thus 6-year-old Sophie, who read the classics such as *Little Women* and *What Katy Did* with her mother, claimed nevertheless that her favourite books were based on the Walt Disney films:

AW: Do you get books for presents?
Sophie: Sometimes I ask for them.
AW: Do you remember any that you have asked for?
Sophie: I asked for *Dumbo* and *One Hundred and One Dalmatians*.
AW: Have you seen the film *Dumbo*?
Sophie: Yes.

Ricky, whose passion was the *Ninja Turtles* (a US television series), was firmly situated in the 'emergent' culture tradition:

AW: What else do you do after school? Do you ever read books or anything?
Ricky: I only read Ghostbusters and Turtle books.

In spite of their popularity with children however, such texts are rarely found in schools. Thus, while they fulfil the criterion of providing pleasure and fun, they are not considered suitable for school reading. Just as we found with the mothers, there still exists a clear distinction between the reading matter that is enjoyed in the home and that which is sanctioned in school.

Literacy brokers and guiding lights

Although the English mothers saw reading at home primarily as an enjoyable occupation, they were nevertheless very concerned about their children's education and in most cases were taking steps to ensure that their children did not experience difficulties in school: Sophie's mother had begun teaching her daughter to read with flash cards at the age of eighteen months so that by age 3 she could recognise simple words like 'cat' and 'dog' and 'was reading books by the time she came out of reception class'. Mrs Taylor bought Nadia maths and language-activity books in order to help with school work. Amy's parents enrolled her for speech and drama classes, which they felt would 'help her with exams later'. Ricky's mother attended special classes organised by the school to demonstrate how reading was taught in school. Without exception, the monolingual parents involved in the project were anxious that their children should succeed where they felt that they themselves had failed:

> I wish I'd stayed on [at school]. That's my big regret. I wouldn't like her to make the same mistakes as I did.

> (Mrs Clark)

Involvement in the children's learning was not restricted to parents however. In each of the monolingual families the grandparents played a major part in fostering the children's interest in books and reading. Sometimes, the grandparents acted as role models, as in the case of Nadia.

AW: Do you ever read any other books at home beside your PACT (Parents And Children Together) books?
Nadia: Sometimes I read these, erm . . . interesting books like bird . . . about birds and . . .
AW: And where do you get them from?
Nadia: From my grandpa.
AW: So there are books about birds?
Nadia: And books about plants and some about ants . . .
AW: Are they interesting? Have they got pictures?
Nadia: Yes but they aren't really like pictures like in a book what you read . . . like just interesting.
AW: Are they books for children, do you think, or are they books for adults?
Nadia: I think they're books for like 7- to 11-year-olds . . . But my grandpa's got lots of books . . . He's got all sorts of books about snakes, about birds, about insects . . .
AW: Does he read them?
Nadia: Yes.
AW: And where does he keep them?
Nadia: He keeps them in his wardrobe.
AW: And what's your favourite one that he's got?
Nadia: The one I read sometimes is this white book called *The Reindeer Book*.

Nadia's grandfather, like two of his brothers, had been a London taxi-driver, who, in order to qualify, had had to pass the written examination based on what is often referred to as 'the knowledge'. His early interest in general knowledge has stayed with him all his life and even now at the age of 80, he still reads widely and maintains his interest in subjects as diverse as stamps and medicine. Nadia appeared to have adopted her grandfather's taste in books and her preferred reading matter at the time of the project was her children's encyclopaedia.

Sarah and Sophie's grandparents bought books for their grandchildren. As we saw earlier, Sarah's grandad bought her dinosaur books and Sophie's grandparents bought collections of the classics as well as reference books: 'She'd brought the atlas home from school and he [grandfather] went out the next day and bought her this [an atlas]'.

Table 1 Literacy-related activities at home and in the community: English monolingual children

Type of practice	Context	Participants	Purpose	Scope	Materials	Role of child	Language
playing school	informal: at home	group or individual	play	frequently (girls)	blackboard, books, writing materials	child imitates teacher and/or pupils	English
PACT (Parents and Children Together: home-reading scheme)	informal: at home	parent–child dyad	homework: to improve child's reading	daily	school reading book	child reads and is corrected by parent using 'scaffolding' or 'modelling' strategies	English
comics, fiction, non-fiction	informal: at home	individual or dyad (parent or grandparent/child)	pleasure	frequently	variety of comics, fiction, non-fiction books	child as 'expert' with comics or books; as interested learner reading adult non-fiction, magazines, etc.	English
drama class	formal	group	pleasure and to learn skill	2 hrs a week	books: poetry and plays	child performs in group; recites individual	English
computers	informal	individual or in dyad with friend or sibling	pleasure	frequently	computer games	active participant	English
video/TV	informal	family group or individual	leisure/ entertainment	daily	TV/videos	child listens and watches; discusses with others	English

Some grandparents actually taught their grandchildren to read, as we saw in the case of Simon who learned to read with his grandfather, using the racing tips in a tabloid newspaper.

> When he was 3 or 4 he was always with him ... watched the horse-racing, read the papers, taught him to read when he was in nursery.

Clearly, the transmission of literacy skills in the monolingual English families is not seen solely as the responsibility of parents. In a society where mothers have to work outside the home, it is often the retired grandparents who have the time to take on the role of literacy brokers. The situation in the Bangladeshi-British families was quite different as we shall discuss in the next section.

Formal learning in informal contexts

The Bangladeshi-British children

The out-of-school lives of the Bangladeshi children seem far removed from those of their monolingual schoolmates. Although they too rush happily out of school with their brothers and sisters at 3.30 p.m., they do not go home to an evening of playing schools or computer games. For most of them, formal learning continues long after mainstream school has finished, as the following conversation with 6-year-old Maruf demonstrates:

Maruf: There are eighty three children.
AW: Eighty three children in your Arabic class! And when do you go to that?
Maruf: 7 o'clock to 9 o'clock.
AW: On?
Maruf: A night.
AW: Every night?
Maruf: Monday to Friday.
AW: Monday to Friday! You go for two hours every night! Aren't you tired?
Maruf: I don't feel tired.
AW: No? And who goes with you? Anybody from your class?
Maruf: I go by myself ... And some people go from upstairs ... juniors.
AW: And are you the youngest then?
Maruf: Yes and I'm on the Qur'an.
AW: You're on the Qur'an now.
Maruf: There's Quaida and Ampara and Qur'an.
AW: And you're on the Qur'an now?
Maruf: I'm on the last one.
AW: Are you ... How many teachers are there for eighty three children?
Maruf: There's two.
AW: Only two. Who are they?
Maruf: One is the Qur'an ... you know, all the Qur'an he can say it without looking.
AW: He can ... What's his name?
Maruf: I don't know. And one is ... he can ... he knows all the meanings.
AW: Does he? Does he tell you the meanings?
Maruf: Yes, he does.
AW: So do you just read the Qur'an for two hours? Is that what you do?

Table 2 Literacy-related activities at home and in the community: Bangladeshi-British children

Type of practice	Context	Participants	Purpose	Scope	Materials	Role of child	Language
Qur'anic class	formal: in classrooms or in someone's living room	group of 0–30 mixed age range	religious: to read and learn the Qur'an	approx. 7 hrs a week	Raiel (wooden bookstand), preparatory primers or Qur'an	child listens and repeats (individually or as group); practises and is tested	Arabic
Bengali class	formal: in classrooms or in someone's living room	group of mixed age range. Can be children of one family up to group of 30	cultural: to learn to read, understand and write standard Bengali	approx. 6 hrs a week	printers, exercise books, pens	child listens and repeats (individually or as group); practises and is tested	Standard Bengali
reading with older siblings	informal: at home	dyad: child and older sibling	homework: to learn to speak and read English	approx. 3 hrs a week	English schoolbooks	child repeats, echoes, predicts and finally answers comprehension questions	English
video/TV	informal: at home	Family group	pleasure/ entertainment		TV in English; videos (often in Hindi)	child watches and listens; often listens to and joins in discussions; sings songs from films	Hindi and English

Maruf: Yes but I don't sometimes, I talk sometimes.
AW: You don't!
Maruf: I do.

This conversation gives some idea of the demands made upon children who participate in two very different cultures. For these children, acquiring literacy is a complex business involving several languages. The home dialect of the London Bangladeshis is Sylheti, an unwritten variety of Bengali, and so parents feel that it is important that their children learn to read and write standard Bengali if they are to maintain their own culture. Second, in their mainstream school they have to learn to read and write in English in order to function successfully in Britain. Finally, as practising Muslims, the children must read the Qur'an and therefore attend Qur'anic school and learn to read in Arabic. Already at age 6, Maruf realises that literacy is a serious business and that punishments lie in store for those who do not apply themselves.

The class which Maruf attended every day after school is typical of Qur'anic classes everywhere. The sessions are usually two hours long: few concessions are made to the young age of some of the children and even the smallest are expected to concentrate for long periods:

> In this particular class there are two male teachers, one of whom is working with the more advanced children who are tackling the complicated word structures of the Qur'an. The other group consists of younger children who are in a different part of the room with the second teacher, grappling with sounds and letters and oral verse. Everyone sits on the mat swaying to the sound of his/her own voice. Although on initial appraisal the noise level seems high, little of this is idle chatter. It is the expressed wish of the teachers that children read aloud, partly to assist their learning, but more importantly so that Allah can hear. Children are encouraged to develop a harmonious recitation in unison with the gentle rocking to and fro which accompanies the reading. They are told that Allah listens to his servants and is pleased if they take time to make their reading meaningful . . . 'Now, repeat after me', the teacher requests, 'Kalimah Tayyabh, la ilaha ilallaho, mohammadan rasolallahe'. He tells them to look at him as they repeat. I leave the room on the third recitation of the prayer and notice that the children have not wavered: all remain seated on the floor as they have done for the last hour and a half.
>
> (Rashid, 1996)

Teaching methods are traditional: the teacher reads a phrase and the children repeat after him until they are word-perfect and the process continues with the next phrase. The pattern of listen, practise and repeat is shown clearly in the following extract, also taken from Rashid:

> The teacher stands in the centre and calls upon each child in turn to recite the passage which they have reached in their reading of the religious primer or the Qur'an.
>
> *Teacher*:   Read this, Shuma.
> *Shuma*:   Alif, bah, tah, sayh . . . (*the names of the graphic symbols on the page*)
> *Teacher*:   What was that? Say it again.
> *Shuma*:   Alif, bah, tah, sayh, jim . . .
> *Teacher*:   Yes, that's it, now carry on.

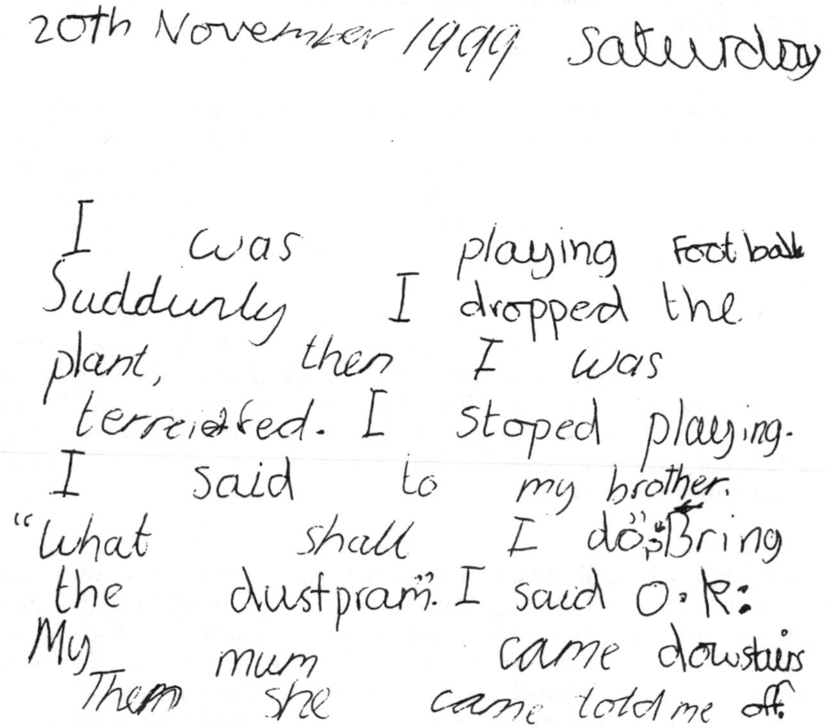

20th November 1999   Saturday

I   was   playing Football
Suddenly   I   dropped the.
plant,   then   I   was
terreiafed. I   stoped playing.
I   said   to   my brother.
"What   shall   I do? Bring
the   dustpram. I said O·K:
My Them mum   came dowstairs
Them   she   came told me off.

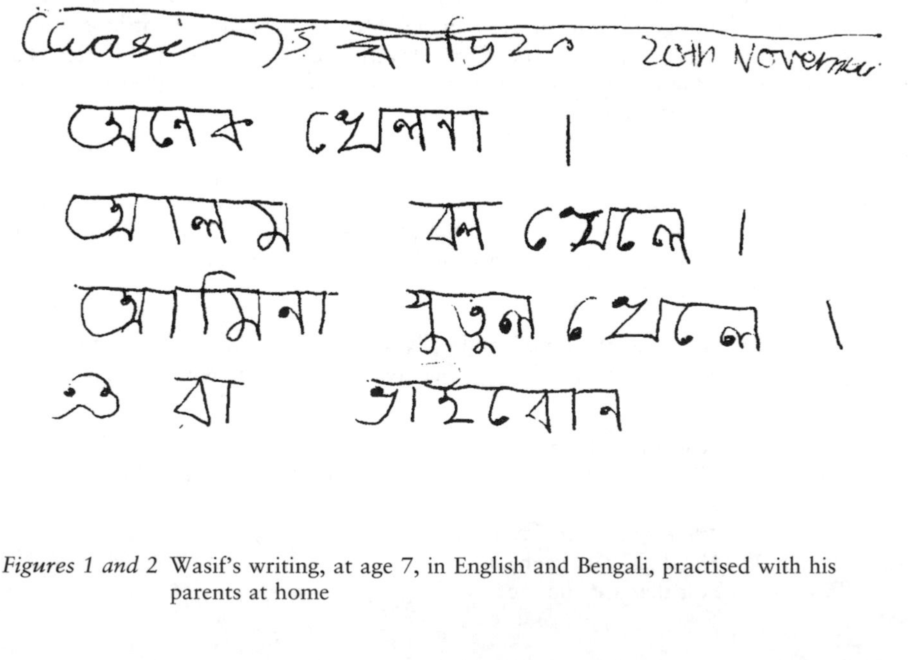

Cuasi   ⟩s ⟨bengali⟩   20th November.

অনেক খেলনা ।

আলম বল খেলে ।

আমিনা ফুতুল খেলে ।

ও বা গাইবোন

Figures 1 and 2 Wasif's writing, at age 7, in English and Bengali, practised with his parents at home

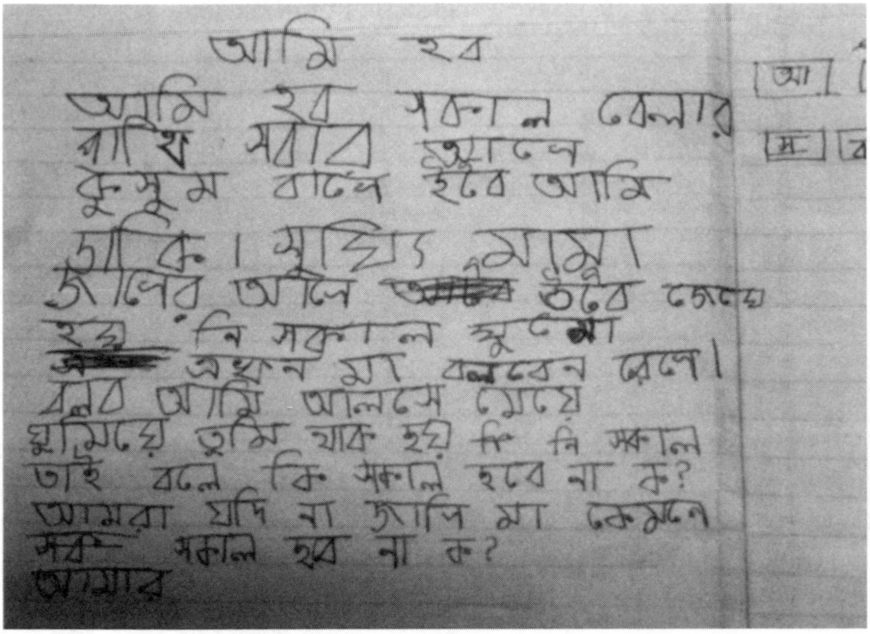

I want to be the morning bird
I'll sing out in the flower garden before everyone else
I'll wake up before Uncle Sun rises
Mother will say crossly, 'Go back to sleep, it's not morning yet'
I'll reply, 'Lazybones, you're still sleeping.
Morning is on its way.
If we don't wake up, how can morning come?
Morning is coming and only your son is awake.'

> From 'The Morning Bird', a poem for children by Kazi
> Nazrul Islam (1899–1976), the 'Rebel Poet of Bengal'

Figure 3 Waseq's writing in Bengali, with English translation below

Table 3 Community class attendance: Bangladeshi-British children

Child	Mon	Tues	Wed	Thurs	Fri	Sat	Sun
M	B	B	B	B	B	A	A
A	A	A	A	A	A	B	B
Sh	B	B	B	B	A	A	
H	A	A	A	A	B	B	
S	A	A	A	A	B	B	
U	A	A	A	A	A	B	B

B = Bengali class. A = Arabic (Qur'anic class). Duration of lessons: 2 hrs

Figure 4 Wasif and Waseq practising their reading together

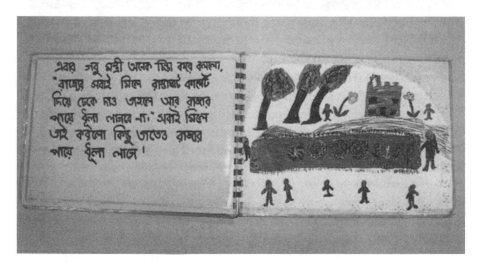

Figure 5 Work from the Bengali community class

Shuma:	jim – jim, hae, kae, d- (*hesitates*) ...
Teacher:	Dal – dal, remember it and repeat.
Shuma:	dal, zal, rae, zae, sin, shin, swad, dwad ...
Teacher:	(*nods*) What's next? Thoy, zoy.
Shuma:	zoy, thoy ...
Teacher:	No, no, listen carefully. Thoy, zoy.
Shuma:	(*repeats*)
Teacher:	Fine. Now say it again from the beginning ...

(Rashid, 1997)

The Bengali classes take place in a variety of locations. Some are held in teachers' houses, some in the children's homes and some in community centres as the one described by Rashid below:

> Situated behind Petticoat Lane Market, this Bengali school is funded through the voluntary sector. It comprises two mobile rooms, the walls bare except for a few information posters made by the children. The room I enter has several rows of desks at which children sit quietly – some writing, others practising words under their breath. At the beginning, the teacher sits in front of the room, then starts to walk around. The children who are mumbling are practising the previous day's work and as the teacher passes around, the voice of the child he is listening to is momentarily amplified so that the teacher can correct if necessary before moving on to the next.
>
> Later the children read, some at a fast pace whilst others read with careful deliberation. When the teacher reaches the child I have come to observe, she reads confidently and eloquently and the few mistakes she makes are firmly corrected. Parts that are not understood are explained briefly in Sylheti ... and the lesson continues in this way to the end.
>
> (Rashid, 1997)

Teaching methods in the Bengali classes are equally traditional: children work on one primer at a time, progressing gradually through the series. As the following conversation indicates, learning Bengali, even if it takes place in someone's front room with a friend's mum as the teacher, is also a serious undertaking:

AW: Tell me what you do, then, on Saturdays and Sundays.
Maruf: I don't come to school.
AW: You don't come to school but what do you do?
Maruf: I go to Bengali school then I come home.
AW: What time do you go to Bengali school?
Maruf: 11 o'clock to 1 o'clock.
AW: And what do you do there?
Maruf: We read Bengali.
AW: And how do you do ... how do you learn that, then? And do you just have one book or do you have a lot of books?
Maruf: There's book two, book three, book four, book five ... there's lots of books.
AW: Lots of books, and which book are you on?
Maruf: Book one.
AW: Book one. Is it hard?
Maruf: Easy!
AW: What do you have to do? Do you have to write in the book?
Maruf: You've got to read it. And sometimes they say, 'You've got to write it without looking'.
AW: Write it without looking and then what do you do?
Maruf: Then if I'm right ... she ... they tell us.
AW: And who is your teacher?
Maruf: There's two, Meli's dad and Jahanara's dad.
AW: Jahanara's dad! Is he the teacher?
Maruf: Jahanara's dad, and Tania ... do you know Tania in Class One?
AW: No.

Maruf: Her mum.
AW: Her mum. And are they strict?
Maruf: They give us . . .
AW: Give you what?
Maruf: Punishment.
AW: What do they do? What punishment do they give you?
Maruf: They talk to us and do you know what Meli's dad does . . . says to pull
           our ear.
AW: He's going to pull your ear?
Maruf: No, you've got to pull it like that.
AW: You've got to pull your own ear. Have you ever had to do that?
Maruf: Never.

Although Maruf is only 6 years old, he spends two hours every day in addition to his mainstream school, in such classes (see Table 3). In contrast with the monolingual group, who engaged mostly in informal literacy practices outside school, the Bangladeshi-British children spent on average thirteen hours per week receiving formal instruction in organised classes. Thus their home literacy differs from that of the monolingual children in many respects. First, it is conducted as group rather than individual or paired activities, and an individual's progress (towards the completion of the Qur'an, for example) is often marked by the whole group sharing sweets or other treats. Second, the notion of 'pleasure' in terms of 'immediate enjoyment' gained from a story read at home is not applicable to the kind of out-of-school reading practised by the Bangladeshi children: learning to read and write in Bengali is seen as entering a cultural world and acquiring a language which was fought over during the violent struggle for independence from Pakistan in 1971: learning to read the Qur'an is necessary for being accepted into the Islamic faith and therefore an adult and serious occupation. Finally, even the task of reading at home in English is quite different for Bangladeshi-British children. In this community where some parents are literate in Bengali but not necessarily in English, home reading usually means children reading their school texts not with mum or dad nor even with grandma or grandpa, but with those members of the family who are already fully proficient in English – that is, the older sisters and brothers.

Booksharing at home

It was 'booksharing' with older siblings that provided some of the most interesting insights into the young Bangladeshi-British children's acquisition of literacy. The combination of cultures and learning styles the bilingual children were exposed to in their daily lives resulted in a unique method of tackling the school reading books at home. When the home reading sessions were analysed, it became clear that the children were blending strategies learned in both their mainstream English school and in their Bengali and Arabic classes. This resulted in what we have termed 'syncretic literacy' (Gregory, 1998), with the repetitions and fast-flowing pace characteristic of the Qur'anic reading grafted on to strategies such as echoing, 'chunking' of expressions and predicting, adopted from lessons in the English school. The transcriptions also revealed that the older siblings employed a series of intricate and finely tuned strategies to support the young readers as they struggled with the text. In the early stages, when reading with a child who was just beginning to read, the supportive 'scaffolding' was almost total, with the older siblings providing almost every word for the beginning reader. As the younger child's proficiency increased however, the scaffolding was gradually removed until the child was able to read alone. We were able to identify the following stages in the scaffolding of the young children's reading:

1   *Listen and repeat*: the child repeats word by word after the older sibling.
2   *Tandem reading*: the child echoes the sibling's reading, sometimes managing telegraphic speech.
3   *Chained reading*: the sibling begins to read and the child continues, reading the next few words until he/she needs help again.
4   *Almost alone*: the child initiates reading and reads until a word is unknown; the sibling corrects the error or supplies the word; the child repeats the word correctly and continues.
5   *The recital*: the child recites the complete piece.

The following two extracts illustrate Stages 1, Listen and repeat, and 3, Chained reading:

Stage 1

Child	*Sibling*
	1 The postman
2 The postman	
	3 It was Tum's birthday
4 was . . . birthday	
	5 Ram made
6 Ram made	
	7 him a birthday card
8 him a birthday card	

Stage 3

Child	*Sibling*
	34 Okhta [This one]
	35 It's
36 It's a whobber. Meg . . .	
	37 Mog
38 Mog catched a fish	
	39 caught
40 caught a fish	
. . .	
44 They cook	
	45 cooked
46 cooked a fish	
	47 and
48 and Owl had a rest. Meg was looking	
	49 looked out

In Stage 3, we see Akhlak and his sister practising 'chained reading': the sister starts and Akhlak continues reading the next few words until he needs help again; the sister then either corrects or provides the word. Akhlak repeats the correction and continues, a process very similar to the 'listen, practise and repeat' that the children are already familiar with from their community classes. These home reading sessions have a very high number of turns and a fast-flowing pace, also characteristic of the Qur'anic classes. It is notable that in spite of the child's young age, the focus is on print rather than on any illustrations. Furthermore, the older sibling's insistence on accuracy from the outset indicates that this is not play but serious work in which the roles of learner and teacher are clearly defined and non negotiable.

The mothers

In the Bangladeshi-British families therefore, we found that reading was a serious activity associated with school work or religion. This respect for books and reading was no doubt inherited from the parent generation, most of whom had been educated in Bangladesh, and who had often had to struggle to become literate against difficult circumstances:

> I finished Class Five and then my mother died just after my engagement, leaving me and my five brothers and two sisters, so I had a lot of responsibilities.
>
> (Mrs Choudry)

> The trouble was there was no legal requirement for school attendance and also you had to provide books and stationery. On top of that, parents had to pay 10 per cent of teachers' salaries, so it was an expensive business sending your children to school, especially for the poor folk, of whom there were many . . .
>
> (Mrs Bibi)

The Bangladeshi-British mothers had learned to read in Sylhet following traditional methods:

> In the classroom all the children would sit in rows. The master would call out the alphabet, or words, or sentences, depending on the level, and then the class would repeat in unison . . . It was successful because there was a cane [*laughter*] you couldn't go far with the master's cane . . . from what I can remember, everything was taught with a lot of testing and memorising.
>
> (Mrs Begum)

Moreover, as Muslims, they were also obliged to read the Qur'an and had to attend Qur'anic class before normal school:

> Arabic learning took place before school started very early in the morning . . . we would have breakfast and go and read for several hours not far from home. Then we would return home, have something to eat and go off to school.
>
> (Mrs Bibi)

There was little room in their lives for reading for pleasure. Learning to read in Arabic at the Qur'anic school had a strictly religious purpose. The only pleasure gained was the satisfaction of pleasing Allah. Reading Bengali literature for pleasure at home was not an option open to these young women either, since, just as in the lives of the older English Londoners, home reading was viewed as an inappropriate activity for a girl. Although one of the mothers now borrows Bengali books from the library, *reading* for most of the Bangladeshi-British mothers means simply '*reading the Qur'an*'. An alternative entertainment to reading books is a practice labelled 'newstelling' by Nasima Rashid (1997). In Spitalfields where they live far from their extended families, the mothers meet regularly to chat and exchange news.

This recounting of events and stories is a group activity and might be regarded as a continuation of the oral tradition practised back home in Bangladesh.

A new paradigm of early literacy?

The children and their families introduced in this chapter reveal the multiple home literacy activities of two communities living within one square mile in the centre of London. They also show the syncretism or 'hybridisation' referred to by Luke and Kale (1997) as they mix and blend practices from home and school into unique new patterns and forms. Yet few of these activities fall within the officially recognised paradigm of preparation for school literacy, which is storyreading with the parent using a 'good book'. The extensive and intensive nature of these 'unofficial' literacy practices in both communities provides a strong argument for a shift in paradigms in the twenty-first century towards one which rethinks the way it authorises the literate and recognises strength in diversity. Fortunately, however, there are some school classrooms where teachers are already building upon the varied literacy experiences of their young pupils.

References

Adult Literacy and Basic Skills Unit (1993) *Parents and their Children: the Intergenerational Effects of Poor Basic Skills*, London: ALBSU.

Department of Education and Science (1975) *A Language for Life* (The Bullock Report), London: HMSO.

Department of Education and Science (1988) *English for Ages 5–11. Proposals of the Secretary of State* (The Cox Report, November), London: NCC/HMSO.

Dyson, A.H. (1997) *Writing Super Heroes*, New York: Teachers' College Press.

Gregory, E. (1998) 'Siblings as mediators of literacy in linguistic minority communities', *Language and Education: An International Journal*, 12(1): 33–55.

Heath, S.B. (1983) *Ways with Words: Language and Life in Communities and Classrooms*, Cambridge: Cambridge University Press.

Luke, A. (1992) 'The social construction of literacy in the primary school', in L. Unsworth (ed.) *Literacy, Learning and Teaching: Language as a Social Practice in the Classroom*, Melbourne: Macmillan.

Luke, A. and Kale, J. (1997) 'Learning through difference: cultural practices in early language socialisation', in E. Gregory (ed.) (1997) *One Child, Many Worlds: Early Learning in Multi-Cultural Communities*, London: David Fulton Publishers.

Padmore, S. (1994) 'Guiding lights', in M. Hamilton, D. Barton and R. Ivanic (eds) *Worlds of Literacy*, Clevedon: Multilingual Matters.

Rashid, N. (1996) *Field Notes from Family Literacy History and Children's Learning Strategies*, Final Report to ESRC (R00021186).

Rashid, N. and Gregory, E. (1997) 'Learning to read, reading to learn: the importance of siblings in the language development of bilingual children', in E. Gregory (ed.) (1997) *One Child, Many Worlds: Early Learning in Multi-Cultural Communities*, London: David Fulton Publishers.

School Curriculum and Assessment Authority (1996) *Desirable Outcomes for Children's Learning in Nurseries*, London: SCAA.

Snow, C. and Ninio, A. (1986) 'The contracts of literacy: what children learn from learning to read books', in W.H. Teale and E. Sulzby (eds) *Emergent Literacy: Reading and Writing*, Norwood, NJ: Ablex.

Street, B.V. and Street, J. (1995) 'The schooling of literacy', in P. Murphy, M. Selinger, J. Bourne and M. Briggs (eds) *Subject Learning in the Primary Curriculum*, London: Routledge.

Wells, C.G. (1985) 'Pre-school literacy related activities and success in school', in D. Olson *et al.* (eds) (1985) *Literacy, Language and Learning*, Cambridge: Cambridge University Press.

CHAPTER 3

GLOBALISATION, LITERACY, CURRICULUM PRACTICE

Allan Luke and Victoria Carrington

Raising Standards in Literacy R. Fisher, Greg Brooks and Maureen Lewis (eds), London: RoutledgeFalmer, 2002, pp. 231–50

Introduction

What is the relationship between economic and cultural globalisation and everyday literacy practices for teachers and students in that most stolid of twentieth-century institutions, the state primary school? What happens when the very institution that was designed for the propagation of print literacy, for the transmission of encyclopedic knowledge, for the inculcation of industrial behaviours, for the development of the post-war citizen, for the domestication of diversity into monocultural identity – the technology of the modern state par excellence – faces the borderless flows and 'scapes' of information and image, bodies and capital? And, no less important, what might happen if we engage in a momentary suspension of belief in current policy-driven preoccupations with pedagogical method, with decoding and basic skills – and ask a larger curriculum question: within the existing walls and wires, capillaries and conventions of the school, how might we construct a literacy education that addresses new economic and cultural formations?

From the prototypical work of economist Harold A. Innis in the 1940s to the work of Marshall McLuhan and the educational psychology of David R. Olson, the legacy of Canadian communications theory is an undertaking that dominant modes of information – from speech to script to print to digital image – have distinctive and identifiable 'biases'. By this Innis (1951) did not mean simple 'prejudice' or 'predisposition'. He and McLuhan, who joined the University of Toronto in the decade after Innis's death, both believed that communications media enabled blended and new conventions and aesthetics of expression, and that communications media powerfully influenced social organisation, spatial and demographic formation, intellectual practice and cognitive habits, and, importantly, the exchange of economic and political power. In work that anticipated current theories of global networks and scapes, Innis (1950) argued that communications technologies had been the agents of 'empire': creating what he called 'knowledge monopolies', reorganising space–time relations between metropolis and hinterland through the use of technology, and thereby shaping and controlling the contours of social identity at the margins in the interests of an imperial centre.

Half a century later, it is an axiom of the 'new literacy studies' (Barton, Hamilton and Ivanic, 2000) that how literacy is shaped as a social practice is linked to larger social structures. How those linkages are established is in part an ethnographic and in part a discourse analytic question: pursued through local analyses of the power relations, knowledges and identities built through literacy education and everyday life. The oft-repeated lesson from the history of literacy is that what people do with technologies of writing and inscription – and, from an educational perspective, what we normatively teach kids to do with these technologies – is shaped in relation to the contexts of work, of consumption and leisure, of citizenship and national ideology, and of varied projects of 'selfhood' and cultural identity. As literacy educators, we can pursue these links between literacy and social formation either by default, by a science that neglects or denies such links, or through a broader understanding of literacy not just as 'social practice', but literacy as curriculum practice.

For educationally acquired social practices with texts and discourses are both 'shaped' by dominant and alternative economic and social relations, and they are potentially 'shaping' of these relations. Following the work of sociologist Pierre Bourdieu (1998), we believe that literacy education involves:

- the teaching and learning of textual *disposition* – that is, the curricular and pedagogic construction of the literate habitus of embodied skills, knowledges and competences;
- the structural *positioning* by schools and teachers of the aspiring literate in relation to social systems and structures – that is, the production and reproduction of relationships to dominant modes of information and means of production;
- the development of the capacities to use literate practice to *position take* in the social and institutional fields of exchange that require literacy – that is, the construction of habits of agency and a sense of and capacity with the relative power of text and discourse in any particular social field.

Literacy – and by association literacy education – are both historically constructed and historically constructive, normative enterprises. In current conditions, they are about the shaping of patterns and practices of participation in text-based societies and semiotic economies.

These conditions raise alien issues for many teachers and teacher educators: How might literacy and literacy education respond to the challenges of new world cultures and economies and, indeed, forms of governance and citizenship? Without falling prey to the traps of taking globalisation as either universal evil or civilising force – the 'mother of all metanarratives' (C. Luke, 2001) – we wish to raise a series of open-ended questions about how to reshape what Richard Hoggart (1956) termed 'uses of literacy' almost a half century ago. Our focus is not on narrowing debates over literacy, basic skills and accountability – debates driven as much by the policy imperatives of funding and restructuring a creaky post-war state schooling infrastructure as by a 'science' of literacy education per se (Luke and Luke, 2001). Instead our concern is with the potential of literacy education as a curriculum practice for the generation of 'student' dispositions, positions and position-takings for viable and powerful life pathways through new cultures and economies, pathways that wind through globalised and local, virtual and material social fields.

This is an introductory view for literacy educators and researchers of these changes, their impact upon local communities and their potential for the transformation of how we see and 'do' literacy education in what remain relatively conventional classroom settings of state primary schools. We use the metaphors of globalised 'flows' to explain the impact of new media, new cultures and new economies on children's identities and developments. We then describe the force of these flows on a regional, small Australian township – Harlow (pop. 1,300) – its school and teachers and how they teach literacy. We document the experience of spatialised poverty – the delete-rious community-specific effects of economic flows on families' and children's life pathways. Our proposed response is an amended curriculum agenda for critical literacy for these children: one that distinguishes a 'glocal', cosmopolitan focus from what we define as 'parochial' and 'fantasy' approaches to literacy education. Our aim, then, is to move yet again away from limiting debates over basic skills and commodified methods into a much broader debate about literacy education as a sustainable and powerful curriculum practice.

The industrial school meets new times

What we call it – 'liquid' modernity (Bauman, 1998), post-Fordist economy and post-modern culture (Harvey, 1988; Cvetkovich and Kellner, 1997; Burbules and Torres, 2000), 'networked' societies (Castells, 1996) – is for those of us who work in class-rooms and teacher training not very important. What seems certain is that many of the patterns and practices of everyday life are shifting and oscillating, albeit unevenly and at different rates, in relation to powerful economic and technological forces that at the least appear beyond immediate local control and, for many communities, belief and comprehension. The effects and consequences of economic globalisation are both spatialised, local and site-specific – with primary resource and manufacturing economies sitting alongside infotech in some communities, with emergent nation states supporting and sustaining peasant economies alongside industrial parks. Any sense that we have hit some kind of decisive millennial shift ignores the non-synchronous character of contemporary change. In most nations and regions, disparate economies and lifeworlds sit in various states of emergence and decay, like radioactive isotopes with persistent half-lives.

The common characteristic seems to be the speed and durability, flexibility and mutability of networks and flows: as bodies and capital, information and image move across increasingly permeable political borders and geographic barriers. The result in the post-industrial West and North is the creation and transformation of cultural and economic 'scapes' (Appadurai, 1996) in local communities. These are sites for the changes in everyday experiences and uses of space and time, the emergence of new practices of work, leisure and consumption, and the writing of blended, hybridised forms of human expression, artefact and identity. Whether in Bangkok or Brisbane, a particular new species and social class of 'world kids' play and learn in shopping malls and basketball courts, on the internet and in schools.

Societies of the North and West are based on complex and blended economies – where means of production entail an increasing majority of working people engaging directly with dominant *modes of information* – concentrated in culture and creative industries, public and private sector, service sector work, and those fast growth sectors involved in the management and movement of imaginary capital, property and consumer goods. Even in strongly resource-driven economies like Australia's, the percentage of workers engaged in the direct exploitation of the natural and biolog-ical world through manual or industrial techniques is in slow but steady decline. In these so-called knowledge economies, human beings' dispositions and position takings occur in those social fields constituted by and regulating regional, national and multi-national flows of ideas and information, capital and bodies, material and discourse artefacts alike. One's capacities to sign and to engage in a universe of signs have principal exchange value in these fields. The institutional and occupational fields themselves shift quickly and, as the citizens of Harlow have discovered, erode tradi-tional life pathways, patterns of work, consumption and leisure.

The pattern of flows moves capital, information and bodies increasingly towards the cosmopolitan centres of world cities, creating culture scapes where the lifeworlds of Sydney and Brisbane are more likely to resemble those of Los Angeles or London than those of their kin in rural and remote communities – in some cases, indigenous and Anglo-Australian communities less than a hundred kilometres away in the bush. In this way, capital, and labour is deterritorialised away from rural and edge city communities [. . .] – at the same time that new forms of information, image and representation are directed through electronic and digital networks to communities at the margins. The irony is that while citizens in these new diaspora increasingly lose their productive capacity and force in key aspects of economic and semiotic production – they are repositioned as global, generic consumers and 'end-users' of goods, government and social services. These same world kids, desiring subjects who form a growth market for textual and material products created by Pokemon, Nike and Virgin, may at the same time be distantiated from the metropolitan and cosmopolitan sites of production of these and other culture industries.

Yet there are few uniform effects on these new diasporas: global flows are mediated and refracted by local variation and response, constituting a push–pull 'glocalisation' effect (Robertson, 1992). Local communities like Harlow become the sites for the playing out of global and local forces, between cosmopolitan heterogeneity and local homogeneity. Yet while mobility, the global flow of bodies across borders – political refugees, migrants, business migrants, guest workers, transnational knowledge workers – is one of the key factors of glocalisation – many areas of poverty are sites of increasing immobility. The underside of shifting capital and employment is that many families are quite literally stuck in locations from which they cannot shift. Others are caught up in a mythic transit between edge cities looking for work and cheap housing.

While in some urban areas the industrial-era phenomena of inner city poverty remains a persistent problem – in Australia, poverty has begun to shift to the hinterlands. These include both traditional farming and rural areas, and, increasingly, suburban edge cities characterised by inexpensive land and housing, often lacking in significant social capital and infrastructure. This phenomenon of spatialised poverty is focused on regional location, where inequality in incomes and local identity reflects a complex interaction of cost of housing, local employment and jobs infrastructure, and the available cultural capital of the population. In such situations, there is little evidence that an educational system in and of itself – without the co-ordination of the availability of other kinds of social, economic and even ecological capital – can alter life pathways on a large scale.

But, as we will see – a key problem is the inability of the educational system to provide the cognitive and textual tools and discourse resources to explicate these changes for the citizens of communities like Harlow, who remain positioned in the flows and fields of globalised economies without capital, without mobility and, indeed, without an analysis. In fact, across Australia, schools and state departments have been slow to make economic and cultural globalisation a key problematic in curriculum and instruction.

To understand the significance of these shifts and the implications they might have for our work as literacy educators, we need to reappraise the genealogy of current approaches to schooling and our approaches to the teaching of print literacy. Earlier generations grew up in an Australian society arranged around an industrial, Fordist model of work, identity and politics. In this society-past, the productive worker (predominantly white and male) could depend on government to provide a basic level of social and economic capital (here defined as equitable and ready availability of non-discriminatory social infrastructure, institutions and networks), including educa-tion, health care, psychic and physical protection, and a relatively secure and stable job market. The nation protected its citizens and guaranteed a better future by warding off migration and diversity, while protecting industries with high tariffs.

In exchange, citizen-workers demonstrated loyalty to both employer and govern-ment, paying taxes, with a highly motivated will to capital and maintaining levels of consumption. In the idealised social model underpinning this economic order, males engaged in paid employment while females reconciled themselves to acceptance of the role of child-bearing and rearing and maintenance of the nuclear family home (Carrington, 2003). In such a lifeworld, transience was a kind of deficit, a risk to encased concepts of community, family and neighbourhood and counterproductive to the expansion of capital.

The industrial school, then, aimed to develop the dispositions to position workers within a particular economy and lifeworld, streaming students into a bifurcated pathway that led, variously, towards university-based and vocational training. In this inter- and post-war schema, literacy – neutral, secular and non-ideological, print-based skills available to all – was defined in relation to the decoding of print-based text, and meaning making around canonical texts that entailed moral and ethical models for secular, industrial society. If, indeed, the education of empire had prepared one to be a colonial subject, the modernist education system that we presently work with prepares and constructs the dispositions of the industrial subject: behaviourally skilled, ideologically and economically patient, and motivated by a will to capital and the maintenance of stable community and nuclear family. That vision is captured and frozen in the cultural and social scapes of the modern basal reading series.

But the social facts of new times weigh heavily on this version of the world. The Australian economic and employment landscape has undergone significant upheaval in the course of one generation: gone is the 'job-for-life' and the promise of a state-funded retirement, gone is the certainty of learning one set of job-related skills sufficient for a life-time's employment; gone is the security of a delineated, hier-archical work order; vanishing is the job market for non-tertiary educated youth; vanished is the job market for the under-qualified and the elderly (Carrington, 2003). In their place are new uncertainties, new flexibilities and new citizen-workers. Prognoses suggest that job and mid-life career shift will increasingly become the norm, rather than the exception.

At the same time, the shift out of a Fordist economy and social order has made cultural and linguistic diversity a focal policy issue. In states like Queensland that might have conceived of themselves and their systems as stable and homogeneous, governments and education systems are contending with the realisation that almost one in five children is of indigenous or migrant backgrounds. New capitalism has created the conditions for the deployment of new and hybridised identities and the emergence of new literate practices, even and perhaps especially in the new hinter-lands of edge cities. The fragmentation of the normative model of identity, community and nation that underpinned the older economic system has placed on educators' tables issues of identity, culture, sexuality or race – whether through presence or absence. Many citizens of Harlow would tell us that the problems they face are due to, variously, Asian migrants who work too hard and cheaply, Aborigines and Torres Strait Islanders who don't work hard and cheaply enough, urban women who should raise families but choose to work, and, indeed, corrupt urban politicians who aid and abet the capital drain on their communities.

Teachers working in 'at risk' communities face a surface set of problems that appear amenable to longstanding approaches. According to the teachers in Harlow, the problems include: an apparent decline in mainstream cultural and linguistic resources required for school success among school-aged children; increasing impatience with conventional pedagogy and curricular approaches; increasing rates of ascertained 'attention deficit disorder' and other symptomologies; and affiliated forms of 'unruliness' and behaviour management problems. In consultations undertaken on behalf of the state government in Queensland in 2000, these phenomena were attributed by teachers to: deficit parenting with a specific focus on failure to read to children at home, absentee parents, overexposure to television, deterioration of the family structure and increased transience, video games and popular culture in all its forms, oral language deficit, and behavioural disorders (Luke, Freebody and Land, 2000). In other words, the response of many teachers is to see what might well be manifestations of the impacts of new economies and cultures as signs of conventional 'lack' in those cultural and discourse resources that we took for granted in monocultural, middle-class communities in the post-war print era.

There is some belated discussion of what these trends might mean for education and schooling systems. The policy responses of Western and Northern educational bureaucracies focus variously on:

- the consequences of information technology for classroom infrastructure and pedagogy, under the assumption somehow that digitalisation will both update and revive pedagogical and curricular systems led by an ageing teaching force;
- the further deployment of a range of compensatory 'pull out' programmes that attempt to address the ostensive needs of culturally heterogeneous and increasingly mobile student populations (e.g. early intervention, learning support, ESL specialist interventions);
- compensatory funding responses to educational exclusion and failure in particular spatial 'zones' hit hardest by economic changes; and, in some states;
- an early debate on the putative human capital demands of new economies.

From a sociological viewpoint, what has been interesting has been how debates over literacy have focused on early intervention and basic skills, especially in the US and UK, with the assumption that testing and accountability systems are the most effective response to the problems of populations and communities displaced, variegated and replaced by new economies. Policy debates over literacy frequently are steeped in deficit terminology, and are struggling to speak to the phenomena of world kids, new family configurations and the diasporic communities that have been adversely hit by these economies. In the face of major economic shift, these debates seem to be at once retro and nostalgic, and attempting to restore or maintain an educational equilibrium around traditionally transmitted and measured print-skill levels among students and schools.

Roughly half of the Australian and North American teaching force is over fifty. For a generation of teachers raised on debates over Cold War ideologies in the curriculum, over deschooling and progressivism, still caught up in the great debate over phonics and word recognition, the issues we have raised here may seem at best medium to long term and, at worst, an irrelevance to the everyday challenges of work intensification in classrooms and staffrooms. Yet the irony is that such changes, and the consequential effects on students' dispositions and social positions, are unlikely to go away, and are proving particularly resistant to the regimes of treatment past (e.g. use of high stakes testing, expansion of specialised early intervention programmes, the roping in of teacher behaviour through standardised and commodified curricula, single-method instruction). And they will continue to remain invisible to an explanatory schema that is still searching out and naming educational problems and human subjects which have morphed into new forms.

Literacy teaching and learning in the new white diaspora

Harlow is an edge-city community caught in the headlights of economic globalisation. It straddles the semi-rural zone between two major highways, each leading to the outermost western fringe of the state's southeastern corner. It sits at the edges of an urban area – about 75 kilometres from the state capital. In its heyday over fifty years ago, it acted as an intermediary service terminus between the city and its outlying grazier and farming communities. But with the decade-long downturn in the adjoining rural communities – exacerbated by drought and deregulation – and with the improvement of direct transportation, communication and just-in-time shipping links between the bush and city, its historical moment, if it had one, has passed. It is caught in a nether world: it is neither a traditional bush community with a long-standing sense of identity and bloodlines, nor is it close enough to the urban centre to participate viably in the service economy. Over the last two decades, Harlow's population has shifted from a long-term base to a significant annual turnover, poorly according to standard measures of literacy. Reading Recovery programmes and special education support generated some short- and medium-term gains but had no visible effect on raising the overall performance profile of the school. The teachers wanted to improve not just baseline reading skills and performance but overall school achievement as well. In their words, they wanted to know what they were doing 'wrong', but they also wanted to know 'what was wrong with these children'. Why weren't they responding to the remedial programmes? Why weren't their reading test scores improving proportionate to the effort of staff?

The teachers – all women ranging from mid-thirties through to retirement age, along with two male staff: the principal and special education teacher – are a stable and experienced staff. They are dedicated to their work and, for the most part, seem to have avoided the industrial alienation and culture of complaint that has become more common in Australian schools. They would view themselves as progressives, as 'child centred' and behind the state system's commitment of equity and social justice. There is none of the high teacher turnover that characterises bush and indigenous community schools. Though many have long histories at Harlow, none of them live in the district, commuting from either of the two larger suburbs 50–60 minutes away. The mismatch of teachers' and students' cultural and economic locations and world views went unremarked in their comments to us.

The teachers' comments reflected these differences in standpoint. We were told that there are few community role models, that welfare parents don't provide supportive print environments, that families move about too much, and that the students' expectations of their futures seem either wildly exaggerated or limited. Clearly, student transience is one of the key difficulties – between Year 1 and 6 the school has a 60 per cent turnover of students. This limits the effectiveness of blanket early intervention programmes. Additionally, the teachers felt that this made its curriculum 'integrity' difficult: 'one step forward and two backwards'. Additionally, they stated, there was 'apathy' in parental commitment. A dedicated and progressive staff, they were worried that kids would end up 'stuck' in the area, on welfare and with limited futures. Over 30 per cent of the children attending Harlow are from single parent families and even more are from welfare families. Taken together, the teachers' comments painted an overwhelming picture of student 'deficit' and 'lack', set against a backdrop of genuine concern, commitment and professionalism.

The other side of the coin emerged in our 'audit' of what the children of Harlow were fluent with. While perhaps not matching the expectations of the teachers, the children in this community have a number of strengths. These include strong social networks in the community, in-depth local knowledge about the geography, demography and culture of their own community, knowledge and skill in handling their allowance and earned money, interest in sports, knowing how to 'make the best' of difficult family and financial situations. When prompted, the teachers acknowledged that the students had extensive knowledge of video movies and cable television programmes, vast knowledge of popular music, fashion and youth culture, and took readily to computer and video games, internet surfing and the new technologies. Additionally, the teachers reported, these children often carry more of the emotional work of their families than do more affluent, middle-class kids and yet are extremely accepting of difference. They are generally well behaved and eager to learn. Reportedly, as a whole the children appear to enjoy school, like their teachers and want to do well.

We worked with the teachers for several days to audit and develop their class-room strategies. Like many other Australian primary schools, Harlow has instituted a 'literacy block' – one and a half hours each day dedicated solely to literacy activities. In this session, basic skills development and consolidation are the focus. Across the school, students engage in sound-letter recognition activities, the development of dictionary and other research skills, decoding strategies, big book reading and activities, cloze activities and some, albeit highly variable, work with functional grammar. In this regard, there was nothing particularly remarkable or unremarkable about the existing practices. These core strategies are part and parcel of the Australian literacy teachers' repertoire for dealing with print literacy. At the same time, the teachers found that there had been poor communication about who was doing what – particularly between lower primary and upper grades teachers – and that they, as a school staff, lacked a shared descriptive metalanguage for (a) describing their practice; and (b) talking about language.

After two days of working with the teachers, the pieces of the puzzle began to fit together for them and for us. If we tracked the children's dispositions and trajectories through the school, across varying patterns of participation and achievement, onto the local high school and out into the world of work, a clear pattern began to emerge. The kids of Harlow were relatively patient and willing to participate in their schooling through and across primary school. This was established in no small part by the school's child-centred environment, the anti-bullying and behaviour management programme and the visible emotional investment in the children by the teachers. Yet that participation was momentary, almost stoic, in the face of larger forces: by the time children hit high school, achievement plateaued or declined, behaviour problems increased, particularly among the boys, and retention rates fell off. The local state high school had one of the highest expulsion rates in the state. Many of the same students who had been average achievers in secondary school, after leaving school would commute to hang out at the shopping malls an hour away, all the while maintaining strong personal commitments to popular culture and Australian team sports.

In our view, students were patiently 'doing time' in a primary literacy programme which was:

- focused on delimited sets of skills and knowledge and was narrow in its focus on now traditional approaches to decoding;
- squarely modernist, pre-digital and anti-popular culture in the form and content of its approach to reading comprehension;
- escapist and irrelevant in its approach to teaching literature.

This programme more or less was 'freestanding' as part of the literacy block study in the morning. When we asked when the kids were taught about the changes in the communities around them – we were told that this wasn't part of the literacy programme but sat in the varied project work and traditional key learning area studies that were part of the 'integrated studies' kids undertook in the late morning and afternoon. Hence, the literacy programme also tended to be:

- disconnected both temporally and thematically from any substantive 'reading of the world' based on specific discourse and field-specific knowledges.

This offered us a possible explanation to the 'rise and stall' scenario of the school's test scores. Put simply, the baseline skills that teachers were attempting to instil in their students were more or less being achieved through a focused and delimited literacy programme, despite high student turnover. Both teachers and students were pursuing this programme in good faith and effectively. That programme had become disconnected and decontextualised on at least three levels. The literacy programme was:

- temporally and programmatically partitioned from the rest of the school curriculum;
- disconnected from the background knowledges, skills and life experiences that the students brought to the classroom; and
- its traditional print format and discourse content were disconnected from a broader analysis of community, of environment, of the experiences and practices of glocalisation.

The biggest difficulty faced by the teachers of Harlow was not simply a question of method. There is no doubt that their whole school plan will focus and co-ordinate their pedagogic efforts, bring them together into a stronger shared vocabulary, and add a few notches to their test scores and affiliated league tables kept in central office. But the teachers and the programme were in some ways caught in their own implicit assumptions about what constitutes 'literacy' and how it should be taught in school. For all their good intentions and hard work, they hadn't hardwired what counted as 'literacy' in the school with the lives of the children and their families – nor were they adept at anticipating and teaching to the kinds of 'literate futures' their students would face as adolescents and young adults.

Critical literacy as a technology for remediating globalisation

We have here provided a shorthand account of how students and teachers in one Australian edge community have experienced economic and cultural scapes of New Times. Is there a simple and happy ending to Harlow's story? Perhaps that the teachers had found the 'right' pedagogy or method, that test scores had risen, that this had set in place the foundations for overall improvements in student achievement, that the communities' and students' life trajectories had shifted as a result. These are the narrative chains underlying current policy interventions in many OECD educational systems. Yet there are competing claims that we need to consider: that basic skills acquisition is necessary, but not sufficient, to turn around the overall educational achievement of the most at-risk students, that higher order thinking, depth of intellectual engagement (Newmann, King and Ringdon, 1997), critical literacy and 'connectedness to the world' (Lingard et al., 2001) have the best chance of 'redesign[ing] social futures' (New London Group, 1996) and altering these kids' dispositions, positions and position-takings.

The story is unfinished. We are continuing to work with Harlow to develop school literacy programmes that bring together a richer, more intellectually demanding and 'contemporary' analysis of these kids' identities and competences, a more cogent understanding of the overlapping and multiple communities that these children inhabit with a balanced focus on code breaking, meaning making, using texts in everyday life and critical literacy. In so doing, we are working within the parameters of a state literacy policy that has an eye equally on basic skills of reading and, as importantly, the emergent multiliteracies required in the cultural landscapes and workplaces of new economies (Luke, Freebody and Land, 2000).

Harlow's dilemma suggests some very different lessons for us: about the inability of education systems and literacy education per se to change life pathways without other kinds of flows of capital and culture across borders and institutions; about the difficulties teachers, researchers and curriculum developers face in understanding both the new knowledges, experiences and skills kids bring to classrooms and the new knowledges, experiences and skills they will need to 'navigate' and 'surf' emergent culture scapes. We conclude with a barely modest proposal for what a critical literacy might entail in conditions of 'glocalisation'.

It was Marx and Engels' contention that the dominant ideas of an age were those that served the interests of particular forms of social organisation, of production and manufacture, and, indeed, of social class. It was Kuhn's contention that scientific paradigms reached crisis points where lifeworlds presented and generated hosts of problems and anomalies that could not be addressed by the redeployment of existing theories and methodologies. Regardless of which of these or other analytic tacts we might take to explain the new blends of literate practices, texts and discourses, skills and developmental patterns at hand, virtually all social science analyses of contemporary social and economic conditions lead us to a similar transit: that education, literacy practices and childhood itself have reached an historical juncture of transition and change, of residual discourses and text forms coexisting and blending with the new, of persistent old inequalities and new ones, of century-old educational practices sitting alongside of ones that have never been seen in classrooms before.

We are of the opinion that while the new communications technologies are a catalyst for economic change and potentially for pedagogic change, they are neither the core problem nor the main answer for teachers and students in what is increasingly resembling a transitional period in the history of schooling. One of the first themes that arose in our discussions with the teachers of Harlow was the assumption that if they just switched to new technologies – that if they just brought in the wires and boxes and went on line – that 'empowerment', engagement with the new economy and so forth would magically occur. While we struggle empirically with the question of which blends of print and virtual skills and knowledges might 'count' for the kids of Harlow, we are painfully aware that it is some time away, perhaps years, before we will have answers about which blends of communications technologies – oral and written, digital and visual, performed and virtual – are optimal for accommodating and articulating some of the new forms of social practice, representation and cognition.

In the meantime, a teaching force with an average age of 47 struggles with a curious cocktail of effects from cultural and economic flows. Answers are at hand. But how we deal with and reshape the kids' use of the old technology of print is as important as, though not mutually exclusive from, their engagement with the new. And in this context the explanatory discourses from conferences, publishers and software peddlers, and professional development experts available to the teachers of Harlow have tended to operate in binary opposition: high tech online facilities and pedagogy will solve the problem and/or low tech, phonics-based programmes will solve the problem. Neither is adequate.

A key lesson that we take away from this case study is that many of the current debates over reading and literacy – the 'available discourses' for talking about literacy education and schooling more generally in new times – are developed and primed to deal with the entry and traverse of children into another universe: a print-based, industrially and economically stable community within which the achievement of rudimentary print literacy was a necessary and, for many, sufficient condition to 'becoming somebody'. The teachers in Harlow were doing their mighty best to describe and contend with the manifestations of a new socio-economic milieu. Yet at the same time they were struggling to recognise, understand and even 'name' it. While they might not have seen it in such terms, in practice they were putting the weight of their efforts into trying to contain and ameliorate the effects of globalised culture and trying to counter the effects of truncated and static life pathways. They were, in many ways, swimming upstream against deteriorating community economic conditions.

Their professional vocabulary for dealing with this – that of 'recovery', of skills versus whole language, of learning disability and oral language deficit, of behaviour management and deficit parenting – led them down a road to simplistic answers, answers that were more about the micromanagement of lessons and plans, to belief in packaged programmes and commodities, rather than towards a re-envisioning of the curriculum, of the students' needs and life pathways, and, indeed, of the kinds of literate dispositions that might effectively vie for position in the social fields of globalised capital. Intervention was more rearguard or, to paraphrase Marshall McLuhan (1966), 'rear view mirror' action. Our view is that neither the available discourses around 'methods' for teaching reading, or about cultural, linguistic and intellectual 'deficits' of children can begin to address the complexity of problems faced by schools and teachers. And while a floor of basic skills has been established, the question of 'preparedness' for this particular construction of adolescence, for school-leaving, for an environment of flight from and to structural unemployment across and between edge communities was still moot.

What might be the shape of critical literacy as curriculum practice – fitted for the analysis, critique and engagement with the lifeworlds of new, globalised and 'glocal' economies and cultures? The points of disconnection between literacy and glocal 'communitas', between old literacy and world cultures are the very nodal points where a rebuilding of the curriculum could begin. We want to argue for a kind of critical literacy that envisions literacy as a tool for remediating one's relation to the global flows of capital and information, bodies and images.

David Olson (1986) described the cognitive effects of the technology of print as the construction of 'possible worlds'. Following Innis, McLuhan and Goody, he argued that the 'bias' of writing was its capacity to take human subjects to other worlds, to traverse the constraints of place and time. Whether in its highly amplified digital form or in its traditional static form, one of the communicative effects of the technology of writing is its capacity to represent in a portable and replicable format times and places that are otherwise inaccessible to place-bound readers. It is this capacity of reading – both traditional and digital – that can provide the basis of a reconceptualisation of literacy as a technology for mediating one's position within globalised flows. As literature teachers have always known, literacy pedagogy can displace and disrupt space, place and time, taking one out of one's immediate

Table 4 Uses of literacy in globalised conditions

Mode	Curriculum practice	Positioning
Parochial literacy	Engagement with local texts and discourses, knowledges and experiences	Material reproduction of position through valorisation of local experience.
Fantasy literacy	Disengagement by taking the reader and writer out of local place, space and time	De-positioning or suspension of position; introduction of 'other' discourses; disengagement with flows.
Glocalised literacy	Engagement with relationship of local to other textual possible worlds	Material repositioning; critical analysis and repositioning of flows; reflexive analysis of other and local texts.

synchronicity – cutting across different spaces and times, and engaging, both virtually and psychically, with specific social fields and markets that otherwise aren't available to, in this case, the children of Harlow. The simultaneous universe envisioned by McLuhan, and before him Innis and Mumford, becomes accessible through one's capacity to read, whether online or off.

That capacity can equally be used – as it was in literature study in Harlow – as a kind of sublimation from engagement with the texts and contexts of glocalisation, a deliberate suspension of the local and pursuit of texts and discourses 'other' to immediate experience. That is, literature study can be enlisted to disengage readers from a 'reading of the world' of globalised scapes and flows. In Table 4 we term this a *fantasy literacy* that aims for a suspension of position in the social fields and scapes of globalisation and a psychic disengagement with flows. While this might have therapeutic purpose, it acts as a pedagogy of disengagement and estrangement from the glocal.

At the same time, the teachers of Harlow used many archetypal strategies, from language experience and 'show and tell', journal writing and project work to make their teaching more 'relevant' to kids' local experiences. These ranged from studies of local wildlife to a regular discussion focus on local sporting events and community activities. Teachers argued that this focus on local texts and discourses increased levels of interest, was important for raising student 'self-esteem'. But it appeared that much of this work did not seem to intellectually or textually 'go anywhere': there was often limited articulation into a broader conversation about how local contexts, experiences and issues 'fit' with the parallel worlds, cultural and economic scapes outside of Harlow. In Table 4, we refer to this as *parochial literacy*, local in scope and focus and reproductive of kids' local discourses, dispositions and positions.

Parochial literacy and *fantasy literacy* are two curriculum approaches with long and distinguished pedigrees, both of which would purport to address the alienation from schooling experienced by at-risk kids such as those of the new white diaspora. These are, respectively: the argument that 'relevance' of curriculum and activity will effectively suture the home–school mismatch and transition problem and the argument that a rich, imaginative literary focus will build self-esteem, expand psychological horizons and world views, and create a 'love of literature'.

Our argument here is that texts – both print and virtual, canonical and popular – and engagement with reading and writing can form a kind of 'trialectical' moment (Soja, 1999) in each learner's life that bridges the 'push–pull' effects of glocalisation. The focus here would be on a 'reading of the local' that connects this with those of other possible worlds, a curriculum approach that focuses students' work with texts on the analysis of the flows of effects between this time–space locality and others.

In Harlow, such an approach to critical literacy curriculum could take multiple forms: using the internet to audit and analyse the global flows of work, goods and discourse that are leading to changes in Harlow, whether by studying the history and economics of the rural sector, the origin of local environmental issues, or patterns of population movement between communities like Harlow (Comber and Simpson, 2001). It could entail using writing and online communication to participate with virtual communities around 'fandom' and popular culture (Alvermann, Moon and Hagood, 1999). Or it could involve reading multiple literary texts that generate or engage intercultural and contrastive historical perspectives on new times, those of economies, cultures and places past, present and future. In these ways, the aim would be to engage children critically in the borderless flows of data, information and image that characterise information economies – using both digital and print media. It would entail working intertextually across various cultural and historical texts and discourses. What this kind of literacy might enable is the modelling of 'position-takings' that actively remediate one's position – both in terms of the capital flows that make forms of work possible and available, but as well to manage the infor-mation flows of images, representation and texts that constitute identity and ideology, and, finally, to engage with other cultures and bodies across time and space.

Conclusions

Our aim in this discussion is to move forcefully not just beyond a great debate over method – that should go without saying – but, as well, a debate between approaches to content and method (from language experience to process writing) that focus on the local, the parochial, the 'at hand', and those approaches that stress the 'wonder', the 'mystery' of 'going elsewhere' through the experience of literature. Both are powerful tools, but, if we are looking for a refashioning of literacy as a normative preparation for a critical engagement with glocalised economies, we would need to begin talking about literacy as a means for building cosmopolitan world views and identity: of enhancing, in Bourdieu's terms, historical memories and contemporary understandings of how these economies of flows actually structurally position (and perhaps exclude) one, how differing dispositions will have different effects in the various fields of flows, and how to actively engage with those fields in agentive and transformative ways. As idealistic as such models might sound, there are viable proto-types in the field drawn from the extensive literature on the teaching of critical literacy and critical language awareness (e.g. Fairclough, 1992; Muspratt, Luke and Freebody, 1997; Comber and Simpson, 2001; Knobel and Healey, 1998). Such models do not discard basic knowledge of print codes, syntactic metalanguage, enhanced automaticity of skill, or metalinguistic awareness, but they ensure that they are lodged within broader curriculum contexts that are not anachronistic, disconnected, dated, or simply intellectually infantile.

Will such approaches to literacy alleviate the patterns and consequences for the children of Harlow and like communities across North America, the UK, New Zealand and Australia? Not in and of themselves. The picture of change and risk here shows that schools and education systems can make a difference, but that that difference is contingent on the availability and flows of other kinds of capital and power as well. At the same time, though, cases like Harlow tell us with some certainty that the answer lies as much in re-envisioning literacy education as curriculum practice as it does fetishising the teaching of basic print skills.

References

Alvermann, D.E., Moon, J.S. and Hagood, M.C. (1999) *Popular Culture in the Classroom*, Newark, DE: International Reading Association.

Appadurai, A. (1996) *Modernity at Large: Cultural Dimensions of Globalisation*, Minneapolis: University of Minnesota Press.

Barton, D., Hamilton, M. and Ivanic, R. (eds) (2000) *Situated Literacies*, London: Routledge.

Bauman, Z. (1998) *Globalization: The Human Consequences*, London: Polity Press.

Bourdieu, P. (1998) *Practical Reason: On the Theory of Action*, London: Polity.

Burbules, N. and Torres, C. (eds) (2000) *Globalisation and Education: Critical Perspectives*, New York: Routledge.

Carrington, V. (2003) *Landscaping the Family in New Times*, Amsterdam: Kluwer.

Carrington, V. and Luke, A. (1997) 'Literacy and Bourdieu's sociological theory: a reframing', *Language and Education* 11(2): 96–112.

Castells, M. (1996) *Rise of the Network Society*, Oxford: Blackwell.

Cvetkovich, A. and Kellner, D. (eds) (1997) *Articulating the Global and the Local*, Boulder, CO: Westview Press.

Comber, B. and Simpson, A. (eds) (2001) *Negotiating Critical Literacies in the Classroom*, Mahwah, NJ: Lawrence Erlbaum.

Fairclough, N. (ed.) (1992) *Critical Language Awareness*, London: Longman.

Harvey, D. (1988) *The Conditions of Postmodernity*, Cambridge: Polity Press.

Hoggart, Richard (1956) *The Uses of Literacy*, Harmondsworth: Penguin.

Innis, H.A. (1950) *Empire and Communications*, Oxford: Oxford University Press.

—— (1951) *The Bias of Communications*, Toronto: University of Toronto Press.

Knobel, M. and Healey, A. (eds) (1998) *Critical Literacies in the Primary Classroom*, Rozelle, NSW: Primary English Teachers Association.

Lingard, R., Ladwig, J., Mills, M., Christie, P., Hayes, D., Gore, J. and Luke, A. (2001) *Queensland School Longitudinal Restructuring Study: Final Report*, Brisbane: Education Queensland.

Luke, A. and Luke, C. (2001) 'Adolescence lost, childhood regained: on early intervention and the emergence of the techno-subject', *Journal of Early Childhood Literacy* 1(1): 91–120.

Luke, A., Freebody, P. and Land, R. (2000) *Literature Futures: The Queensland State Literacy Strategy*, Brisbane: Education Queensland.

Luke, C. (2001) *Globalisation and Women in Academia: North/South/East/West*, Mahwah, NJ: Lawrence Erlbaum.

McLuhan, M. (1966) *War and Peace in the Global Village*, New York: Random House.

Muspratt, S., Luke, A. and Freebody, P. (eds) (1997) *Constructing Literacies*, Creskill, NJ: Hampton Press.

Newmann, F., King, M.B. and Ringdon, M. (1997) 'Accountability and school performance: implications for restructuring schools', *Harvard Educational Review* 67 (1): 41–69.

New London Group (1996) 'A pedagogy of multiliteracies', *Harvard Educational Review* 66(1): 60–92.

Olson, D.R. (1986) 'Learning to mean what you say: towards a psychology of literacy', in S. DeCastell, A. Luke and K. Egan (eds) *Literacy, Society and Schooling* (pp. 145–58), Cambridge: Cambridge University Press.

Robertson, R. (1992) *Globalization: Social Theory and Global Culture*, London: Sage.

Soja, E. (1999) *Thirdspace*, London: Verso.

PART II

EXPLORING LITERACY AND LEARNING

CHAPTER 4

'YOU MADE IT LIKE A CROCODILE'
A theory of children's meaning-making

Gunther Kress

Before Writing – Rethinking the Paths to Literacy, London: Routledge, 2000, pp. 87–110

Developing a framework

The 4-year-old who said 'My Gawd, I made it like Australia' was clear about her agency in her production of meaning; another 4-year-old was equally clear about her father's deliberate intent in shaping a crocodile in taking bites from his delicately held toast when she said 'You made it like a crocodile.' Whether in describing and commenting on their own making, or their reading of the making by others, meaning is at the forefront of both of their concerns. It seems a reasonable, and I would say *essential* task to develop for ourselves a theory, a working account, of how children make meaning. Of course children tend not to engage in extended theory-making, though frequently they make comments which are so incisive that we can only wonder at the precision of their insights.

In this chapter I will put together a consolidated picture of what children do in meaning-making, to describe, in effect their 'practical theory'. From that I derive my theorist's theory. I will consider several issues as they emerge in a close look at children's meaning-making: 'interest'; the motivated sign; transformation; multi-modality; representation; reading; resources for making of meaning; imagination, cognition and affect; the limits to imagination, representation; and the question of synaesthesia.

Interest

The traditional, and in this century commonsensical view of meaning is that there is a stable system of entities which are available to a fully competent user of a language for the expression of their meaning. In this view there is a system, which an outsider has to learn, has to gain competence in – whether this outsider is a child newly born into the group which 'has' this system, or an adult outsider – an adult learner of the new language. There is no suggestion that the individual who uses a language – or other system of communication – has any effect on that system. This view may have developed for any number of cogent reasons: children do seem to end up speaking or writing the language of their parents – even if, and this contradiction goes unnoticed, the same elders have always been known to complain about the changes, deformations, corruptions, degenerations, introduced by the new generation. 'Foreigners' are either marked out by speaking differently to the 'locals', or have learned to 'blend in' perfectly, to adopt the forms of the new community. There are of course issues of power in this, namely the question as to who has control of the language.

It may also be that the real focus of theory has always been on adult users and uses of the language; and where the focus has been on children it has been in order to see how, or to demonstrate *that* they 'move into' the adult system. In other words, children's meaning-making has been seen from the viewpoint of the adult, which has not permitted an understanding of their actions in their terms. Children's interests have been invisible because of the dominant power of adult interests.

When we struggle to see the situation of meaning-making from the child's point of view – and extend it as a means to explain the adult's world also – the picture changes radically. Children, as all will admit, are not competent users of adult systems; and so we can see what it is they do to make their meanings in the absence of the routinized, practiced, finely honed and quite 'natural' competence of adults. We see that they have 'interests'. Too often these appear as a nuisance to the adult: the child who 'throws a tantrum' because *she* wants to choose her own clothes in the morning – at remarkably young ages, as young as 1½ or 2 in my own wearied experience – is expressing her interest in how she looks, how she will feel for that day. Why do I try to resist her? Partly because there is *my* routine – though my routine would be less interrupted by giving way early. In large part, and at bottom, it is, I think, because I cannot actually imagine that the 2-year-old *can* have a 'real' interest, real dress sense, real knowledge, real understanding; perhaps because she has far less power. Once I concede the right to the child to express her or his interest, and *observe*, I find that there are meanings; that they express and intent; as well as systematic design.

Another serious obstacle to the adult's perception is the fact that children's interests change. A boy making toy cars made one car in which it was crucial to show the car in action: but he also made (among many others) a car which was meticulously produced to be an object devoid of context, so as to express the potencies of the object *and* to give it a different status in terms of realisms. Two girls who made *their* car on the floor of the bedroom wanted a car which was mainly made for getting into and sitting in. So their car became a very different car – without steering wheel, without gear lever, without wheels. Children's interest changes; and as it does, that which is regarded as criterial by the child *about* the car changes; and so what is represented changes. The girls' gendered interest sees cars differently from a boy's – usually, though not necessarily. One of the girls who made a pillow car was making a car with cardboard cut out wheels stuck onto a cardboard box a week later.

'Interest' is a short-hand term for an enormously complex set of factors. My reason for using the term is to find a way out of a seemingly irresolvable difficulty in educational thinking. It is the difficulty of reconciling the apparently total opposition between individuality, meaningful individual action on the one hand, and social determinism on the other – the view that our actions are circumscribed by social convention, constraint and convenience, to such an extent that we act as simple socially determined beings. Neither view is attractive or plausible to me. So I want to ask 'Why did this person make this sign at this point?', and have a better answer than either: 'She (or he) just felt like it', 'I just say what comes into my head'; or, on the other hand 'In this context the rules/conventions of politeness, power, and so on are such that you must do such and such', 'The best form to use is this'. Even in conditions of heavy social constraint people can and do act out of their interest; equally, what seems merely individual is socially constrained.

Interest as an explanatory category comprises at least the following for me: we see the world from our own place, and that place differs from that of our neighbour. One reason 3- and 4-year-olds draw adult figures with such enormously long legs topped by a short body and large head is not just limited competence, but the fact that from *their* height adults do look like that. Throughout our lives we have had *our* view of the world: that world is the same for millions of others, and that produces commonality of view; but I always see it from my position, and that produces difference of view. There is no need to go here into the usual statements about social and cultural differences: they are obvious.

Interest is a composite of my experience; but it is also a reflection of my present place, and an assessment of my present environment. With my experience – whether as a 5-year-old or a 55-year-old – I stand here now, in a social place, in a physical place. My experience, personally constructed out of my incessant readings through all my life, makes me assess my present position, and its potentials and responsibilities. It makes me read my immediately present social environment, now at this moment in a certain way. These readings are my transformations, my signs made from what is to hand, out of my experiences and in my present social environment. That includes the person or the persons with whom I am communicating. I assess my relationships with them in terms of my wishes, of their and my power, my affective responses, and so on.

All of these together are the source of my making of signs in communication – not simply what has come into my head, because what has come into my head has come from prior cultural and social places; and then, on the other hand, neither is it simply what society, convention, power, constraint tell me I must do, because I act transformatively in my making of signs.

To what extent is this an apt description of the meaning-making of children? I wish to maintain that the principle is the same. The difference is that when children make signs at a young age, necessarily their experience of, and exposure to, social and cultural forms is less, and so it forms a lesser part of their making of signs. Affect is a much greater part of the signs of very young children, and because it is a greater part it is more readily visible. That has led to the mistaken view that the signs of young children are 'merely expressive'. Also, what children 'have to hand' differs; very often what they 'have to hand' is what they have found – objects and materials not considered materials for making signs and messages by their parents, teachers, or carers – and so are often entirely unconventional. In consequence, their objects and texts often resemble the objects and texts of naive art and as such are easily overlooked. What they 'have to hand' also differs conceptually, but the influence of the society and of its culture exerts itself from the earliest stage.

Motivated signs

Signs come about as the result of human action, usually in the context of culture, often with an intention to communicate that sign. The traditional view of the relation of form and meaning, of signifier and signified, is, in the now clichéd words of Saussure's *Course in General Linguistics* (1974), conventional and arbitrary. That is a view which holds that there is no intrinsic connection between the expression of a meaning, and the form which is used to express it. Two examples will illustrate this by now seemingly unassailable common sense, In German the word for the meaning expressed by the English word *tree* is *Baum*; in French it is *arbre*. So there is one meaning, but three forms for its expression. No one can (now) pretend that there is a real reason for the connection between these forms and the meaning. The second example is adopted from the writings of Ludwig Wittgenstein, the Austrian philosopher. If you and I are playing chess (or draughts) and we lose one of the pieces, then it is no great matter to say 'Look, we'll just let this match, or this button, "stand for" the piece – perhaps a pawn in chess – which we need.' And, as these examples are entirely persuasive put like this, they have passed by without (very much) challenge.

When we look at the etymology of *Baum* (the nearest English relative is *beam*) we find that it is related to the present-day German word *biegen*, 'to bend'. It seems that the original meaning of *Baum* was that it was that conspicuously large plant which bends in the wind. Once we know that, then the relation of form and meaning is less arbitrary – we can see the reason, the motivation for calling the plant after an outstanding characteristic. Given that the ancestors of the people who now say *Baum* came from somewhere in the steppes of southern Russia (some four thousand years ago or so), where trees might have been scarce and thus conspicuous in the landscape, it makes even more sense.

In the case of the button/pawn we can argue in the other direction. Assume that I have lost five or six pieces of my chess set, two pawns, a bishop, the queen, a rook. If I have five identical buttons the idea of substituting the buttons for the lost pieces begins to become problematic. I will need distinguishing features: size for instance. But if I had buttons of different sizes, I would not use the biggest button to substitute for a pawn; I would use it to replace the most valuable piece, the queen: size would become a signifier for value, which is a motivated relation. We could then establish *by convention* that size will signify value. Therefore, in our game, the second largest button would become the rook, and so on.

Now we have a clear situation where there is a motivated and conventional relation between meaning and form, namely that the greater the value of the chess piece, the larger the button that is used by us to substitute for it. Making *larger size* mean *greater value* is a matter of a motivated relation of meaning and form; and that latter feature is established by us as our convention. The people who named trees after their characteristic of bending in the wind focused on a particular, noticeable – perhaps to them unusual and astonishing characteristic – and they named the whole thing by it. Their *interest* was reflected in their combination of meaning and form. In the case of a 7-year-old's newspaper, his interest in the team he supports (an affective meaning as much as a factual description) makes him draw the one player taller, wearing boots with bigger spikes, coloured bright red, and so on.

The combination of form and meaning in the signs made by all humans is motivated: *being tall* as a signifier of *power*, but also as a signifier of the child's great affective investment in the star player, his hero, in the football team that he supports. The child selects – no doubt unconsciously – those characteristics which he regards as most important for him in the thing he wants to represent, and he finds the best possible means for expressing them – size, colour (and in this image, the ball in the net of the opposition's goal!). The relation which unites form and meaning is one of analogy: *size* (of the player) can be the analogue of (this player's or his team's) *power*; *the intensity of the red colouring* can be the analogue of *my affective involvement*. This relation of analogy leads to metaphors: *size is power*; *intense red* equals my *affective involvement*. Motivated signs are therefore always metaphors; formed through the process of analogy; which itself is motivated by the sign-maker's interest.

The older children are, the more their signs are likely to focus not just on expressing the things that they want to represent, but to focus also on communication. This involves a recognition of the presence of the people with whom they are interacting; and that recognition increasingly involves attention to the communicational environment: 'with my teacher I need to communicate in this way', 'with my friends I communicate in this way'. In this manner, the sign-maker's interest also begins to include considerations of the needs of the audience as part of the complex considerations in making signs. Signs have to represent adequately what I want to say; *and* they have to say it in such a way that they pay due attention to what I think I want to achieve in this act of communication.

Signs therefore have a double social motivation: once because of who the sign-maker is, and what her or his history has been; and another time because of what the sign-maker assesses the communicational environment to be, and how, consequently, she or he adjusts their making of the sign.

This issue is important because it affects notions of what *learning* is. In a theory founded on the assumption of arbitrarily constructed signs, the task of learning is conceived of in one broad direction: as the cognitive ability to acquire abstract systems of high complexity, which are, in their characteristics of make-up, in their logics, extraneous to the person who needs to acquire them. Language is seen as one such system, and teachers therefore inevitably hold that view of what the child's task in learning is: 'mastering' this complex, abstract system (whether in speech or in writing). 'Failure' by a child in this task therefore is explained as a failure of precisely that kind – an inability to cope with abstract systems, a 'cognitive disability' defined in terms of the logic of this assumption.

Teachers, along with linguists and educational specialists, have a firmly settled notion of language as a system of arbitrarily constructed signs. Their common sense coincides with the specific difficulty which children face in learning to write, namely the move from drawing picture-ideas to drawing sounds. I will return to this question below, when I discuss learning.

Transformation and transformative action

The cultural world into which children slowly have to work themselves is a world which already has form. So children's making of signs takes place in a world which has the complex shape produced by all the previous sign-makers of that culture, in a particular society, all of them always expressing their interest in the making of their signs. As a result, with few exceptions, members of a culture end up as 'acculturated' – all having what appears as the same cultural knowledge, the same values, the same, recognizably similar traits and dispositions. All speak the same language, make signs in all the modes which are available in that culture, in quite similar ways. To all intents and purposes, it looks as though the culture has imprinted itself on us, or we have actively acquired the culture in the sense of making a copy of it for ourselves.

Against notions of copying, imitation, acquiring, however implicitly they may be held, I would like to propose the idea that children, like adults, never copy. Instead I wish to put forward the view that we transform the stuff which is around us – usually in entirely minute and barely noticeable ways. Consider this simple example, a 3½-year-old child, on a walk with his family, is climbing a steep hill; it is difficult for him to get up, and he says 'This is a heavy hill.' My transformative view of meaning-making leads me to say that he had a meaning, something like 'this is really hard, it takes a lot of effort to walk up here'. The closest experience that he may have is lifting or carrying something heavy, for which he has a word. So he uses the word which is available to him as the means of expressing his meaning. In the process he has made a new sign. In this sign the combination of meaning and form is motivated: *heavy* was the form which best expressed his meaning 'this is really hard, it takes a lot of effort'.

But now, *heavy* has a new meaning for him; it is *no longer* the word it was before. In his own use he has transformed it, *conditioned by the practical experience in which he had to make the sign.* He has transformed his own language; the fact that no one around him will follow his use in their sign-making means that no *convention* will develop which will sustain this usage. In other cases, if there is a group which does follow such a use, a convention will develop, as in the 1960s use of *heavy* in youth-culture: 'Heavy man, heavy.'

This is not a view which treats *heavy* as an error, a sign of a mistake in the acquisition of the adults' system. To me it is clear that the child was not attempting to copy *steep*, which is an attribute of *hill* (*a steep hill*), but saying something about his own experience (which was produced by the attempt to climb the hill) and expressing that experience. So while the adult syntax focuses on a quality of the hill – something external to the speaker – the syntax of the child's sign focuses on his experience, internal to him, from which he then makes an attribution to the thing outside of himself: *a heavy hill*. He had other possibilities available to him for making a sign, *hard* perhaps, but he chose *heavy* as the best for his meaning. This is one of countless times when he will use *heavy*, each time to express a new meaning; and as he grows more and more into awareness of his culture's conventions, his uses of *heavy* will come closer and closer to those of that culture. As an adult speaker of the language, his use of *heavy* will come to resemble that of other members of his cultural and social group; and in everyday communication it is most likely that neither he nor those with whom he is talking will find anything at all unusual about his use of the word. To all intents and purposes, he has grown into society, he is, linguistically, fully acculturated. Yet in my view *heavy* for him will bear the traces not only of that one use which I remember but of all others: his *heavy* will be different from the *heavy* of all other users of the language. He has made his own path into that bit of the language.

So, an approach based on the notion of transformation suggests that we arrive at a stage which is sufficiently similar to that of other members of culture, and yet is never identical with it. The former makes communication possible, the latter opens the possibility of individual differences, even for fully socialized and acculturated adult users of language – and of all the systems of communication. What the culture and the society in which I am makes available to me, becomes necessarily the stuff with which I (have to) engage constantly; but how I engage with it is a matter of my *interest* at a particular moment in communication, and in engagement with that stuff.

A view of meaning-making as transformation allows me to give an account of how *we* make *our* paths into language as into all cultural systems. And even though we arrive at very similar places, we have got there by quite different paths, *our* paths.

Multimodality

Children make meaning in a multiplicity of ways and employ a multiplicity of modes, means, and materials in doing so. Many of these means and materials are not recognized by the adult forms of the culture, and so tend not to appear in theoretical discussions of learning, the learning of writing included. The signs which children make, whether with conventional or unconventional means (coloured pencils bought for them, paper supplied; or bits and pieces assembled by *them*) are themselves multimodal. A shiny red cut-out car may involve paper, pencils, sticky tape; and need scissors for cutting out. Paper as a material offers the potential for being drawn on, coloured, stuck together and cut out. As a material, it opens certain possibilities, which cardboard offers less readily. Cardboard offers the possibility of being turned into container, shield, sword, objects for relatively robust physical handling.

All of these offer the possibility of representing through a multiplicity of means, at one and the same time, in the making of one complex sign. Children are therefore entirely used to 'making' in a number of media; and their approach to meaning-making is shaped and established in that way. Children act multimodally, both in the things they use, the objects they make; and in their engagement of their bodies: there is no separation of body and mind. The differing modes and materials which they employ offer differing potentials for the making of meaning; and therefore offer different affective, cognitive and conceptual possibilities. The opportunity offered by paper for being cut out is a physical opportunity, as much as an aesthetic one: it allows the maker of the subject to heighten, to intensify desirable aspects of his or her represented object; to make his or her imagined shapes physical, concrete, objective; to bring them into the world of potential action. It is also an opportunity to perform, physically that highly abstract conceptual/cognitive transformation from flat representation to concrete object, from represented object to real object, and with it the transformation from potential to action.

Children's engagement with print shows how essential this capacity for multiple engagement is. It enables them to treat print, which is too often seen as a uni-dimensional medium, as multimodal, as a complex semiotic system; and it is this disposition, which makes it possible for them to make inroads into the great complexity of alphabetic writing. For children, alphabetic writing is clearly multi-modal: it is blocks of print; letter-shapes; media – such as newspapers, birthday cards, books; genres; it is an aesthetic object which can be used in design; a medium of meaning; a drawing of sound; and so on.

Here we can clearly see how all children make their own paths into literacy. Given the intense multimodality of writing as print, two aspects in particular lead to differentiating paths into writing. One is simply this: in a multimodal system, the child has a choice as to which aspects, angles, features, to focus on, to highlight for herself or himself. This will have a potent shaping influence on that path. The other is the question of 'what is to hand'. Clearly, if the child is in a 'rich' environment of print from the earliest time, the stuff of print will appear to her or to him differently from when it is relatively absent. The issue that I am focusing on here is that of the relation between the kinds of things that were or are to hand for the children in their meaning-making, and what habits of practice, of cognitive and affective engagement they led the child to develop. For me pillows and blankets are in this respect as important as coloured pencils and paper: the former encourage a disposition towards taking everything as being potentially meaningful, and as being capable of use in representation and communication. The latter are important in providing the means of representation and expression of that more distanced kind which is a necessary part of the path into writing.

Pillows and blankets also enable children to develop their sense of arrangement, display and structure. Transforming a room into a whole house requires and fosters high degrees of both abstract and concrete structuring at the same time. Arranging the furniture in a room in this house – setting out the items in the 'kitchen', for instance – requires planning, classification, design and display. All of these are essential in writing; the page is a space that needs to be designed, managed. It is also a space which, like the room in the house, can be transformed. A sheet of paper unfolded is one kind of space, with one kind of potential – to be a picture perhaps, or a space on which to list things, or to write a story on. Once it is folded it can become a newspaper – with front and back page, and inside pages; or a birthday card; several sheets folded become a book.

Equally important is what is to hand conceptually. And here parents' views of language and writing, are crucial. Here it may be that middle-class parents are as limiting for their children as parents who are less focused on writing, less anxious about success in literacy. A view of writing as too abstractly 'language' may prove as limiting as the absence of a view on language altogether.

Two further considerations are crucial. When we think about writing, it is necessary to ask 'What for?' Even in an era when writing dominated the communicational landscape, it was essential to focus on the purposes of writing. There have been countless deep debates about this – arguments which have ranged from personal expression, development, 'growth', to highly specific pragmatic arguments about 'effective communication' seen in a strict and narrow economic context, with many other versions in between, about pleasure, desire and fulfilment. Now, in a thoroughly multimodal context, where in many domains of public communication language is no longer central, the purposes, benefits and limitations of writing (and of reading writing) can be and must be newly examined. As visual modes of communication have become more dominant, language has not just been pushed off the centre of the page (literally – if you look at any tabloid in Britain today, you will *see* the literal meaning of that phrase) it is also changing in its 'internal' form, and in its uses in relation to readers.

The effects of multimodality are far-reaching, and deeply affect the paths into literacy of the children who are growing up in this – for me, new – communicational landscape. They form their paths into literacy unencumbered by nostalgia about the place of writing which besets so many of their parents and grandparents. But in my view it is not just unhelpful, but damagingly limiting to burden them with my nostalgia. It may very well be that the technologies of communication just as much as the information-based economies of the day after tomorrow will actually need and demand, visual modes of representation and communication.

Representation and communication

In the late 1970s I went to a new job, in Adelaide in South Australia, at a college which had a course in journalism. As it was my task to develop new courses, broadly in communication studies, I had to become very interested in this course. It was a transition point in the media and in communication: it involved, on the one side, the introduction of word-processing into the journalistic production process – what soon became more generally developed into 'desktop' publishing. On the other side it involved ENG – electronic news-gathering. The technology which had made that possible was the development of relatively small-sized video cameras. That technology has since developed, though by involving a number of distinct routes, into multimedia production. The quaint metaphor of 'news-gathering' – like collecting seaweed or shells or wild mushrooms at the right moment – gave rise to a vast debate around *bias*, because underlying the metaphor is of course the assumption that just like seashells or mushrooms, the news was out there to be gathered. This debate very quickly developed the understanding that news is 'manufactured' like all messages and signs, as we now think. It is therefore manufactured by particular social actors, in particular social institutions, and inevitably represented their interest – just as, I would say, all signs do.

I am interested in drawing out one further point in this argument, which bears crucially on children's making of meaning, and their learning of writing. The older view of *representation* rested on an assumption of a relatively clear and stable relation between the world 'out there' and the ways of re-presenting that world in systems of signs, whether as words or images or gestures. That assumption could and did sustain particular kinds of beliefs in the characteristics of truth, questions of fact, possibilities of doing things correctly. News-gathering has been replaced by multimedia production: in the latter I can actually *make* the news. I can have, in my data base, images, words, music, background noises of all kinds for a soundtrack, and I can literally *make* the news. I stick together sounds, images, words which I have in my system of representations. Therefore, I cannot possibly sustain a notion of newsgathering or of older notions of truth, fact, objectivity, correctness. *I* make the representations, out of *my* interest. My best possible attempt at making news now is to construct a parallel text – but a fictive text – to events which I think are happening in the world.

My point in introducing what may seem like a somewhat abstract theoretical debate is to try to point forcefully to an inescapable characteristic of the communicational and representational world into which children are moving, and in which, to a considerable extent, they already live – in which they make their paths into literacy. Their communicational world is already one in which the relation between the world and its representation, a relation which was an unshakeable common sense as recently as thirty years ago, no longer exists. That common sense was founded on representation as reference, the stable relation between the world of signs and the world of reality, 'out there'. The new common sense will be founded on representation as sign-making, with a more difficult link to the real world, 'out there'. It seems to me absolutely essential to understand that new world – even if we may not approve of it. Without our understanding, the paths of children into social sign-making, whether in writing or in images will become more difficult. Above all, that path, that process, will become the domain for carrying out deeply unenlightened, nostalgic and pessimistic moral and ideological struggles – with children inevitably as the losers, unless we are clear about what is happening.

Reading

Reading is our means of engaging with the world. That engagement takes place in a multiplicity of ways, in a multiplicity of dimensions. Children take print to be a multisemiotic medium, and then subject that medium to the most rigorous and sustained analysis imaginable. In 'taking in the world' we transform it, on the basis of a few fundamental principles: form is the best possible guide to meaning, the internal organization of the sign is the best possible clue to the organization of the meanings of the sign-maker. In the transformative act of reading we all constantly form signs which have an 'internal' representation, and these internal representations then function as the basis of new 'externally' represented signs. This activity changes the reader's own internal representational system, and it enables the reader to participate in changing her or his culture's system of representation. If children are unable to make signs externally, in some or many modes, they are cut off from participating in the constant remaking of their group's systems of representation and communication. Equally seriously, they are cut off from the benefits of 'objectification', which enable me to see, when I have written something, what it is that I know or think, and to take a distanced relation to it.

The internal making of signs in reading changes not only the representational system of the reader, it makes her or him able to act differently as a result of that change. A child who has developed – from energetic, enthusiastic expression of circular 'scribbles' – the shape and idea of circles, is now able to use circles to make new signs: wheels for instance, and from wheels 'car as wheels', snowmen, ghosts, pumpkins. Of course all these newly made signs further transform the sign of circle, much in the way in which I described the transformation of the word *heavy* earlier in this chapter. The ability to act differently has a transformative and constructive effect on who the sign-maker is, and becomes: from the ability to do, to a different sense of being. Words such as *liberating* are often used, though other words such as *competence, potential,* even *skill, ability* name important aspects of what I think happens.

Reading is therefore one central component – in literate cultures – of the formation of who we are and can be. That does not mean that non-literate societies produce lesser humans: many so-called 'oral' cultures have a wider range of representational and communicational resources at their disposal and in everyday use than so-called 'literate cultures'. I think here of my (extremely) marginal knowledge of Australian Aboriginal societies which use a complex variety of means of representation as a matter of course – in different domains at different times: speech of course, organized often in complex narratives; drawing, whether in the sand or on bark, or on a rock face, with different colours or not; the body as expressive, in dance, mime; or as object for decoration; message sticks. All of these are elaborated into highly articulate means of expression. The fact that such societies can still be called 'illiterate' is a problem of western language- and writing-focused cultures; though it has of course been made into a problem for those societies, through the power of western colonizers.

The sign-making process in reading is, at one level, the same as the sign-making process in writing. Readers make signs out of their interest; that is they draw from the object or text in front of them the features which correspond to their interest, and form their new internal sign on that basis. The important *social* difference is that writing is the making of a sign externally, which therefore can act in affecting others in being the reason for their making of new signs. This becomes amplified through the effects of media for those who do have access to them.

Because the signs formed in reading are made out of the interest of the reader, when that interest does not coincide broadly with the interest of the writer, readers may shift their reading, so to speak, into an oppositional or *resistant* reading in which formal aspects of the text that is read are read as signs of the writer's ideological intent, which is to be resisted. This introduces the issue of the boundaries to reading, one aspect of which is the question of the boundary of the sign. One common-sense assumption is that writers do, and have the right to, fix the boundaries of the sign, so that reading beyond those boundaries is not legitimate. There are important considerations here for the teaching of reading. The effect of different approaches can be to produce readers who *will* consider it improper to exceed the boundaries of the sign made by the writer. This does not imply that their reading is not transformative none the less. Other approaches may produce readers who habitually refuse to accept these boundaries. There are deeply significant social metaphors at issue here – and the potential to produce more authoritarian or more liberal personalities.

The implications for a curriculum of reading are therefore vast; and the fierce debates which surround this specific matter bear testimony to the fact that they are well enough understood at some level.

Resources for making meaning

We commonly tend to think of resources for making meaning in quite abstract terms. In Michael Halliday's theory of language (1985), grammar is seen as a resource for making meaning. In this section I would like to be more encompassing, and talk about the quite abstract as well as the very concrete. I will start with the very concrete.

Throughout this chapter I have referred to 'what is to hand'. What the childish eye falls on as materials for making exceeds in entirely unpredictable ways the conventionalized expectations of any adult. I have mentioned a considerable range of materials and objects already, and the list is an open-ended one. The real point about this voracious appetite for semiotic recycling is the child's ever-searching eye, guided by a precise sense of *design*, both for material and for shape. The materiality of the stuff out of which they choose to make their signs is in itself meaningful. The pillows in the girls' car suit better than an upturned drawer because they represent the comfortableness of cloth-covered car seats. [. . .]

From this point of view it is revealing to see how these selections change with age; and how they may be influenced by gender. Predictably enough the choice is wider and freer at earlier ages; and it seems to be less gendered – in my experience at least – but it is not free of its influence. Children are drawn into the semiotic web of culture through a vast array of signs – in which the family and its practices and values are centrally important. But there are countless other messages, and again not only those usually focused on. Toys, for instance, are sign-objects which code meanings about a society's view of different ages of childhood: soft plastic, or furry, in bold colours early on; perhaps simple shapes in polished or painted wood. Then, as the ages of children for whom the toys are designed increase, the materials change: metal might appear – they become harder, more angular; the colours change. Of course the range of things which are drawn into the world of toys also changes. The domain of toys constitutes a communicational system, in which differing ideas of being a social human are suggested, and forms of social life explored.

I made the point earlier that there are deep logics at work in the materials of meaning-making – with effects on the conceptual, cognitive and affective organization of children. But children act on materials also. Consider again, the example of a sheet of paper discussed earlier: it can be used as a flat sheet, for drawing on or writing on; once it is folded its potential changes. If it remains a material object, it offers opportunities for cutting out regular patterns along the newly made spine – producing complex symmetrical shapes when they are folded flat afterwards: snowflakes, trees, but also 'Australia'. If the folded sheet becomes a surface for receiving representations, then the folding changes its generic potential – to book, newspaper, birthday card. That change may seem both obvious and simple; it does, however, have far-reaching consequences: if the now-folded sheet has become a newspaper, then it requires the child to produce whatever text it is that makes a newspaper; similarly, if it is a card.

In other words, the simple act of folding the sheet has implications for the child's exploration of what texts are, what layout is, how newspapers actually look and what is done with them. These are transformations of the material stuff which have effects well beyond the merely material. Another way to think about this is to say that the separation of material stuff and non-material, abstract conceptual stuff is untenable in the actual making of signs, by children at least.

But there are also abstract, cognitive/conceptual materials which are to hand. Children have to make these for themselves, in slow, persistently energetic fashion.

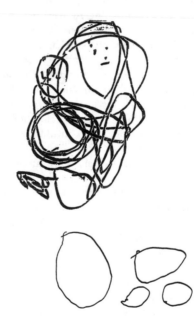

Figure 6 From circular scribbles to circles

Figure 6 illustrates both the notion of 'what is to hand' and the child's own action in developing his (in this instance) resources of representation. The three images represent a sequence that took place over about a year and a half. The top image, circular scribbles, was made at about the age of 1½. The child's energetic circular motion seems to be merely expressive, though even at that age he would often accompany his drawing with some descriptive commentary. By the second image 'circularity' is clearly apparent; the third image represents circles which he had drawn, each on a separate sheet. There is clearly a constant development going on; from one instance to the next (with very many instances between the ones shown here) there is transformation, with a gradual refinement of the abstracted and generalized circle-shape. Each of these instances represents 'what is to hand' for the child, which can be used in the development/transformation to the next. Once the circles are 'what is to hand', the child can use these to make a complex sign, using metaphor, design and deliberateness, and intention.

My second example is from a child at the age of 5½. On vacation with her family in France, travelling in the car, she said 'The thing I hate about France pedestrian crossings is / the cars get to choose. / But it's great when you're in a car / because then VVRRAAAM' It seems clear enough what is to hand, and what is being made entirely newly out of what is to hand. She wants to say things which I understood to have been something like the adjective *French*, the noun 'priority', and some exuberant, and joking expression of her sense of the relation of pedestrians and cars, and her pleasure at being in a car at this moment. She fashions these signs from what she has to hand, namely, the noun/name *France*, which she makes into a different syntactic sign, an adjective; the meaning of *priority* is analysed by her, and expressed in terms of its analytically derived components (changing, in the process from the possessive *have priority*, to the action *get to choose*). And for the expression of her affective meaning she changes mode, using sound and other physical expression as a material to express her feeling directly.

The point here is not to list the kinds of (abstract) resources which are available to her, but to make clear what these processes are, and what their effects are. As with the material aspects of 'what is to hand', here too the different resources have differential potential and effect. It is by starting from that realization, that we may be able to construct curricula of representation to meet our aims, and the needs of the younger generations.

Imagination, cognition and affect

Imagination is an aspect of the processes of sign-making; of necessity it is always 'internal', for when its effects are expressed as 'outward' signs it has again become a part of public social semiosis. Imagination is a form of sign-making in which the boundaries to sign-making, the chains of signs, are potentially unlimited, and are not subject to the usual social constraint. It is dependent on and enhanced by the ability to engage in free movement among forms of (internal) representation – not confined, for instance, to staying within language, or the visual, or the tactile, but able to range freely across modes. The formation of signs is clearly the same kind of activity as that which we call imagination; a sign is a metaphor; metaphor involves the new expression of individual interest, and is therefore always in a sense a facet of imagination.

Imaginative activity takes place in any medium, though it is the case that society, perhaps particularly in formal education, in its focus on written language, acts to inhibit or suppress that activity of 'free ranging across' for most members of that society. That does not apply to the Arts, but the very fact that they are treated as a quite separate domain indicates the extent of the separation. The different media make different kinds of imagination possible; and impose their limitations on imaginative activity. The difficulty of translation between texts and signs in different media is evidence of the different potentials of the various modes.

One question to ask therefore is precisely about the limitations and possibilities of each medium. The visual, for instance, seems to permit in many cases much more subtly graded expression than the verbal. In the visual semiotic there is a rule, for instance, about the meaning of *distance* between viewer and object viewed – something broadly like familiarity, solidarity, intimacy, formality; but clearly variation of distance is infinitely variable. In language I can say 'quite far', 'quite close', 'very close' and use a range of other forms, but there is a clear limit to the number of such variations. In the visual mode there is no such limit: the distance between myself and the object I look at is infinitely variable. Similarly with the possibilities of signifying meaning through colour: the range is infinite in the visual semiotic; and limited, relatively in language by the existence of colour terms.

Forms of teaching, as much as other social practices, can, over time, engender dispositions which impose limits to imagination, yet forms of teaching could equally be designed to open up its possibilities. At the moment the easy move across media 'mentally' – synaesthesia – is discouraged. The brain's capacity for translation from one mode into another is not seen as a quality to be fostered. If it were, the imaginative capacity of humans in western culture would be entirely different.

If cognition is the same kind of mental activity as that which we consider to be imagination, then the freeing of one will have positive effects on the other. This is entirely traditional thinking; but it may be possible to think freshly about this in the light of a theory which treats both as the same activity: one, cognition, is dependent on the existence of articulations of units and their relations in a particular medium; the other, imagination, is dependent on actively moving across media and modes, always going beyond the boundaries set by convention in a particular mode. In my view imagination and cognition are entirely and closely related. What we have learned to call 'cognition' works with established modes and their elements, and stays – in so far as that may ever be possible – with one mode. What we regard as imagination works across all the modes – in so far as it is not suppressed by socially induced 'habits of mind'. Cognition works with, and depends on, sign-making by using established kinds of units and their relations, respecting what can be generally referred to as the established boundaries; and where it does not, it is clear about the transgression of boundaries. Imagination goes beyond units and exceeds boundaries as its normal mode of action.

Lastly a word about affect. It seems to be the case that, as biological beings, we have different dispositions towards the world, differential preferences in relation to our senses. One child might prefer physical three-dimensional representation, another the distanced representation of drawing or writing. Another child might prefer to express herself or himself through the body, in dance or gesture. Compelling a child to forget his or her preferred mode will have affective consequences. Cultural groups have developed preferences in relation to modes and forms of expression. School necessarily imposes some further selection. These all have their influence on the child's affective disposition towards modes of representation and communication. In thinking about affect it is important to be aware of the relatively fine distinctions between cultural groups, within broader categories such as 'Western European', or even 'English' (rather than 'British', or 'Welsh' or 'Scottish'). Within multicultural 'English' society there are cultural groups strongly oriented towards writing; and not oriented strongly towards bodily forms of expression. Other groups within that society are much more oriented towards spoken language, and are freer in their use of the body as a means of communication. Children from both kinds of group can end up in the same 'English' classroom. The very broad distinctions of 'West African', 'South Asian', 'Mediterranean' maybe too uselessly general, but they allow us to think, for instance, about the different cultural uses of the body as a vehicle of representation and communication. The difference between 'South Asian dance' and 'African dance' may suggest the distinctions I have in mind. In multicultural Britain or Australia or Germany, all these appear in one classroom. The consequences for the affective response by children in that classroom are impossible to calculate, but need to be imagined by a teacher.

Beyond that, there is the question of affect generally. The affective state of a child coming from her or his home to school in the morning will influence how that child will and can respond to an explanation, a task, given or set by the teacher. Affect 'colours' all activity, and cognitive action in particular. Again this is simply restating, in some ways, what is commonsensical: a warm, supportive, encouraging atmosphere in the classroom has positive effects on the ability of children to learn; and equally the opposite will be incontrovertible. Affect can dampen or enhance our perform-ance, and the transformative tasks and processes of synaesthesia may be particularly prone to that. At the moment we know very little about all of this; and we know very little because the issue is not quite respectable on the public agenda. It may well be that we can no longer afford the luxury of such disdain.

References

Halliday, M.A.K. (1985) *An Introduction to Functional Grammar*, London: Edward Arnold.
Saussure, F. de (1974) *Course in General Linguistics*, trans. Wade Baskin, Glasgow: Collins.

CHAPTER 5

WHERE ARE THE CHILDHOODS IN CHILDHOOD LITERACY?

An exploration in outer (school) space

Anne Haas Dyson

Journal of Early Childhood Literacy, 2001, 1(1): 9–39

Introduction

> [In Montessori's classroom] we find messages like the following: 'Happy Easter to Engineer Talani and Headmistress Montessori. Best wishes to the director . . .' and so forth . . . If [reading and writing] are used only . . . [for] whatever the teacher thinks up . . . [the child's] activity will not be manifest in his writing and his budding personality will not grow.
>
> (Vygotsky, 1978: 117–18)

Writing early in the last century, Vygotsky used children's neatly written renditions of adult-modelled texts as symbols of literacy teaching gone awry. As experienced composers in speech, play, and drawing, children had 'the right stuff (Wolfe, 1979) for travel into the spheres of school literacy. But to make this journey, they had to begin within social worlds that allowed them some space for decision-making, or else their agency – their 'budding personalities' – would be hampered, not furthered, by this new medium.

At the beginning of the next century, we collectively know a great deal more than Vygotsky did about the development of literacy in early childhood. His view however, is no less radical. In the USA, for example, a wave of reductionism has gripped the schools, and many state curricular guidelines equate children's learning with adults' teaching of orderly lists of literacy knowledge and know-how. To illustrate, in California, children are first to 'see good models, edit others' writing, and *then* 'generate their own' written language (California Department of Education, 1998: 61; emphasis added). Children will thus progress linearly from 'the skills of forming uppercase and lowercase letters and using letter and sound knowledge to write words' at ages 5 and 6, through the writing of sentences and, then, paragraphs with topic sentences at ages 8 to 9 (California Department of Education, 1998: 31).

It is hard to imagine anyone writing against children forming letters or using 'sound knowledge', but it is equally hard to imagine that such a linear mapping could account for children's literacy learning. For, given the smallest bit of manoeuvering space, children's 'budding personalities' disrupt the best-laid literacy plans. Consider for example, the 6- to 7-year-olds in Ms Rita's class (USA first grade). They are illustrating studied space facts, which are listed neatly on a chart; the facts include, for example, that 'the earth orbits the sun,' and that 'there are 9 planets'. The children copy a chosen fact and then spin off into outer child space.

Denise and Vanessa are illustrating that 'the earth orbits the sun.' As they work, they consult a picture in a reference book, and then they try to reconcile the heavens above, populated with 'Great Grandma, my grandpa') with the pictured expanse of the Milky Way, which, perhaps, people in heaven use for 'milk in their cereal'. When the girls are nearly done with their planet-filled, multi-modal text, they add a space robot – who soon gets long hair and a t-shirt, becomes a singer, and has a little girl robot named Precious. When those robots get antennae they look, for heaven's sake, like radios! 'It's K-M-E-L [the local hip hop radio station],' they say. Then they slip from the official school space into the unofficial one, and, under the expansive buzz of classroom voices, they sing the opening to Coolio's (1995) 'Gangsta's Paradise' rap: 'As I walk through the valley of the shadow of death.'

What are the implications of children's potential for such unruliness? Should teachers tighten the borders and build fortresses around spaces for child agency? Should they allow only blanks to be filled in, story starters to be completed, books with decodable words to be read, perfectly edited thank you notes (or accurate illustrations) to be displayed? Is such tightening particularly important for the 'at risk' (i.e. for children most apt to be viewed as academically unruly)?

In this chapter, I argue against these responses and for the centrality of childhoods to literacy development – that is, for the centrality of the cultural symbols and practices through which children construct their own varied childhoods. These cultural resources reveal children's powers of adaptation and improvization – their symbolic and discourse flexibility; and it is children's exploitation of these cross-cultural childhood strengths (Stephens, 1995; Sutton-Smith, 1997) and their ways of stretching, reconfiguring, and re-articulating their resources, that are key to literacy learning in contemporary times.

To make this argument, I venture into the outer spaces of an official school curriculum in an urban primary school in the San Francisco East Bay. Drawing on a current project in Rita's classroom, I sketch a portrait of a contemporary childhood, suggesting the range of symbols and textual practices that may guide and, indeed, become the very symbolic stuff of children's early school composing. Against the backdrop of the classroom space unit, I highlight the participation of two children Denise and her peer Noah. Using key events from their case histories, I illustrate the recontextualization processes (processes of transporting and transforming cultural material across practice boundaries) that account for the children's textual untidiness in their literacy growth. To envision development in this way, however, growth must be imagined not as movement along a linear road, but as increasingly deliberate movement among expanding social spheres.

To frame this effort, I introduce below the dialogic vision of language and of development that guides it. Then, because methodological details are available elsewhere (see for example Dyson, 1999a, c), I describe the project data set only briefly and then take readers into a classroom universe, illuminating its outer spaces, where the children rule. I close the chapter by connecting this effort to underline the *childhoods* in childhood literacy in contrast to the narrowing gravitational hold of selected, idealized childhoods.

Slip-sliding words and spinning children: re-imagining developmental trajectories

> The immobility of our world is an illusion. We spin. We speed through space. We circle the Sun. We live on a wandering star . . . [But] the mind would rather cede revolution to the universe than relinquish the solace of solid ground.
>
> (Sobel, 1999: 153–4)

It was, as readers may recall, a cosmic struggle in Renaissance times to release the earth from its stable place in the heavens, to see ourselves as spinning through space 'on a wandering star'. It belies common sense.

There have also been theoretical, if not cosmic, struggles to release oral and written texts from a stable place in the universe, to see them as spinning through social space in communicative chains, anchored only in the coordinated efforts of specific people in specific encounters before, once again, slipping away (Bakhtin, 1986). In such a theoretical vision, people interactively rotate within, and revolve through, social space by means of wandering words. As composers and readers, producers and consumers, they fix textual meaning only momentarily within the shifting social constellations (Bakhtin, 1981; Hanks, 1996).

Consider, once again, Denise and Vanessa, now singing out on their school playground; they are singing play songs that surface only within the social constellation of other children, especially other African-American girls. Their songs are composed of wandering words; they echo not only contemporary popular culture but also Motown music of the seventies (Jackson, 1972), the rock 'n' roll of the fifties (Day, 1958), and the play rhymes of black rural childhoods at the turn of the century and, no doubt, beyond that too (Jones and Hawes, 1972). Listen to a few verses of 'one' play song, transcribed from an audiotaped performance by Denise and Vanessa:

> Rockin' robin/tweet tweet, tweet-a-leet
> Rockin' robin/tweet tweet, tweet-a-leet [see Jackson, 1972; and Day, 1958]
> Mama in the kitchen/Burning rice
> Daddy on the corner/Shooting that dice
> Brother in jail/Raising H
> Sister at the corner/Selling fruit cocktail [see Jones and Hawes, 1972]
> Rockin' robin/ tweet tweet, tweet-a-leet
> Rockin' robin/tweet tweet, tweet-a-leet
> Batman and Robin/Flying in the air
> Batman lost/His underwear
> Robin said/I'll buy you a pair
> But you don't know/What size I wear [parody of contemporary superhero]
> Rockin' robin . . .

The children's familiarity with these verses allowed them to appropriate their words and recontextualize them in new contexts, as in Vanessa's response below to my query about a popular singer nicknamed 'Batman':

> Vanessa: Not the Batman that flies through the air.
> Not the Batman that lost his underwear
> But Batman. He black and he fine.

Thus, 'Batman' has the potential for many different meanings, and the source of those meanings is not the word itself but 'the social matrix within which discourse is produced and understood' (Hanks, 2000: 166). The interdependence of textual meaning and shifting social constellations is key to understanding childhood agency and the development of childhood literacy.

Symbolic agency in childhood spaces

Although the particularities of childhoods vary across historical time and cultural space, all over the globe, children like Denise and Vanessa use available symbolic, textual, and cultural resources for their own childhood pleasures (Stephens, 1995; Whiting and Whiting, 1975). They are both conservators and innovators of cultural traditions and, most strikingly, they are 'scavengers of form and theme' (Goldman, 1998: 143; Opie and Opie, 1959). In this scavenging, young child 'scavengers', as well as older youth, may appropriate popular media material (e.g. its content and genres) as a means of cultural production, that is, as a means of constructing social affiliations, expressive practices, and imaginative worlds (e.g. Dyson, 1997; Marsh, 1999).

For example, when Denise and Vanessa played 'radio stars' on the playground, their textual toys were the soul songs and the raps marketed to their older relations but overheard, by them (for a full report of this phenomenon, see Dyson, 2001a). One day Denise and Vanessa were concerned about a classmate's 'spying' on them. During recess, Denise 'made up' a 'rap' about this situation. Her effort to maintain a driving beat and a consistent pattern of syllable stresses and rhymes led to some lexical nonsense, which she soulfully admitted during her performance:

> Denise: It's called, 'Why You in My Bus'ness?' (*sternly*)
> (*rapping*) Why you in my bus'ness?
> Cause I *got* you/In my far-*is*-mus
> And I *had* you/In my char-*is*-mus/my *bus*'ness
> Why you gotta be/In the *bus*'ness?
> (*In an R & B [Rhythm and Blues] musical style*) I don't know these words
> I'm saying/So please forgive me for my words

Denise and Vanessa illustrate the 'genius of composition' described by McDowell (1995), that is, children's 'almost amoebic ability' (p. 53) to make ready use of any textual material for expressive and communicative purposes and for aesthetic performance (cf. Willis, 1990). Their sense of competence is rooted in their familiarity with certain ways with words (which Bakhtin would call 'genres'); their sense of agency, of possibility, comes from recontextualizing, that is, from rearranging, re-articulating, and stretching their ways with words (processes displayed in Vanessa's exuberant 'Not-the-Batman-that-flies-through-the-air' response).

Literacy learning and social location

Children's symbolic flexibility, and, moreover, their cultural worlds as *children* seem absent from most accounts of childhood literacy, including 'child-centered' ones (for discussions, see Dyson, 1995, 1999b; Newkirk, 2002). When children enter the school's atmosphere, they are often fixed within its hierarchical patterns. Words indexing texts and social constellations beyond its stratosphere are of little interest, little relevance. In literacy research itself, learning to manipulate written symbols is seen most often as a fragile business, best suited for childhoods centered around school-valued practices (Snow *et al.*, 1998).

But children enter school with the words and symbols indexing their prior travels on Bakhtin's voice-strewn landscape, that is, in families, churches, sidewalks and playgrounds, neighborhoods, radio waves, and screens of all kinds. Recontextualization processes – process of differentiation and translation of cultural material across symbolic, social, and ideological borders (Bauman and Briggs, 1990) – seem at the heart of developing a functional place for written language in a symbolic repertoire (Dyson, 1999a, 2001). Children must stretch familiar resources from their communicative experiences into new social constellations if they are to participate meaningfully in the literacy practices of school. In a dialectic fashion, children must reframe the written medium within familiar social constellations, if they are, not only to make sense of, but moreover, to understand why they might want to make sense through, manipulating written graphics.

Thus, by children's own actions, the singular classroom context becomes dynamic, multilayered worlds (Dyson, 1993). Theoretically, children's recontextualizing of cultural material (e.g. of genres, social relations, discursive content, particular symbols, and composing skills – and potentially, varieties of language[s] themselves) across practice boundaries has the potential to make that material available for deliberate reflection and use (Bakhtin, 1981; Dyson, 1999a, in press, b, Moll *et al.*, in press; Nelson, 1996; Vygotsky, 1987). A more deliberate use of written symbols – a use that reflects children's learning about the symbolic, social, and ideological 'options, limits, and blends' of practices – is what literacy development entails (to build on the non-literacy focused work of Miller and Goodnow, 1995: 12).

Moreover, development as 'the tightening or the recontextualization of situation-bound understandings' situates literacy learning within a diversity of developmental pathways, since children bring to school strikingly varied symbolic and communicative experiences (Clay, 1998; McNaughton, 1999; Miller and Goodnow, 1995:13). As Rockwell (1999:122) argues, the larger social processes of children's lives always 'penetrate the space of schooling,' although, I would add, they are not always recognized, acknowledged or responded to. Thus, children's developing literacy knowledge is an integral part of their developing social and ideological knowledge about the place of their experiences in school.

The trajectories of evolving practices

In the project in Denise's classroom, I focus on children's appropriations of diverse cultural material for school composing. Analysis of ethnographic data has revealed that children draw deeply upon non-academic social worlds to negotiate their entry into school literacy; those worlds provided them with agency and meaningful symbols, including those from popular music, films, animated shows, and sports media. The resulting texts could lack a 'definite generic skeleton,' that is, a clear genre home, to use a descriptor from Bakhtin's (1981: 59–60) analysis of literary history. Nonetheless, as children engaged in recontextualization processes, they linked textual practices from a diversity of social worlds, seemingly making themselves more at home in school.

In my project, I view the production of a text, like Denise's and Vanessa's multimodal 'space fact,' as a Vygotskian minimal unit of analysis (Vygotsky, 1987). Such productions maintain and display the intertextual linkages between children's engagement with official school literacy and their engagement with textual practices from other sources. Studying these minimal units, these literacy events, has allowed me to untangle the intertextual threads that index the children's present literacy activity in their experiences, for instance, as (pretend) radio singing stars and, beyond that, as radio consumers (or video watchers, superhero enactors, church goers, and so on). The events, then, are a window to the landscape of a contemporary childhood and to its diversity of cultural symbols, textual practices, and communicative media. Moreover, using data collected from individual children over time, I have been able to trace their pathways into school literacy, as they juxtapose, interweave, and sometimes deliberately differentiate kinds of speaking voices or genres.

In tracing these pathways, I find useful Hanks' (1996) notion of evolving communicative practices. He views practices as exemplified by genres, or schemas for social action (after Bakhtin, 1986), which are key aspects of 'habitus' (after Bourdieu, 1977) – that is, of a group's disposition to perceive and act upon the world in certain ways. As communicative practices, genres are neither rigid types nor formless inventions; they are potential ways of producing meaning, shaped by formal symbol systems, by the existent social constellation, and by strategic improvization.

Hanks is not interested in children's textual unruliness or their development in school places, but he is interested in the ways practices interweave, differentiate, and, more generally, evolve over historical time and across social space. He traces the trajectories of practices by following their enactment in particular events. Trajectories become visible as producers orient themselves to particular social constellations by, for instance, adopting particular words or phrases that appeal to, or appease, the current social scene, or by using indexical elements (like personal pronouns or demonstratives) that situate producers among other participants. In these and other ways, language users establish linkages to their 'spaces of engagements' (Hanks, 1996: 245).

By linking key events from Denise and Noah's case histories, I intend to illustrate how recontextualization processes undergirded the complex convergence of – and differentiation of – practices in their spaces for school literacy. The children used similar processes in the same classroom, but they differed in their developmental paths (i.e. in the nature of their converging practices and the 'limits, blends, and options' thus made salient). Moreover, these paths were not just linearly unfolding but expansive, as the children used written words to more deliberately maneuver through social space.

Entering children's spheres: the project data set

Denise and her peers attended an elementary school officially described as having the 'greatest crosstown span' in this East San Francisco Bay district (i.e. the greatest socioeconomic mix). Approximately half the school's children were African-American, approximately a third European-American, and the rest were of varied Latino and Asian ancestries.

Denise's teacher, Rita, was highly experienced, having begun teaching in the London primary schools of the 1960s. Rita's curriculum included both open-ended activities (e.g. writing workshop, where the children wrote and drew relatively freely, followed by class sharing) and more teacher-directed ones (e.g. assigned tasks in study units, in which children wrote and drew as part of social studies and science learning).

In any classroom there are both official and unofficial social spheres (D'Amato, 1987; Goffman, 1961). In the unofficial world, I met a small group of friends, all African-American: Denise, Vanessa, Marcel, Wenona, Noah, and, less centrally involved in the project, Lakeisha (who was in pull-out programs for tutoring and counseling support). During the course of an academic year, I documented through observation and audiotaping this group of children's participation in school activities, especially but not exclusively composing events. I observed as Rita circulated among the children, or alternately wrote in her own journal and guided child writers. Although I was, in the main, a quiet, passive observer, I did query focal children when confused by their actions. In addition to observing, I also photocopied all 20 class members' written work. I collected data over an 8 month period, approximately 4–6 hours per week.

In analyzing this data, I catalogued (and verified with the help of the research project assistant, Soyoung Lee) all media references in the children's talk and writing. I also examined the chronologically organized data for each case study child, noting key, theoretically illustrative events. Key events were those that displayed intertextual linkages between official school and non-school practices; and that, moreover, highlighted children's negotiations across symbolic, social, and ultimately, ideological boundaries.

Although the focal children shared a cultural landscape (i.e. they had favorite sports teams, listened to the same radio station, saw many of the same videos, shared a religious discourse of God and the devil), they drew differentially on that landscape as they entered into school literacy. And so it was for the two children featured herein, Noah and Denise (whose case intersects with that of Vanessa, her 'best fake sister'). Their cases illustrate both commonality in recontextualization processes and distinctiveness in the communicative frames within which each embarked on school literacy journeys. (Extended case history of Noah is available in Dyson, 2001c; and of Denise in Dyson, 2001.)

Children in composing spaces: plotting journeys into school literacy

> A machine, if shot into outer space never to return, would simply go on being a machine; after it ran out of fuel or traveled beyond guidance, it would still be a machine. A human mind necessarily embodied, if shot into outer space never to return, would die as soon as it went beyond its sustaining connections and references . . .
>
> (Berry 2000: 49)

Denise and Noah's journeys into school literacy were shaped not only by official curricular purposes, relationships, and tools, but also by unofficial child relationships and by their stores of experience and knowledge – their cargo of resources. They did not reveal these resources by pulling them out, one by one, from a back pack in a variant of show-and-tell. They revealed them in response to particular tasks, both teacher organized and child initiated. During writing events in Rita's class, they revealed and made use of many cultural materials that figured into their lives as children, and they did so in ways that reflected understood forms of agency and familiar communicative practices.

I formally introduce Denise and Noah below, summarizing their composing events in the fall of the year, before the space unit began. I then discuss their participation in the space unit, which helped welcome them back in January from the winter holidays. Finally, for each child, I briefly sample key events that allow insight into the recontextualization processes through which they continued to construct school literacy practices.

Denise

Six years and two months when school began, Denise had gotten her first radio when she was five; it was a Christmas present from her father. Denise loved to sing, and she often sang along with the radio on car rides with her mother and older brother, with whom she lived. Moreover, Denise enjoyed emotion-filled and rhythmic voices wherever she found them. Outside official events which involved the whole class (in which she herself said she was 'shy'), she often slipped into an emotion-filled, if playful, role. Once, explaining to Vanessa about being teased on the school bus, she dropped to the floor, raised her hands to the heavens, and moaned, Why me? Why me?' (which was quite amusing, we three thought).

Although Denise learned to encode and decode faster than most of her classmates, she, like them, produced her first prose entries by appropriating brief forms from the class-generated 'things to write about' list. These forms provided children with textual frames within when to insert content that 'I like', 'I saw' or 'I went to'. During the fall of the year (from September through December), Denise inserted Vanessa's name into these framing devices (e.g. 'I like ____' or 'I went ____'), and Vanessa inserted hers. 'I want [went] to Vanessa has [house] today,' Denise wrote. 'Vanessa wit [went] to my party' was another. Denise and Vanessa accompanied their writing with detailed drawings of themselves, checking on each others' preferences for hair baubles and outfits. These texts of personal experience were actually bits of fiction, since Denise and Vanessa's relationship was confined to school.

Denise's easy slippage into dramatic performances for others' amusement, her alertness to musical, emotion-filled language, and her sisterly play will all be evident in the data excerpts to come.

Noah

Six years and one month when school began, Noah enjoyed watching movie videos with his family and playing video games or watching cartoons with his fraternal twin, Ned (in another classroom). Like Denise and Vanessa, he enjoyed singing songs of all kinds, although he seldom played radio star.

During composing time, Noah could become deeply involved in an imaginative world, especially when he was drawing some melodramatic happening involving power swirls and fire bursts. His drawing and accompanying narration borrowed characters, plot elements, themes, and visual images themselves from the popular media. They supported Noah's play with compelling themes of good and evil, with villains and heroes, and with physical power and physical vulnerability.

Despite Noah's imaginativeness, he was quite serious and straightforward about official expectations for writing. Like Denise, he too appropriated brief framing devices from the official world. And, also as with Denise, Noah's tendency to lean on official patterns led him to write personal experience texts that were, in fact, fictional. After dramatizing a scene from the film *Jurassic Park*, Noah wrote I wt [went] to tll [the] zoo I sa[w] Dinosaurs,' which, one would have to say, was not likely.

Noah's easy slippage into the communicative practice of constructing visually dramatic worlds and his alertness to the language that marked school boundaries will both be evident in the data excerpts to come.

The textual journeys of Noah and Denise now come in for closer inspection against the backdrop of the classroom space unit. Although there are complex issues embedded in the children's events, my focus here is on the recontextualization processes through which they constructed the trajectories of their evolving practices.

Enacting the official space unit

During the space unit, the children were officially guided into galactic space through a myriad of activities, involving varied media and diverse genres. The unit was undergirded by a focus on stance toward reality (i.e. a concern with facts, fiction, or opinion). It is 'really hard to tell' what's real or not on the topic of space, Rita explained, and even accepted 'facts' can change. The study unit included a study of the night sky and the planets ('facts' that seem like 'fantasy') and a viewing of *Star Wars* (a 'fantasy' that includes some 'facts' and one which is sometimes considered 'ersatz high culture' [Jenkins, 1992: 22]).

Illustrating facts

The children's first composing assignment was to produce illustrated facts, alone or in self-chosen teams. Illustrating a fact was not, in and of itself, a familiar genre or communicative practice. In making the assignment – and the fact – meaningful, the children could cover a great deal of social and symbolic ground, as their singular composing event became a space of intersecting spheres of action.

For example, in the earlier vignette on Denise and Vanessa's event, the children's official relationship with their teacher, experienced through practices of book consulting and class concept discussions; their unofficial relationship as friends, realized through practices involving collaborative play; their community relationships as church goers who participate in practices enacting beliefs about a heavenly afterlife – all this cultural material resulted in a hybrid event, constructed from resources that indexed their participation in overlapping official and unofficial worlds.

Noah's 'illustrated fact' event yielded a seemingly more coherent text than the girls' did – but his event was less a space of intersection than one juxtaposed to the official world. Noah's physical artefact, a drawn scene featuring a laser dual, could have been an illustration of the listed fact that 'The movie Star Wars came out nearly twenty years ago.' But Noah's fact was that 'There are nine planets' – a fact he neither copied nor orally referenced. At the beginning of the work period, Noah immediately began drawing an intergalactic space battle (with the open admiration of his peer Cedric). Indeed, Noah drew intergalactic space battles for all of the space unit composing activities, including a thank you letter to a class helper, and a homework assignment to share space facts with family members.

The apparent coherence of Noah's event came, then, from being situated within a familiar communicative practice – constructing visually dramatic worlds. His illustrated fact included the usual suspects of his many media-inspired drawn dramatizations: a good guy, bad guys, and 'fire power' (i.e. a clearly labeled TNT blast – not the result of space age technology).

Both Noah's disposition to visually enacted adventures, and Denise's to sisterly play and performative voices allowed them agency in this new school task, and their resulting events contained within them developmental challenges, including differentiating both the symbolic possibilities of print, voice, and pictures and the social goals and values of official and unofficial practice. The children's response to the reporting task discussed below also evidenced recontextualization and the challenges it generated.

Reporting facts

In the reporting practice, children were to perform as knowledgeable students for interested others. Among its variants were dialogue games, in which partners asked each other 'Did you know that ...?' and reported 'I learned that ...' to Rita and the class. At the end of the space unit, the children wrote in their writing books about what 'I learned,' and this is the assignment of interest here.

As that work session began, Noah, Vanessa, and Denise made their way to the rug, writing books in hand. In reconstructing the children's actions below, I turn first toward Noah.

Noah's official event – and an unofficial encounter

Noah settled himself on the rug and wrote his name on his page (unnecessary in his writing book, a bit of a textual practice that floated in from the broader school sphere). He watched his friend Marcel, who had retrieved the book *Space Case* (Marshall, 1980), in order to spell *space*. That title, though, seemed to remind Noah of a television adventure similarly named, one in which multi-species children, lost on a renegade space ship, confront varied evil others and solve near disasters. Thus, Noah situated the current task within his regular practice of constructing visually dramatic adventures.

Noah *did* begin by writing, his oral language assuming the slow, deliberate pace of a child just learning 'to draw speech,' (Vygotsky, 1978: 115): 'Space [pause] case [pause] ses [pause] there was.' But he only wrote as far as *the* (of *there*), and then he drew (not wrote) a space ship. 'There was some stars,' he next intoned, and he drew those stars. And then, in an animated voice that soon erupted in a burst of sound effects, the space ship 'blast[ed] off' unexpectedly and went 'all the way into space.' The person at the controls threw TNT, and there was a burst of fire power: 'BLEW::::!'

As Noah became more deeply involved in his drawn space adventure Vanessa loudly reread her writing:

> 'I learned that the movie *Star Wars* was made –'
> '20 [years ago],' piped up Noah, sure of the next word in this oft-repeated fact.
> 'A long time ago,' said Vanessa firmly, letting him know he was wrong.
> Still, that fact, or its rhythm, seemed to stay in Noah's mind, because when he finished his drawing, he wrote that the 'space [ship] come from 2 years.' (Later he revised the 2 to 20.)
> 'Is this your fact?' I asked.
> 'Uh huh,' said Noah affirmatively. 'It's on *Space Cases*. . . . They're supposed to fight bad guys.'

Noah, the visual dramatist, hung on to his adapted written fact, as he earlier had to *I went* and *I saw*. Those words were not so much mediators of his efforts to recall facts as lifelines that secured him to the official world, whose purposes seemed to elude him. And yet, when Vanessa interrupted his efforts for an unofficial interlude, Noah adopted with ease the agency of a written practice:

	Vanessa hands Noah a note. He reads it:
Noah:	'I like Noah. Denise.'
Denise:	I did not write that! *(firmly)*
Vanessa:	*(to Denise)* Yes you did. *(to Noah)* She told me to give it to you.
Denise:	No I didn't.
Vanessa:	O:::. Don't believe her. She's just shy.
	Noah now writes his phone number for Denise and hands it to her. (Exchanging phone numbers is a common unofficial literacy practice, one not previously associated with gender play.)

Denise: Lucky I ain't no teenager. (In other words, Denise does not have to engage
in this now gendered practice; she is only 6. Denise throws Noah's phone
number away, which irritates him.)
Noah: De *nise*!

The dumped phone number ended the unofficial event. Noah's official event was
done now, too, and he left the rug. In fact, nearly all the children were done now,
and the rug became the site of a class lesson. Denise and Vanessa, still composing,
moved to a table. (So did I.)

Denise's official event

Although Vanessa, by now, had written two variants of space facts listed on the
facts chart, Denise had struck out to do 'something on my own.' That something
began with the appropriate official opening and two statements that were on topic
if slightly contradictory (see Figure 7):

Figure 7 Denise's text on 'What I Learned about Space'

The first two lines of text in the figure read: 'I learned that space is a good place to be. If I lovd [lived] in that place I would died [die].' 'You can't be using that word [died],' Vanessa told her, as though *die* were a bad word for sure. Denise then wrote an apology, orienting herself more centrally under unofficial stars, as the transcript excerpt reveals:

	Srey [Sorry] Ms Rita
Denise:	(*to Vanessa*) Better now?
	Being playful now with Vanessa, Denise recalls, not a taught fact, but their robot child, Precious – the child they first drew with those radio antennae:
Denise:	I'm gonna write, 'Oh Precious.' Precious, she got on my nerves . . . 'Oh Precious. You done it. You done it. Oh Precious you done it.' I would say it in a mean voice. 'OH PRECIOUS! YOU DONE IT! I'm GONNA (*unclear*) YOU! YOU DONE IT!'
Vanessa:	Write it in big ol' letters!
Denise:	(*does so and then reads*) 'OH PRECIOUS! YOU DONE IT!'
Rita:	Denise! Be quiet!
	Denise looks startled, mildly embarrassed, and then smiles and writes her last line:
	Sre [sorry] boys and girls (That is, 'Sorry I disturbed you.')

Denise's composing actions indexed her relationship as a dutiful student recalling 'what I learned,' an irritated (but playful) mother whose child had 'done it' now, and a polite human being, sorry for forgetting quite literally where she was.

Summary

Both Denise and Noah covered social and symbolic ground in these events. Noah's official written text, like his initial free composing ones, remained relatively distanced from, and juxtaposed to, his major symbolic efforts, which were mediated primarily by talk and drawing. Denise's written text was more centrally located as a mediator of her symbolic actions, but those actions were quite socially freewheeling. In interaction with Vanessa, she negotiated symbolic media, using a visual means to convey spoken meanness, but she slipped into and, then, out of that playful time and space, writing an apology to her real-time class. Conveying deliberately studied facts was not, for Noah nor Denise, a recurrent, routine way of using written language, that is, a practice that (at that point, in that event) guided and sustained their agency. In contrast, the children understood gender play and they collaborated, adapted, and improvised in conflicting but never incoherent ways.

In the following sections, I use intertextual linkages to briefly continue the trajectories of children's communicative practices. For both children, I point out textual threads to 'what I learned,' considering how the children assumed that informative voice. My own space limitations do not allow me to present the complexities of the children's travels. However, I can at least suggest that there is no straight, no singular developmental path, be it imagined as a textual evolution (requiring only exposure to modeling) or as an evolving apprenticeship (requiring only expert guidance). Rather, as I aim to explain, entering into particular school practices requires that children both draw upon and differentiate the symbolic, social, and ideological complexities of the very communicative frames that allow them entry in the first place.

Noah's textual journeys

During the winter and spring months, the converging and diverging trails of Noah's visually enacted dramatizing led first into written stories, as he rode the words of an easy-to-read book and kept his eye on a video adventure. That same practice of visually enacted dramatization was linked to his first self-initiated 'What I learned' piece (i.e. one in which he recalled and revoiced information about a school studied topic).

When these grand textual adventures began, Noah had already adopted a conversational stance in his personal texts, losing much of his syntactical awkwardness in that genre. 'Me and My Bother play wheth [with] my frey [favorite] Gamy [game],' he wrote, and that video game was, to use his spelling, 'DK*eK Cotree2' – *Donkey Kong Country 2*. Fictional composing however, became a strictly drawn and orally enacted affair until Noah met Little Bear (Minarik, 1957), a character in a series of books for beginning readers.

Little Bear is a sweet bear cub who lives in the woods. He progresses through his written narratives primarily through participating in dialogues comprised of short declarative sentences, often enacting a mild conflict. For example, in the excerpt below, Little Bear announces his desire to fly, which will figure in Noah's own story production:

> 'I'm going to fly to the moon,' said Little Bear.
> 'Fly!' said Mother Bear. 'You can't fly.'
> 'Birds fly,' said Little Bear.
> 'Oh yes,' said Mother Bear. 'Birds fly, but they don't fly to the moon. And you are not a bird.'
>
> (Minarik, 1957: 37–39)

In the last chapter in the cited book, Little Bear explicitly says, 'I wish that I could sit on a cloud and fly all around,' and his mother explicitly says 'You can't have that wish' (p. 52). Little Bear does receive one wish – a 'surprise' birthday cake (p. 35).

In contrast to Little Bear, Donkey Kong, a big uncouth gorilla, and his friends, the chimps Diddy and Dixie, do not talk. As Noah himself confirmed: 'They just play. They run and be happy.' Nonetheless, there are written graphics in the video experience: in game materials, the initials DX (plus a star) appear on a wooden sign (indicating Donkey Kong Country), and words containing Os typically sport a star inside those Os. During the game, the initials DK appear on barrels, which often hide one of the Donkey Kong characters; and each of the letter icons K, O, N, and G appear in floating boxes, which the monkeys try to jump up (perhaps, fly up) and bump.

Despite their semiotic differences, the Donkey Kong creatures and Little Bear are all furry animals drawn in iconic, rather than more realistic, styles, and all are embedded in a series of narratives, that is, in sequenced events situated in imagined worlds. Their similarities seemed to strike Noah, who interrupted his reading group's engagement with Little Bear to announce that 'I'm gonna get a little tiny baby gorilla. My mommy said Friday I would get one. I gotta get some bananas . . .'.

Although Donkey Kong and Little Bear seemed to come together in Noah's welcoming imagination, their symbolic and social incompatibility became evident in his composing efforts. Noah wrote a story that, orally and iconically was about Donkey Kong but, orthographically, was about Little Bear. Indeed, Noah did not draw a Donkey Kong story, nor a Little Bear story for that matter. Rather, his media-influenced dramatic practice, centered around visual symbols, seemed selectively encoded within (and sometimes surrounded by) textual structures appropriated from the official world, as illustrated by the event excerpts below.

Although he is sitting by Denise and Vanessa, Noah talks mainly to himself, planning, rereading, and monitoring his written efforts. (See Figure 8):

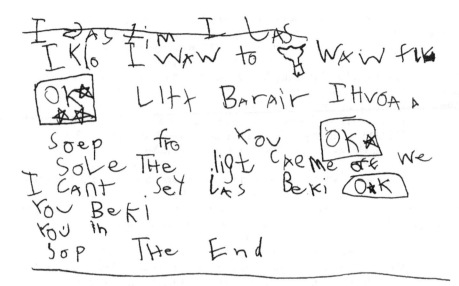

Figure 8 Noah's 'Donkey Kong' text

Noah: (*writing and rereading I Klo*). 'call, I call, I call' (*writing I waw to waw fly*) 'I, wish, wish'

Noah now pauses in his writing and draws a tiny flying monkey, commenting to no one in particular:

Noah: This is Donkey Kong.
Anne: Donkey Kong? (*I had expected Little Bear.*)
         Noah proceeds silently to write OK, accompanying those letters with stars and containing them in a box. He turns to me:
Noah: And that says, 'OK.' It's a Donkey Kong monkey ... The monkey says he wants to fly ... Donkey Kong Country, deep in the jungle. (*said in a deep voice*)

An attentive Noah has appropriated Little Bear's story and, particularly, his utterances for a Donkey Kong tale. However, Noah's next recontextualized utterance jars the attentive but confused me – and I jar Noah. Noah writes:

Litt Barair I HavoA (Little Bear I have)
A soep fro you (a surprise for you)

Anne: That's not about Donkey Kong is it?
Noah: (*working to explain his text to me and, seemingly, to himself too*) Oh,
            he he – bears live in some – no. They don't live in the jungle. It [the
            text] got both of them inside it. (*big breath*) Donkey Kong was in the
            video game. The monkey and the little monkey was in the video game.
            The little bear was playing with me and my brother ... [That is, all the
            animals were home with him.]

Noah continues writing, adding sentences about 'suddenly' the lights going off (apparently because of the impending 'surprise') and, then, someone saying, 'can't see.' Noah's intense concentration is interrupted by Denise, who has a story to tell:

Denise: Last night I spilled some Skitters [a food] on my homework. I was crying.
Noah: I was too! I was too!
Denise: I messed up my homework all up.
Noah: I was crying too because my mommy yelled at ME:: because I, DID IT,
            WRONG:: And my daddy came mad at me. And I said, 'O K::, Daddy,
            O K::, Daddy.' My Daddy is so crazy sometimes.

Noah returns to his writing. He continues the generic structure of a Little Bear story, but his evaluative tone is strikingly different. He includes another boxed and starred *OK*, but he does not silently write it, as before. This *OK* is not primarily iconic but orally expressive, like the *OK*s of his homework story.

Noah: 'Jus' be quiet, OK::?' (*writing Jas BeKi O*K*)
            When I ask who is talking, Noah says that the little girl monkey is telling
            the little boy monkey to 'Just be quiet, O K::?' (*with exasperated tone*).
            He then finishes his story:
Noah: 'YOU be quiet.' (*writing You Be Ki*)
            'You, YOU in, shut up!' (*writing you in sop*)

Noah had engaged in a story writing practice by recontextualizing material from diverse sources. That recontextualizing necessitated some negotiating among the conventions of different symbolic media, and it led as well to a highlighting of the social expectations of different worlds. When Noah read his story to the class, Rita, securely anchored in the official world, interpreted his piece as a Little Bear story. Noah's peers, however, responded to one strong index of the text's hybridity: that blunt 'Shut up,' which the gentle Little Bear would never say (although the uncouth Donkey Kong characters might and Noah, upset by his daddy, might want to too). Rita did not allow children to say 'Shut up.'

Noah's peers gasped and then giggled when he read that sentence to them. Rita herself did not attend to this laughing but commented, 'He didn't have any time for a picture because he was so busy writing a Little Bear story, right?' (apparently not noticing the tiny drawing). Noah said nothing, but he grinned at his peers' response and when Lakeisha asked him to 'read that end again,' he complied by rereading the whole story.

As the school year unfolded, Noah continued to grapple with the textual complexities and possibilities raised by reframing familiar cultural material in school contexts. For example, soon after the Donkey Kong/Little Bear event, Noah more conventionally blended the visual conventions and icons of animated media with print media. He ended 'a scary story', written in the dialogic style of a Little Bear text, with a written 'The End' around which were draped cartoon characters – a Looney Toon cartoon convention.

In another event, Noah used animation to enact a self-initiated 'I learned that' genre. This event occurred in the midst of a classroom study of silk worms. One day, as Noah sat at a table with a plastic container of such worms, he wrote that 'I learned that silk worms can't eat hard leaves like regular leaves because they will die,' a revoicing of Rita's caution that the worms would eat only mulberry leaves.

When Rita came by, Noah talked with her about the silk worms. 'They're scared in there,' Noah said. 'They do like this', and he lifted his head up and looked stiffly around. Implicit in his talk was a characterization of silk worms as fellow creatures whose emotions and intelligence are expressed through bodily features and movement (the qualities exploited in visual media, particularly animation). Later, after Rita left, Noah began an animated visual adventure at the bottom of his paper. He drew a silk worm on a large leaf. Then, to convey movement, he drew zigzagging lines, all the while making 'munching' noises. Finally, he added wings, commenting that the worm had turned into a moth.

This event was more coherent, more textually sensible than his earlier 'I learned that' event. He coordinated visual, print, and oral material to enact what he had learned, and, in so doing, he also coordinated narrative, or storytelling, and informative voices. Thus, Noah's path to the 'I learned that' practice was not a linear one constructed in stages, although it did evolve over time. That path was also not located within a singular school practice, although involvement in that adult guided and monitored practice mattered. However, Noah's path was constructed as he blended and differentiated practices and the cultural resources they entailed, not all of which originated in school. Noah, like all the children, was not just moving forward in the official school world; he was negotiating complex social worlds by adapting, stretching, and transforming his resources.

Denise's textual journeys

During the winter and spring months, Denise too continued her textual travels; like Noah's, her personal texts were becoming more conversational and, in her case, often contained words whose rhythm or drama seemed to appeal to her. My 'god dad is moving because he wants to see his whole generation,' she wrote [spelling corrected] – and she couldn't suppress a grin when she read that phrase 'whole generation' to her class. When her dad said he might take her to Water World, a local amusement park, she wrote that she said 'what you are keding [kidding],' dramatically performing her words for Wenona, her tablemate that day. (Rita could not understand Denise's text, until Denise performed it for her too: 'WHAT !!??!! You are *kid*ding!', thereby demonstrating the symbolic tensions between oral and the written still to be articulated and resolved.)

Denise also maintained her engagement in collaborative play with emotion-filled, often rhythmic voices. As readers may recall, Denise's capacity for composing extended, coherent pieces was first evident on the playground in her radio play. Indeed, she leaned on these old resources to construct pathways to new practices. However, even more so than Noah's visual adventures, the actual content of Denise's collaborative verbal play had difficulties traversing the borders of school spheres. (The collaborative composing strategies involved, however, traveled more easily; see Dyson, 2000.)

To suggest those difficulties, one day Denise and Vanessa collaboratively wrote a short R & B song by re-voicing popular lyrics. The resulting product, however, never saw the official stage, in part because, as Denise said, Rita probably wasn't 'used' to this style of song. 'Teen-age-er' songs were part of the children's unofficial play, glamorized futures – and adults' (including their parents') voiced concerns. A similar fate was dealt an extended 'cap' Denise wrote (in the African-American tradition, a humorous verbal put down [Smitherman, 1994]), in which the Disney movie character Pocahontas insulted her.

Denise had a sense of what words would fly in what social spheres. Indeed, she and Vanessa even played with the ideological tensions behind lyrical composition. After a lesson in which Rita emphasized the limits of money as a cause of love and happiness, Denise and Vanessa worked on a class assignment about their wishes for the future. Denise drew herself as a popular African-American performer, Tina Turner, singing 'What's Love Got to Do with It' (1983). Denise wrote those title words as though they were coming out of Tina Turner's head. She joked that she was going to make a ten thousand dollar bill coming out of her head too – which she did not do, although the complex links between stardom, popular song and wealth surfaced orally.

As Denise finishes her drawing, Vanessa reads her completed three wishes to Denise:

Vanessa: Listen. (*reading*) 'I wish that Denise will stay my friend. I wish the earth clean, and I wish my granny gets better.'

Denise now writes her own three wishes. 'I wish,' she says to herself as she begins.

Vanessa: (*starts singing*) Got no money/All I got is you baby/Don't need nothing else/ I got you baby . . .

Denise: (*has just reread 'I wish' and now says loudly*) I MADE A LOT OF MONEY!

Vanessa: (*singing*) Ain't got no money/Ain't got no thing but you now/ I got lo::ve . . .

Denise did not write that she wished she had money. She wished 'the earth was feld [filled] with love' and that Vanessa 'wold [would] still be Precious.' Both girls' actions reflected the social and ideological boundaries salient to them and, also, writing's potential to maintain or disrupt them.

Although appealing words and, indeed, wishes had to be monitored, Denise did find some available words in the official world that she used to construct pathways into new textual areas. The words did not come via a little bear but via a grand musician of words – the poet Eloise Greenfield.

Throughout the year, Rita's class orally performed poetry, especially that of Greenfield, an African-American poet who consistently renders child interests, including loving relationships and music, in literary voices. Moreover, Greenfield, like Denise's favorite radio station, features African–Americans and often renders her musical language in African-American Vernacular English, which the focal children generally spoke. From Greenfield's poems, Denise appropriated discourse features common to many kinds of musical or poetic texts (Tannen, 1989) – rhyme, repetitive phrases, and dramatic dialogue, the same features she appropriated from radio songs.

Denise initially lifted appealing images, phrases, and lines from these books, fitting them into varied spaces on her writing book pages. However, from the particularly appealing book *Honey I Love* (Greenfield, 1978), Denise and Vanessa both appropriated not only lines (e.g. 'Love don't mean all that nasty stuff,' 'I love a lot of things') but a whole textual form that occupied a page space – the 'I like' poem. Denise used Greenfield's repetitive structure and, optionally, her conversational rhythm and persistent rhyme, as evident in Denise's written love of peas – a food she really did not like at all (she was just playing):

I like apples/I like peas
I like bananas/On the trees
I like oranges/I like trees
And you all know/that I like peas
I'm not playing now/I like me.

In another 'I like' poem, this one about her family likes, Denise slipped out of her appreciative voice to comment on her dislikes – and to insult Vanessa for acting like she's 'all that' (something special). However, Denise not only acknowledged her slip textually and quickly stepped back into voice, but, at the end of the poem, she apologized (apparently to Rita, who explicitly disapproved of written insults):

I like to be helping my mom
I like to be with my brother
I do not like when Vanessa be
like she all that and
Mean to me and back to I like poem
I like going to Water World with My Dad
. . . [omitted lines]
You know I said about Vanessa I am so
so sorry [spelling corrected for ease of reading]

Denise's more deliberate moving in and out of voice, and in and out of social spheres of propriety, suggest her own clear sense of the bounded social and aesthetic sense of the 'I like' poem, relative, for example, to her earlier 'What I learned' piece.

Indeed, it was Denise's attraction to rhythmic voices that accounted for a coherent textual response to a 'What I learned' assignment. The assignment was part of the freedom and slavery unit, a regular one in local schools. In the course of this unit of study, Denise's teacher Rita included many informative texts and, also, fictional and poetic ones informed by the history of the pre-Civil War period in the US. For example, Rita played (and taught the children the words to) the folk singer Pete Seeger's version of 'Follow the Drinking Gourd' (which Denise and Vanessa interpreted as 'Follow the Drinking God,' who made the Milky Way and the North Star followed by escaping slaves). Rita also played albums by, shared a video about, and discussed the artistic skill of the African-American female a cappella ensemble Sweet Honey in the Rock:

'Do you want your freedom?' one of the group sings.
'Oh yeah,' echo the others, joined by the voices of Rita and the children.

Among book media, Rita chose to read (and Denise and Vanessa chose to reread) Faith Ringgold's *Aunt Harriet and the Underground Railroad* (1992), whose own text appropriates songs, and she also taught the class to recite Greenfield's (1978) poem about Harriet Tubman:

> Harriet Tubman . . .
> Didn't come in this world to be no slave
> And wasn't going to stay one either
> . . .
> She ran to the woods and she ran through the woods
> With the slave catchers right behind her
> And she kept on going til she got to the North
> Where those mean men couldn't find her
> Nineteen times she went back South
> To get the three hundred others
> She ran for her freedom nineteen times . . .

As a culminating activity, Rita asked the children, once again, to write a piece to show what they had learned. She said that they could write whatever kind of piece they wanted, but that they should include facts that they had learned. Children, who were African-American, Asian-American, and European-American, positioned themselves differently in the ongoing study, becoming sharers of facts, commentators on social evils, or story tellers. (Noah, unfortunately, was home with a serious bout of asthma.)

Denise herself began, like Vanessa, as a sharer of facts about Harriet Tubman, but, as she proceeded, the dramatic storyteller emerged. She revoiced utterances linked to many others, among them Ringgold, Greenfield, Seeger, and Sweet Honey in the Rock:

> Aunt Harriet wasnt a slave
> for Log. She was born a
> Slave. She ran back to
> sav 300 PePal. She said
> We Are going To be free.
> But I will follow The Drinking GorD North.
> We did it Said HarrieT
> yes yes yes yes yes yes
> But WhaT if he beats us?
> Cit [Can't.] We are SafE now.

The piece reflected Denise's alertness for dramatic voices, which had so characterized her movement in unofficial realms, but it was also a coherent piece that demonstrated knowledge of a study unit – that is, it mediated a semantically consistent conversation, even though its words had traveled through varied communicative chains before anchoring, temporarily, in Denise's event.

Like Noah, and all the focal children, Denise appropriated diverse cultural material, and she did so in ways that reflected understood forms of agency and familiar communicative practices. Inherent in this recontextualization of cultural resources were developmental challenges – challenges revealed when she, like Noah, crossed boundaries of symbol systems, social relations, and ideologies. Her challenge was not to master certain kinds of static textual structures (a 'story' a 'report') but to assume certain social voices. Although her behaviors – and her budding personality – differed from Noah, she too began by appropriating brief official text frames and then ventured out, trying on, combining, and even deliberately steering clear of appropriating certain kinds of textual voices in certain kinds of social scenes. One could never predict the particularities of her journeys but, along the way, they made sense, as I, the reframer of her efforts, followed the textual threads; those threads linked the actions of Denise as an aggressive singer who, nonetheless, was sorry for 'her words,' through a range of aggressive written deeds and sweet apologies, to the poetic sharing of Denise as a history student knowledgeable about a famed figure 'who didn't take no stuff' (Greenfield, 1978).

Toward childhoods and literacies

> I'd heard about that planet quilt often, but I'd never seen it. What I had pictured was a kind of fabric map – a plaid Canada, a gingham US. Instead the circle was made up of mismatched squares of cloth no bigger than postage stamps, joined by the uneven black stitches of a woman whose eyesight was failing . . .
>
> (Tyler, 1998: 261)

When I began this piece I amassed a collection of textual stuff – a patchwork of quotes, field notes, and bits of old papers I rather liked. And then, energized by the opportunity, disciplined by the due date, and guided by a sense of genre expectations and malleability, I began to cut, sculpt, and dump, trying to unravel the stitches of previous textual boundaries, to thread new connections, add new material, have another go.

What I was having a go at was young children's own textual stuff, accumulated on their life journeys and their efforts to compose something that would, perhaps, amuse, please, or just pass muster, given their understanding of their place amid the social constellations. In so doing, I have hoped to place childhoods themselves center stage in the study of literacy development. This repositioning has consequences for how development itself is described and, in my view, for how childhoods themselves are valued.

Through the textual exploits of Denise and Noah, I have hoped to illustrate the non-linearity of literacy development. The key to understanding this non-linearity lies not in close up views of the patchwork quilts themselves but in stepping back and examining the recontextualization processes through which they are constructed. Through these processes, children's 'budding personalities' – their identities and their histories – are potentially made manifest.

I imagine, with some trepidation, a hurried and harried reader, skimming this patchwork, trying to decide whether or not to bother with its words. What, my imagined reader asks, could cartoons have to do with science reports? How in the world could raps link to historical texts? But (I protest) these are not the appropriate questions. They assume, incorrectly, that written language learning is neatly bounded from learning other symbolic systems; the questions seem to assume too that child learners are dedicated apprentices, hovering exclusively around designated experts.

To understand literacy development, questions must include those focused on what children do within a communicative space (and, of course, on the nature of the provided spaces), on the forms of agency children exercise, and the materials they themselves deem relevant to the social action at hand. Such a focus revealed herein that, within the classroom Rita guided and, more particularly, within Noah's journeys, animated cartoon creatures did converge with and diverge from written and, indeed, real ones. And crafted raps, composed with an ear for the dramatic and an eye toward audience sense and sensibility, did inform Denise's gravitation toward, and use of, certain school texts. Both children were still beginning their textual travels, but they were beginning in symbolically, socially, and ideologically complex ways that eclipsed the sparse California classroom guidelines earlier shared. (For more theoretically informed discussions of classroom conditions, which stress the diverse ways that children may enter into school literacy activities, see Clay, 1998; Genishi *et al.*, 2001; McNaughton, 1999.)

The emphasis in this chapter on literacy learning as a process of text appropriation and recontextualization, rather than one of pure invention or diligent apprenticeship, recasts the usual developmental story. Rather than a kind of ancient Greek adventure, unfolding in a space removed from the local (Bakhtin, 1981), it becomes a (post)modern novel, actualized through children's play with, and organization of their everyday textual stuff. Unlike the cultural differences literature of twenty years ago (see for example Brice-Heath, 1983), it resists spinning some childhoods off into a separate 'diversity' orbit. Rather, it aims to problematize views of idealized childhoods that launch the young straight into the literate heavens, as well as views that assume oppositional relationships between kinds of media (e.g. print and audiovisual) and between kinds of genre (e.g. story and report).

The accentuation here on human adaptability and flexibility highlights both the variations in children's application of a range of literacy means, and the interplay of sociocultural and instructional factors that may shape those variations. It challenges the increasing economic, political, and cultural constraints on childhoods' spaces all around the world (Stephens, 1995). Children's potential to adapt cultural resources in response to changing conditions – to be playful – seems key, not only to furthering literacy development, but also to furthering sociocultural lives on a fragile, ever-changing planet.

References

Bakhtin, M. (1981) 'Discourse in the Novel', in C. Emerson and M. Holquist (eds) *The Dialogic Imagination: Four Essays by M. Bakhtin*, pp. 259–422. Austin: University of Texas Press.

Bakhtin, M. (1986) *Speech Genres and Other Late Essays*. Austin: University of Texas Press.

Bauman, R. and Briggs, C.C. (1990) 'Poetics and Performance as Critical Perspectives on Language and Social Life', *Anthropological Review* 19: 59–88.

Berry, W. (2000) *Life Is a Miracle: An Essay against Modern Superstition*. Washington, DC: Counterpoint.

Bourdieu, P. (1977) *Outline of a Theory of Practice*. Cambridge: Cambridge University Press.

California Department of Education (1998) *Reading/Language Arts Framework for California Public Schools*. Sacramento: California Department of Education Press.

Clay, M. (1998) *By Different Paths to Common Outcomes*. York, ME: Stenhouse.

Coolio (1995) 'Gangsta's Paradise', *Gangsta's Paradise* [CD]. New York, NY: Tommy Box Music Inc.

D'Amato, J.D. (1987) 'The Belly of the Beast: On Cultural Difference, Castelike Status, and the Politics of School', *Anthropology and Education Quarterly* 18: 357–60.

Day, B. (1958) *Rock-in Robin* [record].

Donkey Kong Country 2 (1986) video game, by Stamper. Redmond, WA: Nintendo.

Dyson, A. Haas (1993) *Social Worlds of Children Learning to Write in an Urban Primary School*. New York: Teachers College Press.

Dyson, A. Haas (1995) 'Writing Children: Reinventing the Development of Childhood Literacy', *Written Communication* 12: 3–46.

Dyson, A. Haas (1997) *Writing Superheroes: Contemporary Childhood, Popular Culture, and Classroom Literacy*. New York: Teachers College Press.

Dyson, A. Haas (1999a) 'Coach Bombay's Kids Learn to Write: Children's Appropriation of Media Material for School Literacy', *Research in the Teaching of English* 33: 367–402.

Dyson, A. Haas (1999b) 'Transforming Transfer: Unruly Children, Contrary Texts, and the Persistence of the Pedagogical Order', in A. Iran-Nejad and P. D. Pearson (eds) *Review of Research in Education: Vol. 24*. Washington, DC: American Educational Research Association.

Dyson, A. Haas (2000) 'On Reframing Children's Words: The Perils, Promises, and Pleasures of Writing Children', *Research in the Teaching of English* 34: 352–367.

Dyson, A. Haas (2001a) 'The Stolen Lipstick of Overheard Song: Composing Voices in Child Song, Verse, and Written Text', in M. Nystrand and J. Duffy (eds) *The Rhetoric of Everyday Life*. Madison: University of Wisconsin Press.

Dyson, A. Haas (2001b) 'Writing and Children's Symbolic Repertories: Development Unhinged', in S. Neuman and D. Dickinson (eds) *Handbook on Research in Early Literacy for the 21st Century*. New York: Guilford Publications.

Dyson, A. Haas (2001c) 'Donkey Kong in Little Bear Country: Examining Composing Development in the Media Spotlight', *Elementary School Journal* 10: 417–433.

Genishi, C., Stires, S. and D. Yung-Chan (2001) 'Writing in an Integrated Curriculum: Pre-kindergarten English Language Learners as Symbol-makers', *Elementary School Journal* 10: 417–433.

Goffman, E. (1961) *Asylums: Essays on the Social Situation of Mental Patients and Other Onmates*. Garden City, NY: Anchor Books.

Goldman, L.R. (1998) *Child's Play: Myth, Mimesis, and Make-believe*. London: Routledge.

Greenfield, E. (1978) *Honey I Love*. New York: Harper & Row.

Hanks, W.F. (1996) *Language and Communicative Practices*. Boulder, CO: Westview Press.

Hanks, W. (2000) *Intertexts: Writings on Language, Utterance, and Context*. Lanham, MD: Rowan & Littlefield.

Heath, S.B. (1983) *Ways with Words: Language, Life and Work in Communities and Classrooms*. Cambridge: Cambridge University Press.

Jackson, M. (1972) *Rockin' Robin* [record]. New York: Motown Record Company.

Jenkins, H. (1992) *Textual Poachers: Television Fans and Participatory Culture*. New York: Routledge.

Jones, B. and Hawes, B.L. (1972) *Step It Down: Games, Plays, Songs, and Stories from the Afro-American Heritage*. New York: Harper & Row.

Jurassic Park (1993) film, directed by Stephen Spielberg. USA: Universal Pictures.

McDowell, J. (1995) 'The Transmission of Children's Folklore', in B. Sutton-Smith, J. Mechling, T.W. Johnson and F.R. McMahon (eds) *Children's Folklore: A Source Book*, pp. 293–308. New York: Garland.

McNaughton, S. (1999) 'Developmental Diversity and Beginning Literacy Instruction at School', in J.S. Gaffney and B.J. Askew (eds) *Stirring the Waters: The Influence of Marie Clay*, pp. 3–16. Portsmouth, NH: Heinemann.

Marsh, J. (1999) 'Batman and Batwoman Go to School: Popular Culture in the Literacy Curriculum', *International Journal of Early Years Education* 7: 117–31.

Marshall, E. (1980) *Space Case*. New York: Dial Books.

Miller, P. and Goodnow, J.J. (1995) 'Cultural Practices: Toward an Integration of Culture and Development', in J.J. Goodnow, P.J. Miller and F. Kessel (eds) *Cultural Practices as Contexts for Development, No. 67: New Directions in Child Development*, pp. 5–16. San Francisco: Jossey Bass.

Minarik, E.H. (1957) *Little Bear, An I Can Read Book*. New York: HarperCollins.

Moll, L., Saez, R. and Dworin, J. (2002) 'Exploring Biliteracy', *Elementary School Journal*.

Nelson, K. (1996) *Language in Cognitive Development: The Emergence of the Mediated Mind*. Cambridge: Cambridge University Press.

Newkirk, T. (2002) 'The Revolt against Realism: The Attraction of Fiction for Young Writers', *Elementary School Journal*.

Opie, I. and Opie, P. (1959) *The Lore and Language of School Children*. London: Oxford University Press.

Pocahontas (1995) film, directed by Mike Gabriel and Eric Goldberg. USA: Walt Disney Pictures.

Ringgold, F. (1992) *Aunt Harriet's Underground Railroad in the Sky*. New York: Crown.

Rockwell, F. (1999) 'Recovering History in the Study of Schooling: From the *longue durée* to Everyday Co-construction', *Human Development* 42: 113–28.

Smitherman, G. (1994) *Black Talk: Words and Phrases from the Hood to the Amen Corner.* Boston, MA: Houghton Mifflin.

Snow, C. Burns, S. and Griffin, P. (eds) (1998) *Preventing Reading Difficulties in Young Children.* Washington, DC: National Academy Press.

Sobel, D. (1999) *Galileo's Daughter: A Historical Memoir of Science, Faith, and Love.* New York: Walker & Co.

Stephens, S. (ed.) (1995) *Children and the Politics of Culture.* Princeton, NJ: Princeton University Press.

Sutton-Smith, B. (1997) *The Ambiguity of Play.* Cambridge, MA: Harvard University Press.

Tannen, D. (1989) *Talking Voices: Repetition, Dialogue, and Imagery in Conversational Discourse.* Cambridge: Cambridge University Press.

Turner, T. (1983) What's Love Got to Do with It', *Private Dancer* [CD]. Hollywood, CA: Capitol Records.

Tyler, A. (1998) *Patchwork Planet.* New York: Random House.

Vygotsky L.S. (1978) *Mind in Society.* Cambridge, MA: Harvard University Press.

Vygotsky L.S. (1987) *L.S. Vygotsky, Collected Works: Volume 1, Problems of General Psychology.* New York: Plenum Books.

Whiting, B.B. and Whiting, J.W.M. (1975) *Children of Six Cultures: A Psycho-cultural Analysis.* Cambridge, MA: Harvard University Press.

Willis, P. (1990) *Common Culture: Symbolic Work at Play in the Everyday Culture of the Young.* Boulder, CO: Westview Press.

Wolfe, T. (1979) *The Right Stuff.* New York: Farrar, Straus, & Giroux.

CHAPTER 6

LEARNING AS PUZZLE SOLVING

Peter Geekie, Brian Cambourne and Phil Fitzsimmons

Understanding Literacy Development, Stoke-on-Trent: Trentham Books, 1999, pp. 1–26

Introduction

> [human learning] presupposes a specific social nature and a process by which children grow into the intellectual life of those around them.
>
> (Vygotsky, 1978: 88)

Children learn to see the world through the eyes provided by their culture and learn culturally specific ways of communicating, thinking and solving problems through sharing their consciousness with others. Vygotskian theory proposes that learning precedes and promotes mental development. Instruction should therefore identify those tasks which children cannot manage alone but can complete with assistance.

However, no theory is ever complete and Vygotsky's explanations of learning and development have been elaborated and developed in a number of significant research studies in the last twenty years. Accounts of learning have been built on a Vygotskian foundation by such researchers as Jerome Bruner, David Wood and Barbara Rogoff. These people are participants in what has been called 'a quiet revolution' in developmental psychology, a revolution which involves the recognition of children as social beings who, through social interaction, 'acquire a framework for interpreting experience, and learn how to negotiate meaning in a manner congruent with the requirements of the culture' (Bruner and Haste, 1987: 1). As a way of discussing some of the insights into the nature of learning offered by these and other researchers, we turn to an example taken from informal observations of adults and children interacting in natural settings.

> Liam is the grandson of one of the authors. During visits to his daughter's home Peter was struck by how closely the exchange between his daughter and her child paralleled the behaviour of mothers in formal research studies. It will be used for that very reason: because it demonstrates that the best theoretical accounts of learning and instruction are those which can be validated by reference to what real people do in natural contexts.
>
> One present Liam received on his third birthday was a jigsaw puzzle of a fire engine. One fireman was at the steering wheel talking on a telephone. Another was uncoiling a large hose. Others were climbing out of the cabin onto the street.

When Jacqui, his mother, first sat down with him to do the puzzle she tried to use the picture on the puzzle box as a guide but this proved to be of no use. Liam clearly did not understand the nature of the task. He was unable to connect the picture with the puzzle. So she decided to try to do a section at a time.

The ladder on top of the fire engine was a prominent feature of the puzzle, occupying about a quarter of its total area, so she started there. As she handled the pieces she talked about them.

'Let's find all the ladder pieces. Is this a bit with the ladder on it? All right, let's find another one. What about this one? It's got ladder on it. And that looks like a fireman's hat. See? Let's see if they go together. Here. Help me put them together. I'll hold this piece while you push the other one. That's right.'

She did most of the work, getting Liam to 'help' find pieces of the puzzle and put them together. She worked down the puzzle following the same routine with each section of it. The pieces with parts of the hose on them. The pieces with the number plate. The pieces with parts of the wheels. She talked about them, saying what they were, pointing to the identifying features of each piece, showing how the features of one piece matched with features of its neighbouring pieces, and coercing Liam's assistance in putting them into place.

When the puzzle was finished Jacqui discussed the picture with Liam, looking at the picture as a whole rather than as an assemblage of parts.

'Look Liam, that man is driving isn't he? And he's talking on the telephone too. Can you see him? And can you see the men walking down the steps? Show me where they are.'

And so on.

They did the puzzle again. And again the next day. Soon Liam became a more active partner in the activity. It wasn't long before he was doing most of the puzzle himself while his mother watched, guiding him with clues and cues when he seemed unable to go on by himself.

'You need a piece with the hose on it. Can you see one? Is that it? Does it fit? Well, see if you can find another one with the hose on it.'

And Liam started to ask questions.

'Mummy, does this piece go here?'

In a surprisingly short time he was able to do it himself with almost no assistance. And he talked to himself as he did it. At first he used the cues provided by his mother.

'There's another piece of ladder. Does this go here?'

He joined the piece of puzzle successfully to a neighbouring piece.

'Here's the man with the telephone.'

He put this piece into position and looked at his mother.

'Is that right?' he asked. Jacqui nodded.

Next he began to generate his own cues. Where Jacqui had emphasised one feature of a particular piece, Liam now focused on another. The pressure gauge instead of the hose. The fireman's boot instead of the wheel. And he used his own terms.

'This is the clock,' he said picking up the piece with most of the gauge on it. 'And here's another bit of clock.' He joined them.

He picked up a piece of the number-plate. 'Here's the writing. And here's some more writing.' He joined the two pieces together.

After a few more days he could complete the puzzle on his own. Mostly he worked in silence, finding pieces and putting them together in a systematic way. He didn't always work from the top down any more. He was capable of starting anywhere. He sometimes constructed the outline first, leaving a gap in the middle and completing that part last. But the talk hadn't disappeared completely. Sometimes it surfaced again, especially when he needed confirmation that what he had done was correct.

'That's the piece I was looking for,' he said on one such occasion, and he tried to put it in the puzzle. Obviously uncertain about the accuracy of what he had done, he turned to his mother. 'Is that right? Does that piece go right here?' he said, pointing at it. And Jacqui nodded in reply.

Sometimes his mother intervened if he seemed to have completely lost his way. For example, Liam would sometimes look blankly at the piece in his hand, not trying to do anything with it.

'Can you see the writing on that piece?' his mother would say. He would look at her and then back at the piece in his hand. 'Now, where's the writing on the picture?'

Liam would try the piece against a part of the number-plate already completed on the puzzle.

'That's right,' his mother would say, and he would put it into place.

How does this incident illustrate our theoretical position on learning? We have organised our answer to this question under a series of headings to highlight key aspects of the learning process.

Principle one: learning is often a mutual accomplishment

It is important to recognise in the interactions between Liam and Jacqui the complementary nature of teaching and learning. Jacqui did her best to simplify and structure the activity of jigsaw puzzle construction for her son. At the same time Liam cooperated with his mother in an activity which he did not understand at first. He participated at his own level of understanding and his behaviour determined what Jacqui did. Barbara Rogoff (1989) explains this relationship between learning and instruction well when she writes that

> Adults do not simply solve problems and report their solutions, nor do children passively observe adults and extract the relevant information spontaneously. An adult assesses a child's current understanding of the material and adjusts the scaffolding to support the child's developing skill, while the child simultaneously adjusts the pace of instruction and guides the adult in constructing the scaffold.
> (Rogoff, 1989: 69)

Rogoff's observation that children actively (although usually unconsciously) shape adult's contributions to any instructional session is a crucial insight into the nature of learning. Learning is collaborative, not adult-driven.

Principle two: children often learn through guided participation

Liam had assembled puzzles before, but they had been the type that required him to place shapes in matching spaces in a board. The construction of a full picture from a set of interlocking pieces was something new. And although he had almost no idea about how to proceed, he watched and listened and took part when his mother invited him to 'help' put together pieces of the puzzle. This is a clear instance of what Barbara Rogoff has called 'guided participation'. Liam learnt the purpose of the activity, as well as the manipulative skills required, by participating. At first his participation was minimal and his involvement required a great deal of guidance and support, but gradually, as his competence grew, his mother allowed him to take more and more responsibility for completion of the task.

In other words, Liam's learning depended on his being involved in the activity, from the beginning, at his current level of competence. The truly significant thing is that although his initial involvement was slight, his competence grew as his mother encouraged and allowed his involvement.

Principle three: children profit from the support of more competent people

What is involved in these interactions between mother and child is what David Wood (1988a) refers to as the development of expertise. The expert is someone whose existing knowledge base in a specific area is both large and well organised. Expertise, Wood says

> structures the process of perception and memorisation. This makes thinking and acting fast, smooth, accurate and sensitive to error, novelty and unusual events.
> (Wood, 1988a: 76)

The recognition of novelty, and the ability to cope with it, is especially significant in understanding the differences between the mental functioning of adults and children. We might all find novel situations overwhelming but, as Wood points out, children are 'novices of life in general'. Like adults, children are limited in the amount of information they can deal with at one time. But they are further restricted by their limited experience of life. They are less likely to recognise a new problem as being like a similar one encountered previously. Their limited knowledge base makes it less likely that they will perceive structure and organisation in new situations. They will experience high levels of uncertainty more often than adults because they know so much less about the world. So it becomes necessary for children to enlist the assistance of someone more experienced, someone more expert. That person is often an adult who simplifies and structures the experience for them, breaking the task into more manageable sub-tasks and helping them to attend and remember; to organise and plan their activity. By so doing adults help children to overcome their limitations and make it possible for them to complete tasks which they could not manage independently.

This is what Jacqui is doing during Liam's encounter with the puzzle. She is constantly prompting Liam to attend to certain things, indeed to specific features of certain things, and she keeps reminding him of what they have done on previous occasions to complete the puzzle. She also decides how the task is to be attacked; how it is to be broken into sub-tasks that she thinks Liam will be able to manage. She is, in effect, allowing him to use her capacity to attend, her memory and her ability to choose appropriate strategies to complete the task. She is, to use a phrase from Bruner (1986), acting as 'consciousness for two'.

It is here that cognitive psychology connects with Vygotsky's work. Children who can, with assistance, complete tasks that they could not manage alone are working in what Vygotsky called a 'zone of proximal development'. The adult is helping to further develop 'ripening' functions; that is, those abilities that the child possesses but only employs when prompted to do so by a more competent other. Within this theoretical framework, adult intervention is instrumental not just in overcoming the child's immediate information overload, but in actually promoting development and shaping its direction.

There was also something far more fundamental involved in Liam's growth of expertise as a puzzle solver. As Wood (1988b) has pointed out, in order to become expert in a particular activity children have to learn what their intentions in that activity are *supposed* to be. Once Liam understood the purpose of jigsaw puzzle construction and how he could participate appropriately in the activity, he was able to engage in purposeful, independent problem solving behaviour. This is a basic feature of learning that is central to our discussion of young children engaged in learning to write.

Principle four: effective instruction is contingent instruction

The involvement of adults who simplify and structure learning for the child does not imply direct instruction or adult control of learning. As Wood said, effective instruction involves 'leading by following'. It is essentially responsive rather than directive.

Wood's investigations of the nature of effective instruction focused on mothers instructing their four year old children in the construction of a wooden pyramid made up of several interlocking pieces. After the tutorial session the children were tested to see if they could build the pyramid independently. It was discovered that those who had learnt best were those whose mothers behaved 'contingently', in accordance with two 'rules'. The first rule specifies that failure on the part of a child to complete a sub-section of the task should cause the mother to increase her level of control. For example, if a child failed to respond to an instruction to find the big blocks, a mother following this rule would intervene more directly, perhaps by pointing to the blocks that were needed. If this brought no response, the mother might then arrange the big blocks so that the child had only to push them together to complete that section of the model. If the child still failed to respond, the mother could take her level of intervention to the final stage by actually assembling them while the child watched. In other words, the mother behaved contingently in this situation by progressively increasing her control over the act of pyramid construction.

The second rule specifies that instruction following success in completing part of the task will result in a mother providing less help or exercising less control than before. So if a mother suggests that the four big blocks should be found and the child responds by picking them up and trying to join them, the mother would withdraw and allow the child to try to complete the action independently. The mother in this situation is again behaving contingently, but now by decreasing her level of control over the construction of the model. The rules describe an inverse relationship. As the child's competence in model construction increases, the mother's level of control over the construction decreases.

One would argue that the superior pyramid builders' learning was more effective not because of the mother's teaching style but because they were just better at solving problems. To check this possibility Wood and his colleagues repeated the research study, this time matching mothers with children other than their own. Once again it was the tutor's contingency of response which seemed to be the critical factor. Children instructed by adults who behaved contingently were better at constructing the model independently.

Jacqui's tutorial behaviour, like that of the most successful mothers in Wood's research, was characterised by contingency of response. She took as much control as was necessary to keep the puzzle construction moving forward at an acceptable rate. At first Liam watched and took little part in the activity. But it was not long before he tried to do parts of it for himself. And as soon as he showed an interest in trying to take over any part of the activity, Jacqui immediately withdrew and allowed him to do so. In Bruner's (1983) observations of two mothers and their infant boys, he commented that the changes in interaction between the mothers and their children over an eighteen month period might well be summed up by: 'where there was once an observer, let there now be a participant'. This sums up Jacqui's interactions with Liam equally well. It looks as if this process of 'handover' is a fundamental aspect of learning. And it is significant that Edwards and Mercer (1987), in their study of groups of ten year olds involved in discussions with their teachers at school, also observed a transfer of control of learning from the adult to the children. It seems that it is a constant in learning across age groups.

Principle five: it is not interaction itself but the quality of the interaction that contributes to better learning

The research cited above suggests that interaction in itself is not enough to promote successful learning. Recent research studies have investigated aspects of the relationship between social processes and learning and these provide a more detailed picture of the nature of effective tutorial interaction. For example, Barbara Rogoff and her colleagues have examined the effect of collaborative planning on learning. She concludes that children 'appear to benefit from participation in problem solving with the guidance of partners who are skilled in accomplishing the task at hand' (Rogoff, 1990: 169). The more expert other must possess expertise which can be passed on to the novice. But social interaction, even with an expert guide, is not enough. The quality of the interaction is of crucial importance in determining the effectiveness of the learning which takes place.

In one study (Radziszewska and Rogoff, 1988) adult-child and child-child pairs were given a shopping list and a map of an imaginary downtown area with stores at which the items on the list could be purchased, and were asked to plan efficient shopping routes. Participants were later asked to complete a similar exercise independently, to establish whether they had mastered the task. In general, collaboration in adult-child pairs led to better performance on the test tasks than the collaboration in child-child pairs. But they also found that children who performed well among the adult-child groups had engaged in 'shared and guided decision making' during the first part of the study. By contrast, those who performed poorly when asked to complete the task independently had been matched with adults who used inefficient planning strategies and dominated the interaction. These partners did not talk about the strategies which might be used or involve the children in making decisions about what should be done. This was not true of Jacqui's conversations with her son. As soon as Liam had a broad understanding of the nature of the activity she began to ask him to share decisions with her (Is this the right piece? Does this one go here? etc.).

It appears, then, that children are most likely to learn effectively guided by an adult who is expert in the task being attempted, who involves them in shared decision making and discusses those decisions with them.

Principle six: language is the means through which self-regulation of learning behaviour develops

Possibly the most significant aspect of the exchanges between Liam and Jacqui is the role language played in them. Jacqui talked constantly as she modelled jigsaw puzzle construction. She talked about what she was doing and why she was doing it. She described the pieces of puzzle in terms of the distinguishing features of each piece and how those features related to other pieces. And then when the puzzle was complete, she talked about the completed puzzle, directing Liam's attention to its elements, making him aware of it as a picture.

According to the study by Radziszewska and Rogoff, another feature of the collaboration between adults and children that seemed to contribute to effective learning was that the adults often engaged in 'strategic thinking aloud'. They not only used efficient strategies but also talked aloud about what they were doing. This is exactly what Jacqui did and Liam's rapid learning seems to testify to the effectiveness of her approach.

The role of language in learning goes beyond this, however. When Liam was able to take an active part in constructing the puzzle, and even when he could complete it independently, language remained an integral part of the activity. First he used his mother's talk as a model to guide him in his completion of the task. As Vygotsky (1978: 28) has said, the talk shaped the activity into a structure just as a mould gives shape to a substance. The conversations with his mother continued to guide him. He used her words and phrases to focus his attention on the features of the puzzle which were relevant at each point in its completion and to cue his memory of what was to be done and in what order. Liam had learnt to use the dialogue with his mother to regulate his own behaviour.

It did not stop there. He then began to generate his own words and phrases, exercising conscious control over what he was doing, and even sometimes providing a metacommentary on his actions (e.g. 'That's not the piece I'm looking for. This is.'). And even when he had mastered the puzzle, working quickly and quietly on his own, language still surfaced at times. But the direction clearly seems to have been from the control of his behaviour by his mother, to overt self-direction and finally to internalised self-direction. We cannot be absolutely sure that covert language did exercise control over his behaviour as he worked quietly on the puzzle, but the general direction of his use of language as he learnt the puzzle certainly seems to suggest that this is what happened.

Principle seven: learning depends upon the negotiation of meaning

Imagine a child being asked to describe one of a series of six drawings of a man so that a listener could identify it. Each man holds either a small balloon or a large balloon which is either red, green or blue. Each drawing can be identified by a statement discriminating it from all other possible choices (e.g. 'Point to the man holding the small red balloon'). It has been found that children under seven are likely to provide ambiguous messages for a listener (e.g. The man has a green balloon). Similar results have been found when children are asked to listen to messages instead of giving them. Children under seven are likely to react to an ambiguous message like 'Show me the man with the green balloon' by choosing one of the two possible choices instead of seeking clarification by asking a question ('a big balloon or a small one?'). These studies reveal aspects of the difficulties young children are thought to have with referential communication; that is, the ability to produce clear spoken messages and to recognise when heard messages are not clear (Robinson, Goelman and Olson, 1983; Robinson and Robinson, 1985; Robinson and Whittaker, 1986; Robinson and Whittaker, 1987).

Peter Lloyd has brought a sociolinguistic perspective to the study of referential communication (1991, 1992, 1993). To understand referential communication, he says, the reciprocal nature of conversation must be considered. Success or failure in communication is seen from this perspective to depend on the negotiation of understanding through conversation, especially the asking of questions designed to bring responses which will clarify, confirm or elaborate on information previously received. Lloyd found that while younger children were much more likely to produce inadequate messages, they were also much less likely to respond to an inadequate message with a request for further information. In other words they are much less likely to engage in a negotiation of meaning with their conversational partner.

Lloyd (1990) also speculates about why young children apparently find it difficult to detect and deal with ambiguity. In everyday life, he says, adults respond to children's feedback, providing support for them when they seem puzzled or uncertain. The familiar adult is not just a resource from whom young children can obtain needed information, 'but also an extension of the child's cognitive and communicative system – a communicative support system' (1990: 64–69). Lloyd argues that in normal situations adults make dialogue with young children possible by performing a number of communicative functions. These functions include focusing the child's attention on what is relevant; simplifying and interpreting information for the child; holding information in working memory for the child's use; reminding the child of what is known and what the goal of the dialogue is; alerting the child to communicative success and failure; and shifting the child to an alternative procedure when the present one is failing. He suggests that when this 'communicative support system' fails to function in the usual way, children start to behave in an aberrant manner. They might, for example, stop asking questions and agree with whatever the adult suggests, as they often do in the experimental situation. It is not, therefore, the behaviour of children which is strange in such situations but the behaviour of adults.

Jacqui provides Liam with communicative support. As a result, although he is only three, he does ask clarifying questions of his mother. He asks, 'Does this piece go here?' and 'Is that right?', looking at his mother for confirmation. He is capable of jointly constructing meaning with his mother in the pursuit of a mutual goal. His mother responds to the clues he gives (which are often non-verbal) indicating uncertainty and confusion, and she guides him and 'fills in' for him to ensure that their interaction can continue. This certainly supports the claim that, in natural situations, children are capable of quite sophisticated negotiation of meaning through language at an early stage of their development, albeit with people with whom they share a common background of experience and close emotional ties and whose primary aim, when they talk with their children, is to sustain the dialogue by whatever means.

Competence in referential communication would seem to be essential to children if they are to learn with, and from, other people. At school, children need to be able to determine the teacher's referential intent in order to learn. Yet, as we have said above, the research evidence suggests that young children have difficulty in recognising when they do not understand and in seeking information to clear up confusions in communication. The fact that Liam seemed able to seek confirmation through questioning at a much earlier age than research findings indicate, suggests that children might go to school far better able to negotiate meanings than has previously been thought. Perhaps teachers should give more attention to creating circumstances which make it easier for children to ask questions and resolve misunderstandings. Certainly the excellent teachers we have worked with, do this without conscious effort. They get to know their children very well, they build a background of shared experience which forms a basis for talk, and they allow children to use the linguistic competence they bring to school with them (including their know-ledge of how to use language to get things done). In their classrooms the negotiation of meanings is visible to those who trouble to look, and learning proceeds smoothly because the focus is on the construction of meaning and the maintenance of communication.

Conclusions

We have gone to some lengths to make our assumptions and beliefs about learning clear. We have positioned ourselves with those who believe that learning is social and collaborative in nature. This is not to say that children learn only through social interaction. But it does mean that learning can only be adequately understood if its social nature is taken into account. Learning is social both in what is learnt (for example, writing is a valued social achievement) and in the learning process (that is, the dialogue which facilitates learning and eventually becomes the basis for thought itself). This position is basically Vygotskian and Barbara Rogoff sums it up when she says that

> individual development of higher mental processes cannot be understood without considering the social roots of both the tools for thinking that children are learning to use and the social interactions that guide children in their use.
>
> (Rogoff, 1990: 35)

The most casual observations reveal that when children have trouble in learning something, they naturally turn to more competent others to help them through their difficulties. And our prolonged observations of children learning to read and write have convinced us that they very often achieve far more with assistance than they could have managed alone. This raises a crucial question: how important is adult intervention in children's learning? It should be clear from what we have said that social interaction facilitates understanding and promotes development, and it helps children to relate what they have learnt independently to what is known, by people generally. But is teaching a prerequisite for learning? And if this is not the case, then what exactly is the role of instruction in learning?

In any discussion about the nature of the relationship between instruction and learning we need to recognise that learning is primary. Different sets of assumptions about learning will necessarily produce different approaches to instruction. Rogoff, Matusov and White (1996) identify three models of instruction based on specific positions on learning. First is the 'adult-run' model which corresponds with 'theoretical notions that learning is a process managed by experts who transmit knowledge to learners'. Second is the 'children-run' model of instruction which corresponds with 'theoretical notions that learning is the province of learners who acquire knowledge through their active exploration'. The third is a 'community of learners' model which corresponds with 'the theoretical stance that learning involves transformation of participation in collaborative endeavour'. The models differ essentially in where the responsibility for promoting learning is placed. The first two positions are one-sided. In adult-run instruction, the teacher manages the learning activities and is seen to be centrally responsible for promoting learning in the child. In children-run instruction, children choose their own activities while the adult's main responsibility is to provide an enriched and stimulating learning environment. By contrast the community of learners model involves mutuality of responsibility despite 'some asymmetries in roles and responsibilities'.

Debates about competing approaches to literacy instruction are really concerned with the different views of learning upon which the approaches are based. Our own position on learning implies an approach to instruction much like that which is embodied in a 'community of learners' model. In a classroom operating in accordance with this model, responsibility for learning is shared. Adults and children will be collaboratively engaged in learning activities, with the adults often guiding and supporting the children's learning. Amongst other things, the children learn to participate in the management of their own learning. Everyone works together, with everyone being a resource for everyone else (Rogoff, Matusov and White, 1996). [. . .]

The type of instructional model which functions in any classroom, inevitably tells the children what types of learners the teacher considers them to be. This means that the teacher who . . . involves the children in collaborative thinking and hands control to them as they are able to accept it, tells the children that they are capable of incidental learning and independent problem solving.

We are claiming that learning which is social and collaborative will not only lead to more efficient learning but will also produce better learners. We have cited a number of psychological studies in support of this position but it is our experience in classrooms over many years which has really been the primary influence on what we believe. . . . We are not psychologists, nor are we sociolinguists or anthropologists. We are educators. We began our working lives as teachers of primary age children and as we became researchers, the questions we asked and the answers we formed were still related to our personal experience of teaching children to read and write. [. . .]

We believe learning involves collaborative puzzle solving and a transformation of participation, with the adults passing control to the children as they seem ready to accept it. Such adults will be supporting and guiding the children's thinking rather than prompting and organising it.

References

Bruner, J. (1983) *Child's Talk: Learning to Use Language*. Oxford: Oxford University Press.

Bruner, J. (1986) *Actual Minds, Possible Worlds*. Cambridge, Mass.: Harvard University Press.

Bruner, J. and Haste, H. (eds) (1987) *Making Sense: The Child's Construction of the World*. London: Methuen.

Edwards, D. and Mercer, N. (1987) *Common Knowledge: The Development of Common Knowledge in the Classroom*. London: Methuen.

Lloyd, P. (1990) Children's communication. In Grieve, R. and Hughes, M. (eds.) *Understanding Children*. Oxford: Blackwell.

Lloyd, P. (1991) Strategies used to convey route directions by telephone: a comparison of the performance of 7-year-olds and adults. *Journal of Child Language*, 18, 171–189.

Lloyd, P. (1992) New directions in referential communication research. *British Journal of Developmental Psychology*, 10, 385–403.

Lloyd, P. (1993) Referential communication as teaching: adults tutoring their own and other children. *First Language*, 13, 339–357.

Radziszewska, B. and Rogoff, B. (1988) Influence of adult and peer collaborators on children's planning skills. *Developmental Psychology*, 24, 840–848.

Robinson, E., Goelman, H. and Olson, D. (1983) Children's understanding of the relation between expressions (what was said) and intentions (what was meant). *British Journal of Developmental Psychology*, 1, 75–86.

Robinson, E. and Robinson, W. (1985) Teaching children about verbal referential communication. *International Journal of Behavioural Development*, 8, 285–299.

Rogoff, B. (1989) The joint socialization of development by young children and adults. In Gellatly, A., Rogers, D. and Sloboda, J. *Cognition and Social Worlds*. Oxford: The Clarendon Press.

Rogoff, B. (1990) *Apprenticeship in Thinking: Cognitive Development in Social Context*. Oxford: Oxford University Press.

Rogoff, B., Matusov, E. and White, C. (1996) Models of teaching and learning: participation in a community of learners. In Olson, D. and Torrance, N. *The Handbook of Education and Human Development: New Models of Learning, Teaching and Schooling*. Cambridge, Mass.: Blackwell.

Vygotsky, L. (1978) *Mind in Society: The Development of the Higher Psychological Processes*. Cambridge, Mass.: Harvard University Press.

Wood, D. (1988a) *How Children Think and Learn*. Oxford: Blackwell.

Wood, D. (1988b) Aspects of teaching and learning. In Richards, M. and Light, P. (eds) *Children of Social Worlds; Development in a Social Context*. Oxford: Polity Press. p. 199.

PART III

EXPLORING ORAL TEXTS

CHAPTER 7

DEVELOPMENT THROUGH DIALOGUE

Neil Mercer

Words and Minds, London: Routledge, 2000, pp. 131–66

Introduction

This chapter is about how children learn to use language for collective thinking, and how other people help them do so. It is also about how the process of communicating with language contributes to children's intellectual development. To begin, here is some talk which I recorded while three children were playing together at home. Kay was 5 at the time, while her brother Alec and his friend Robert were both 9. She was listening to them telling each other jokes of the question-and-answer type.

Sequence 1: What a joke!

Robert: What's the difference between

Alec: (*interrupting*) Between a pelican and another pelican? Well, there's not much difference! (*laughs*)

Robert: No, between a banana and an elephant? Try lifting it. If you can't lift it, it's likely to (*loud noises from Kay*) to be a banana – to be an elephant.

Kay: What did the hippopotamus do when he's, uh, in the park?

Alec: I don't know.

Kay: Plays football (*giggles*).

Robert: Ho, ho, ho (*false laughter; Alec sighs*).

We can see that Alec and Robert have learned a common genre structure for joke telling, based on a question-and-answer sequence. This involves the joke teller leading their listener along an apparently predictable line of thought to a surprising, unexpected conclusion. It seems that Kay has also learned the structure of this genre; but she does not share their conception of how to use it to make a funny joke. Joke telling relies on learning the genre, because audiences usually need to know this is the type of dialogue in which they are involved. (As illustrated by the occasional need for repair remarks like 'It was a joke' when this shared frame is not established.) To be successful the joke teller must do more than use a structure; they must build up the right kind of cohesive content. This is a rhetorical skill based on cultural ground rules. The boys share past experience of hearing these kinds of jokes and through this they have formed implicit criteria for what 'counts' as an appropriate, funny answer. It seems that Kay has not yet been drawn into this communal way of thinking.

However, children do seem to grasp the basic rhetorical and dialogical quality of joking quite early in life. Sequence 2 is an extract from a recording the researcher Dianne Horgan (1988) made of a conversation with her daughter Kelly (who was nearly 3 years old at the time).

Sequence 2: Do you love me?

Kelly: Mommy, do you love me?
Mother: Yes.
Kelly: Do you love me to HIT you? Ha, ha!

This example not only illustrates Kelly's developing understanding of humour, but also the awareness she has already developed of different meanings of the word 'love'. Verbal humour is not an incidental, peripheral part of human thinking; it is one manifestation of how language is involved with making collective sense of experience. Becoming able to tell jokes involves an appreciation of some important aspects of the relationship between minds: that you can usually take as 'common knowledge' the familiarity of your audience with appropriate genres; that if you know something that other people do not, surprises can be engineered; and that your listener's understanding of a word can be shaped by the contexts in which you offer it. As children communicate with people around them, they are learning to perceive and understand the world from the perspective of being a member of a community. This means their thinking is becoming more collective. But they are also becoming aware of the significance of the distinction between their knowledge and understanding and that of other people. So, as they communicate, they are also learning how to take account of people's individuality when thinking collectively.

In an activity with children aged 7–13 in which pairs were each given a slightly different version of a route map, the partners, using only spoken language, had to resolve these discrepancies and help one of them find a route to their intended destination. Anne Anderson (1991) and her fellow researchers found that the most striking age-related variation was that the younger children hardly ever used questions to find out what their partner knew, or to check that they understood the information they had been given. Yet asking questions is one of the best strategies for getting this kind of task done successfully. There is also an apparent paradox in that young children often bombard adult companions with questions. But this is not so paradoxical if we remember that the effective use of language depends not just on knowing communicative techniques or strategies, but realizing when to use them in particular situations. The younger children still had to learn how to link minds together effectively in this particular kind of task.

A socio-cultural perspective on development

Recent psychological and anthropological studies of adult–child relations, observed in many cultures, support the view that growing up is an 'apprenticeship in thinking', an induction into ways with words and ways of thinking (e.g. Brice-Heath, 1983; Rogoff, 1990). The extent to which language is used to make matters explicit to young cultural apprentices seems to vary considerably between societies (and even between communities within them). Amongst some social groups, adults seem to rely quite heavily on the ability of children to make sense for themselves of what they are learning, while in others explanations are provided regularly. In some societies, demonstration rather than verbal explanation is preferred as a method of teaching

– for example amongst the Navajo, who consider language a sacred gift which should be used sparingly (Rogoff, Mistry, Göncü and Mosier, 1993). Nevertheless, throughout the world, conversation is one of the most important means by which children seek and receive guidance. One of the principal researchers in this field, Barbara Rogoff, calls the process of children's induction into the intellectual life of their community 'guided participation':

> Guided participation involves collaboration and shared understanding in routine problem-solving activities. Interaction with other people assists children in their development by guiding their participation in relevant activities, helping them adapt their understanding to new situations, structuring their problem-solving attempts, and assisting them in assuming responsibility for managing problem solving.
>
> (Rogoff, 1995: 93)

This 'socio-cultural' explanation of cognitive development depicts children's emergent understanding as the product of the collective thinking of generations, made available to children through observation, joint activity and communication. This contrasts with more biological and individualistic psychological accounts of cognitive development, in which abilities and understanding are seen as emerging through natural growth and individual discovery (e.g. Tudge and Winterhof, 1993). Socio-cultural explanations recognize the role that parents and other people play in helping children learn.

Guidance through dialogue

Of course, adults do not only allow children to participate in activities, they also deliberately provide them with information and explanations and instruct them in ways to behave. But this need not be thought of as a one-way transmission process. Children may take an active role in soliciting help or obtaining information and transforming what they are given into their own new understanding. They can also contest what they are given, and gain understanding from engaging in argument. I can illustrate these points through the next sequence of dialogue. Have you ever felt, during a conversation with a child, that a shift in their understanding has taken place as a result of gaining some new information? I remember feeling this during a conversation with my daughter Anna, which happened when she was 2 years old. At that time, I was regularly recording our talk in joint activities. On this occasion, the topic of our conversation had continued from a little earlier the same evening, when for the first time she had seen bats flying round the house. I had pointed to the eaves, where I had said the bats slept.

Sequence 3: Bats in the roof

Me:	What did you think of the bats?
Anna:	What?
Me:	Did you like the bats?
Anna:	Yeh.
Me:	Think of those bats now, they're out flying around now. Aren't they?
Anna:	They not going – are they lying on the roof?
Me:	What about them?
Anna:	Lie on the roof.

Me:	Oh yeh.
Anna:	They not, but not inside.
Me:	Yeh, I think they do go inside the roof.
Anna:	But not in.
Me:	You don't think so?
Anna:	Not in!
Me:	Not in the roof? I think they go inside the roof. That's where they go to sleep in the day.
Anna:	(*sounding confused*) But they, they not gong *in*side it.
Me:	Why? (*laughing*) Why do you think that?
Anna:	(*also laughing*) But they are not going inside it.
Me:	They can get inside it. There are little kind of holes round the edge of the roof, at the top of the walls and they creep in there.
Anna:	They go there to bye-byes now?
Me:	Yeh – no, they go to bye-byes in the day. They're just coming out now.
Anna:	Are they not going to bye-byes now?
Me:	No, they go to bye-byes in the day, in the morning, and they fly around all night. They get up at night and go out.

It seems that our earlier conversation, while watching the bats, had left Anna with some intellectual dissatisfaction with what she had heard me explain about the creatures' lifestyle. This motivated her to raise the issue of whether the bats' habit was to sleep lying on the roof, when I had offered the (apparently less believable) story that they slept inside it. When I would not confirm her existing belief, it can be seen from the transcript that she reiterated it five times, continuing to do so until I offered a more elaborated explanation of how the bats might enter the roof. She seemed to accept this explanation as reasonable, because in her next statement she asked if the bats were now going 'there' to sleep. As we continued on this topic, it became apparent to me that she did not understand that the bats were nocturnal, and so I tried also to explain this feature of their lifestyle.

An interesting point to note about Sequence 3 is that both the topics for which I provided Anna with explanations were raised by her, not by me. The developmental psychologist Jean Piaget suggested that one of the motivations for intellectual development was the 'cognitive conflict' that periodically arises between children's experience of the world and their understanding of it (Piaget, 1985). He saw this as happening mainly through children's direct involvement with the physical world, but also through communication with other children exposing them to alternative conflicting perspectives. However, Piaget may have underestimated the importance of the role that adult–child conversation plays in development. Young children's direct experience of the world usually takes place in social settings, and is often accompanied by talk about it. That is, new experiences are likely to be mediated by language. What is more, conversation is one of the most important kinds of experience that children have; there is no reason to think that the information they gain through it is any less significant than that obtained by other means (such as by seeing, touching, and so on).

Nevertheless, Piaget's notion of 'cognitive conflict' is still very useful. The information children gain through language may well be, or at least appear to be, incompatible with experience gained in other ways, or with their existing understandings formed through past experience. Language provides both a means for generating a motivating kind of cognitive conflict – and also a means for resolving it, by engaging in some joint thinking with an adult, as Anna did with me. Using language, children can actively test their understanding against that of others, and may use argument to elicit relevant information and explanations from adults about what they perceive – and what they want to know. There is little doubt that children who are unable to ask more knowledgeable people about the world they are discovering, either because adults are uncooperative or because the children themselves lack the communicative ability or confidence to do so, are being denied valuable learning experience as developing thinkers (Collins, 1996).

Interactions with parents and other older people also provide young children with ways of using language that they can appropriate and adapt for later use. A good example of this comes from Mariëtte Hoogsteder's observations of adults and children engaged in the play task of assembling blocks of increasing sizes on to a spindle. When one 2-year-old made a mistake in choosing a block, his father pointed out his error and remarked 'that's a joke, I think', at which the boy took the block away and tried again. Later, the boy decided to rebuild the tower himself. As he was doing so, the following interaction took place.

Sequence 4: Building blocks

Child:	Shall we continue with this one?	(*Child selects too small a block and places it on the spindle.*)
Father:	Well yes, do you think so?	
Child:	(*laughs*) <u>Joke</u>!	
Father:	Oh.	(*Child takes off the wrong block and selects the right one.*)

Hoogsteder suggests that the boy had taken the wrong block on purpose, so that he could turn the tables and tease his father as he had been teased himself. The father's earlier guidance led to learning of a kind he may not have envisaged. The boy appropriated his father's ironic comment on his earlier effort ('that's a joke, I think') and used it in conjunction with his 'wrong' choice to make an original, creative contribution to the dialogue. In this way, the child not only created his own 'joke' but also demonstrated to his father that he had some understanding of how the blocks should be put together.

The Russian literary scholar Bakhtin said that we take the words we use from other people's mouths (Bakhtin, 1981). The meanings of words are generated in context, through dialogue, and when we speak we almost always do so in partial response to what others have said. We 'appropriate' ways of using language from the people with whom we interact. The relevance of Bakhtin's ideas for analysing Sequence 5 is fairly clear. This is an extract from a conversation with two young girls which was recorded by my colleague Janet Maybin in her research on children's informal talk. They are telling her about the sister of one of them, who had got pregnant.

Sequence 5: She did the best thing

Janet:	So does your sister live quite near you?
Nicole:	She lives with us
Karlie:	Cause [she's only quite young
Nicole:	[she's young, she's sixteen
Janet:	Ah right
Karlie:	She did the best thing about it though, didn't she, Nicole?
Nicole:	She didn't tell a soul, no-one, that she was pregnant

Karlie: Until she was due, when she got into hospital, then she told them
Nicole: On Saturday night she had pains in her stomach and come the following
               Sunday my mum was at work and my sister come to the pub and my
               aunt Ella was in it and my sister went in there and said 'I've got pains
               in my stomach' so my auntie Ella went and got my mum, and took her
               to hospital, and my mum asked her if she was due on and she said 'No,
               I've just come off' and when they got her to hospital they said 'Take her
               to maternity'. My mum was crying!
Janet: Your mum didn't realise she was pregnant?
Nicole: No, and my mum slept with her when she was ill!
Karlie: My dad said she did – Terri did the best thing about it – her sister's
               Terri
Nicole: Or if she did tell, as she's so young, she weren't allowed to have him
                                                                    (Maybin, 1994)

We can see that Nicole quotes her sister and the hospital staff in her account of this
unusual childbirth. Karlie also recycles language from an earlier event, but in a less
obvious way. We first hear her expressing her opinion that Nicole's sister 'did the
best thing about it'. Later, though, these same words emerge as an apparent quotation from her father. It seems that she was so impressed by her father's comment
that she appropriated it for her own use. Although her father may not have made
his comment in a self-conscious attempt to guide Karlie's moral development, by
recycling his remark she implicitly supports the moral sentiments that it expresses –
or at least she shows that she felt they were appropriate sentiments to voice in this
later conversation with another adult (the researcher). For children, 'recycling' the
language they hear may be an important way of assimilating the collective ways of
thinking of the community in which they are growing up.

Providing a 'scaffolding' for learning

Teachers commonly use techniques like 'elicitations', 'recaps' and 'reformulations'
when interacting with students. These techniques are deliberate guidance strategies
for generating a common frame of reference during an episode of teaching-and-
learning. James Wertsch (1985) observed parents of young children using two other
rather similar techniques. The first, which he calls 'establishing a referential perspective', is when an adult responds to a child's apparent lack of comprehension by
referring to other shared knowledge. Imagine, for instance, that while on a country
walk a parent says to a child: 'look, there's a tractor'. If this reference fails (that
is, the child does not seem to realize which object is being referred to), the adult
may then say something like 'can you see, that big green thing with enormous wheels
in the field?' In doing this, the adult is drawing on resources of common knowledge
to build a shared contextual frame of reference, based on the reasonable assumption
that the child's understanding of basic features like colour and appearance will help
them identify the strange object in question. Coupled with this technique, adults use
a kind of reverse process which Wertsch calls 'abbreviation'. This is when, over the
course of time, an adult begins to assume that new common knowledge has been
successfully established, and so, when talking to the child, makes progressively more
abbreviated or cryptic references to what is being discussed. For example, the next
time the same parent and child are out in the countryside, the parent may first point
out 'another big green tractor', but then later just refer to 'the tractor'. In these ways,
by gradually and systematically creating and assuming more common knowledge,

adults support and encourage children's developing understanding of language and the world it describes.

To use any of these teaching techniques effectively, an adult has to make careful judgements about what a child understands at any one point in time, to base their communications with the child upon these judgements, and adapt the kind of intellectual support they give the child to take account of their developing knowledge and understanding. If they do so systematically while engaged in a joint activity with a child, the adult can enable the child to make progress which they would not have been able to do alone. The adult's intellect provides a temporary support for the child's own, until a new level of understanding has been achieved. To provide this 'scaffolding', as Jerome Bruner and others have called it (e.g. Wood, Bruner and Ross, 1976; Maybin, Mercer and Steirer, 1992), an adult may not only offer useful information and guiding suggestions, they may even intervene to simplify slightly the task in hand. (As, for example, when an adult helps a young child get started on a jigsaw puzzle by assembling all the edge pieces.) Effective 'scaffolding' reduces the learner's scope for failure in the task, while encouraging their efforts to advance. 'Scaffolding' helps a learner to accomplish a task which they would not have been able to do on their own. But it is a special, sensitive kind of help which is intended to bring the learner closer to a state of competence which will enable them eventually to complete such a task on their own.

Creating an intermental development zone

The notion of 'scaffolding' is closely related to one of the ideas of the Russian psychologist Vygotsky. Vygotsky suggested that the usual measures of children's intellectual ability, such as IQ tests, are too static and decontextualized to be of real educational value. He pointed out that children differ in their responsiveness to guidance, instruction and opportunities for learning. So two children who currently have reached a similar level of, say, mathematical understanding, could be expected to achieve similar results in a standardized maths test. But, given (as he put it) 'good instruction' by a teacher, one of those children might very quickly grasp new mathematical concepts and computational skills, while the other – even if similarly motivated – might only be able to make a little progress. By measuring the difference between the original independent capability of each child and what they were able to achieve when given some intellectual guidance and support, educators could make a more useful, dynamic assessment of these children's educational potential and needs. The difference between their original and eventual achievement was what Vygotsky called each child's *zone of proximal development* (often today referred to by the acronym ZPD). In his last major work, he returned to this concept and used it to argue that 'Instruction is only useful when it moves ahead of development' (Vygotsky, 1978). That is, good teaching should draw children just beyond their existing capabilities to 'stretch' their intellect and so help them to develop. He seems to have wanted the concept to be used to ensure that individual children received teaching appropriate to their potential, rather than their actual, achievements. Vygotsky's conception of the ZPD embodied his view that intellectual development is something sensitive to dialogue and situational factors, a process by which *intra*mental (individual) processes can be facilitated and accelerated by *inter*mental (social) activity.

I went back to Vygotsky's original account of the ZPD while writing this book, and also read again what several other socio-cultural researchers had written about it (e.g. Newman, Griffin and Cole, 1989; Wells, 1996; Cole, 1996). This made me realize that I have developed a rather different conception of a 'zone' of intellectual development. This is probably because I am less interested than Vygotsky in assessing individuals and more in understanding the quality of teaching-and-learning as an 'intermental' or 'interthinking' process. For a teacher to teach and a learner to learn, they must use talk and joint activity to create a shared communicative space, an 'intermental development zone' (IDZ) on the contextual foundations of their common knowledge and aims. In this intermental zone, which is reconstituted constantly as the dialogue continues, the teacher and learner negotiate their way through the activity in which they are involved. If the quality of the zone is successfully maintained, the teacher can enable a learner to become able to operate just beyond their established capabilities, and to consolidate this experience as new ability and understanding. If the dialogue fails to keep minds mutually attuned, the IDZ collapses and the scaffolded learning grinds to a halt.

Like Vygotsky's original idea of the ZPD, the concept of an 'intermental development zone' still focuses attention on how a learner progresses under guidance in an activity, but in a way which is more clearly related to the variable contributions of both teacher and learner. The IDZ is a continuing event of contextualized joint activity, whose quality is dependent on the existing knowledge, capabilities and motivations of both the learner and the teacher. Vygotsky suggested that 'good', appropriate instruction could influence development. But if we say that the contribution of a teacher is significant in determining what a learner achieves on any particular occasion, we must accept that this achievement is a joint one, the product of a process of interthinking. The progress of the two hypothetical mathematics students I mentioned above might well be greatly affected by who taught them, because teachers do not offer the same quality of continuing intermental support, and individual students respond differently to the same teacher. This has obvious implications for researching cognitive development and evaluating the process of teaching-and-learning. As well as observing the progress a learner, or a class of learners, makes with the support of a particular teacher through a particular activity, we should also observe how the teachers and learners use language and other means of communicating to create an IDZ during the activity. I will return to these ideas a little later, in relation to teaching-and-learning in school.

Learning together

As well as learning from the guidance and example of experts, children (and novices of all ages) also learn the skills of thinking collectively by acting and talking with each other. Any account of intellectual development based only on the guidance of young people by older members of their community would of course be inadequate. As members of a younger generation, we often rebel against the learning that our elders prescribe, and often question the values inherent in the given knowledge of our community. We use language to generate some of our own common understandings and to pursue our own interests. Each generation is active in creating the new knowledge they want, and in doing so the communal resources of the language tool-kit may be transformed. Yet even the rebellious creativity of a new generation is inevitably, in part, the product of a dialogue between generations.

I now want to look at some examples of children involved in activities without an adult present. The nature of the collective thinking involved is usually very different in such circumstances. Language offers children a means for simulating events together in play, in ways which may enable the participants to make better sense of the actual experiences on which the play is based. The Dutch psychologist Ed Elbers

(1994) has provided some excellent examples of children engaged in this kind of play activity. Like many children, when they were aged 6 and 7 his two daughters enjoyed setting up play 'schools' together with toy animals. They would act out scenarios in which, with one of them as the teacher, the assembled creatures would act out the routines of a school day. But Elbers noticed that one typical feature of their play school was that incidents which disrupted classroom life took place with surprising frequency. Sequence 6 is one such example (translated by Elbers from the Dutch). Margareet is the elder girl, being nearly 8 years old, and here takes the role of the teacher. Elisabeth, her younger (6-year-old) sister, acts out the role of a rather naughty student.

Sequence 6: Play school

Margareet:	Children, sit down.
Elisabeth:	I have to go to the toilet, Miss.
Margareet:	Now, children, be quiet.
Elisabeth:	I have to go to the toilet.
Margareet:	I want to tell you something.
Elisabeth:	(*loud*) I have to go to the toilet!
Margareet:	(*chuckles*) Wait a second.
Elisabeth:	(*with emphasis*) Miss, I have to go to the toilet!!
Margareet:	OK, you can go.
Elisabeth:	(*cheekily*) Where is it? (*laughs*)
Margareet:	Over there, under that box, the one with the animals on, where the dangerous animals ... (*chuckles*) under there.
Elisabeth:	Really?
Margareet:	Yes.

In this sequence we can again see, as in earlier sequences, a child appropriating an adult's way with words. 'Now, children, be quiet' is exactly the kind of teacher-talk that Margareet will have heard every day in 'real' school. But Elbers suggests we can also interpret this sequence as an example of children reflecting together on the rules which govern their behaviour in school, and how the robustness of these rules can be tested. They can play with ideas of power and control, without risking the community sanctions which 'real life' behaviour would incur. Teachers normally have to be obeyed, and children are not meant to leave the class during lessons – but given the legitimate excuse of having to go to the toilet, how can a child not get her way? Sometimes, in setting up this kind of activity, the girls (out of role) would discuss how best to ensure that such disruptive incidents occurred. For example:

Sequence 7: Setting up the play school

Margareet:	You should choose four children who always talk the most; those children must sit at the front near the teacher. It'll be fun if they talk.
Elisabeth:	(*to one of the toy pupils*) You, you sit here and talk, right?
Margareet:	The desks are behind each other, then they can only ... then I have to turn round all the time, if the children talk.

These kinds of examples illustrate something important about how language use in play activities may contribute to children's development. Language can be used by them to simulate social life, to create virtual contexts in which they can use dramatized activity to think together about the ways in which life is carried out in the communities in which they are cultural apprentices.

Maybin (1994) asked children in her project to wear radio microphones so that she could record their conversations throughout the school day. Sequence 8 is part of such a recording for a girl of 11 called Julie, which begins while she is doing a mathematics problem in class with a partner. She then goes out to the girls' toilets and eventually returns to the classroom.

Sequence 8: In and out of class

Julie: Three pounds twelve I make Tom Ato. Back in a second. Miss can I go to the toilet please?
Teacher: Yes all right.
(*Sound of Julie's heels as she goes down the corridor. When she enters the toilets the acoustics on the tape change abruptly, with the tiled walls making the voices echo. Carol and Nicole are already there*)
Julie: Oh, hi. Where did you get your hair permed?
Nicole: (*indistinct*)
Julie: You're not going out with Sasha, are you?
Nicole: Yea.
Julie: Are you?
Nicole: Yes, I hope so (*laughs*)
Julie: You've, got darker skin than me, I've got a sun tan. (*pause*) (*to Carol*) I should think so too, it's disgusting, that skirt is! Aii ... don't! (*Nicole starts tapping her feet on the tiled floor*) Do you do tap dancing? (*both girls start tapping their feet and singing*)
Julie and Nicole: 'I just called to say I love you / And I mean it from the bottom of my heart.'
Julie: Caught you that time, Carol – ooh! What's the matter, Carol, don't show your tits! (*laughs*) (*to Nicole*) I went like this to Carol, I says, I pull down her top, I went phtt 'don't show your tits!' (*Nicole laughs*)
(*Julie leaves the toilets, walks down the corridor, re-enters the classroom and sits down*)
Julie: Turn over – six plates of chips – oh I've nearly finished my book. I've got one page to do.

(Maybin, 1994)

Maybin points out that the conversation in the toilets seems to belong to a different world from that of the maths classroom. The frame of reference changes completely. In the toilets, the girls are no longer students but young adolescents jointly interpreting their femininity. Yet in doing so they are still recycling earlier language experience, transforming the 'given' into the 'new', using *risqué* words and song lyrics that they have appropriated from older children or adults.

In the informal setting of the girls' toilet, Julie and her friends have no problems in sharing ideas and developing shared understandings about their experiences of life. But this does not necessarily mean that they know how to use language effectively for thinking together in other kinds of situations, or that they will inevitably learn all the communication strategies they will need from each other or from the informal guidance adults provide outside school. For example, Maybin's research of children's informal conversations captured little 'exploratory' talk in which reasons are made explicit and ideas are critically considered. Of course, play activities may not generate any obvious need for such talk. But observational research in classrooms on children's activities in pairs and groups generally shows that much of it is unproductive, with more 'disputational' than 'exploratory' talk happening. Sequence 9, for example, is a fairly typical episode of interaction amongst a group of four 11-year-olds writing together at the computer, recorded by the teacher and researcher Madeline Watson. The three girls (Jenny, Katy, Annie) have sat down at the screen in such a way that the fourth member, Colin, has had to get a stool and sit behind, sometimes leaning on the girls' shoulders. He has made it clear that he thinks the girls lack computer expertise, and that he should tell them what to do.

Sequence 9: At the computer

Jenny:	No	*Katy goes to press DELETE.*
Annie:	Now delete. Yeh. That's it. And then nuh (*sounds out the letter n*)	*Jenny pushes her hand out of the way. Colin pushes over and goes to press the key.*
Colin:	For God's sake.	*Jenny pushes Colin's hand out of the way.*
Katy:	Stop it Colin.	*Colin gets off stool.*
Colin:	You're not doing any of mine (*speaks in aggressive high voice to Katy*).	
Annie:	Now space.	*Raises hand towards keyboard.*
Katy:	(*high pitched – arguing with Colin*) I know. She's just doing the title.	
Annie:	No a bit – delete one of those spaces. There you have to	*Annie leans across Jenny at keyboard to press DELETE.*
Katy:	(*still arguing with Colin*) We're meant to be doing the title. It's the title.	
Annie:	Hang on.	*Jenny pushes Annie's arm up off the keyboard.*

This is the kind of talk which gives group work a bad name. Classroom research has shown that the educational potential value of collaborative activity is often squandered because students do not communicate effectively. [. . .]

The nature of children's communication in these contexts might be shaped more by what the linguist Michael Halliday calls the 'interpersonal' function of language than by its 'ideational' function as a tool for getting their task done (Halliday, 1978). There is no avoiding the interpersonal function of language, of course. All interactions, however much focused on a joint intellectual task, must involve participants in an intersubjectivity, a way of orientating to each other's minds. We cannot, and should not, try to ignore the interpersonal function of language, but we can try to help participants ensure that interpersonal orientations are compatible with what they are trying jointly to achieve.

Educating children in collective thinking

The communication problems we have been considering are not only found in school. In all situations, in work and at home, people – often despite their good intentions – find it difficult to communicate effectively. This is not surprising. The ground rules of everyday communication are usually taken for granted, and there may be little encouragement from other people to reflect and improve on how things are normally done. Some ways of using language to get things done may not be used much in the informal activities of everyday childhood life, and so children can hardly be expected to learn them. This offers a clear and useful role for schools, which are special institutional settings created for guiding intellectual development. Education should help children to gain a greater awareness and appreciation of the discourse repertoire of wider society and how it is used to create knowledge and carry out particular activities. It should give them access to ways of using language which their out-of-school experience may not have revealed, help them extend their repertoire of language genres and so enable them to use language more effectively as a means for learning, pursuing interests, developing shared understanding and generally getting things done.

Throughout the 1990s my colleagues and I began to produce classroom-based activities for developing children's use of language as a tool for thinking collectively. The background and first stages of this research were described in my earlier book, *The Guided Construction of Knowledge* (Mercer, 1995). In the most recent five-year phase of this research, Lyn Dawes, Rupert Wegerif, Karen Littleton and I have been working closely with primary teachers in Milton Keynes to develop a practical programme of 'Talk Lessons' for children aged 8–11. These lessons have a careful balance of teacher-led and group-based activities. We have designed teacher-led activities to raise children's awareness of how they talk together and how language can be used in joint activity for reasoning and problem-solving. These teacher-led activities are coupled with group-based tasks in which children have the opportunity to practise ways of talking and collaborating, and these in turn feed into other whole-class sessions in which teachers and children reflect together on what has been learned (Dawes, Mercer and Wegerif, 2000). We have also created computer-based activities using specially designed software. As other researchers have also found, computer-based activities can be excellent for stimulating and focusing children's discussion (Littleton and Light, 1999). [. . .]

In order to evaluate the Talk Lessons, we have made comparisons between children in 'target' classes who have done them, with 'control' classes of similar children who have not been involved in the programme. Compared with children of similar age, experience and background in the same city who have not done the lessons – and compared with their own prior selves before doing them – children who have done the programme discuss issues in more depth and for longer, participate more equally and fully, and provide more reasons to support their views. Our analysis of recordings of the group activities shows that the improved ability of the 'target' children to think together critically and constructively can be related directly to the structure and content of their talk. [. . .]

The target children offered opinions and gave reasons to support them. They asked for each other's views and checked agreement. They made relevant information explicit and built their common knowledge effectively. They engaged critically and constructively with each other's ideas, by challenging suggestions and offering their own reasons and alternatives. They actively sought each other's ideas. They may not have always reasoned well, or allowed each other the conversational space that they perhaps ought, but they were using language as a tool for joint, rational thinking.

Encouraging exploratory talk

The quality of their discussions can be related to the idea of 'exploratory talk', which I define as follows:

> *Exploratory talk* is that in which partners engage critically but constructively with each other's ideas. Relevant information is offered for joint consideration. Proposals may be challenged and counter-challenged, but if so reasons are given and alternatives are offered. Agreement is sought as a basis for joint progress. Knowledge is made publicly accountable and reasoning is visible in the talk.
>
> (Mercer, 2000: 98)

Such talk embodies a valuable kind of 'co-reasoning', with speakers following ground rules which help them to share knowledge, evaluate evidence and consider options in a reasonable and equitable way. It is an effective way of using language to think collectively, and the process of education should ensure that every child is aware of its value and able to use it effectively (Lyle, 1993; Barnes and Todd, 1995; Teasley, 1997). However, observational research evidence suggests that very little of it naturally occurs in classrooms when children work together in groups. Most of the talk observed tends to be 'disputational' or 'cumulative' only involving some of the children and amounting to no more than a brief and superficial consideration of the relevant topics.

When a teacher asks students to 'discuss' a topic, the teacher is usually expecting a certain quality of interaction to take place. A competitive disputation, or the passive acceptance by most members of a group of one assertive person's viewpoint, would almost certainly not be what any teacher had in mind. But one other clear finding of classroom research, including my own, is that teachers rarely make such expectations clear and explicit (Mercer, 1995). That is, the ground rules which are used for generating particular functional ways of using language – spoken or written – are rarely taught. In all levels of education, from primary school to university, students usually seem to be expected to work out the ground rules for themselves.

Identifying exploratory talk

Although talk which has exploratory features can be identified by a careful, detailed and fairly laborious analysis of recorded discussion, my colleague Rupert Wegerif and I designed a convenient computer-based method which helps us locate this kind of co-reasoning activity. [. . .]

With this computer-based text analysis we did two things. First, we looked back at the transcripts and videos to check whether the frequent occurrence of the key words, e.g. 'because', 'if' and 'why', was a reliable indication of the occurrence of talk of an exploratory, co-reasoning kind. We were able to confirm that this was so. Where we located a high incidence of 'because', 'if', and so on, we regularly found evidence that children were engaged in critical, constructive discussion. Next, we made a quantitative, statistical comparison of the incidence of the key words in the talk of the 'target' and 'control' groups, to see if children who had done the Talk Lessons used them more frequently. This showed us that the children who had done the Talk Lessons used these words significantly more than the children who had not. In other words, the Talk Lessons had fulfilled our aim of guiding children into an 'exploratory' way of using language to think together (Wegerif and Mercer, 1997). [. . .]

Another interesting fact was that the 'target' children appeared to have improved their individual reasoning capabilities by taking part in the group experience of explicit, rational, collaborative problem-solving. These results therefore support Vygotsky's claim about the link between intermental (social) activity and intramental (individual) development.

Of course, we cannot be sure exactly what the 'target' children learned from their experience that made the difference. It may be that some gained from having new, successful problem-solving strategies explained to them by their partners, while others may have benefited from having to justify and make explicit their own reasons. But a more radical and intriguing possibility is that children may have improved their reasoning skills by 'internalizing' the ground rules of exploratory talk, so that they became able to carry on a kind of silent rational dialogue with themselves. That is, the Talk Lessons may have helped them become more able to generate the kind of rational thinking which depends on the explicit, dispassionate consideration of evidence and competing options.

The role of the teacher

The role of the teacher in talking and learning is undoubtedly crucial. In some Mexican research we tried to see whether the better teachers were providing a more effective 'scaffolding' for their students' learning, and to identify kinds of learning they appeared to be encouraging (Wegerif, Rojas-Drummond and Mercer, 1999). Our analysis of the recordings covered several features of classroom interaction, including teachers' uses of questions. We looked at the content of tasks, activities and discussions, at the extent to which teachers encouraged students to talk together, and the kinds of explanations teachers provide to students for the tasks they set them. The results of this time-consuming and complex analysis can be summarized as follows. We found that the more effective teachers could be distinguished by the following characteristics:

1   *They used question-and-answer sequences not just to test knowledge, but also to guide the development of understanding.* These teachers often used questions to discover the initial levels of students' understanding and adjust their teaching accordingly, and used 'why' questions to encourage students to reason and reflect on what they were doing.
2   *They taught not just 'subject content', but also procedures for solving problems and making sense of experience.* This included teachers demonstrating to children the use of problem-solving strategies, explaining to children the meaning and purpose of classroom activities, and using their interactions with children as opportunities for encouraging children to make explicit their own thought processes.
3   *They treated learning as a social, communicative process.* This was represented by teachers doing such things as organizing interchanges of ideas and mutual support amongst students, encouraging students to take a more active, vocal role in classroom events, explicitly relating current activity to past experience and using students' contributions as a resource for building the 'common knowledge' of the class.

There is, of course, much more to effective teaching than the use of particular talk techniques. The better Mexican teachers and those who were less effective were all using elicitations, recaps, reformulations, and so on. The crucial difference between the two sets of teachers was how and when they used them, and what they used them to teach. They differed significantly in the extent to which they helped children to see the relevance of past experience and common knowledge, and in the opportunities they provided for children to explain their own understanding or misunderstanding.

The findings of our research are in accord with those of other researchers in various parts of the world. It is therefore useful for teachers to become aware of the techniques they use in dialogue and what they are trying to achieve by using them. A teacher is not simply the instructor or facilitator of the learning of a large and disparate set of individuals, but rather is a potential creator of a 'community of enquiry' in a classroom, in which individual students can take a shared, active and reflective role in the development of their own understanding (Lipman, 1970). The students are apprentices in collective thinking, under the expert guidance of their teacher. The quality of their educational experience, and to some extent at least their commitment to their own education, will be affected by the extent to which what they are doing in class has continuity, a comprehensible purpose and scope for their own active participation. The teacher has to use classroom activities to develop IDZs with students, and among students, to fulfil these conditions. In addition, the teacher has to guide children in how to talk and work together and agree some clear ground rules for making it happen. [. . .]

Conclusions

I have concentrated in this chapter on the ways in which language use is involved in the development of children's understanding, and their induction into ways of using language for collective thinking. In the early part, I explained how an influential group of psychologists have redefined cognitive development as a dialogue, rather than a process of individual discovery and growth. From this 'socio-cultural' perspective, the guidance of children into ways of thinking collectively is a vital aspect of human development, and one in which language is necessarily closely involved. I illustrated how this kind of guidance happens in casual, incidental ways, as adults and children go about their joint activities, and in more structured kinds of teaching-and-learning. I suggested that the concept of an 'intermental development zone' (IDZ) is useful for explaining how dialogue supports the process of teaching-and-learning.

Young people learn a great deal about how to think collectively from interacting with each other. As the younger generation, there are lessons that they can only learn amongst themselves, away from the guiding or constraining influence of their elders. They may be more or less receptive to the guidance adults offer on any particular occasion, but nevertheless they will actively participate in many informal dialogues with adults which contribute to the development of their own understanding and skills in communication. In such dialogues, knowledge of generations is shared and children acquire some valuable tools for creating knowledge together.

I also suggested, however, that out-of-school everyday life does not provide many children with adequate experience or guidance in the use of language as a tool for collective thinking. It is not to their benefit, or to that of society in general, that they should be expected to discover or infer this kind of important cultural knowledge for themselves, or to live their social lives without it. Such experience and guidance can, and should, be provided by schools. . . .

References

Anderson, A.H., Clark, A. and Mullin, J., 'Introducing information in dialogues: forms of introducing chosen by young speakers and the responses elicited from young listeners', *Journal of Child Language*, 1991, no. 18, pp. 663–87.

Bakhtin, M., *The Dialogic Imagination*, Austin, TX, University of Texas Press, 1981.

Barnes, D. and Todd, F., *Communication and Learning Revisited*, Portsmouth, NH, Heinemann, 1995.

Cole, M., *Cultural Psychology: A Once and Future Discipline*, Cambridge, MA, Harvard University Press, 1996.

Collins, J., *The Quiet Child*, London, Cassell, 1996.

Dawes, L., Mercer, N. and Wegerif, R., *Thinking Together*, Birmingham, Questions Publishing Co., 2000.

Elbers, E., 'Sociogenesis and children's pretend play: a variation on Vygotskian themes', in W. de Graaf and R. Maier (eds) *Sociogenesis Re-examined*, New York, Springer, 1994.

Halliday, M.A.K., *Language as a Social Semiotic: The Social Interpretation of Language and Meaning*, London, Edward Arnold, 1978.

Heath, S.B., *Ways with Words: Language, Life and Work in Communities and Classrooms*, Cambridge, Cambridge University Press, 1983.

Hoogsteder, M., *Learning Through Participation* (Doctoral Thesis published as Monograph), Utrecht, University of Utrecht, 1995.

Lipman, M., *Philosophy for Children*, Montclair, NJ, Institute for the Advancement of Philosophy for Children, 1970.

Littleton, K. and Light, P. (eds), *Learning with Computers: Analysing Productive Interaction*, London, Routledge, 1999.

Lyle, S., 'An investigation in which children talk themselves into meaning', *Language and Education*, 1993, vol. 7, no. 3, pp. 181–96.

Maybin, J., 'Children's voices: talk, knowledge and identity', in D. Graddol, J. Maybin and B. Stierer (eds) *Researching Language and Literacy in Social Context*, Clevedon, Multilingual Matters, 1994.

Maybin, J., Mercer, N. and Stierer, B., ' "Scaffolding" learning in the classroom', in K. Norman (ed.) *Thinking Voices*, London, Hodder and Stoughton, 1992.

Mercer, N., *The Guided Construction of Knowledge: Talk Amongst Teachers and Learners*, Clevedon, Multilingual Matters, 1995.

Newman, D., Griffin, P. and Cole, M., *The Construction Zone*, Cambridge, Cambridge University Press, 1989.

Piaget, J., *The Equilibration of Cognitive Structures*, Chicago, IL, University of Chicago Press, 1985.

Rogoff, B., *Apprenticeship in Thinking: Cognitive Development in Social Context*, New York, Oxford University Press, 1990.

Rogoff, B., 'Observing sociocultural activity on three planes: participatory appropriation, guided participation and apprenticeship', in J. Wertsch, P. del Rio and A. Alvarez (eds) *Sociocultural Studies of Mind*, Cambridge, Cambridge University Press, 1995.

Rogoff, B., Mistry, J., Göncü, A. and Mosier, C., 'Guided participation in cultural activity by toddlers and caregivers', *Monographs of the Society for Research in Child Development*, 1993, vol. 58, no. 7.

Teasley, S., 'Talking about reasoning: how important is the peer group in peer collaboration?', in L. Resnick, R. Saljo, C. Pontecorvo and B. Burge (eds) *Discourses, Tool and Reasoning: Essays on Situated Cognition*, Berlin, Springer Verlag, 1997.

Tudge, J.R. and Winterhof, P.A., 'Vygotsky, Piaget and Bandura: perspectives on the relations between the social world and cognitive development', *Human Development*, 1993, vol. 36, pp. 61–81.

Vygotsky, L.S., *Mind in Society: The Development of Higher Psychological Processes*, Cambridge, MA, Harvard University Press, 1978.

Wegerif, R. and Mercer, N., 'A dialogical framework for researching peer talk', in R. Wegerif and P. Scrimshaw (eds) *Computers and Talk in the Primary Classroom*, Clevedon, Multilingual Matters, 1997.

Wegerif, R., Rojas-Drummond, S. and Mercer, N., 'Language for the social construction of knowledge: comparing classroom talk in Mexican pre-schools', *Language and Education*, 1999, vol. 13, no. 2, pp. 133–50.

Wells, G., 'Using the tool-kit of discourse in the activity of learning and teaching', *Mind, Culture and Activity*, 1996, vol. 3, no. 2, pp. 74–101.

Wertsch, J., 'Adult-child interaction as a source of self-regulation in children', in S.R. Yussen (ed.) *The Growth of Reflection in Children*, Orlando, FL, Academic Press, 1985.

Wood, D., Bruner, J. and Ross, G., 'The role of tutoring in problem solving', *Journal of Child Psychology and Child Psychiatry*, 1976, vol. 17, pp. 89–100.

CHAPTER 8

GROUP WORK

Learning through talk

Roy Corden

Literacy and Learning Through Talk: Strategies for the Primary Classroom, Buckingham: Open University Press, 2002, pp. 81–108

British primary schools have, since the early 1970s, generally been organized with children seated around tables in small groups. The fostering of collaborative, investigative learning is often given as the prime justification for this arrangement. However, although group seating has been a prominent feature of classroom organization in primary schools, prior to the National Oracy Project, there was little evidence that teachers were planning for talk in any systematic way. Research on classroom organization has consistently confirmed the view that a great deal of group work in primary schools is either ineffective or inappropriate. The HMI survey (1978) of primary education made no mention of the kind of collaborative and expressive talk recommended by the Bullock Report (DES 1975), or the purposeful discussion described by researchers such as Johnson and Johnson (1990: 77), who state that cooperative learning is not:

- having students sit side by side at the same table and talk with each other as they do their individual assignments;
- having students do a task individually with instructions that the ones who finish first are to help the slower students;
- assigning a report to a group where one student does all the work and others put their name to it.

The ORACLE survey (1975–80) found that although grouping had become a major feature of classroom organization, collaborative work was rare (see Galton *et al.* 1980; Simon and Willcocks 1981). Of the 58 classes observed, 50 used an informal layout but throughout the observation period, 90 per cent never organized collaborative group tasks. The survey found that most children spent their time in school working alone, individually and silently. Only 18.6 per cent of the time was spent on interaction with peers and a meagre 1.5 per cent of time was allocated to group interaction. HMI (1982) stated that the aims, objectives and methods for promoting oral language needed to be more clearly defined and Alexander *et al.* (1992) recommended that teachers give more consideration to matching seating arrangements to teaching and learning purposes, rather than organizing classes into groups as a matter of course. Ofsted (1993) found that although classes were organized into small groups, children worked independently on individual work tasks. Galton *et al.* (1999) conclude that the organization within primary classrooms has hardly changed since the original 1976 ORACLE survey. Although teachers now appear to be spending more time in group and whole class teaching, the pattern of interaction has remained fairly constant and 'children still mostly sit grouped around tables, but still work mostly alone' (Galton *et al.* 1999: 105). What research and reports confirm is that we have been seduced by the colourful, bustling, busyness of the primary classroom, which has, in effect, masked a lack of quality teacher–pupil interaction.

Group work and learning

> Cooperation is working together to accomplish shared goals and cooperative learning is the instructional use of small groups so that students work together to maximise their own and one another's learning.
>
> (Johnson and Johnson 1990: 69)

Barnes and Todd's (1977) seminal work on collaborative learning illustrated its importance in the development of children's cognitive understanding. The National Oracy Project (see Norman, 1992) highlighted the learning potential of peer group discussions which are reflective and hypothetical and where speech is tentative and exploratory. Des Fountain and Howe (1992: 146) suggest that children need 'worthwhile opportunities to work together in small groups, making meaning through talk'. In the USA the value of dialogue in scaffolding children's comprehension skills has been demonstrated by Palinscar and Brown (1984), while Rosenblatt (1989: 173) argues that teacher–pupil and peer–peer dialogue and interchange is a vital ingredient in helping children make connections between the reading and writing processes:

> Group interchange about the texts of established authors can also be a powerful means of stimulating growth in reading ability and critical acumen. When students share their responses and learn how their evocations from transactions with the same text differ, they can return to the text to discover their own habits of selection and synthesis and can become more critical of their own processes as readers. Interchange about the problems of interpretation and a collaborative movement toward self-critical interpretation of the text can lead to the development of critical concepts and criteria of validity of interpretation. Such metalinguistic awareness is valuable to students as both readers and writers.

Achievement in group work

Researchers in the USA have made great claims for the effectiveness of group work in enhancing motivation, developing social skills and raising levels of academic achievement. Slavin (1983a) devised a number of structured approaches to competitive-cooperative group work such as TGT (team games, tournaments) and STAD (student-teams achievement divisions). The CLIP (cooperative learning implementation programme) (Robertson 1990) focused on collaborative learning and aimed to promote prosocial skills and academic achievement. In the UK, Mercer (1991) and Moore and Tweddle (1992) investigated the role of CAL (computer assisted learning) and explored its potential for pair and group work. Slavin reports that his methods can develop social relations, improve children's self-esteem and increase student achievement. Johnson and Johnson (1990: 71) make similar claims and offer evidence to suggest that group cooperative learning can promote higher achievement than an individual competitive approach. They argue that promoting positive interdependence and individual accountability in group work results in higher achievement, more positive relationships and higher self-esteem. Sharan (1980) also concludes, though rather more tentatively, that team learning methods result in enhanced academic achievement in comparison with a more traditional teaching approach. Sharan and Shaulov (1989) point particularly to benefits in terms of social development and motivation, arguing that cooperative groups typically generate devotion and application to a task. Sharan (1990: 182) concludes that group investigation: 'fosters more positive attitudes towards learning, more motivation to learn, and more cooperative patterns of behaviour among classmates in multi-ethnic groups, than does the typical presentation–recitation method'.

Despite these claims, there has been some debate over whether group work produces results superior to those obtained from individual or whole class teaching. Bennett and Blundell (1983) suggest that children are likely to spend more time on task when working in traditional rows than when working in groups. However, other studies (e.g. Hertz-Lazorowitz, 1990) show that time on task is substantially higher during collaborative group work than in whole class activities.

Determining when and whether children are on or off task is highly problematic. As Hastings (1990) has pointed out, children can develop various ploys to give the impression of being on task when they are actually doing very little. Similarly, children can appear to be off task, when in reality they are thinking. Dyson (1987: 397) notes that 'off task behaviour may in fact contain some of the children's most intellectually skilful behaviours'. I have numerous examples of children making significant contributions to discussion following apparent off task behaviour. In one such example a group were discussing the Beatles song 'Eleanor Rigby'. They were investigating the meaning of the words 'Father Mackenzie wiping the dirt from his hands as he walked from the grave'. One group member appeared to withdraw from discussion. He leaned back in his chair and actually turned away from other group members. However, he suddenly turned back to face the group and said, 'no no it means two things it means he's wiping away the dirt mud of burying her and he's wiping her away at the same time'.

It is extremely difficult to conclude whether group work is more academically effective than whole class or individual work because the measurement of achievement is not easy to determine. Moreover, there is a difference between product and process outcomes. The criteria for achievement will be different for investigative 'open tasks' that require higher order thinking than for closed 'information gathering tasks'. Bennett and Dunne (1992) found a difference in the amount of abstract talk during work on English and maths tasks, the former generating 20 per cent of the total and the latter almost zero. A low proportion of abstract talk was also found to occur in technology and computer tasks. Bennett and Dunne suggest that action tasks, which for example require children to make things, demand a different kind of activity than many English tasks, which require children to discuss issues and make decisions unrelated to action – that is, they do not have to produce something, a main learning outcome of such tasks being the *process* of discussion. The point is that group work should be just one of a whole repertoire of organizational arrangements within the classroom. As with any other arrangement it should be used only when it is appropriate to do so. If children happen to be engaged in a task that requires individual attention and concentration, the educational milieu should reflect this need. It is organizational lunacy to seat children face to face around a table if their learning need at that particular time requires a little peace and privacy. Attempting to compare academic results in whole class, individual or group work situations is a difficult and somewhat futile task. Effective teaching requires a variety of contexts, including whole class, small group and individual learning scenarios. Academic achievement is facilitated by a careful match between learning objective, classroom organization, task and teacher intervention.

Group work in a literacy hour

The literacy hour, organized into whole class and guided and independent working groups, provides opportunities for children and teachers to engage in purposeful interactive discourse to meet differentiated learning objectives. Managing independent group work is considered to be one of the most challenging aspects of the literacy hour by many teachers. Indeed the NLSF training pack devotes a section to this issue and many LEAs have advised schools to establish shared and guided reading sessions before attempting to introduce independent reading groups. At first glance this seems surprising, since most primary school classrooms have been organized into small groups since the early 1970s. Teachers' anxieties would appear to confirm research which shows that, while children have been organized into groups, they have rarely been engaged in cooperative or collaborative group work (Bennett 1985; Mortimore *et al.*, 1988; Tizard *et al.*, 1988). Research also suggests that children have been accustomed to working within a particular teaching and learning culture, where they can call for, and expect to receive, the teacher's attention on demand. As Bennett and Dunne (1992: 125) suggest, 'A central feature of the typical primary classroom is the atmosphere of "busyness" which is accentuated because the bulk of the interactions between teachers and pupils are on an individual basis, and to attend to different children's needs the teacher must continually move rapidly around the classroom'.

Teachers have found themselves having to respond to multitudinous demands, not only because the children have expected it but also because the structure necessary for supporting group work and encouraging independent, cooperative interaction has been inadequate. The classroom of one experienced and particularly gifted primary teacher I worked with in the National Oracy Project had the 'busy, bustling' milieu. It looked exciting, imaginative and highly interactive. After viewing video recordings of her classroom practice, the teacher concluded that, although she thought she was engaging in quality interaction with the children, she was merely 'putting out forest fires'. We rationalized her approach by:

- focusing on specific curriculum subjects;
- dealing 'collectively' with issues in groups;
- structuring tasks carefully;
- matching the type of group to the nature and purpose of the task;
- establishing ground rules for group work.

The result was dramatic. The classroom retained its busyness, but we described it as 'buzz with a purpose'. However, the most significant development was the increase in time the teacher was able to spend with a group of children in 'quality interaction', where she could scaffold their learning appropriately and effectively. This was in 1989, nine years before the introduction of a literacy hour and the current concept of guided and independent groups. Similar experience is noted by Bennett and Dunne (1992), who describe teachers' astonishment at the decline of demands from children following the successful implementation of cooperative groups.

Making group work work

Although the organization of students into small groups may increase the potential for meaningful discourse, it does not mean they will automatically engage in productive collaborative discussion. Evidence from some studies indicates that students working in groups interact cooperatively for only a small percentage of the time (Galton *et al.*, 1980; Alexander, 1992). Other studies show how the same tasks can generate different student responses in terms of the quality of talk and collaboration that emerge (Crook, 1991; Jones and Mercer, 1993). Moreover, McMahon and Goatley (1995) found that without specific instructions from the teacher, student-led reading groups tend to use an asymmetrical discourse pattern more commonly associated with formal whole class teaching.

Evidence from longitudinal studies (Norman, 1992) and other empirical research (Hoyles *et al.*, 1990; Mercer, 1995) confirm the view that successful peer-group work depends on students having a shared understanding of the purpose of the task and a joint conception of what they are trying to achieve. However, some studies show how students' interpretations of the ground rules may differ in important ways from those of their peers and/or teachers (Rohrkemper, 1985; Mercer *et al.*, 1988). For example, while some students working in reading groups may see it as an opportunity to explore and interrogate texts collaboratively, others in the same group may see it as an opportunity to exhibit individual knowledge and demonstrate an ability to get the correct answers. There is evidence that when teachers bring ground rules for discussion into the open, it can lead to improved motivation and levels of performance among students (Prentice, 1991; Dawes *et al.*, 1992). However, a substantial body of research shows this practice to be uncommon and that students usually receive little help in understanding and appreciating the ground rules for group discussion (Mercer and Edwards, 1981; Hull, 1985; Phillips, 1992; Elbers and Kelderman, 1994). Moreover, some studies illustrate how students' traditional conceptions of school learning contexts can inhibit collaborative discussion (Edwards and Mercer, 1987; Barnes and Sheeran, 1992; McMahon and Meyers, 1993). Teachers in the National Oracy Project identified a number of key features of successful group work in reading and group discussion activities, where both process (the interaction) and product (the cognitive outcome) are important.

Features of successful group work are:

- use of hypothetical, explorative language;
- individual initiatives being accepted and developed by the group;
- participation of all group members;
- discussion developed through discourse rather than dispute, that is: through challenge, evaluation, reasoning and justification (based on evidence from texts) rather than through intuitive, unqualified personal feelings;
- absence of excessive diversion from the task (either external interference or internal disruptive behaviour);
- avoidance of premature and unsatisfactory consensus.

Teachers found that for these features to be encouraged, it was useful to consider a number of issues before, during and after the task. Before the task, the activity must be:

- well-planned and structured;
- carefully organized;

- thoroughly resourced;
- appropriate for the learning objective.

During the task, the teacher should:

- introduce the activity and establish a collaborative working climate;
- clarify expected outcomes (working process and end product);
- ensure children have a clear understanding of the ground rules for group work;
- ensure children have a clear understanding of respective roles and interdependency;
- intervene appropriately and effectively.

After the task, there should be:

- an evaluation of learning (group process and individual learning);
- reflection, reinforcement and consolidation of learning;
- an identification of key aspects for further development or investigation;
- a method of rewarding all participants.

Planning and structuring group work

Research has shown that collaborative interaction won't happen simply by seating children together and instructing them to work as a group. Children need to understand why they are being asked to work as a group and to see the relevance and usefulness of what they are doing. They also need to appreciate what it means to work in a group: to recognize individual and collective responsibilities. Getting children to discuss the benefits of collaborative learning and to negotiate the ground rules is an essential prerequisite to successful group work. Similarly, for group work to be successful it needs to be carefully matched to its intended purpose, and organized accordingly. Moreover, it should be remembered that pair or group work is only a suitable form of classroom organization if the task requires a cooperative response and the children's learning is likely to be enhanced by working collaboratively. The kind of group should be determined by the nature of the task and the purpose of the activity.

One particular primary school I worked with in the National Oracy Project developed a whole school approach to group work. The staff found they needed to:

- get children to value group work and establish ground rules;
- identify appropriate tasks for group work;
- recognize the social and cognitive demands of group tasks;
- organize different kinds of groups for different tasks and purposes;
- develop pair and group work techniques;
- develop children's metadiscoursal skills.

Successful group interaction depends on the cooperation of the children and their willingness to make it work. Children, like adults, are more likely to cooperate if they know why they are doing something and appreciate the benefits of what they are doing. The best way to do this is:

- To provide children with a task where they have to work cooperatively, pool knowledge and skills, and share information.

- Following the task, ask the children to talk about how it felt to work as a team. What benefits did they get? How was it more enjoyable than having to work alone?

Establishing the ground rules for group work

After conducting extensive research in primary schools, Kagan (1985) concludes that successful group work requires a degree of tolerance, mutual understanding and an ability to articulate a point of view. In collaborative work, children are expected to discuss, reason, probe and question. Such skills, argues Kagan, are not innate but have to be taught. Children need to understand the rules and expectations associated with this mode of working. The ground rules for group work need to be made explicit. The best way to achieve this is to engage the children in an activity which focuses their attention on the process of group interaction and encourages them to draw out their own list of rules. For example, explain to the children that they are going to design a 'rules for group work poster'. Organize the class into groups and get each group to:

- individually write a list of rules for when they are working in a group;
- share and discuss the individual lists;
- identify any common rules;
- draw up a group list of main rules;
- collect the group lists and from these, draw up a class list of common rules for group work;
- discuss the list with the class, suggesting modifications and additions;
- agree on a final set of rules.

The teacher should:

- display the rules where everyone can see them;
- ensure that everyone abides by the rules;
- ensure that the rules are enforced.

Primary age children will often identify the following rules:

- don't shout;
- don't all talk at the same time;
- listen to each other;
- give everyone a chance to say something;
- help each other out;
- share ideas;
- take people's ideas seriously;
- don't make anyone feel silly;
- everyone should join in.

It is important for children to develop their understanding of both negative and positive elements and to see what is and what is not useful. One useful strategy to use when introducing group work is to place a cassette recorder on the table and ask the children to switch it on when they begin a discussion and switch it off when they have finished. Replay the recording and ask the children to discuss what they hear. They will often identify for themselves many of the issues the teacher would want to address. Children I have worked with have said things like:

- there's too much noise;
- everyone's shouting;
- everyone's talking at once;
- you won't let anyone else say anything;
- you don't listen to other people;
- you don't say anything;
- we're not discussing, we're just arguing;
- we're supposed to listen to everyone's point of view.

Roles in groups

Having an explicit set of rules helps children to self-regulate. It can also ensure that all group members participate. Teachers in the National Oracy Project found that primary children rarely opt out of well-organized group activities (a feature also noted by Bennett and Dunne, 1992), However, the American researchers Salomon and Globerson (1989) showed that some children can devise work avoidance strategies, and they identify what they call 'free riders', 'suckers' and 'gangers'. Free riding occurs when children opt out of work and allow others to complete a task. Low ability children may do this if the task is challenging and other members of the group are clearly more able. The low ability child can become marginalized and have no apparent use. High ability children may also free ride if they feel the task is too easy or is moving too slowly for them. The sucker effect can occur when children, who are usually motivated and enthusiastic, are allowed by others to do most of the work. They then feel they are being exploited and do not contribute effectively. Gangers are those children who may collectively reject a task and simply go through the motions of working. The ORACLE study (Galton *et al.*, 1980) identified 'attention seekers', who tend to move around the classroom and interrupt other children, thus eliciting the teacher's attention. At the other extreme are 'hard grinders' (Galton and Willcocks 1983) or what Pollard (1985) describes as 'goodies'. These are children who conform to teacher's expectations and remain on task for extended periods of time. However, children who are 'eager participants' (Galton *et al.*, 1999), keen to engage in whole class question and answer sessions, may be 'solitary workers' and prefer to work individually, rather than as collaborative group members. 'Intermittent workers' are perhaps the most difficult to spot because they tend to work when they feel they are being observed by the teacher but move off task whenever an opportunity arises.

In some activities, assigning key roles to children can be counter-productive and may inhibit the natural flow of ideas. However, in other tasks, cooperation can be facilitated by children having clear roles to play within an overall structure. This issue is discussed in some detail by Bennett and Dunne (1992: 147), who suggest the following key roles in a group of four:

- *Coordinator*: to keep the group on task, to ensure contributions from all, to guide discussion or activity.
- *Data gatherer*: to take notes or summarize ideas, to clarify ideas and to read aloud from some materials when appropriate.
- *Secretary*: to record group answers or materials, to act as spokesperson when reporting to the class.
- *Evaluator*: to keep notes on the group process (how well individuals in the group are working together), to lead any evaluation at the end of the session.

Stages in group discussion

From her work in the ORACLE study Tann (1981) identified three key stages in the discussion process:

- *The orientation stage*: involves children in defining problems, interpreting the task and setting limits on the activity.
- *The development stage*: involves children in generating ideas and using reasoning strategies.
- *The concluding stage*: is marked by increasing acceptance of each other's ideas and more progressive focusing on the specific strategies necessary for a successful resolution of the problem.

Robertson (1990: 195–6), reporting on the CLIP, suggests that children need time to develop group work skills and that they go through several 'naturally occurring' stages before operating at their most productive level. She discusses five stages of development:

- *The orientation stage*: where group members find out about one another and their place in the group.
- *The norm establishment stage*: where members develop shared expectations of behaviour and learn to organize themselves into an effective team.
- *The conflict stage*: where group members test one another and the teacher. This conflict is not necessarily a signal that something is going wrong and that groups should be changed. It is often a signal that groups are on track, moving towards productivity. Conflict will naturally happen and is an opportunity to learn problem solving and interpersonal skills.
- *The productivity stage*: which is generally the longest stage in the life of a group where group members focus both on the task and interpersonal relations.
- *The termination stage*: where group members look back at their experience together and deal with the problems of parting. They look toward experiences with a new group and consider what they have learned that they can take with them.

It should be noted that Tann's (1981) work was conducted under controlled conditions and recorded through systematic observation, and that Robertson's (1990) work took place in the USA and was concerned with cooperative learning in maths. My own observations of children working on English tasks in naturalistic classroom settings indicate that the interactive process is not quite so predictable or sequential. Successful group work in most literary activities is characterized by talk which is tentative and explorative. Interaction is dynamic and unpredictable, as children appear to go off at a tangent, leap ahead or backtrack. Discourse is characterized by the false starts, hesitations, rephrasing and changes of direction noted by Barnes (1976: 28). The group process is also, to an extent, determined by the nature of the task and the particular learning context created by the teacher and the task structure.

Group tasks

Mercer (1992: 221) argues that 'the education value of any classroom talk between children, with or without a teacher present, may hinge on how well a teacher has set up the activities and environment for generating and supporting suitable kinds of talk'. Lyle (1993: 195) points to the importance of teachers encouraging children to see themselves as responsible learners by designing activities which 'ensure children pose questions, make observations, contribute opinions'. However, this is no simple matter. Bossert *et al.* (1984) show that certain kinds of task organization are likely to create particular learning contexts, which will in turn influence the way that children interact. Barnes (1976) suggests that learning through discussion needs to be planned and carefully resourced by the teacher in order to provide the appropriate context for discussion. Teachers should organize and introduce tasks according to the intended purpose. Too little structure for some kinds of task may result in chaos and pupil anxiety; too much structure for investigative tasks may inhibit discussion. Barnes and Todd (1977: 84) refer to tasks which are *loose* or *tight* and show how this affects patterns of interaction. Their distinction reflects the difference between activities where the teacher has one particular solution in mind and those where alternative solutions are acceptable. They cite one particular group of girls who, despite assurances to the contrary, determined that a task was tightly directed, and as a consequence displayed anxiety and a frantic search for the one correct answer. Barnes (1992) explains that tasks requiring 'exploratory talk' do not require pupils to learn new information but to manipulate what they already know, and explore possibilities.

Cowie and Ruddock (1988) (cited in Bennett and Dunne, 1992: 71) differentiate between:

- *Discussion tasks*: where there is an onus on process and the sharing of ideas. The subject matter is likely to be interpretative or controversial – for example, a poem, narrative text, magazine article or newspaper report. The outcome may be a group decision or consensus, or the development of individual interactive skills and cognitive understanding.
- *Problem solving tasks*: where a number of alternatives may be critically evaluated, for example a sequencing, prediction or deletion activity. The outcome may require a group consensus or individual decisions that are reached after group discussion.
- *Production tasks*: where children work collaboratively to produce a group response – for example, the dramatization of a text, or the adaptation of a text for a film. A jigsaw activity, where children work on different aspects of a topic to achieve a group goal (such as writing an information book about ancient Egypt), is an example of a production task.

Bennett and Dunne (1992: 190) suggest that group work is particularly valuable for problem solving tasks, but show that the kind of abstract talk which is a feature of English tasks 'is more difficult for children to generate and is less fluent than talk relating to action'. Doyle (1983) and Galton (1989) also argue that ambiguous tasks are more challenging and much more likely to produce anxiety and uncertainty. Cohen (1994) suggests that exploratory tasks, which require higher-order thinking skills, depend more for their success on the quality of interaction than do routine information gathering or practical tasks. In planning work, the nature and ambiguity of tasks and the degree of children's personal sense of freedom and ownership needs to be considered. Table 5 exemplifies tasks that may fit within a loose–tight continuum.

A further distinction between tasks is made by Deci and Ryan (1985), who differentiate between those which are inherently interesting to children and those which may be less interesting but necessary for learning and development. This is an important point because the degree of inherent interest can impact on children's

Table 5 Organization of tasks

Loose	Intermediate	Tight
Discussing a controversial issue such as fox hunting.	Discussing a poem, chapter or short story and evaluating its literary quality.	Reading aloud accurately and with expression.
Free choice reading.	Reading and evaluating a variety of story openings.	Reading, discussing and answering literal-level comprehension questions.
Writing in a personal journal.	Writing in a particular genre or poetry form.	Reading and understanding key aspects of a non-fiction text and writing a summary.

motivation and behaviour. Teachers need to be aware of potential differences in the level of children's intrinsic interest and motivation and to plan accordingly, thinking about such things as introduction, timing, pace, groupings, activities and teacher intervention. For successful group learning to occur, teachers need to consider the relationship between the social, communicative and cognitive aspects of talking and learning and to structure tasks carefully in terms of social interdependence and cognitive demand.

Social and cognitive demands of group work

Group work places considerable social as well as cognitive demands on children. In discussing an issue or solving a problem they develop their understanding within a social context. Table 6 shows how children talk to explore, hypothesize and evaluate while simultaneously maintaining and developing the social framework.

Group discussion can deteriorate into what Mercer (1994) calls disputational talk, where group members simply argue their own viewpoint and don't consider those of others. To be of value, some kinds of group discussion need to be informed, where children bring to the task essential background experience and knowledge. This must be planned for and provided by the teacher in order to establish a productive context for talk. I once recorded a group of Year 6 children discussing the sale of the Mappa Mundi (it caused something of a storm when this famous medieval map of the world was put on sale some years ago). The children made an admirable attempt to discuss whether, as a 'board', they should sell or retain the map but after a short while a long silence ensued. It was suddenly ended by the comment, 'Oh let's flog the bastard!' Similarly a Year 3 class I was working with was engaged in an environmental topic using texts such as *The Iron Man* by Ted Hughes (1968) and *Dinosaurs and All that Rubbish* by Michael Foreman (1972). The teacher and I decided to jigsaw an activity and to place the children in different roles so they would argue a case from various perspectives: for example, a farmer, a local resident, an environmentalist, a local councillor. The task was a failure because we had expected the children to role play without knowing enough about the roles. We decided to try again but this time spent some time developing the children's knowledge and understanding of what it means to be an environmentalist who wants to protect land, or a farmer who wants to sell it. The activity was a huge success.

Table 6 Analysis of group discourse: social and cognitive functions

Social	Utterance	Cognitive
Initiating	'What if say he's poaching and that's why he's out late and he's moving dead careful?'	Setting up hypothesis
Supporting and extending	'You might be right, yeah 'cos he he's got dogs hasn't he Jas?'	Evaluating and constructing a question
Contradicting	'No he hasn't . . . he hasn't got a gun . . . it doesn't say does it . . . anyway 'cos he's got dogs doesn't mean he's a poacher does it?'	Raising new questions and putting an alternative view
Relating to personal experience	'I went with me Uncle Ted once after rabbits and he didn't have dogs or a gun.'	Qualifying/reasoning
Eliciting	'Where does it say . . . it doesn't say anywhere . . . look it only says he moved stealthily.'	Using and advancing evidence from the text
Supporting	'No but like his wax jacket and leggings he's got on . . .'	Providing descriptive details from the text

In designing tasks, teachers need to consider the cognitive demands and social skills required to undertake activities cooperatively. Devising activities that are appropriate for cooperative rather than individual outcomes is a challenge. However, once the learning purpose is determined, and it is clear that group work is appropriate,the necessary organization becomes clearer. Biot (1984) suggests that it is most appropriate to begin cooperative group work with simple, tight production tasks, where children are clear about the procedure and the expected outcome, before moving on to introduce collaborative problem solving activities with looser, more abstract discussion. Lyle (1993) found that structured activities with well-defined rules helped to keep pupils on task for extended periods of time. Certainly my own experience of working with teachers and children in the National Oracy Project would confirm the effectiveness of the two-stage approach advocated by Galton and Williamson (1992), where task and context demands are increased gradually as children develop their skills and confidence. Points to consider might be:

- What are the social and cognitive demands of the task?
- Is the task suitable for cooperative/collaborative working?
- What kind of group is most suitable for the task?
- How will the task be introduced and children's curiosity and enthusiasm aroused?
- Are the resources and materials suitable and sufficient?
- What is the teacher's role during the task?
- Are the children clear about the task in terms of process (how they are to work) and product (what they are expected to produce)?
- What response/feedback/reward will be given on completion of the task?

Kinds of group

There are numerous kinds of group to serve different purposes. One way to ensure that successful interaction occurs is to make the group match the purpose. Galton and Williamson (1992) identify a variety of groups, as shown in Table 7.

Bennett and Cass (1988) and Bennett and Dunne (1992) found task-related talk to be highest in cooperative groups. The following types of group were used by teachers in the National Oracy Project:

- Friendship
- Mutual interest
- Mixed interest
- Targeted (jigsaw/rainbow)
- Mixed attainers
- Selected attainers
- Single gender
- Mixed gender

In the UK, Bennett and Cass (1988) studied the effects of group work on high, average and low attaining pupils and found that high attainers performed well, irrespective of the kind of group they were in. However, low attaining groups fared badly, confirming other research which suggests that low attainers seem to lack the necessary skills to interact and learn effectively in groups. Homogeneous grouping according to achievement is a feature of the NLSF that has drawn criticism from primary teachers, used to operating with heterogeneous groups. Such resistance is based largely on the suggestion that teachers who group children according to attainment create unequal social structures within their classrooms. Cairney and Langbien (1989) state that low achieving groups are *interrupted* far more frequently by teachers than are high achievers. The perception of teachers interacting with children and intervening in their learning as *interruption* is an unfortunate legacy of Piagetian

Table 7 Classification of group type, task and outcome

Type	Task demand	Intended outcome	Example
Seated group	Each pupil has a separate task	Different outcomes: each pupil completes a different assignment	Writing stories on themes chosen by the pupils
Working group	Each pupil has the same task	Same outcome: each pupil completes the same assignment independently	Mathematics worksheet
Cooperative group	Each pupil has a separate but related task	Joint outcome: each pupil has a different assignment	Making a map
Collaborative group	Each pupil has the same task	Joint outcome: all pupils share same assignment	Problem solving, e.g. discussing a social or moral issue

Source: Galton and Williamson (1992: 10)

thinking. The reason for grouping children according to their attainment and educational needs is so that learning objectives, resources and teacher input can be matched appropriately in order to meet those needs most effectively. It seems positively bizarre to recognize that children have different needs but not to differentiate in terms of teacher support. What teacher, with a class of beginning, intermediate and advanced swimmers, would not allocate them to different parts of the pool and provide differentiated activities and support? What is important is for groups to be organized flexibly and according to children's needs, rather than rigidly and as an organizational expediency.

Gender differences

> They [pupils] should be taught to listen to others, questioning them to clarify what they mean, and extending and following up the ideas. They should be encouraged to qualify or justify what they think after listening to other opinions or accounts, and deal politely with opposing points of view.
>
> (DfEE, 1995a: AT1)

The National Oracy Project found gender differences between the discourse patterns of boys and girls, confirming the findings of other research (Galton *et al.*, 1980; Swann, 1992). Norman (1990: 22) claims that 'boys tend to talk more, interrupt more and be more aggressive while girls defer to others' ideas and are more tentative'. It was found that boys often speak in a challenging, confronting way and girls in a comforting reassuring way, indicating that girls tend to criticize others in more socially acceptable ways. Tann (1981) found that girls tended to be more consensus-seeking than boys and would refrain from challenging or critically evaluating each other's views. Phillips (1988) showed that while boys frequently deviated from a task, girls tended to remain on task and, in mixed gender groups, were often the ones to adopt a steering, focusing role. Moreover, Holden (1993) found that girls used a far higher proportion of abstract language when engaged in English tasks than did boys.

Gender differences are particularly noticeable when children work in pairs around a computer. Boys will tend to dominate an activity and assume control of the 'technology'. Video recording of children in National Oracy Project schools illustrated that, during computer-based activities, even where boys were contributing little to a discussion, they invariably took up a central seating position and retained ownership of the keyboard. Baddeley (1991) points to the danger of over-generalization with regards to gender issues and asserts that some boys will be quiet and unassertive and some girls will confidently hold their own. Nevertheless, the general decrease in quantity and depression of quality of girl's talk in mixed gender groups is a matter of concern.

Computers and group work

There is some evidence to suggest that computers can promote discussion and encourage collaborative learning (King 1989; Mercer and Fisher, 1992; Fisher, 1993; Hill and Browne, 1994). However, such evidence is not conclusive. Although computers may have the potential for offering collaborative learning contexts, merely providing computers and software in classrooms will not automatically enhance the quality of children's interaction. While computers can generate a high level of on task talk, much of this talk reflects *procedural* ways of thinking. For example, Kumulainen (1994: 51) found that 'the Imaginative, Hypothetical, Experiential and

Heuristic functions hardly occurred in children's language interactions at the word processor'. Fisher (1993) found that rather than redrafting significant features of their work, children focused mainly on editorial features of spelling and punctuation, while Mercer (1994: 29) suggests that 'discrete, serial, closed problem-solving tasks generate very little extended continuous discussion of any kind'. Computers, therefore, far from encouraging exploratory talk, can produce a didactic, instructional learning context, where children are offered a very limited set of feedback responses.

The Spoken Language and New Technology (SLANT) Project examined how primary children use talk when they are seated around computers. A major conclusion was that the success or failure of computer-based talk depends more on the quality of teacher–pupil interaction than on the nature of the software or on child–computer interaction. Mercer and Fisher (1992: 354) claim that although the quality of computer software is important, it is the joint activity of teachers and pupils that will determine the quality of the learning.

They suggest that:

> the main defining influence on the structure and outcomes of a computer-based activity will be that of the teacher, through any initial 'setting up' of the activity, through the nature of the interventions he or she makes during the activity, and through the ways (before and after the time spent at the screen) that pupils are enabled to relate the activity to other educational experiences.

For computers to generate interactive discourse, teachers need to:

- choose software carefully to ensure that high quality feedback is offered to children;
- establish learning contexts which encourage exploration and collaboration;
- provide a seating arrangement that is likely to aid collaborative talk;
- ensure that children understand the ground rules for group work;
- develop discursive strategies so that children are able to hypothesize, reason and justify;
- make explicit the purpose and collaborative nature of the activity;
- intervene effectively once activities are under way.

The Talk, Reasoning and Computers (TRAC) Project (Wegerif and Mercer, 1996) has confirmed that children who understand and can implement ground rules for collaborative discussion can use spoken language more effectively as a learning tool. My own experience confirms the view that the learning potential of computers for collaborative work is significantly diminished if children are unable to implement essential ground rules for cooperative learning. Computer activities do have the potential to generate talk, but work around a computer amplifies the need for children to possess group work strategies and metadiscoursal skills. [. . .]

Developing metadiscoursal skills

General rules for group work need to be supplemented by developing children's awareness of the roles they can play in discussion and the features of talk which are helpful and productive or unhelpful and unproductive. An essential element of successful group work therefore is the development of children's metadiscoursal awareness: that is, their understanding of group interaction and their ability to monitor, control and reflect on their own use of language. Unfortunately, ground rules often remain implicit, possibly as a result of primary teachers' unwillingness to 'impose' on the children's understanding of the world. However, as Edwards and Mercer (1987: 59) argue, 'there is no reason why children's acquisition of the modes of discourse and thought required by education should entail their loss of other, "real world" perspectives'. Hardman and Beverton (1993: 147) argue for the development of a metalanguage, which they say will enable children to 'reflect upon and evaluate their own discussions and increase their understanding of what the characteristic features of talk are and how they contribute to discussion'. According to Bruner (1986) it is this process of objectifying in language what we have thought, and then turning around on it and reconsidering it, that allows us to develop our understanding.

As a National Oracy Project coordinator, I worked with a teacher and her class of 39 Year 3 children in a city primary school. The class could euphemistically be described as 'challenging' and the teacher was concerned that the children might not possess the necessary social skills to enable them to engage in effective discourse. We embarked on a consciousness raising exercise to develop the children's understanding and appreciation of group work. They had tape-recorded themselves during discussions and critically evaluated the results. With the help of the teacher, the children had then drawn up their own set of ground rules. The following extract is a two-minute snapshot taken from a total discussion which lasted for 18 minutes before the teacher intervened, and continued for a further 16 minutes following her intervention. The children have been looking at various interpretations of *The Three Little Pigs* story. The class has been organized into small groups and each group has been given the task of discussing and designing a house to be built in a particular material. The material this group has to work with is straw. [. . .]

1	*Kerry:*	The door's here like this . . . the straw's got to go round the window.
2	*Leslie:*	The straw's got to go round it hasn't it 'cos it isn't a square door.
3	*Carl:*	Yeah . . . no . . . but . . . [all the children start to talk at once].
4	*Martin:*	Just wait a minute and listen to Carl's advice.
5	*Carl:*	Well . . . the door'll have to be that high and then the window'll have to come about there [indicates on the drawing].
6	*Katy:*	I haven't had a speak yet.
7	*Martin:*	Right . . . Kate . . . see what you can say.
8	*Katy:*	Well do you want me to tell you what you can do for the knob . . . just curl some of the straw around tight and put it in . . . make a space . . . [all the children start to talk at once].
9	*Martin:*	Come on . . . let's listen to Kerry.
10	*Kerry:*	Could've been a bit of wool there rolled up.
11	*Leslie:*	Or we could have a piece of cotton wool.
12	*Sarah:*	Cotton wool . . . cotton wool's better.

[The discussion continues until the children's attention is focused on the roof.]

13	*Sarah:*	What we could do round there is get a piece of straw and make it stronger . . . right?
14	*Leslie:*	Show us.
15	*Martin:*	Straw . . . you mean tons of straw just bungled together?
16	*Sarah:*	No . . . I mean like a piece of strong straw that isn't bent and we can tie it round with the straw on the roof.
17	*Kerry:*	Like that [demonstrates with a piece of straw]?
18	*Leslie:*	Yeah . . . I've got a book . . . she's right . . . she's right . . . it is like that.
19	*Kerry:*	It's not very good for tying round is it?
20	*Sarah:*	Yeah but you could get a long piece of paper and colour it an orange brown and tie it round.

[The teacher now joins the group.]

21	*Teacher*:	How are you doing?
22	*Martin*:	We're still thinking about the door handle.
23	*Leslie*:	Because we don't know if it's card or wood.
24	*Sarah*:	We could have a bit of tissue paper or straw.
25	*Teacher*:	What do you think about a wooden door?
26	*Leslie*:	Oh yeah, a wooden door.
27	*Carl*:	A wooden door . . . how'd we do that?
28	*Teacher*:	Do you want to have a look in the books we took the story from?
29	*All*:	Yeah.
30	*Teacher*:	Sit where you are and I'll bring them to you.

Martin is obviously playing a leading role in the discussion. When the teacher and I first viewed the video recording, our initial thoughts were that Martin was dominating the discussion. However, after we had analysed the entire transcript, it became clear that he was actually preventing another group member (Leslie) from doing just that. Most of Martin's gatekeeping utterances are not to hold the floor for himself, but to let others in. Without his intervention it is likely that some group members, such as Carl and Kerry, would have been marginalized if not excluded. The maturity of Martin's interjections is impressive: for example he brings the group to order and offers the floor to Carl (4). He brings in Kate (7) and Kerry (9) and invites Sarah to expand on her idea (15). The teacher's intervention is also interesting. She recognizes the children have reached a point in the discussion where they need some guidance. She identifies the problem, ascertains their need, and with the minimum of fuss, equips them with the necessary resources to continue unaided for a further extended period.

It is worth reiterating that this group of Year 3 children were part of a class of 39 pupils in a city school. The class included one statemented child and a number with special educational needs. Small group interaction in this classroom is successful because the teacher:

- negotiates with her class the ground rules for group work;
- develops children's metadiscoursal skills and awareness;
- presents the group with appropriate tasks which require collaboration;
- is aware of group dynamics in formulating groups;
- makes the purpose of tasks explicit to the children;
- provides adequate resources;
- intervenes appropriately and effectively.

Small group work within a constructivist framework for learning

Building upon the work of others (Reid *et al.*, 1982; Scott *et al.*, 1987), the National Oracy Project adopted a useful theoretical framework in which individual, pair, group and whole class work all had a part to play:

- *Engagement or orientation*: arousing interest and establishing the topic, issue or problem to be investigated. Teacher and children establish existing knowledge and understandings. New information and stimulus is provided.
- *Exploration or elicitation*: relating existing knowledge and understanding to new information and stimulus. Clarifying existing beliefs, feelings and understandings.

- *Transformation or restructuring*: engaging in activity in which the learners extend their knowledge and understanding. Investigating, exploring and evaluating ideas.
- *Presentation and review*: Offering new knowledge and understanding to a critical audience. Reviewing and evaluating the learning experience.
- *Reflection and application*: Thinking and talking about what has been learned and considering how previous understanding has changed. Considering ways in which new understanding will impact on future learning.

Table 8 Example of learning stages in developing knowledge about the language of advertising

Learning stage	Explanation	Example
Engagement or orientation	Pupils encounter new information or material. This could be through teacher talk, reading, listening to radio or watching TV extracts, examination of texts from a variety of sources, a field trip or a visiting speaker.	Teacher introduces the idea of examining radio advertisements. Pupils record examples of radio advertisements on tape in order to investigate and evaluate the persuasive language used.
Exploration or elicitation	This involves giving pupils time and a structure to enable them to make sense of the information for themselves. Small group discussion is vital at this stage.	In groups pupils listen to their recorded advertisements. They discuss and evaluate the language used. Pupils choose one example to play to the other groups giving reasons for their choice.
Transformation or restructuring	Pupils are required to focus their thinking, sort out their ideas, make decisions and use their knowledge.	In the same groups, and bearing in mind the radio advertisements they have heard, pupils decide on an imaginary item to sell, its uses and sales points. Pupils produce a radio advertisement for their product.
Presentation and review	This is the stage when ideas are presented to an interested audience. It could be a presentation to the whole class or it could be pairs, pairs–groups, groups etc.	Each group plays its advertisement to other groups and answers questions from peers about the product and the way they chose to advertise it.
Reflection and application	This is a time for considering what groups have been doing, how the work went and the final outcome. Decisions may be made about follow-up work.	The teacher discusses with each group how they collaborated, the nature of their advertisement and how each person contributed to it. The teacher also explores with the group reasons for language choice and register.

It was recognized that at each stage the children may be working individually, in pairs, in small groups or as a whole class. The stage of engagement refers to the initial focusing of attention on a particular topic, issue or problem. During the exploration stage the children will be having their attention focused on the subject to be studied. They may be sharing a common experience which could involve listening to the teacher, watching a video, or going on a visit. At the transformation stage, children may be organized in several ways depending on the nature of the task. The teacher's main purpose should be to provide an opportunity for children to use the ideas and concepts that have been explored and to share their understanding of these in some way, perhaps through a jigsaw activity. It is at the exploration and transformation stages that the kind of investigative, hypothetical language, so crucial to the construction of meaning, is most prominent. The presentation stage offers children a chance to gain feedback through constructive criticism and evaluation. This can occur on a one-to-one basis between children, between teacher and child, within a whole class scenario, or through the envoy system. During the reflection stage, children need to be given space and time to consider their own learning and to identify areas for clarification and development. Table 8 shows pupils going through the different stages as they investigate the language of advertisements.

This learning framework proved to be of immense value when members of the National Oracy Project were attempting to analyse audio and video recordings of small group interactions and teacher intervention. Initially the general focus of attention was on the nature of activities and children's interaction, either without the teacher's presence or with minimal teacher intervention. However, it became increasingly clear that the teacher has a crucial and central part to play in scaffolding children's learning. As children's needs are diverse and dependent on their stage in the learning process, appropriate teaching roles will vary, with different roles being 'more' or 'less' appropriate at any particular time. Failure to recognize this repertoire of roles and to intervene, as and when necessary, limits teachers' effectiveness as enablers of children's learning. [. . .]

References

Alexander, R. (1992) *Policy and Practice in Primary Education*. London: Routledge.

Alexander, R., Rose, J. and Woodhead, C. (1992) *Curriculum Organisation and Classroom Practice in Primary Schools: A Discussion Paper*. London: DfEE.

Baddeley, G. (1991) *Teaching, Talking and Learning in Key Stage 2*. Sheffield: NATE/NCC Publications.

Barnes, D. (1976) *From Communication to Curriculum*. Harmondsworth: Penguin.

Barnes, D. (1992) The role of talk in learning, in K. Norman (ed.) *Thinking Voices: The Work of the National Oracy Project*, London: Hodder and Stoughton.

Barnes, D. and Sheeran, Y. (1992) Oracy and genre, in K. Norman (ed.) *Thinking Voices: The Work of the National Oracy Project*. London: Hodder and Stoughton.

Barnes, D. and Todd, F. (1977) *Communicating and Learning in Small Groups*. London: Routledge & Kegan Paul.

Bennett, N. (1985) Interaction and achievement in classroom groups, in N. Bennett and C. Deforges (eds) *Recent Advances in Classroom Research (British Journal of Education Psychology* monograph series, no.2).

Bennett, N. and Blundell, D. (1983) Quantity and quality of work in rows and classroom groups. *Educational Psychology*, 3(2): 93–105.

Bennett, N. and Cass, A, (1988) The effects of group composition on group interactive processes and pupil understanding. *British Educational Research Journal*, 15: 19–32.

Bennett, N. and Dunne, E. (1992) *Managing Classroom Groups*. Cheltenham: Stanley Thornes.

Biot, C. (1984) *Getting on Without the Teacher* Sunderland: Centre for Educational Research and Development, Sunderland Polytechnic.

Bossert, S., Barnett, B. and Filby, N. (1984) Grouping and instructional organisation, in P. Peterson, L. Wilkinson and M. Hallinan (eds) *The Social Context of Instruction* Orlando, FL: Academic Press.

Bruner, J. (1986) *Actual Minds, Possible Worlds.* Cambridge, MA: Harvard University Press.

Cairney, T. and Langbien, S. (1989) Building communities of readers and writers. *The Reading Teacher,* April: 560–7.

Cohen, E. (1994) Restructuring classrooms: conditions for productive small groups. *Review of Educational Research,* 64: 1–35.

Cowie, H. and Ruddock, J. (1988) *Cooperative Group Work: An Overview.* London: B.P. Educational Service.

Crook, C. (1991) Computers in the zone of proximal development: implications for evaluation. *Computers in Education,* 17(1): 81–91.

Dawes, L., Fisher, E. and Mercer, N. (1992) The quality of talk at the computer. *Language and Learning,* October: 22–5.

Deci, E. and Ryan, R. (1985) *Intrinsic Motivation and Self Determination in Human Behaviour.* New York: Plenum.

DES (Department of Education and Science) (1975) A *Language for Life* (the Bullock Report). London: HMSO.

Des Fountain, J. and Howe, A (1992) Pupils working together on understanding, in K. Norman (ed.) *Thinking Voices: The Work of the National Oracy Project.* London: Hodder & Stoughton.

DfEE (Department for Education and Employment) (1995a) *English in the National Curriculum.* London: HMSO.

Doyle, W. (1983) Academic work. *Review of Educational Research,* 53(2): 159–99.

Dyson, A. (1987) The value of time off task: young children's spontaneous talk and deliberate text. *Harvard Educational Review,* 57(4): 396–420.

Edwards, D. and Mercer, N. (1987) *Common knowledge: The Development of Understanding in the Classroom.* London: Methuen.

Elbers, E. and Kelderman, A. (1994) Ground rules for testing: expectations and misunderstandings in test situations. *European Journal of Psychology of Education,* 9(1): 111–20.

Fisher, E. (1993) Characteristics of children's talk at the computer and it relationship to the computer software. *Language and Education,* 7(2): 97–114.

Galton, M. (1989) *Teaching in the Primary School.* London: David Fulton.

Galton, M. and Willcocks, J. (eds) (1983) *Moving from the Primary Classroom.* London: Routledge & Kegan Paul.

Galton, M and Williamson, J. (1992) *Group Work in the Primary Classroom,* London: Routledge.

Galton, M., Simon, B. and Croll, P. (1980) *Inside the Primary Classroom.* London: Routledge.

Galton, M., Hargreaves, L., Comber, C., Wall, D. and Pell, A. (1999) *Inside The Primary Classroom 20 Years On.* London: Routledge.

Hardman, F. and Beverton, S. (1993) Co-operative group work and the development of metadiscoursal skills. *Support for Learning,* 8(4): 146–50.

Hastings, N. (1990) Questions of motivation. *Support for Learning,* 7: 135–7.

Hertz-Lazarowitz, R. (1990) An integrative model of the classroom: the enhancement of cooperative learning, in R. Lazarowitz and N. Miller (eds) *Interaction in Cooperative Groups: Theoretical Anatomy of Group Learning.* London: Cambridge University Press.

HMI (Her Majesty's Inspectorate of Schools) (1978) *Primary Education in England.* London: HMSO.

Holden, C. (1993) Giving girls a chance: patterns of talk in co-operative group work. *Gender and Education,* 5(2): 179–89.

Hoyles, C., Sutherland, R. and Healey, I. (1990) Children talking in computer environments: new insights on the role of discussion in mathematics learning, in K. Durkin and B. Shine (eds) *Language and Mathematics Education.* Buckingham: Open University Press.

Hull, R. (1985) *The Language Gap*. London: Methuen.

Johnson, D. and Johnson, R. (1990) What is cooperative learning? In M. Brubacher, R. Payne and K. Rickett (eds) *Perspectives on Small Group learning: Theory and Practice*. Ontario: Rubicon.

Jones, A. and Mercer, N. (1993) Theories of learning and information technology, in P. Scrimshaw (ed.) *Language, Classrooms and Computers*. London: Routledge.

Kagan, S. (1985) Dimensions of cooperative classroom structures, in R. Hertz Lazarowitz, S. Kagan, S. Sharan, R. Slavin, C. Webb (eds) *Learning to Cooperate, Cooperating to Learn*. Netherlands: Kluwer Academic/Plenum.

King, A. (1989) Verbal interaction and problem-solving within computer-assisted cooperative learning groups. *Journal of Educational Computing Research*, 5(1): 1–15.

Lyle, S. (1993) an investigation into ways in which children talk themselves into menaing. *Language and Education*, 7(3): 181–97.

McMahon, S.L. and Goatley, V.J. (1995) Fifth graders helping peers discuss texts in student led groups. *The Journal of Educational Research*, 89(1): 23–34.

McMahon, S.L. and Meyers, J.L. (1993) *What's Happening Here? A Comparison of Two Literature Discussion Groups*. Paper presented at the National Reading Conference, Charleston, SC.

Mercer, N (1991) Computers and communication in the classroom, Unit 7, EH232. *Computers and Learning*. Milton Keynes: The Open University.

Mercer, N. (1992) Culture, context and the construction of knowledge, in P. Light and G. Butterworth (eds) *Context and Cognition*. London: Harvester Wheatsheaf.

Mercer, N. (1994) The quality of talk in joint activity at the computer. *Journal of Computer Assisted Learning*.10: 24–32.

Mercer, N. (1995) *The Guided Construction of Knowledge: Talk Amongst Teachers and Learners*. Clevedon, OH: Multilingual Matters.

Mercer, N. and Edwards, D. (1981) Ground rules for mutual understanding: a sociopsychological approach to classroom knowledge, in N. Mercer (ed.) *Language in School and Community*. London: Edward Arnold.

Mercer, N., Edwards, D. and Maybin, J. (1988) Putting context into oracy: the construction of shared knowledge through classroom discourse, in M. Maclure, T. Phillips and A. Wilkinson (eds) *Oracy Matters*. Milton Keynes: Open University Press.

Mercer, N. and Fisher, E. (1992) How do teachers help children to learn? An analysis of teachers' interventions in computer-based activities. *Learning and Instruction*, 2: 339–55.

Moore, P. and Tweddle, s. (1992) *The Integrated Classroom: Language Learning and IT*. London: Hodder & Stoughton.

Mortimer, P., Sammonds, P., Stoll, L., Lewis, D. and Ecob, R. (1988) *School Matters*. Wells: Open Books

Norman, K. (1990) *teaching, Talking and Learning in Key Stage 1*. Sheffield: NATE?NCC Publications.

Norman, K. (ed.) (1992) *Thinking Voices: The Work of the National Oracy Project*. London: Hodder & Stoughton.

Ofsted (Office for Standards in Education) (1993) *The New Teacher in School*. London: Ofsted Publications.

Palinscar, A.S. and Brown, A.L. (1984) Reciprocal teaching of comprehension, fostering and comprehension monitoring activities. *Cognition and Instruction*, 2: 117–75.

Phillips, T. (1988) On a related matter: why 'successful' small group work depends upon not keeping to the point, in M. Maclure, T. Phillips and A. Wilkinson (eds) *Oracy Matters*. Milton Keynes: Open University Press.

Phillips, T. (1992) Why? The neglected question in planning for small groups, in K. Norman (ed.) *Thinking Voices: The work of the National Oracy Project*. London: odder & Stoughton.

Pollard, A. (1985) *the Social World of the Primary School*. London: holt, Rinehart & Winston.

Prentice, M. (1991) A community of enquiry, in *Talk and Learning 5–16: An In-service Pack on Oracy for Teachers*. Milton Keynes: The Open University.

Reid, J., Forrestal, P. and Cook, J. (1982) *Small Group Work in the Classroom*. Perth: Western Australia Education Department.

Robertson, L. (1990) Cooperative learning à la CLIP, in M. Brubacher, R. Payne and K. Rickett (eds) *Perspectives on Small Group Learning*. Oakville, Ontario: Rubicon.

Rohrkemper, M. (1985) Individual differences in students' perceptions of routine classroom events. *Journal of Educational Psychology*, 77(1): 29–44.

Rosenblatt, L.M. (1989) Writing and reading: the transactional theory, in J. Mason (ed.) *Reading and Writing Connections*. Boston, MA: Allyn & Bacon.

Salomon, G. and Globerson, T. (1989) When teams do not function the way they ought to. *Journal of Experimental Social Psychology*, 26: 168–83.

Scott, P., Dyson, T. and Gater, S. (1987) *A Constructivist View of Learning and Teaching in Science: Children's Learning in Science Project*. Leeds: Centre for Studies in Science and Mathematics Education.

Sharan, S. (1980) Cooperative learning in small geoups: recent methods and effects on achievement, attitudes and ethnic relations. *Review of Educational Research*, 50: 241–71.

Sharan, A. and Shaulov, A. (1989) Cooperative learning, motivation to learn and academic achievement, in S. Sharan (ed.) *Cooperative Learning: Theory and Research*. New York: Praeger.

Sharan, Y. (1990) Group investigation: expanding co-operative learning, in M. Brubacher, R. Payne and K. Rickett (eds) *Perspectives on Small Group Learning* Oakville, Ontario: Rubicon.

Simon, B. and Willcocks, J. (eds) (1981) *Research and Practice in the Primary Classroom*. London: Routledge.

Slavin, R. (1983a) *Cooperative Learning*. New York: Longman.

Swann, J. (1992) *girls, Boys and Language*. London: Blackwell.

Tann, S. (1981) Grouping and group work, in B. Simon and J. Willcocks (eds) *Research and Practice in the Primary Classroom*. London: Routledge.

Tizard, B., Blatchford, D., Burke, J., Farquar, C. and Plewis, I. (1988) *Young Children at School in the Inner City*. Hove: Lawrence Erlbaum.

Wegerif, R. and Mercer, N. (1996) Computers and learning through talk in the classroom. *Language in Education*, 10(1): 47–64.

CHAPTER 9

DISCOURSE, CONVERSATION AND CREATIVITY

Ron Carter

Investigating English Discourse, London: Routledge, 1997, pp. 154–70

Introduction

This chapter examines some practical and pedagogical issues in the design and implementation of materials at the interface of language and literature, with particular reference to the teaching of English as a second or foreign language. In order to achieve this practical focus, theoretical issues are necessarily never far from the forefront of discussion. There are therefore core questions such as: what is literature? What is literary competence? What kind of materials development is best suited to teaching which enhances both linguistic and literary competence? Such questions are not new but answers to the questions, however preliminary and provisional, must continue to form the basis for any prospectus for further development in this field.

A main point in the argument is that an extension of fuller *language awareness* and of the enhanced interpretive skills which should go with it are instrumental to a prospectus for future materials development. In particular, it is argued that course books for the teaching of English should exploit the opportunities provided by recent work in the domain of language awareness and that, if language awareness becomes a more central component in all course books, then the need for *separate* books which seek to integrate language and literature will not exist to the same degree.

Much of the data illustrated here is drawn from the CANCODE project, a corpus-based project designed to collect and analyse samples of everyday conversational discourse. The project data exemplifies in places considerable creative facility with language on the part of many speakers; greater awareness of such creativity in ordinary language can be a valuable starting point for an enhanced language and literary awareness. In order to build towards the overall argument, the chapter begins with a brief review of materials development at the interface of language and literature study during the past ten years or so.

Literary materials 1983–93

During the 1980s materials for the teaching of literature in the context of English language teaching have operated according to a number of common theoretical and strategic principles. Among the underlying theoretical assumptions are first that literature is made from language, and that sensitivity to language use is a strong basis for the development of an understanding of literary texts and, particularly in the case of non-native users of a language, often a secure and practical way to unlock the different levels of meaning in such texts. Second, suitably selected literary texts can provide a motivating and stimulating source of content in the language class-room, serving as a basis for discussion and interpretation in which the response of the individual learner is encouraged. Third, the skills of decoding literary texts are transferable to most language learning contexts in which meanings, because they are not always immediately transparent, have to be experienced, negotiated, or 'read' in the sense of interpreted between the lines. Such principles stress the mutual rein-forcement and support of literary and linguistic skills and underlie an essentially integrated view of language and literature.

Pedagogically, two main principles can be isolated: an activity principle and a process principle. An activity principle means that students are more than merely passive recipients of interpretations generated by a teacher or assimilated from books of literary criticism. Instead, students actively participate in making the text mean. In this activity they are supported pedagogically by a range of strategies of the kind widely used in the EFL classroom: rewriting, cloze procedures, jumbling texts, role-play, prediction tasks, and so on. A process principle means that students are more likely to appreciate and understand texts if they experience them directly as part of a process of meaning creation. Process-based approaches are learner-centred and seek to encourage students to respond to the text not exclusively as a complete artefact or finished product but rather more to the text as an unfolding process in which the relationship between form and meaning is shown to be central. The learner-centred activities outlined above serve also to stress the unfolding and evolving nature of the reading and interpretation of literary texts. Skills in interpretation are likely to be more successfully fostered if both activity and process principles operate at the same time. For further discussion see Carter and Long (1991).

The materials developed during these years have had different inflections according to context, purpose and audience. For example, some more advanced materials have involved learners in more linguistic-stylistic analysis (e.g. Carter and Long, 1987); some materials (e.g. Gower and Pearson, 1986) have been more traditionally literary in orientation, providing detailed reference to literary and cultural history. Some materials have been more eclectic, drawing on a wider range of literary and non-literary texts to encourage the building up of literary competence through interaction with the text, the textbook and others in the class (e.g. Boardman and McRae, 1984; McRae and Pantaleoni, 1991).

All these materials are characterised, however, by being additional or supple-mentary to mainline language course books. They reflect a teaching context in which language courses and literature courses are taught separately and in which integrated courses in language and literature are not integral to either. In the remainder of this chapter a main argument is for the need to build upon the advances of the past decade but at the same time to switch the focus to the place of language awareness in language and literacy development and to the place of literary texts in all language course materials (e.g. Sheperd *et al.*, 1992).

Some core questions

In order to provide such a focus, some core questions have to be posed. The main ones are: What *is* a literary text and how does it differ from other kinds of text? What is the relationship between literary uses of language and everyday uses? What is literary competence and how does it differ from general linguistic competence?

What is literacy development and are there major differences between literacy development in a first language and literacy development in a second or foreign language? Is there such a thing as pre-literary competence (that is, a set of skills basic to the development of a subsequent fuller literary competence)?

The provision of answers to such leading and complex questions depends on many more years of extensive research than have currently been undertaken, but continually to pose the questions is a necessary part of all processes of text selection, materials design and of competence testing in relation to language and literature in language learning.

Basic material: the arbitrariness of the sign

It can be safely assumed that colour words are among the first words learned in a language (see Wyler, 1992: 43ff.), allowing as they do a necessary contact with the identity of things and providing the language user with a vital means for distinguishing and differentiating within the material world. **Red, yellow, green, black, white, brown** and **blue** are thus central to the semantic structure of the lexicon of English, and the words are normally assimilated both early in a learning sequence and with relative ease. The centrality and coreness of such words often means, however, that they are extended into a range of compounds and combinations which result in changes in meaning. It also means that such words are available as basic signs for states of mind and feeling, for marking core cultural properties and for shaping attitudes and interactions, usually through processes of idiomatic extension. Taking a core word such as **green**, therefore, we can have the meaning of green as a core colour, as in the first example, but also:

green	=	She is wearing a green skirt.
green	=	They are playing on the green.
Green Cross Code	=	Children must follow the 'Green Cross Code' when crossing the road and when green means go.
green light	=	Give somebody the green light.
greens	=	Eat up your greens (green vegetables) and you'll be healthy.
Greens	=	I'll always vote for the Greens (the Green party) because of their concern for the environment.
greenhouse	=	Tomatoes should normally be grown in a greenhouse; 'the greenhouse effect' is altering weather patterns across the world.
green	=	She's rather green about such things (innocent, inexperienced).
green	=	You've done well to pass the examinations. I'm very green (envious).
green	=	In contrast with 'orange' as the colours of Catholic Republicanism and Protestant Unionism, respectively, in the conflict in Northern Ireland (e.g. an Orangeman).

In a first-language learning environment such meaning extensions to the word **green** and its morphological derivatives are learned in the process of naturalistic exposure to the language in its cultural contexts; in most second- or foreign-language learning environments the specifically cultural, idiomatic and, to a considerable extent, simply *arbitrary* meanings of the sign are normally withheld on the grounds that they are problematic for learners. However, to tidy up the language to this extent may be simultaneously to remove opportunities for recognising and interpreting non-literal forms and meanings in ways which lay a valuable basis for reading and interpreting a variety of texts, including literary texts. McRae (1991) has explored this domain with particular reference to differences and distinctions between referential and representational language. The productivity that results in the derivatives of **green** within prevailing socio-cultural frameworks is immanent in everyday conversational interaction, not just in literary creation.

One essential element in the literariness of language is that there is no single or simple one-to-one correlation between the language used and the meanings produced. Meanings have to be read from the language and the context of use. Such a process of negotiation also pays due attention to the arbitrariness inherent in many language forms, which may require a reorientation to what was supposed to be their point of reference in the world, even a relearning of the frames of reference within which differently possible worlds are created. The process may also require an understanding that more than one meaning can exist as part of the message. To know the word **yellow** is also to know its associations with cowardice; to know the word **blue** is also to know that in English its plural in nominal form ('the blues') is connected with feelings of depression as well as with an associated style of music from the deep South of the United States; to know the word **green** is to know the colour, its natural, vegetative associations *and* its additional considerably more non-literal, representational and arbitrary meanings.

Idioms, metaphors, proverbs and other extensions to what is assumed to be the core of a language are frequent across all languages and may, indeed, be in themselves more core than the construction of language courses would suggest. They are often embedded within the cultures which are intrinsic to that language and therefore do not readily translate between and across languages. But awareness of such features and interpretations of them allows access to these cultural embeddings, providing in the process opportunities for interpreting meanings which are communicated with varying degrees of indirectness and obliqueness.

As a preparation for subsequent reading of complete literary texts such awareness is valuable in this connection but the language learner is also learning that words have extended meanings as well as learning those meanings themselves, that meanings often have to be negotiated, that language is something to be learned *about* as well as learned, and that language is not just a fossilised code but a productive resource of great creative potential.

Playing with words

The simultaneous holding of more than one meaning within the communicative layers of a message is basic to a very wide variety of language use, from everyday conversation to the most elaborate literary texts, and in the context of language and literacy development may therefore be better included in the language course and not separated off into the literature course. Very young children possess the capacity for telling and receiving jokes which depend for their effect on a recognition of creative play with patterns of meaning. For example, first-language learners of English encounter in the school playground creative exchanges such as the following:

Q: What is black and white and read all over?
A: A newspaper.

They can also give varying explanations for a newspaper headline such as the following:

> General flies back to front

– both instances of which depend on recognising dual meanings created by the phonology (read/red) and syntax of English (front is both a noun and a preposition).

Advertising language also depends crucially on creative play with language and on the cultural discourses of society within which the language is embedded (see, in particular, Cook, 1992; also Moeran, 1984; Tanaka, 1992). For example, an advertisement for a motor car which states that it is 'A car for the 90°s' holds simultaneously together the possibility that it is a car in which you can travel at great speeds (90 m.p.h.), that it is particularly suited to very hot weather (90 degrees – the temperature reaches the nineties Fahrenheit), and that it is ultra modern and in tune with expectations for the decade (the 1990s). To provide learners with such a text and working collaboratively with them to decode it is also to provide them with an especially rich set of possibilities for learning language, for learning about language and for the development of literary competence. All the texts discussed so far have required some engagement and interaction on the part of the reader/interpreter; the reader has been positioned in a creative conversation or dialogue with the text.

So-called ordinary, everyday discourse is frequently patterned creatively so that it is memorable and striking, displaying a play with the more stable forms of language in ways which make them less stable. In the process the limits of idioms, fixed expressions and other pre-patterned regularities are stretched and creatively deformed and reformed. The names of shopfronts are a good example of this creative design, playing with common collocations and idioms in order to make language used to describe the products they offer part of the presentation. Here are examples of a chain of health food shops in Southern Ireland:

> Nature's Way
> Mother Nature
> Back to Nature
> Open Sesame
> In a Nutshell
> Wholesome Foods
> The Whole Story
> Fruit and Nut Case
> Naturally Yours
> Grain of Truth
> Simple Simon
> Nature's Store
> Just Natural

Most of these words and phrases (many of them fixed expressions or idioms) are connected with nature and a simple way of life and are creatively exploited to promote the sale of food which is either organically grown or which is defined as having particularly health-giving properties. For example, words like **grain, nut, nutshell, store, whole** and **wholesome, sesame** (seeds) are all words used to describe specific foods or specific qualities associated with such food; and they are then combined into fixed expressions such as 'in a nutshell' or 'grain of truth', which draw attention to themselves as expressions and are made memorable by their unusual association with the sale of health food products. The examples here illustrate a basis for aware-ness of literary and cultural uses of language. Terms such as 'literary' and 'cultural' are used with a small 'l' and a small 'c' (see McRae, 1991). In other words, creativity and cultural embedding are not the exclusive preserve of canonical texts but are pervasive in the most everyday uses of language (see also Alptekin and Alptekin, 1990; Gibbs, 1994 and from the point of view of practical language teaching resources, Prodromou, 1990).

Creativity in conversation

It is not just in the more deliberately planned contexts such as journalism, joke-telling and advertising that we find embedded cultural references, extended uses of linguistic forms, metaphors and idioms, and language in general being creatively manipulated. Everyday conversation reveals uses of language that are strongly asso-ciated with criteria for 'literariness', that is with the uses of language that characterise texts held by members of given speech communities to be 'literary'. One of the more negative aspects of the communicative movement in language teaching that has domin-ated the last couple of decades is an overemphasis on the transactional uses of language (i.e. the transacting of information, goods and services) at the expense of interactional uses (i.e. for the creation and reinforcement of social relationships) and creative uses. In McCarthy and Carter (1994) in particular that trend is criticised in an attempt to formulate what a language-teaching syllabus based on a notion of language as discourse would entail. However, the communicative urge has been a double-edged sword, and the very desire for authenticity in communication has led language practitioners to look more and more towards real spoken data, where day-to-day creativity and cultural embedding leap to the fore again.

Empirically based studies in discourse analysis continue to reveal the pervasive-ness of creativity in everyday discourse and to recognise that so-called literary tropes such as metaphor and metonymy (as well as figurative imagery in general) play a seminal part in the construction of interpersonal relationships. Recent studies by Tannen (1989), McCarthy and Carter (1994), Brazil (1995) and McCarthy (1997) recognise that casual conversation intrinsically creates a space within which speakers can fulfill what would appear to be a basic need to insert a more personal or person-ally evaluative position into the ongoing discourse. It is as if the relationships which are so important a part of casual conversation cannot be fully realised without an element of verbal play and inventiveness; and it is as if verbal play and creativity in talk are in essence interactive and interpersonal in character, that a fundamental casual conversational strategy is to engage and involve others and that there is an underlying recognition that, although, as Cook (1996) suggests, casual conversation is often a space-filling discourse, it comprehends so much more than the transfer into the space of information.

Tannen (1988: 71) has commented extensively on this feature of conversational discourse and with particular reference to repetition (see Figure 9). Crystal (1995: 413) has summarised and himself glossed this position in a clear and helpful way, drawing on the above data examined by Tannen herself in her book *Talking Voices* (Tannen, 1988).

Crystal (1995: 413) comments:

> Not only does it readily admit linguistic deviance, it displays many of the formal features which are traditionally thought to be 'literary', such as metrical rhythm, syntactic parallelism, figurative language, alliteration and verbal repetition . . .

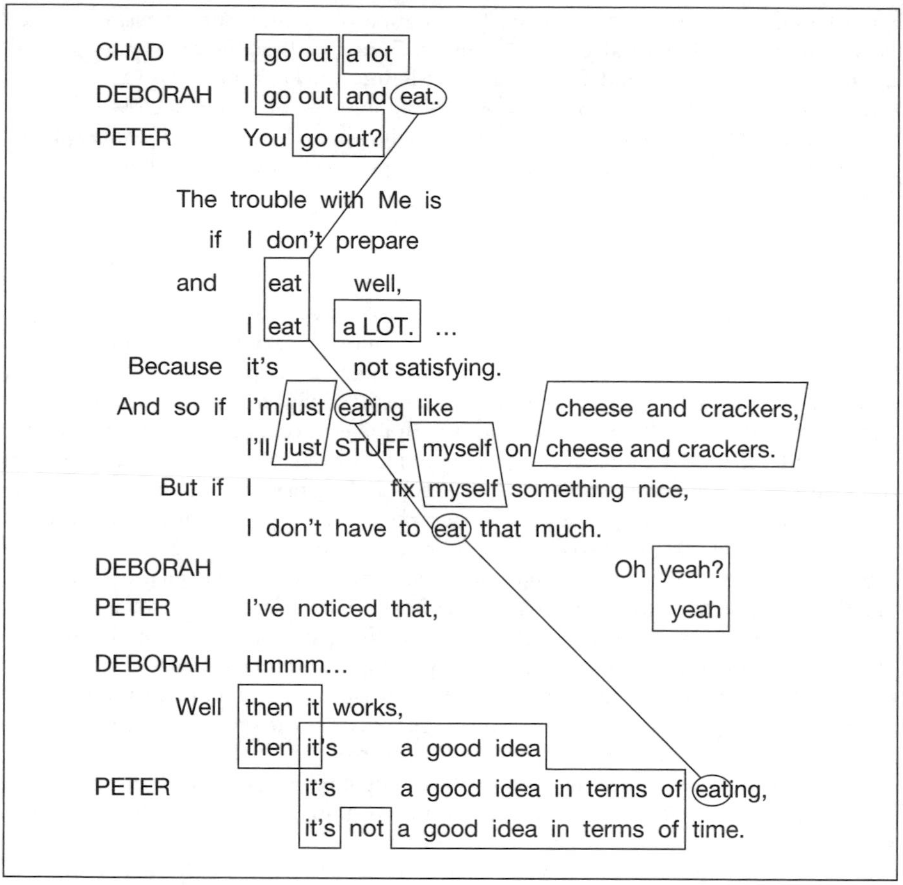

Figure 9

The literariness of a conversation is not immediately obvious ... Transcribed in a conventional manner, it is difficult to see anything of interest taking place. Laid out differently, several patterns begin to emerge and a more informed comparison can be made with the crafted conversation of drama. Only the lexical patterns are shown: several other links can be found between certain grammatical words (*I, if*) and there are signs of phonological repetition too (*in terms of time, lot/not, just/stuff/much*).

(For a study which also parallels poetic structure with language structure in a non-literary event – livestock auctions – see Kuiper and Haggo, 1984.)

In the following extract from CANCODE data, a not dissimilar pattern of phonological echo and lexical repetition occurs (is the relationship between 'bob' and 'Bob' in the fixed idiom 'Bob's your uncle' accidental?) alongside a further creative extension of an idiomatic phrase ('to get/have a finger in every pie').

B: Yes, he must have a bob or two.
A: Whatever he does, he makes money out of it. Just like that.

B: Bob's your uncle.
A: He's quite a lot of money tied up in property and things like that. He's got a finger in all kinds of pies and houses and things. A couple in Bristol and one in Cleveland I think.

Further scrutiny of naturally occurring, informal conversational data of the kind collected as part of the CANCODE project appears to refute the notion that speakers are not normally creative in their daily uses of language and that certain fixed linguistic structures, idioms in particular, cannot be unfixed. Instead, numerous examples show that speakers can engage in creative play with idiom: here are two teachers talking about their classes:

A: The second year I had, I started off with 37 in the class, I know that, of what you call dead wood, the real dregs had been taken off the bottom and the cream, the sour cream in our case, up there had been creamed off the top and I just had this dead wood, I mean it really was and he was so impressed with the job I did with them and the way I got on with them and he immediately said, how do you feel about taking a special class next year? And I took one from then on.
B: Rather you than me.

The idiom structure here is creatively transmuted in the play with **cream** (which is good) and **sour cream** which is not good and between metaphors of **down** and **dregs** which are not good and **up** and **top** which are good. Here idiomatic and fixed expressions are used almost in the manner of extended metaphors but they are deployed in order to comment on the world in some way rather than to describe it. They are frequently evaluative in a manner which confirms Gibbs's hypothesis (see Gibbs, 1994) that idioms are never just neutral alternatives to semantically equivalent, literal transparent expressions. They nearly always display a marked interpersonal orientation.

Irony and sarcasm are also common features of much conversational discourse. Indeed, fixed expressions can be deployed to critically ironic purpose; as in the following conversational extract from CANCODE data (based on the phrase 'And pigs might fly' – a fixed phrase used to frame an unlikely event), when a friend, who is notoriously unreliable at remembering to repay debts, promises to repay a small loan the following day:

A: Thanks I won't forget this time. Till tomorrow OK?
B: Brian, can you see those pigs over my left shoulder, moving slowly across the sky . . .
    [*A and B burst into laughter.*]

As in this example, the witty, ironic effects depend on shared knowledge; here both participants are aware of the phrase 'And pigs might fly' which is 'echoed' by B and which needs to be interpreted indirectly by A by drawing on such mutual understanding.

Ironic utterances are to an extent culture-specific and may cause problems for learners who are not suitably acculturated: in Britain, for example, remarks about the weather are frequently given an ironic preface such as:

Lovely day, isn't it?
Warm enough for you?
Just right for a day on the beach

– all of which refer to weather which is cold and inclement and which require a listener to work out that the referential propositions advanced do not obtain directly or literally. The listener furthermore interprets the speaker as making a critical, evaluative comment on current meteorological conditions. Irony belongs within a range of contextually generated effects such as sarcasm, satire, understatement and hyperbole which produce meanings that are non-literal and that require listeners to make indirect, interpretive inferences.

That such communicative features are common in conversations (particularly in informal casual discourse) reinforces the view that ordinary language can be pervasively unordinary and can involve the creation and interpretation of patterns which enjoy a family resemblance with those more usually designated literary.

Morphological creativity

Another kind of creativity which students of literature have to contend with, especially in modern poetry, is morphological creativity, whereby derivational potential is creatively exploited. Vizmuller-Zocco (1985) sees lexical derivation as belonging to 'that linguistic competence which is based on creativity', while Howden (1984) sees the native speaker's knowledge of existing derived words and what the potential for choice is as centrally important; she also stresses the interrelationships of meaning set up by new combinations of stems and affixes. Such creativity is surprisingly common in everyday talk, and can be used as the basis of a bridge towards its more daunting manifestations in literary texts. Here are some examples from the Nottingham University CANCODE Corpus of speakers exploiting the -y suffix in non-institutionalised word-forms to create diffuse and evaluative meaning.

> [*B, who is preparing food, has asked A to get her a bowl.*]
> A: You said you wanted the little ones as well. Want the little ones?
> B: Not really ... sort of **salady** ... that fruit bowl would be ideal.
> [*A is describing some newfangled shoelaces she has bought.*]
> A: They're well sort of like lycra, **elasticky** sort of stuff.
> [*A and B are deciding where to go for the evening.*]
> A: Cos there's a really nice place me and Myra go to.
> B: Oh I don't want a romantic **mewsy** pub

On another occasion, using the -ing inflexion, a speaker 'derives' a verb from a noun while telling a story of a dangerous game he and his friends played as children, rolling down industrial spoil heaps inside old lorry tyres. He intensifies the nightmarish rolling movement:

A: And you'd just roll, like **circusing** right the way down and get right up the top.

This is not inherently different from the poet Seamus Heaney's morphological creativity in describing the flight of a snipe: 'as he **corkscrews** away / into the vaults / that we live off' ('The Backward Look').

In another extract in the corpus, two women are assembling a portable baby-cot which involves twisting the metal parts until they become rigid. Note how speaker B uses morphological creativity, this time with a prefix (instead of using the more conventional 'loose' or 'slack'), to satirise her own mistake in the twisting movement:

A: There, that's solid now.
B: I think I've made it **unsolid** . . . sorry . . . I've done it the wrong way round, have I.

We find parallels of this in poetry, with the 'hot **unasking** sun' and 'the friendless and **unhated** stone' in W. H. Auden's poem 'As He Is'. To make such parallels between conversation and literary text is not to demean literary text in any way. As Widdowson (1975: 36) points out, it is the randomness of such occurrences in conversation as opposed to their *patterning* in literary text which is the significant difference. What the literary and conversational contexts cited have in common is their ability to bring together elements that are normally separated in the language code, to borrow again an observation from Widdowson (ibid.: 57). It is this common property that the teaching of literature and language can exploit.

Morphological creativity can be combined with satirical cultural reference too, as in this extract where a hostess (speaker A) is apologising to her dinner guests (one of whom is speaker B) that they are a little short of home-grown vegetables. The extract reinforces with real data our comments above on the breadth of lexical extension and shared cultural reference that accrues to a basic term such as **green**:

A: And so I'm afraid we're a bit sort of erm challenged **greenwise**.
B: **Greenly** challenged.
A: We're **greenly** challenged so erm sorry about that.

Here we have the morphological creativity of **greenwise** and **greenly** combined with an oblique cultural reference to phrases such as **visually challenged, physically challenged**, etc., as current 'politically correct' euphemisms for 'blind' and 'disabled', just as being 'green' (growing one's own vegetables organically, etc.) is a politically correct stance. The pun works on several levels, and it is significant that the joke is jointly created by the two speakers, emphasising the high degree of shared cultural knowledge and convergence. Along the scale from everyday conversational punning to literary text we find parallels in journalistic satire. The following example is taken from a newspaper article on left-handedness:

> These . . . figures come from a survey held by the Left-Handers' Club . . . the national mouthpiece of the **dexterously challenged**.
>
> (*Observer*, 1994)

The importance of awareness of multiple meanings has also been mentioned. Speakers play on these spontaneously by exploiting the real, immediate context for humorous effects, just as ready-made jokes exploit fictitious contexts. In the next conversational extract, a group of young female students are taking tea together, and two such ambiguities are exploited within a very short stretch of text:

A: Yeah, did you ever do . . . erm erm . . . oh what was she called erm Cynthia.
B: Did I ever do Cynthia.
A: [*laughs*]
B: [*laughs*] Can't say, did you.
     . . .
A: Oh this is wonderful, Bakewell tarts.
B: Tea and tarts.
A: [*laughs*] tea and tarts.

B: [*laughs*] tea with
A: Tea with tarts [*laughs*] ... tarts with tea.

'Do' is exploited for its sexual ambiguity and 'tarts' for its meanings of (a) a sweet pastry item and (b) a slang term for a prostitute.

These examples are some of the many kinds of linguistic creativity that one finds in a corpus of everyday conversation. They have in common with literary language that language is being made to 'stick out' from its context of use. Casual conversation is classically marked by a high degree of automatic and unconscious routine language use, but, now and again, speakers make their language draw attention to itself in some way, displacing it from its immediate context, a phenomenon Widdowson (1992: 26) has argued to be a fundamental characteristic of poetic language. It can therefore be argued that to use in the language class only those types of dialogue that are transparent and transactional and devoid of richness, cultural reference and creativity is to misrepresent what speakers actually do and simultaneously to lose an opportunity for interesting language awareness work of the kind which may be an ideal precursor to enhanced literary awareness.

Semantic density: grading the text

It is clear that some instances of language require a greater effort of processing. One reason for this is that they possess a greater semantic density. Stretches of language or texts such as the advertisement for 'A car for the 90°s', involving as they do a greater element of creative play with language and a layering of patterns at different levels, generally demand more processing effort than the semantic reordering of the word **green** as a colour to the phrase 'on the green' in which the word refers to a stretch of (mostly) green parkland. Similarly, idioms such as 'bumper to bumper', as in 'the traffic was bumper to bumper', are semantically transparent when compared with idioms such as 'to smell a rat' or 'to be on the ball'. Proverbs such as 'don't cry over spilt milk' allow real-world analogies to be drawn or semantic extensions to be made in a relatively more straightforward way than is normally the case with proverbs such as 'every cloud has a silver lining', which involve more indirect and metaphoric processes of decoding and interpretation.

The following examples of the names of shopfronts for hairdressers' shops in Britain involve varying degrees of creative play with language (and are indeed essentially *literary* in such verbal play), and require competence in recognising a multilayering of effects; but some names are more semantically dense and require a greater processing effort than others which are less oblique and less multilayered in the creation of meaning:

Highlights	Brush Strokes
Way Ahead	Cut Above
Headlines	Hair Comes Linda
Shampers	Hair and Share Alike
Cut 'n' Dried	Headcase
New Wave	

'Way Ahead', for example, is more transparent in its straightforward link between hairdressing and 'head' and its suggestion that hair styling in this shop puts you at a social advantage over others, as does 'Cut Above', from the idiom 'to be a cut above the rest, meaning to be superior, though this example demands more idiomatic knowledge, as does 'Cut 'n' Dried', a patterned semantic equation between the idiom and cultural behaviour (a confident, no-nonsense approach) as well as a literal link between cutting and drying hair. 'Shampers' too requires a specific cultural knowledge of the drinking of champagne (colloquial word 'shampers' and its phonetic analogy with shampoo) in contexts of high living. 'Brush Strokes' obliquely suggests 'art', while 'Headcase' (meaning 'crazy', 'lunatic') suggests a zany, youthful environment, and so on.

As we have seen proverbs, idioms, metaphors, jokes and texts such as newspaper headlines, advertisements and some titles/names for shops involve language use which is central to the culture patterned in and through that language. A further processing effort is therefore required in the case of those texts which invoke specific frames of cultural reference, for without the relevant cultural knowledge interpretation becomes a much more testing procedure. For example, children's jokes such as:

Q: Waiter, we're getting hungry. How long will the spaghetti be?
A: Each piece is about 15 centimetres.
Q: What's the difference between a teabag and Everton?
A: A teabag stays in the cup.

demand knowledge which is culture-specific (knowledge that Everton is a Liverpool-based football club with a poor FA 'Cup' record; or knowledge that spaghetti consists of long strips of pasta in addition to the linguistic knowledge that 'long' can be both an adverb of time and an adverb of measurement.

Jokes are generically diverse and range from straightforward verbal punning as in the instances above (p. 163) to jokes which allude to or reproduce specific sets of sociocultural assumptions. Thus, in the following example:

British Rail announces: Coffee up 20p a slice

the comic equation of coffee (a liquid) with the word 'slice' (normally applied to pieces of bread or to cake) together with the sizeable cost of the increase combine to reveal much in public attitudes to British Rail; for example, that British Rail is believed to provide a poor but expensive service; that food and beverages served on British Rail are expensive and of poor quality; that the coffee, in particular, is barely drinkable and is more like bread or cake in its consistency (see Chiaro, 1992).

And some texts allude in ways which require specific literary knowledge. For example, a camping shop with an advertising slogan:

Now is the winter of our discount tents

may only be processed on one level by readers not acquainted with a key speech from Shakespeare's *Richard III* (for this and further similar, examples, see McCarthy, 1992).

On the other hand, some effects produced in conventionally identifiable contexts such as poetry are less semantically dense. Poems by Dylan Thomas which contain phrases such as 'all the sun long' or 'once below a time' (based on the fixed phrases 'all the day long' or 'once upon a time') obtain their effects from, for example, a basic substitution of 'sun' for 'day', creating a suggestion that the sun shone through the day. Alternatively, titles such as Dylan Thomas's 'A Grief Ago' allow grief to be measured in temporal terms by substitution of a noun describing the emotion for the more usual noun measuring time such as hour, week, month or year. Recognising such patterns is instrumental to understanding the effects which such patterns produce. Producing them, as a British actress did recently in a television interview (commenting that a 1950s film she had appeared in was 'four husbands ago'), is a marker of a linguistic inventiveness and creativity which all 'ordinary' language users possess.

In this section it has been suggested that texts from various sources can be utilised to promote the development of skills of interpreting, inference, reading between the lines, that such texts could be included as a natural and normal component in language teaching materials at all but the most elementary levels, and that such texts can be graded and thus appropriately sequenced according to the relative degrees of processing effort required of them.

Language awareness: opening a door to literary competence

The above arguments are for learners to engage earlier in second- or foreign-language learning processes with samples of non-literal, representational language. Such engagement entails processes of interaction with and interpretation of language use. A necessary prerequisite for this kind of interaction and interpretation is a fuller awareness of language itself as a medium. This requires of learners that they become more reflective as learners, that is, that they become more conscious of texts and stretches of language as containing messages which need to be negotiated for meaning. In addition to interpreting language use they need to be aware of how they have made interpretations and to reflect on interpretive procedures, learning, in other words, how to learn better to interpret and engage with such texts as a result of more conscious operations.

The orientation here is parallel to that advocated by, among others, Ellis and Sinclair (1989) who have constructed teaching materials designed to enhance both awareness of the nature of the language system being learned and consciousness of the learner's own procedures for learning the language. Ellis and Sinclair's work underlines that a more conscious reflective language learner is a more effective language learner. For further arguments on the relationship between language awareness and language learning, see Donmall (1985); Hawkins (1987); James and Garrett (1992); Carter (1994); Bardovi-Harlig *et al.* (1991); Holborrow (1991).

Conclusions

One of the main theoretical and practical implications of this chapter is that the term 'literature' is not defined in any exclusive sense. The position adopted here is close to that established by Carter and Nash (1990), exemplified with comparisons of conversational data and literary texts by McCarthy (1994a, 1994b), and developed more fully in pedagogy by McRae (1991) and McCarthy and Carter (1994). It is that of recognising the co-existence of literature with a capital 'L' (canonical literature) and of literature with a small 'l' (the latter is the title of McRae's 1991 book – examples of texts, ranging from proverbs to jokes, to advertisements, which can be read as displaying literariness). Such a position may be felt by some, especially teachers of literature, to demean texts valued by a cultural community as of canonical status; the argument here is that, far from demeaning literary texts, it reveals and endorses the creativity inherent in much 'ordinary' everyday language use.

Literary uses of language and the necessary skills for its interpretation go routinely with all kinds of text, spoken and written. Literature exists at many different levels for different people in different communities but it is argued here that literary language is not simply any use of language. The main argument in this chapter is that literary language will always be patterned in some way and will involve a creative play with these patterns. The patterns may also involve words or structures which are representational and not intended to be read literally. The patterns invite involvement on the part of a reader or hearer who then has an option to interpret the text as the context and circumstances of the language use appear to him/her to demand. This patterned, representational 'literary' aspect of language is central to language use, though it will of course occur with greater density in some texts than others. The sooner language learners can come to appreciate this central component of language, the sooner they appreciate that they themselves and other users of language are essentially creative. In the future pedagogies and related tests for literary language development are likely to be all the richer for recognising this reality.

Acknowledgement

This chapter is a rewritten version of a paper entitled 'Discourse and creativity: bridging the gap between language and literature' in Cook, G. and Seidlhofer, B. (eds) *Principles and Practice in Applied Linguistics: Studies in Honour of H.G. Widdowson* (Oxford University Press, Oxford, 1995). The paper was co-written with Michael McCarthy, to whom I am grateful for allowing me to draw on the original source.

References

Alptekin, C. and Alptekin, M. (1990) 'The questions of culture: EFL teaching in non-English speaking countries', in Rossner, R. and Bolitho, R. (eds) *Currents of Change in Language Teaching* (Oxford University Press, Oxford) pp. 21–6.

Bardovi-Harlig, K. *et al.* (1991) 'Developing pragmatic awareness: closing the conversation', *ELT Journal* 45, 1, pp. 4–15.

Boardman, R. and McRae, J. (1984) *Reading Between the Lines* (Cambridge University Press, Cambridge).

Brazil, D. (1995) *A Grammar of Speech* (Oxford University Press, Oxford).

Carter, R. (1994) 'Language awareness for language teachers', in Hoey, M. (ed.) *Data, Discourse and Description: Essays in Honour of Professor John Sinclair* (Collins, London and Glasgow).

Carter, R. and Long, M. (1987) *The Web of Words: Exploring Literature through Language* (Cambridge University Press, Cambridge).

Carter, R. and Long, M. (1991) *Teaching Literature* (Longman, Harlow).

Carter, R. and Nash, W. (1990) *Seeing through Language: A Guide to Styles of English Writing* (Blackwell, Oxford).

Chiaro, D. (1992) *The Language of Jokes: Analyzing Verbal Play* (Routledge, London).

Cook, G. (1992) *The Discourse of Advertising* (Routledge, London).

Cook, G. (1996) 'Language play in English', in Maybin, J. and Mercer, N. (eds) *Using English: From Conversation to Canon* (Routledge, London) pp. 198–234.

Crystal, D. (1995) *The Cambridge Encyclopaedia of the English Language* (Cambridge University Press, Cambridge).

Donmall, G. (ed.) (1985) *Language Awareness* (CILT, London).

Ellis, G. and Sinclair, B. (1989) *Learning How to Learn English* (Cambridge University Press, Cambridge).

Gibbs, R.W. (1994) *The Poetics of Mind: Figurative Thought, Language and Understanding* (Cambridge University Press, Cambridge).

Gower, R. and Pearson, M. (1986) *Reading Literature* (Longman, Harlow).

Hawkins, E. (1987) *The Awareness of Language*, rev. edn (Cambridge University Press, Cambridge).

Holborrow, M. (1991) 'Linking language and situation: a course for advanced learners', *ELT Journal* 45, 1, pp. 24–33.

Howden, M. (1984) 'Code and creativity in word formation', *Forum Linguisticum* 8, 3, pp. 213–22.

James, C. and Garrett, P. (eds) (1992) *Language Awareness in the Classroom* (Longman, Harlow).

Kuiper, K. and Haggo, D. (1984) 'Livestock auctions, oral poetry, and ordinary language', *Language in Society* 13, pp. 205–34.

McCarthy, M. (1992) 'English idioms in use', *Revista Canaria de Estudios Ingleses* 25, pp. 55–65.

McCarthy, M. (1994a) 'Spoken discourse markers in written text', in Sinclair, J.M., Hoey, M. and Fox, G. (eds) *Techniques of Description* (Routledge, London) pp. 170–82.

McCarthy, M. (1994b) 'Conversation and literature: tense and aspect', in Payne, J. (ed.) *Linguistic Approaches to Literature* (English Language Research, Birmingham).

McCarthy, M. (1997) *Spoken Language and Applied Linguistics* (Cambridge University Press, Cambridge).

McCarthy, M. and Carter, R. (1994) *Language as Discourse: Perspectives for Language Teaching* (Longman, London).

McRae, J. (1991) *Literature with a Small 'l'* (Macmillan/MEP, Basingstoke).

McRae, J. and Pantaleoni, L. (1991) *Chapter and Verse* (Oxford University Press, Oxford).

Moeran, B. (1984) 'Advertising sounds as cultural discourse', *Language and Communication* 4, 2, pp. 147–58.

Prodromou, L. (1990) 'English as cultural action', in Rossner, R. and Bolitho, R. (eds) *Currents of Change in English Language Teaching* (Oxford University Press, Oxford) pp. 27–39.

Tanaka, K. (1992) 'The pun in advertising: a pragmatic approach', *Lingua* 87, 1–2, pp. 91–102.

Tannen, D. (1988) *Talking Voices: Repetition, Dialogue and Imagery in Conversational Discourse* (Cambridge University Press, Cambridge).

Vizmuller-Zocco, J. (1985) 'Linguistic creativity and word formation', *Italica* 62, 4, pp. 305–10.

Widdowson, H.G. (1975) *Stylistics and the Teaching of Literature* (Longman, Harlow).

Widdowson, H.G. (1992) *Practical Stylistics* (Oxford University Press, Oxford).

Wyler, S. (1992) *Colour and Language: Colour Terms in English* (Gunter Narr Verlag, Tübingen).

CHAPTER 10

DRAMA, LITERACIES AND DIFFERENCE

Helen Nicholson

Where Texts and Children Meet, Eve Bearne and Victor Watson (eds), London: Routledge, 2000, pp. 113–22

Introduction

Drama, as a particular mode of artistic representation, uses different forms of literacy to tell stories and communicate ideas. In the English curriculum, attention has been drawn to verbal qualities of drama, to the ways in which it encourages skills in speaking and listening, and the textual study of dramatic literature. However, as a cultural practice, drama includes more than verbal literacy; drama makes meanings through the languages of movement, visual images, sound and music as well as through the spoken word. Indeed, as a dynamic medium of social communication, drama is constantly changing, and the various ways in which experiences are presented and represented as dramatic texts reflect the complexity of the art form.

In contemporary theatre and dramatic practices, while the literary playscript has maintained an established place, drama that is created around visual images, sound and movement has become increasingly visible. The work of physical theatre companies, black and Asian practitioners and multimedia performance artists has led to debates about the representation of gender and ethnicity, for example, and to a renewed interest in how the body is portrayed and read. Supported by postmodern theories of representation and identity, in which it is acknowledged that selfhood is consciously constructed and interpretations of the body are culturally produced, artists and performers have reframed dramatic imagery, narrative and design. With a renewed interest in how the interplay between sound, word, movement and image creates dramatic meanings, contemporary dramatists have experimented with the juxtaposition of different artistic forms, and have made explicit references to the intertextuality of drama.

Within this creative and intellectual climate, the idea that each drama is a cultural and social text has become widely accepted in educational discourse. The consequences of this shift in thinking is leading to a more inclusive model of drama education, where attention is paid to the various ways in which the dramatic form itself is interpreted, as well as the process of exploration of content or theme. In this context, a wide variety of dramatic styles are included in the curriculum, with attention drawn to the ways in which the content of the drama, the ideas expressed in it, are inseparable from the values associated with different dramatic practices and forms.

What is particularly interesting about the practice of drama, including the performance of more conventionally written playscripts, is that participants operate simultaneously on a number of levels – ideas, thoughts, feelings and values are created and represented in physical, verbal, aural, kinaesthetic and visual texts at one and the same time. Daphne Payne gives a description of the multiple texts that constitute drama practice:

> Drama is not speech, but action. It is a mode of expression which utilises a whole range of communication skills – words, certainly . . . but also facial expression, body language, mime, movement, dance – all those channels of communication of which the human body is capable in order to convey meaning.
>
> (Payne, 1998)

How these different 'languages' of drama are combined, how the different textual elements interact, and how the semiotics of time, space, movement and gesture are created and read, is dependent on the particular ways in which ideas are symbolised and constructed, and the particular use made of dramatic genre, style and form. Drama draws on a complex web of different sign-systems which involve a range of physical senses; as practitioners young learners are invited to explore not only how drama is read, but how it is seen and heard.

In this chapter I shall argue that drama, as an intertextual art form, enables children to explore the multiple texts and textures implicit in a range of dramatic forms. I shall explore how learners might use and develop their abilities as encoders and decoders of visual images, aural texts, movement and literary forms to make drama which has personal and cultural significance. Indeed, it is precisely because dramatic texts are *multimodal* – combining the different textual modes of visual, aural, verbal and kinaesthetic languages – that drama develops a range of literacies, often ignored in a curriculum that has been traditionally dominated by written language.

Dramatic literacies

The term 'literacy' has not always been associated with drama education. Most usually it is identified with the written word, although an increased consciousness of the influence of new forms of cultural communication, particularly in media and electronic texts, has led to an awareness of the need to provide a wider description of what it means to be literate in today's technological society. In this context, literacy has gained a wider definition; the term is now variously applied to practices such as the ability to work with computers, to read and interpret a musical score, and to decode and compose visual images.

In this expanded definition of literacy, the emphasis is not only on the ability to *read* texts with a degree of competence, but to *practise* the skills and crafts associated with particular forms of literacy. For example, if I were to describe myself as computer-literate, it would be reasonable for you to expect me to work out how to use a computer program with some degree of proficiency. Similarly, it is difficult to imagine how someone might be described as musically literate if they have absolutely no ability to play an instrument or sing. Likewise, to be visually literate is usually understood to entail some knowledge of how images are composed. Literacy is not associated with passivity; it is an active process of interpretation and exploration. As Jane Gangi points out, 'literacy allows a kind of thinking that is reflective, interpretive and abstract, one which promotes questioning' (Gangi, 1998: 53).

In this context, to speak of 'dramatic literacies' is to raise questions about the range of artistic practices involved in making drama. Literacy, in dramatic terms, is not primarily concerned with reading words on a page (although this may be part of the process); it includes an awareness of how different signifiers such as space, vocal colour, intonation, gesture, movement, design, costume, lighting combine to communicate in sound, image and movement. The practice of drama, in primary and secondary schools, from the most simple of classroom improvisations to the most complex professional productions, involves a synthesis of different semiotic vocabularies.

In the secondary-school curriculum, drama has a very particular place precisely because it encourages students to experiment with a wide range of artistic languages. As practitioners, students use the multimodality of drama to shape ideas, to explore situations, to represent experience. Described more simply, when students make drama they are putting together visual images, sounds, movement and speech in creative ways. As members of an audience, they not only take account of the action, but interpret such aesthetic qualities as the scenography, the use of space, the movement and aural elements of the drama. Making, performing and responding to drama does not imply that different semiotic vocabularies are isolated from each other. Rather, dramatic literacy entails a recognition of how the various textual elements included in dramatic practices are woven and integrated into a coherent whole.

In past practices, the tendency has been to offer students experience of drama in two quite separate ways. On the one hand, the drama curriculum has often focused on the exploration of ideas through role play and improvisation; while, on the other, there has been the reading of plays, most usually, in the secondary school, undertaken in English lessons. However, by placing an emphasis on the multitextuality of drama, I am suggesting that these two approaches to drama might be productively combined. The act of reading plays is itself a creative process, which involves an exploration of the ways in which visual, kinaesthetic and aural texts interact. Similarly, when students are creating improvised drama or role plays, their work is enriched by an explicit awareness of how the various textual elements of drama combine to make meanings. Furthermore, to return to Jane Gangi's definition of literacy, both sets of practices can be interrogative, reflexive and interpretive, particularly where they are taught with an explicit focus on the relationship between the content of the drama and the use of dramatic form. The following example, based on the teaching of a play-script, gives one illustration of how students might be encouraged to interpret and question the ways in which different elements of drama contribute to creating an atmosphere that illuminates the thematic content of the play.

A class of Year 7 students (aged 11 and 12) were reading Alistair Campbell's play, *Anansi*, in both their English and Drama lessons. The teacher aimed to encourage them to explore the play's thematic content of the slave trade and to develop an awareness of the effects of the play in performance. She divided the class into small groups, with each group taking responsibility for different aspects of play production, such as set, lighting and costume designers, sound technicians and directors. However, she also wanted the students to become aware of how the different aural, visual and kinaesthetic signifiers of theatre work together, and much of the work was undertaken collaboratively; the whole class were involved in acting the script, with time structured for the work of the specialist small groups. In one lesson, the class worked on the opening scenes of the play. It begins with a title and a stage direction:

The Good Ship Hope: West African Coast, 1791

Listen ... hear the last sounds of a ship preparing for an Atlantic voyage. The Boy is seated at a desk, reading and writing. His father, the Captain, consults ledgers and maps.

(Campbell, 1992: 2)

The play is set in three locations on a ship – the cabin, on deck and in the hold. However, the action moves between the ship, and 'a forest full of stories'. This presented the group of set designers with something of a problem. The teacher had given some guided questions to the group, anticipating their initial frustration with the constraints of small-scale theatre design and their preference for the resources of a major Hollywood film studio. Her questions asked the students to consider the practicalities of quick scene changes, the dramatic atmosphere they wanted to create, and how the actors might use the space. Similarly, the sound technicians were baffled by the stage direction, but quickly discovered their significance as creators of dramatic atmosphere. After some discussion, the groups shared their ideas. They discovered the necessity to invoke a similar dramatic atmosphere in different forms of design. As a starting point, they decided to create an atmosphere invoked by the word 'hopelessness'. It was an inversion of the ship's name, which the students recognised as dramatic irony, and which acknowledged the play's dramatic exploration of slavery. But 'hopelessness' is, in itself, too abstract a concept for designers to realise; it is difficult to give a literal portrayal of the word in sound or in furniture or props. A further brainstorm, in separate groups, made the idea more concrete. The visual design of the play took shape; hopelessness was symbolised by dark covers over wooden desks, tatty maps and ledgers, and the suggestion of claustrophobia through enclosing the stage space with beams that looked like stakes. The sound of the ship was created by rattling chains, a rhythmic soundscape of chanting sailors pulling ropes, and an underscore of flapping sails, which, the students suggested, would continue through the dialogue of the opening scene.

In many ways, these highly creative and inventive designs were only realised because the teacher outlined specific constraints that accompany the processes of making theatre, and offered the students guidance in the form of structured questions that helped them solve the problems. However, as a result of this work, they were able to develop an understanding of the visual and aural qualities of a playscript which might have been overlooked if they had read the play as if it were a novel (focusing primarily on narrative and characterisation) and without considering the extra-dialogic features of the script. As Elaine Aston and George Savona point out, 'the habits of reading cannot be unproblematically transposed across differential forms. The dramatic text must be read on its own terms' (Aston and Savona, 1992: 72). And these terms include the visual, aural, kinaesthetic and verbal languages in the drama, without which the layers of symbolic meanings inherent in the playscript would remain unquestioned.

The concept of dramatic literacy is inclusive. It extends to drama practices that are primarily based on improvisation as well as those that are script-led. What all these practices share, when taught with cognisance of the range of languages that make up drama, is a sense of critical distance from the process of making meanings and communicating in and through drama. Indeed, dramatic literacy entails an ability to analyse the dramatic process, and reflect explicitly on how dramatic meanings are continually created, re-negotiated and redescribed. However, because drama is an art form that is physical as well as intellectual, dramatic literacy can be shown in the form itself, through creative use of the body as well as articulated in written or spoken language. This kind of open-ended learning invites speculation, reflexivity and questions, where it is recognised that drama offers a symbolic interpretation of experiences, thoughts, feelings and ideas, with all their contradictions and ambiguities.

Drama, differentiation and learning styles

The emphasis on learning in drama and the acquisition of a dramatic literacy has sometimes been criticised for taking an inadequate account of the individual needs of different children. Such a curriculum, it has been argued, is too prescriptive, too focused on learning outcomes, and overly preoccupied with meeting predetermined assessment criteria. Indeed, if drama lessons were so inflexible, and took no account of those delightfully unexpected moments of insight and creativity, it would indeed be a just criticism; planning for effective learning requires us, as teachers, to meet the needs of individual students. This entails careful consideration of the different ways in which individual children learn.

Theories of learning have emphasised that, unsurprisingly, students learn in a variety of ways. Drawing on psychological research, Michael Fielding has pointed out that students prefer to use different sensory channels to help them learn: some students have developed an ability to learn by using an auditory sense, while others are visual or kinaesthetic learners. He offers the following description of these learning styles.

> Auditory students prefer to learn mainly through talking or hearing ... Visual learners are helped most when they can see a visual equivalent or encounter the thing or process itself in a visual way ... Kinaesthetic learners have a need to touch and get physically involved in the work.
>
> (Fielding, 1996: 88)

If students are to be supported in their learning, Fielding argues, there is a need to recognise the different ways individual children habitually learn, and to accommodate and extend their approaches to learning in classroom practice.

It is interesting that Fielding's description of different learning styles so closely mirrors the visual, aural, verbal and kinaesthetic languages of drama I identified earlier. What this suggests is that learning *in the dramatic form itself* inevitably includes a wider range of learning styles than many other subjects in the curriculum, and that this suits the abilities of a greater diversity of children. Perhaps this, too, explains the success of the methodology of drama practice to teach other curriculum areas, and accounts for why students who are labelled low achievers often appear to do rather well in drama. Because drama is multitextual, the art form itself provides students with different points of entry into the work, and different ways of becoming involved.

Planning for differentiation in drama, therefore, takes account of the different ways individual students learn and includes a variety of dramatic forms, genres and styles. This extends to both the processes of making drama and the art form itself. For example, a Year 8 class (12- and 13-year-olds) were recently investigating the plight of World War II evacuees in their drama lessons, where the teacher explicitly aimed to encourage the students to sustain roles, create a dramatic atmosphere and to use dramatic form to communicate with others. As a way of encouraging empathy, she showed the group pictures, which helped the visual learners; a soundtrack, which encouraged auditory learners to enter the drama; and asked the class to create a slow-motion mime, which appealed to those who were primarily kinaesthetic learners. The lesson was structured so that initially each element was explored separately: the children were invited to discuss the power of the image, the mood of the soundtrack and the dramatic effectiveness of their first attempts at the mime. Gradually, however, the teacher led the group in bringing these different activities together, and the class developed a mime that took account of the visual image (projected on to the studio wall), with the soundtrack playing in the background. It was a satisfying experience for the students, who used their particular abilities as learners to build on their understanding of role and situation and understood how different dramatic signifiers might be synthesised to create a strong dramatic atmosphere.

The range of teaching and learning strategies included in this lesson gave the children different points of entry into the drama. However, because all the students were involved in each activity, they were able to support each other both in developing a wider repertoire of learning styles and in gaining an explicit understanding of the effectiveness of dramatic convention and style. Experienced learners are able to use a variety of approaches to learning. In practice, while the recognition of different learning styles may be a useful way of identifying students' individual needs and structuring group work, any rigid categorisation of their abilities risks labelling children rather than enabling them. As teachers we have a responsibility to encourage students to develop a diversity of learning styles and, as teachers of drama we are entrusted with extending students' knowledge and understanding of dramatic art. Such an approach to teaching and learning has implications for progression and curriculum planning.

A fully differentiated drama curriculum takes account of students' individual needs by including a variety of learning styles, and supports them in tackling areas of difficulty. Furthermore, a curriculum that provides equality of opportunity will introduce students to a range of dramatic forms and styles and encourage them to interpret them inventively; in the Year 8 class I described, for example, there were two children with hearing impairments, who would have been excluded had the drama been dominated by spontaneous improvisation, and a child in a wheelchair, whose expressive use of gesture provided a focal point for the mime. As Michael Fielding points out, 'learning is about development, not stasis or dependency' (Fielding, 1996: 90).

The process of becoming an independent learner involves the student recognising *what* they have learnt, and *how* they have acquired their knowledge, skills and understanding. According to drama educator Michael Fleming, 'progression towards increased independence in drama starts with both teacher and learner having a clear idea of what they are doing, knowing why they are doing it, and being able to assess to what extent the aims have been achieved when the activity is completed' (Fleming, 1994: 135). In other words, if our students are to progress into independent learners, as teachers we need to make the aims of the work, the processes of learning and the assessment criteria explicit to them. However, when this is combined with an approach to dramatic literacy, this does not have to equate with rigidity or an over-prescriptive and unimaginative approach to the subject. On the contrary, if progression in drama is linked to dramatic literacy, and if this involves questioning, invention, speculation and reflexivity, then, this will be reflected in the aims of the drama curriculum. Such a drama curriculum will be structured with this in mind, enabling students to frame questions, to take account of the unexpected, and to evaluate and speculate within the dramatic form itself and as a critical response to the work of others. It is an approach to drama education which combines approaches to learning in the subject of drama with approaches to learning itself.

Communities of learners

Underpinning this argument lies the assumption that drama is a collective enterprise. Drama in schools is practised as a group activity, and this makes very specific demands on students and their teachers. The multitextual qualities of drama as an art form require students to produce a coherence in their work, where the visual, kinaesthetic, aural and verbal elements of the work complement and support each other. As individuals, students also need to find ways of working together to create drama that reflects their interpretations of the play-script or their shared understanding of the content or theme. This places specific demands on young people, particularly in an age when much social activity is influenced by the introspective and isolated pastimes associated with new technologies, and in an educational climate where individualised learning is valued above the achievements of a group.

In this context, the challenge to drama teachers is how to encourage the kind of collective classroom culture that is the prerequisite of good drama practices. Indeed, students themselves often cite the ability to cooperate (or otherwise) as one of the main reasons for the success or failure of their work in drama. The problem, it would appear, is not that students are unaware of the need to work together to create effective drama, but that they lack the skills and strategies to realise their good intentions. In this final section of the chapter, I shall focus on how an explicit recognition of the multimodality of drama can enable students to develop practices that foster successful learning communities.

As a drama teacher, one of my aims is to encourage students to make, perform and respond to drama in ways that have personal and cultural significance for them. In this context, there is a balance to be achieved between creating drama that has artistic integrity and accommodating the different ideas of individual members of the group. However, reader response theory suggests that the meanings of drama are subject to interpretation and reinterpretation; works of art contain, as Merleau-Ponty has described, not just ideas, but 'matrices of ideas' which are in themselves open to interrogation (Merleau-Ponty, 1973: 90). This means in practice that drama often works best when it offers alternative perspectives and, rather than creating drama showing a single narrative viewpoint, leaves room for ambiguity, with some information withheld, and some questions unresolved and thus open to further interpretation.

Through the process of working, drama teachers can create a culture of collaborative learning that invites students to exchange ideas, to experiment with alternative perspectives and interpretations, to raise questions, to reflect and speculate. Dispelling the myth that cooperation always means agreement between individuals is both part of the process of creating a community of learners, and it is also integral to dramatic form itself. Indeed, experimenting with how visual, aural, verbal and kinaesthetic signifiers can be juxtaposed to create 'matrices of ideas' is a sophisticated skill, but one that students, by the age of 11–13, are well able to achieve. For example, if a situation seems to demand a sombre atmosphere, what happens if everyone is showing through facial expression or gesture that they are trying to be cheerful? What further questions does this raise? It is a process of opening questions, and finding modes of representation that, in themselves, invite further speculation and reflection. Within this climate, the intention is to demonstrate to students that tensions cannot always be resolved, that drama may be interpreted in different ways. Learning to live with ambiguity is both part of the process of working collaboratively and the process of making art.

A community of learners who work well together can live with and accommodate unresolved tensions. In practice, this requires teachers of drama to structure the process of working carefully, and to provide students with the apparent constraint of limited artistic choices. Imaginative work, as Sharon Bailin points out, is most likely to be achieved when students have access to the rules and conventions of dramatic form (Bailin, 1998: 48). Indeed, it is only when students can understand

and interpret dramatic conventions that they have the independence to break them. This requires learners to experiment with the different textual elements of drama, and find inventive ways of juxtaposing or contrasting the visual, aural, kinaesthetic and verbal qualities of the work. It is the kind of independence that comes from mutual respect and inter-dependence between individuals, where it is recognised that drama holds multiple viewpoints, multiple forms of representation and raises multiple questions. A community of learners, in the drama classroom, will learn to value difference.

References

Aston, E. and Savona, G. (1991) *Theatre as Sign System*, London: Routledge.
Bailin, S. (1998) 'Creativity in Context', in Hornbrook, D. (ed.), *On the Subject of Drama*, London: Routledge.
Campbell, A. (1992) *Anansi*, Walton-on-Thames: Thomas Nelson.
Fielding, M. (1996) 'Why and How Different Learning Styles Matter: Valuing Difference in Teachers and Learners', in Hart, S. (ed.), *Differentiation and the Secondary Curriculum: Debates and Dilemmas*, London: Routledge.
Fleming, M. (1994) *Starting Drama Teaching*, London: David Fulton Publishers.
Gangi, J. (1998) 'Making Sense of Drama in an Electronic Age', in Hornbrook, D. (ed.), *On the Subject of Drama*, London: Routledge.
Merleau-Ponty, M. (1973) *The Prose of the World*, trans. J. O'Neill, Evanston: North-western University Press.
Payne, D. (1998) No Sound, No Speech, No Drama? Unpublished paper delivered at the National Drama Conference, April 1998.

PART IV

EXPLORING VISUAL TEXTS

CHAPTER 11

SEEING, THINKING AND KNOWING

Evelyn Arizpe and Morag Styles

Children Reading Pictures: Interpreting Visual Texts, London: RoutledgeFalmer, 2002, pp. 222–42

> We can never neatly separate what we see from what we know . . . in the hands of a great master the image becomes translucent. In teaching us to see the visible world afresh, he gives us the illusion of looking into the invisible realms of the mind . . . if we only knew how to use our eyes.
>
> (Gombrich, 1960: 329–31)

> By looking at the drawings of my reception class and analysing their discussions during out study of *Zoo*, I have found that children can see the most incredible things beyond what they might be assumed to know.
>
> (Rabey, 2001)

We began our research after many years of combined expertise in teaching reading to pupils and undergraduates and with considerable experience of reading picturebooks with children. We were already well versed in most of the standard theoretical and practical texts published in Britain and the USA about teaching reading, children's literature, reader-response theory and the role and scope of picturebooks. We thought we were quite well educated in visual literacy when the project started; now we know we were wrong! Two years on, after much reading of art history, art education and aesthetics, and revisiting and supplementing a fairly basic knowledge of psychology (though we did read comprehensive digests of psychological approaches to visual literacy), as well as dipping into relevant reading within media education and related disciplines, we realise what an enormous body of literature exists on this topic and how many different disciplines impinge on it. This wide reading has underpinned the analysis of our findings and we have used it to support or challenge our arguments and contentions.

The appeal of pictures

Picturebooks are the primary literature of early childhood and the most challenging examples demand highly interactive reading. As far as we are aware, nobody has ever before collected such intensive data on how children from 4 to 11 actually read pictures. All the evidence in our study pointed to the pleasure and motivation children experienced in reading these texts, and the intellectual, affective and aesthetic responses they engendered in children across the ability range and from different cultural and linguistic backgrounds. Pictures in picturebooks provide equality of access to narratives and ideas that would otherwise be denied to young readers. As Perkins points out: 'It is not so often the case that we can learn in the presence of compelling objects that engage our senses, allow for many kinds of cognition, connect to many facets of life and sustain our attention. We look and we see meaning upon meaning, all more or less immediately accessible' (1994: 5–8).

Gombrich has argued that the visual image is more effective than spoken or written language in evoking an affective response from the reader. Similarly, in discussing the affective pleasure in pictures, Nodelman asserts: 'my pleasure seems to be emotional rather than intellectual – a sensuous engagement with the colours, shapes and textures' (1996: 115). Kiefer also talks about 'the complex nature of aesthetic response. It involves affective as well as cognitive understandings, and it may change over time' (1995: 12). However, Benson reminds us of the limitations of our study, too (1986: 135).

> Art objects, including pictorial art, are specifically made to favour their being experienced aesthetically. If I speak of my experience of a picture, I am in part reformulating in verbal symbolic terms my visual apprehension of the pictorial sign. If I speak of what it is the picture signifies, then I am translating from a pictorial symbolic system into a verbal symbolic system. Translation always and inevitably involves transformation and distortion. . . . The picture, especially the picture as a work of art, is a mediation of an idea. That idea is embodied in the perceptible qualities of that picture, qualities which are so presented by the artist to the spectator as to guide the experience along particular paths. Talk of the picture is a further mediation.

Reading picturebooks – an intellectual activity

> To read the artist's picture is to mobilise our memories and our experience of the visible world and to test his image through tentative projections. . . . It is not the 'innocent eye', however, that can achieve this match but only the inquiring mind that knows how to probe the ambiguities of vision.
>
> (Gombrich, 1960)

It was no surprise to find that children were extremely good at analysing the visual features of texts; that was our hunch before the research started and it was supported by our findings. Children noticed, admired, wondered at and puzzled over diverse visual features produced by Browne and Kitamura in *Lily*, *The Tunnel* and *Zoo*. Most children took on board with equanimity the challenges of surrealism, the widespread use of intertextuality, postmodern games of suggestiveness and inconclusivity, the many layers of meaning offered up by the texts. They read colours, borders, body language, framing devices, covers, endpapers, visual metaphors and visual jokes. They responded with alacrity to the various invitations offered by the different texts and recognised that hard work and endeavour were required to get as much out of the books as they could. While there was an obvious line of development in children's ability to interpret visual texts, the trajectory by age was not always clear cut.

Most children were deeply engaged by our chosen picturebooks and keen to discuss the moral, social, spiritual and environmental issues they raised. Our choice of texts was vindicated by the children's overwhelmingly positive responses to them. They wanted to read them, talk about them, reflect on them, revisit them, draw in response to them; and even when they were amused (as in parts of *Lily* and *Zoo*), the overwhelming impression we had was of the children's serious intellectual delight provoked by these picturebooks. Furthermore, although the three texts were very different in style, tone, design, mood, story line, they were all sophisticated, multi-layered picturebooks and they all provoked deep, intelligent responses in young readers.

Reading picturebooks – the affective dimension

In her seminal work on reader-response theory, Rosenblatt (1978) underlines the importance of children making 'personal connections' in their reading in order to engage actively with texts and draw on their own experience. Significant numbers of children in our study had strong emotional reactions to our chosen picturebooks. In some cases, this was highly personal and individual, as in the case of Sam who seemed to take great comfort from *The Tunnel*. Children frequently used personal analogy to try to understand the feelings of characters or animals in the books and their responses were often sympathetic and thoughtful.

Moral issues held the children's attention; this was particularly noticeable in those who read *Zoo*. Such was the seriousness and zeal of the children's interpretations that in *Lily*, which was lighter in tone than Browne's books (though it was also mysterious and slightly menacing) and far removed from ethical matters, many found undertones which spoke of environmental issues. Kitamura had no conscious intention of saying anything about the ever-increasing problem of rubbish in the urban landscape in this book, but many children noticed overflowing dustbins and litter and interpreted these details as references to pollution and the spoiling of the planet. It certainly shows children's active search for meaning and Kitamura may, indeed, unconsciously have revealed his own views.

Drawing in response to picturebooks

The decision to include drawing as part of the data collection was almost an afterthought and we were delighted by the quality of some of the art work and what we could learn from it about the children's knowledge and emotional responses to the picturebooks they were studying. In the case of the younger children, their drawings often showed understandings they were unable to articulate. It also taught us much about how children develop as artists. There is no doubt that the bold, spontaneous compositions of the early years metamorphise into more recognisable, but usually duller representations as children strive for realism as they get older. Benson explains this with reference to Gardner's work: 'the preschooler's freedom to use form independently of specific content soon disappears from the work of most children. Instead, the work of 8 or 9 year olds comes to exhibit an increasing precision, regularity, linearity, concern for detail, neatness and command of geometrical form, but it lacks the liveliness of work completed at an earlier age' (1986: 123). Or as Gardner puts it himself: 'It is the pursuit of the realistic and the literally true which casts its spell on the individual in middle childhood' (1980: 142).

An unexpected finding was the strong correlation between the quality of the children's drawings and the input from their teachers prior to and during the research study. We were lucky enough to have two class teachers (one of whom was Kate Rabey, an art educator) who were specialists; one was a humanities teacher who had worked intensively with the pupils on deconstructing image before our study began. Both teachers had clearly influenced the children in the receptive and productive modes, as artists (as the quality of the drawings in those two classes will testify), but also as skilled observers of visual texts. We also noticed that particularly gifted individuals will always buck the trend.

Revisiting picturebooks

We decided to revisit one-third of our original sample to see if there were any significant changes in the responses made by the children several months after the initial interviews. Early observations had suggested that the more acquainted children were with a multi-layered picturebook, the deeper and richer their responses. Having selected a mixture of children, from those already making sophisticated analyses of image to those just beginning that journey, and adding a few whom we found interesting along the way, we set about asking questions which were more demanding than the first time round and which focused on the book as a whole and the artist's likely intentions. For example:

- What goes on in your head as you look at pictures?
- How do you think the artist decides what to write as words and what to draw as pictures?
- Tell me about the way Satoshi Kitamura draws lines.
- How do the endpapers of *The Tunnel* take you into the story?
- What is Anthony Browne trying to tell us about the differences between humans and animals in *Zoo*?

We also repeated a few of the original questions which the children had found challenging initially and asked for new drawings in response to the text.

At first we found the re-interviews a little disappointing as few children had made great strides in their understanding. While most children returned to the books eagerly enough and remembered a great deal about their earlier encounters with them, there was little evidence of any major new thinking. However, after we scrutinised the transcripts we became aware of small, subtle developments. Amy (now 5), for example, pounced on *Zoo*, declaring: 'I just noticed a funny difference I never noticed before the colour helps you find the differences between the animals and the humans' (Amy had meticulously searched for what she called 'changes' in Browne's work the first time round). Her statement about the mother was more clear cut than before: 'Mum is sad and she thinks the animals should be going free.' She also told us that 'I imagine the pictures. I see them with my brain', while Yu (4) concluded that 'I think of pictures when I go somewhere else.'

Erin's (7) thoughtful interpretation on the first visit was again evident on re-interview. Her summing-up of *Zoo* as a whole showed her usual insight: 'Humans change into animals to learn how it feels; animals look a bit like humans so they know what it's like to be free.' She liked Browne's work because 'it makes you keep thinking about things'. Perhaps most noteworthy was Erin's different style of drawing. Her first picture is spontaneous, attractive and expressive, full of the experimentation she enjoyed in Browne's work; five months later she seems to have entered the phase which Davis (1993) calls 'literal translation' and she is now more concerned with naturalism and a sense of morality, so evident in the drawings of the older pupils.

During the re-interviews, children also spotted details in the pictures that they had not noticed the first time round. Unsurprisingly, the pictures were more memorable than the words. Some pupils produced art work which was more elaborate and detailed than the first time round. In all cases, the children went a little further in their understanding of the picturebooks and some of them came up with new insights. Such was true of Dave (now 9), with regard to the fairytale theme and gender roles in *The Tunnel* and Carol (now 11), who in the first interview had been very observant of visual features such as colour and line, but now focused on the word/image dynamics in *Lily*.

I like this bit because Nicky's just a little creature in amongst these other big ones and she (Lily) hasn't worked out any of those bits and he's still got them in his mind which is really good and she's just eating dinner and telling her mum a completely different story. [Without pictures] you wouldn't know what he saw, you wouldn't have his side of the story.

The revisits may have yielded less evidence than we had hoped for because the experience was less intense for the pupils than the first time round and because there was no opportunity for discussion with their peers. Furthermore, apart from being a richer learning context, the discussions were the only part of the data collection where the researchers were free to behave more as teachers and intervene to move the children's learning on. Kate Rabey, who was in the unique position of being class teacher as well as researcher, found that revisiting *Zoo* with the whole class led to extraordinary developments in the children's thinking, mostly manifested in their drawing.

Oracy, language and learning

Language is inextricably linked to our study, not least because we were dealing with children's oral responses most of the time. The pupils' use and understanding of language is what divides them into different ability groups in the English classroom and determines the way they are taught. Knowledge of the English language was evidently important, particularly in the case of bilingual learners, but also in terms of cultural beliefs about language itself (such as value and use). Gender differences were also made manifest through language, as girls tended to be more articulate and forthcoming than boys. Finally, the language children hear and read in the various visual media that surround them – comics, television, films, computer games – filters into their response to picturebooks as well as providing them with a tool to understand and discuss the pictures.

Talk was operating to promote the children's learning since discussing the pictures with others gave children opportunities to operate at a higher cognitive level and demonstrate the capacity to turn around their own schemata and construct them afresh – a sort of *visible thinking*. The young learners also demonstrated a metacognitive ability to step back, and observe themselves as readers going through a series of deductions almost like scientific reasoning, confirming whether their hypotheses were right.

Although we did not set out to conduct a detailed linguistic analysis, the various careful readings of the transcripts resulted in two main observations: one was the way the children struggled to find the words that would communicate their understanding, excitement or doubts to others (both researchers and peers), so that even readers who were shy and/or unsure about their English made an attempt to express their thoughts; the second was how the pupils' choice of words reflected the internal thought processes that occurred as they looked.

Related to the first finding is the way some pupils' language changed as they became more confident about the pictures. Kathy Coulthard describes bilingual readers like Sam, Mehmet and Manisha, whose lack of English was positively challenged by Browne's text. It was also observed among native English speakers and in the children's attempts to find and use technical terms to describe aspects of the pictures, such as pattern, shape, line or perspective.

Mines' doctoral thesis is based on an analysis of how children from different ethnic minority groups read *The Tunnel*. She noticed that certain words appeared more frequently in her transcripts once the children became more involved and 'their reading became more tentative and exploratory and, as it did so, their language became less certain' (2000: 204). She refers to the repetition of words like 'think', 'because', 'might' and 'probably', which indicate an awareness of different possibilities of interpretation. Although we did not quantify systematically the appearance of this type of language throughout our interviews, we did note the frequent use of these same terms, alongside other words and phrases expressing deductions ('so that's why', 'now that means', ''cos you can see that', 'because the Mum said') and opening up hypotheses ('maybe the artist thinks', 'he might not be', 'by the looks of him a vampire', 'so perhaps Nicky knows').

Kiefer (1995) classified the oral responses from her subjects according to four Halliday's functions of language: informative, heuristic, imaginative and personal. We found examples of all of these functions in our transcripts, some of them very similar to those mentioned by Kiefer. This is evidence not only of the way children use language functions to make meaning, but also of the range of different expressions children choose to convey this understanding. We found examples of other types of language usage, including:

- questioning the text ('It makes you think why is that there?')
- explaining ('I can show you a scary bit.')
- wondering ('It makes you think someone must have been there . . .')
- analogising ('If I rescued my brother, I would feel happy as well.')
- asking questions ('Where's the woman who is knitting then?')
- exclamations ('Look! Oh, there's something there.')
- personal involvement ('I'd be surprised if . . .')
- awareness of metacognitive implications ('It makes me think . . .')
- explanations ('It's saying that . . .')
- speculation about the plot ('I wonder what's going to happen . . .')
- speculation about the characters ('What she could do is . . .')
- contesting ('I don't agree with . . .')
- awareness of the author ('Maybe the artist thinks . . .')
- agreeing with others ('I think the same as X.')
- justifying opinions ('Because he said . . .')
- comparison ('How would you like to be locked up in a cage?')

Cultural factors

Given that our study was concerned with children who were situated in a particular cultural and educational context, it is important to mention some of the social factors that may have influenced their responses. The discussion of these issues raises a host of questions that are beyond the scope of this study and we can only point to some of the directions which further research could take. The most influential factors, all linked together by their relationship to language, were the following: ethnicity, gender and popular visual media culture. With the exception of Mines' research on children's 'cultural literacies', none of the studies on children's response to visual texts have covered these issues.

Ethnicity

After repeated analysis of the transcripts, we have come to the conclusion that there were no serious differences between children for whom English was an additional language (some of whom are multilingual or emergent bilingual, but we will call bilingual in this chapter) and native English speakers in terms of their appreciation and interpretation of visual texts. The former category includes a diverse range of children, several of whom had recently arrived in Britain and others who were third generation, say, Turkish-British, and fluent in English. In fact, Kathy Coulthard's work movingly documents the insightful comments made by several bilingual children with little experience of the English language or culture. What happened was that an inviting, multi-layered picturebook allowed them to show just how capable they were at making meaning from a text.

Perhaps most central of all is the notion of teacher expectation. All the children in our sample, however inexperienced at reading and/or speaking English, were invited to make sense of a high-quality picturebook. It so happened that none of our chosen books made any concessions to different cultural traditions; nor were there any images of black or Asian children in them. The books were not chosen to teach English; they were chosen because they were worthwhile texts. Of course, as with any valuable reading experience, the study was also bound to have a positive impact on the learning of English. The researchers believed that the children would get a lot out of the books and treated them all as intelligent readers. As Kathy Coulthard put it, 'when the primary focus was no longer the words, the children were able to fly'.

Unlike Mines, we were not exclusively looking at the relationship between children's ethnic backgrounds and their response to the texts; however, some issues came through, given that about a third of the interviewees turned out to be bilingual and/or from a cultural background that was not mainstream English. Approximately 35 per cent of the interviewed pupils came from varied ethnic backgrounds. The sample included pupils from Asian, African and Caribbean backgrounds, as well as Kosovo Albanians, Italians, Chinese, Greeks and Turks.

In her doctoral study, Mines (2000) used *The Tunnel* with three groups of 5- and 6-year-olds with distinct cultural backgrounds: Bangladeshi newcomers, second-generation Bangladeshi immigrants and English children from rural Sussex. As well as detailing her own analysis of the picturebook, Mines studied the transcripts with codes based mainly on Barthes' semiotics. Barthes' cultural code, in particular, links the text to the real world and builds on readers' social and intertextual knowledge. This is particularly relevant to a text like *The Tunnel* where the limits of the 'real world' are blurred and knowledge of other texts is required to make sense of the story.

Mines contends that the reader approaches the text as a cultural being, bringing to the transaction with the text their own experiences of life and the world in order to make the new culture less strange. Thus, for example, the recent immigrants to Britain saw snakes and dragons in the forest, while the Sussex children recognised the references to familiar fairy stories. Mines found cultural differences in each group's reading, particularly with respect to their response to (a) the everyday objects in the book, (b) intertextual references, (c) the ideology of the text, and (d) the secondary world within the text.

Some of the children in our study were the same age and from similar backgrounds as those described by Mines. Kathy Coulthard analysed the responses of recent immigrants from Tanzania, Turkey, Mauritius and Nigeria, and her findings in this area are not dissimilar to those of Mines. In terms of the everyday objects in the book, these children showed interest in them but, like Mines' first group, were less likely to try to place them within the narrative unless prompted to do so. As to intertextual references, Sam, for example, was able to connect *The Tunnel* to traditional narratives from his own culture. Mines speaks of the ideology of the text in terms of the sibling relationship and the criticism or acceptance of Jack's attitude to his sister. We did not find such a marked acceptance or criticism of this behaviour, although most children commented on it. Finally, talking about the secondary world within the text, we also found that it was older and native English speakers who were more aware of the fairy-tale alternative, as opposed to the ones who wanted to make more literal sense of the events in the story.

Our findings and observations about cultural influences also coincide with those of Mines, in that we also found this particular picturebook (but also the other two) had the ability to transcend cultural differences precisely because it allowed children of all backgrounds to bring in their personal and cultural experiences in order to make sense of the story for themselves. Mines emphasises the importance of providing these students with an opportunity to speak, of taking into account their previous experience, both personal and genre-related, and their ability to talk about emotions and values such as fear, love, hate, boredom and freedom.

Gender

None of the previous studies on response to visual texts mention the issue of gender even though gender analysis has been carried out in various studies on children's response to literature (Sarland 1991; Davies 1993; Arizpe 2001a). The questionnaire on reading choices did not reveal great differences between the preferences of boys and girls in the early years. Their responses began to differ more significantly with age. In the first years of primary, both boys and girls said they enjoyed picturebooks and stories. Later, although picturebook-reading declines, more girls mentioned picturebooks and more boys preferred 'stories'. In the later years of primary both began to read more magazines and comics. Also, girls at all stages preferred books and television over computer games, but boys begin to prefer computer games from about age 7 although they watched as much television as the girls. 'Action'-type books, films and programmes were more frequently mentioned as boys grew older and, although many girls also included them, they also showed more interest in narratives dealing with emotions and relationships. These differences become even more marked at secondary school (Millard 1997).

In terms of the response to the picturebooks in the study, the gender issue can be approached from different angles. In the first place, there are the picturebooks themselves. An immediate analysis reveals that the female characters in all three books appear as emotionally stronger than the male characters, a factor not consciously considered when selecting the books for the study. Lily never shows any fear, while her (male) dog is terrified by real or imaginary monsters; Rose conquers her terror to rescue her brother; it is the mother in *Zoo* who makes the most insightful comment on the day's events. Browne's male characters come over as rather insensitive, even bullying (Dad in *Zoo*).

One of the main issues in *The Tunnel* is gender differences and this was reflected in the immediate association made by many of the children to the wallpapers and backgrounds: flowers for girls and bricks for boys. Other stereotypical comments were common: girls are quiet, they like reading; boys are noisy, they like active games. The children's own gendered experience seemed to be the basis of these responses: boys tended to identify with Jack's excitement at finding a tunnel and his impatience with Rose's fears, but then found their expectations literally 'frozen' as Jack is imprisoned in stone and depends on his sister to be freed, while girls could relate to Rose's terror and immersion in a fairy-tale fantasy world. In *Zoo*, the boys seemed to relate easily to the brothers (eating, wrestling, feeling bored), yet at the same time also became aware of the contrast with the animals' situation. In the end, the readers' expectations of stereotypical gender roles were subverted in *The Tunnel* and in *Lily*, while *Zoo* might have led them to question so-called masculine, insensitive attitudes.

This links with another aspect of gender which is the identification of readers with the characters. The confidence and bravery of Lily and Rose made it much easier for the girls to put themselves 'in their shoes'. More girls than boys commented on the feeling that they were 'there', in the story, particularly in the case of Rose. Both boys and girls talked about the family in *Zoo* as being a bit like their own family. To the question of 'How does it make you feel when she rescues her brother?' apropos *The Tunnel*, more boys answered 'don't know', while the girls tended to immediately say 'happy'. It is hard to know whether this was because the boys had not really thought about it or whether they were reluctant to reveal their feelings. The latter explanation is perhaps closer to the truth, given the next two observations on gender differences.

Boys were, perhaps, slightly less willing than girls to keep on looking and thinking, particularly when faced with difficulties in the visual text. This was observed by all the researchers in all the schools. Boys generally became more impatient with the questions and were more likely to say 'I don't know' when faced with anything perplexing. However, boys took as long as the girls – if not longer – when drawing, an observation that suggests that boys may find it easier to express themselves through this type of activity rather than through words. This is linked to the final way in which gender differences were manifest, which was in the girls' willingness to talk and in their generally being more articulate. Both girls and boys tended to make comments comparing situations in the books with their personal experiences. However, the boys tended to be objective while the girls expressed their feelings more openly. Although this may have had something to do with all the interviewers being female, the fact that some of the more experienced male readers were more forthcoming than those who were struggling with print, suggests that this particular observation may have more to do with confidence than anything else.

This leads us to a tentative conclusion regarding gender and response to visual texts, which is that differences are more apparent in inexperienced readers who are less confident, not only about their ability to understand, but also to express their thoughts in front of others. Using a medium which boys usually enjoy – drawing – is one way to build up their confidence. It is also important to find pictorial texts that reflect images of masculinity with which boys can identify – images that incorporate the positive side of masculinity, but also bring out qualities more associated with caring and sensitivity. Browne's recent *My Dad* is a good example. Could it also be the case that the differing qualities of boys and girls' engagement with the texts was indicative of a different 'voice' even among such young respondents (see Gilligan, 1982)?

Popular culture

As we mentioned, the questionnaire results reveal that children's lists of favourite television programmes, films, videos and computer games were much longer than those of picturebooks. In all age groups computer games were preferred over books and television, although the lists of games were not as long as the lists of programmes and films and there were 43 out of 486 children (8 boys and 35 girls) who said they did not play computer games, while only a small handful did not watch television or videos. Pupils engaged with a wide range of media texts, from those designed for children to those intended for adults – many mentioning extreme examples of both types in the same list. (One 9-year-old girl, who included *Winnie the Pooh* and *Dirty Dancing* in the same list was the most extreme example!) The lists grew much longer in the later years of primary school, with many children running out of space on the questionnaire form. In this multi-media world, is it possible to find out how exposure to these different types of visual texts affects the reading of picturebooks?

During the interview, with the aim of finding out the relationship between other visual media and picturebooks, we asked children whether other types of images helped them to read pictures in books. In most cases, children answered that it did not help or that they couldn't think how it might help, but some of those who answered 'yes' came up with responses that revealed interesting aspects of how they 'look', not only at television, computer games and comics, but also how this influences looking at picturebooks. As they compared and contrasted different media, several points emerged.

The movement of the narrative was one of the points of comparison. Children spoke of moving through the narratives in a comic book or on the computer screen, guided by the pictures which help keep the reader 'on track'. Other points of comparison were the visual conventions used in comic books and on screen which are also used in picturebooks, such as speech bubbles or speed marks. Not a single child failed to recognise that Rose is running in the forest, that the snail in *Zoo* is moving fast, and that Nicky is shaking in *Lily*. This knowledge may be reinforced in school, but it has clearly been acquired at an early age. Oliver at the age of 5 explained to the interviewer how speech and thought bubbles work in books like *Asterix* and *Tin Tin*. Many children were also familiar with terms like 'slow motion', '3D', 'pause', and used them regularly in their responses.

Some children emphasised the differences between the viewing processes required by each medium, usually referring to the commonplace, but (we would argue) mistaken, assumption, that media texts automatically encourage passive viewing while books require active engagement. According to the children, television and video involve watching and listening, while reading a picturebook involves 'thinking', 'concentrating' or 'imagining'. However, this did not apply to computer games because as Sofia (8) said: 'Sometimes on the computer games you have to think really carefully what to do before a go.' Also, as Lauren (11) suggested, playing computer games was like reading picturebooks because 'you can make up your own imagination and make a story in your mind'.

Another point of contrast, linked to the previous one, is that media texts were perceived to be dynamic while pictures in books are static. Dan (7) compared the transformations in *Zoo* with the way they would have appeared on television, pointing out that because there was no movement in books:

> [in the picturebook] you can't see the whole body changing into animals. In cartoons, they are moving and change at the same time, so you can see different parts of the body changing into different parts at different moments.

Yet description as well as colour was thought to help make a reader understand when there is movement in picturebooks. According to Natasha (10), films or videos show what's happening through movement, so it was easier to tell a character was angry on the screen because they use gestures like stamping their feet, while in a picture it is necessary to take in details such as facial expressions. Gemma (9) explained that the use of colour in a picturebook could be an expression of movement, for example where the colours get lighter in the four-picture sequence in *The Tunnel* when Jack returns to his human form.

Another difference with film was pointed out by Ron (10) who said that 'in film you don't see words come up on the bottom of the screen telling you what happened'. So written text is considered one of the determining characteristics of picture-books, while 'noise and voices' are the sound elements of television and video which you can't 'hear' in a book. Some children also mentioned that, with videos, films and computer games, the images were going very fast compared to the images in a book which one can look at more slowly. However, it is also possible to stop a video or film in order to have a closer look, as Mark (7) pointed out: 'When you are playing the game you can always pause it and look at the details and textures of the picture.'

Children were aware of the way visual media can influence someone's thinking, even a dog! According to John (7), Nicky sees the monsters because he's been watching 'TV about all his stuff – he's thinking of all this stuff and when he looks he sees them there, when they are not really there'. Jessica (4) unconsciously revealed the media's influence when she mistakenly called Mrs Hall (a character who is named but not depicted in *Lily*) by the name of Mrs Goggins, the old woman in Postman Pat who also knits. Christina (9) talked about the way a viewer's emotions were influenced by the type of media and, according to how realistic it was: 'even though it's not real it makes me feel that it is a real story and that it really happened and that it's so sad and stuff'. Cartoons, on the other hand, were not real and Christina said they just made her laugh.

The extent to which popular forms of visual culture influence the children's descriptions of their metacognitive abilities is perhaps not so surprising. Polly (6) actually described her thinking processes like 'a computer inside my head' which she can 'switch' on and off. 'I do loads of things in my head', she boasted to the interviewer, even mentally 'watching television' as she did her schoolwork!

At the end of her study, Mines (2000: 201) concludes that: 'The transcripts show how hard the children worked to fill the gaps, and the fact that how they looked at the pictures and what they saw was determined by the mental template they applied to their reading, this being a largely cultural construction.' We agree with these conclusions and, like Mines, feel that much more research is needed on how these cultural constructions influence the meanings children make of the visual. We need to learn more about what role all these factors play in visual literacy. It is also important that these constructions are recognised by teachers and are brought into the classroom. Language and pictures are invaluable tools for taking advantage of the potentially enriching aspects of the children's experiences and at the same time helping overturn stereotypes and prejudices.

Our findings and the National Literacy Strategy

In *Reading Images*, Kress talks about 'the staggering inability on all our parts to talk and think in any way seriously about what is actually communicated by means of images and visual design'. He goes on to celebrate how 'children seem to develop with little help a surprising ability to use elements of visual grammar' (Kress and van Leeuwen, 1996). Despite the expanding visual base of contemporary culture, low status is still accorded to image in education. Pictorial cueing systems do not figure in the skills required for reading in the National Curriculum and the National Literacy Strategy makes scarcely any reference to visual texts.

Analysing visual text, and the relationship between word and image, makes demands on what are often called 'higher order reading skills' (inference, viewpoint, style and so on) and involves deep thinking. Some of the key skills highlighted in the National Literacy Strategy at text level for 10–11 year olds are as follows.

- reading and interpreting texts in which meanings are implied or multi-layered;
- analysing how messages, moods, feelings and attitudes are conveyed;
- articulating a personal response to literature;
- identifying why and how a text affects a reader;
- explaining preferences in terms of authors, styles and themes;
- taking account of viewpoint;
- analysing the success of texts and authors in evoking particular responses in the reader;
- being familiar with the work of established authors and knowing what is special about their work;
- describing and evaluating the style of an individual author;
- identifying the key features of a text etc.

All these categories were covered using our texts over the course of a day with readers of 7 and above; quite a few were explored with children under 6. Although lip-service is paid to such notions in both the National Curriculum for English and the National Literacy Strategy, their content and pedagogy lead to very different practices, where texts are often shared in bite-sized chunks for short amounts of time, with an emphasis on filleting them for phonic or punctuation potential. Fortunately, the most recent emphasis in the National Literacy Strategy has been on creative ways with text, and the glaring hole of oracy is beginning to be incorporated into their materials. There has been encouragement for local initiatives and flexible adaptations have been welcomed in schools which are clearly doing a good job with literacy. There is enough freedom for teachers with confidence and vision to develop literacy in more imaginative ways, including the use of visual texts.

Working on the principles and practices detailed in our research, Kathy Coulthard has, indeed, developed a series of Literacy Hours, helped by teachers and a Literacy Consultant in north London. In particular, ten imaginative Literacy Hours based round *Zoo* and *The Tunnel* have been successfully trialled in Enfield primary schools, using some of the questioning techniques adopted during our interviews and discussions and drawing on the data generated during the project. (In addition, some drama techniques have also been employed and the scope of our research has been extended to include work at word and sentence level.) The outcomes look very promising, as pupils and teachers alike have been overwhelmingly enthusiastic about this work. Some of the most pleasing anecdotal evidence points to the following:

- analysing multimodal texts appears to extend the most academic pupils as much as the least experienced learners;
- pupils were able to transfer the skills they employed in analysing visual text to wholly written texts;
- this type of work proved particularly successful with English as an Additional Language learners.

Memory, creativity and thinking

Imagination and thought appear in their development as the two sides of opposition ... this zigzag character of the development of fantasy and thought ... reveals itself in the 'flight' of imagination on the one hand, and its deeper reflection upon real life on the other.

(Vygotsky, 1986)

Hubbard, an American educationalist, has produced an inspiring longitudinal study based on systematic observations of 6- to 9-year-olds, as she tried to learn more about how children used art in their thinking processes. The teachers tackle literacy in as structured a way as the Literacy Hour in Britain and there are many overlaps between the two approaches. However, the priorities of the American study have to do with memory, creativity and imagination, as well as teaching literacy, and that is what makes the difference. They also include activities like visual response logs where pupils draw and write their personal responses to their reading. As well as teaching reading and writing as enjoyable and worthwhile activities in themselves, with plenty of opportunities for personal choice in subject matter, the American teachers do not neglect the necessary skills of spelling, punctuation, grammar, phonics etc. But crucially, they understand that:

> As we share literature with children and adolescents, we want to foster their genuine reactions and responses – and we want to find ways to link up their own experiences to the ones in the books they read. ... By including visual responses to literature (and responses to visual literature), we can tap into areas that we might not otherwise reach through talk and writing alone. ... In both classrooms, the key role of memory images in the meaning-making processes of the children was a finding that leapt out at us.
>
> (Hubbard, 1996: 309–23)

Sinatra, however, speaking of education in the United States, says something different. He points out that non-verbal modes are rarely taken into account in the curriculum, especially art, and that visual literacy is an unfamiliar concept to educators. His description of what happens to those who do not show a strong verbal development is similar to what happens in the UK:

> We may praise and reward artists, inventors, and technological genuises when they achieve their feats but we do not reward them during their schooling years if their non-verbal strengths interfere with written literacy attainment. For those youngsters who don't attain written literacy early or rapidly enough, we may label these youngsters disabled and subject them to analytical, parts-specific verbal remediation. By doing so we curtail the power of holistic, analogic thinking for those youngsters and minimise the opportunity to cultivate the non-verbal, creative mode in which they may excel.
>
> (Sinatra, 1986: 42)

Perkins (1994: 89) offers the same sort of message, talking about the need to create classroom environments where serious thinking can take place, and outlining the role of art to bring diverse strands of thinking together:

> a culture that honours giving thinking time, establishes it as legitimate, avoids the rush to hasty resolutions, musters time for thinking things through, and allows time for the revisiting and rethinking of things ... [since] well mastered skills are more likely to stand up in new contexts. And diverse practice prepares the mind for a variety of future applications. Unfortunately, in most school settings, skills and knowledge are underpractised or practised only in a narrow range of circumstances. ... Art connects because artists make it connect, because artists strive to express not just the anatomy of bodies but the anatomy of the human condition and of the universe that impinges upon it. If most disciplines build moats, art builds bridges.

There is still much more work to be done in understanding visual literacy, but our results are heartening. When children are given the time they need to look at visual texts and talk, listen, draw, reflect and think about them, the results can be outstanding. When opportunities are provided to privilege visual and verbal skills, instead of concentrating on reading and writing, many children can *fly* intellectually, especially those who are inexperienced with written text or learning in an unfamiliar language. Engaging in exploratory activities with beautiful, challenging visual texts is a worthwhile way to spend time in the primary classroom. The picturebooks amused, provoked, sustained and inspired the children we worked with. In turn, the children's responses have surprised, moved and thrilled us. We hope that this chapter conveys something of our excitement in the enterprise and the deep respect we owe to the young readers whose ways of interpreting visual texts we have struggled to understand, analyse and celebrate.

References

Benson, C. (1986) 'Art and language in middle childhood: a question of translation', *Word and Image*, 2: 123–40.

Davis, J. (1993) 'Why Sally can draw. An aesthetic perspective', *Educational Horizons*, 71: 86–93.

Gardner, H. (1980) *Artful Scribbles*, London: Jill Norman Limited.

Gilligan, C. (1982) *In a Different Voice*, Cambridge, MA: Harvard University Press.

Gombrich, E.H. (1960) *Art and Illusion*, London: Phaidon Press.

Hubbard, R. (1996) 'Visual response to literature: imagination through images', *The New Advocate*, 9: 309–23.

Kiefer, B. (1995) *The Potential of Picture Books: From Visual Literacy to Aesthetic Understanding*, Englewood Cliffs, NJ: Merrill.

Kress, G. and van Leeuwen, T. (1996) *Reading Images: The Grammar of Visual Design*, London: Routledge.

Millard, E. (1997) *Differently Literate: Boys, Girls and the Schooling of Literacy*, London: Falmer Press.

Mines, H. (2000) 'The relationship between children's cultural literacies and their readings of literary texts', Ph.D. thesis, University of Brighton.

Nodelman, P. (1996) 'Illustration and picture books', in P. Hunt (ed.) *International Companion Encyclopedia of Children's Literature*, London: Routledge.

Perkins, D. (1994) *The Intelligent Eye: Learning to Think by Looking at Art*, Cambridge, MA: Harvard Graduate School of Education.

Sinatra, R. (1986) *Visual Literacy Connections to Thinking, Reading and Writing*, Springfield, IL: Ch. C. Thomas.

Vygotsky, L. (1986) *Thought and Language*, A. Kozulin (ed.) Cambridge, MA: MIT Press.

CHAPTER 12

A WORD ABOUT PICTURES

David Lewis

Reading Contemporary Picture Books: Picturing Text, London: RoutledgeFalmer, 2001, pp. 102–23

Introduction

> N: That looks like a fan.
> DL: What is it do you think?
> N: A towel
>
> > (Nathan (N) and the author (DL) reading together from
> > *Time to Get Out of the Bath, Shirley* by John Burningham)

There was a time when it was necessary to defend the idea that the pictures in picturebooks made an important contribution to the meaning of the text. Joseph Schwarcz, for example, summarizes in his Introduction to *Ways of the Illustrator* some of the history of how pictures and illustrations in children's books were dealt with in the past. He shows how limited were the responses of critics and reviewers who saw picturebook images as merely tasteful or drab, beautiful or undistinguished. At best, picturebook pictures were said to 'harmonize' with the written text. Schwarcz saw his own book as contributing to the movement away from this condescending approach to the visual image toward 'the examination of the illustrator's work as a means of symbolic communication' (Schwarcz, 1982: 4). He therefore began with the following questions: 'In what ways does the illustration, an aesthetic config-uration created for children, express its contents and meanings? How do its elements combine and its structures operate so as to carry the messages to which we are asked to relate?' (Schwarcz, 1982: 4). He did go on to ask, 'How does the illustra-tion relate to the verbal text?' but it was the pictures that had to be dealt with first.

It is no longer necessary to defend the right of pictures to be considered in this way. Non-specialists, as well as critics and scholars, are now much more at ease with both the idea and the practice of 'reading pictures'. In this chapter, therefore, I have not attempted a review of all that is currently known about pictures and how they work, but have restricted myself to a discussion of five key features of the visual image and have linked these to examples of children attempting to make sense of picturebook illustrations. I then briefly examine one of the most recent attempts to develop a grammar of the visual image.

Some key features of the visual image

Line

In the extract set at the head of this chapter, Nathan and I are at the beginning of Burningham's book and are looking at the first page-opening after the title page. On the right is the first picture of Shirley in her bath. Her mum reaches out towards her daughter holding a towel in her left hand. The towel is white with sketchy blue stripes, or possibly fold lines, running along its length. The towel hangs downwards from where it is held at one end and Nathan, quite rightly, points out that it looks like a fan. He is in no danger of really mistaking the towel for a fan as the context clearly calls for a towel, but he does have a point. Burningham's sketch-like, non-naturalistic style stiffens the towel somewhat so that it looks more rigid than it should – it does indeed look like a fan. If we look at the image carefully we can see that it is the towel's black outline and the blue marks fanning out downwards that give the impression of stiffness. In other words, we see the shape as a rather fan-like towel because of Burningham's handling of line.

In this case it is the quality of line that is important. Contour lines not only outline characters and objects but can be made to animate them. Quentin Blake's drawing in *All Join In* explodes with movement and energy, his characters leaping from sofas, chasing mice and hurtling down snowy mountainsides. None of this violent and helter-skelter movement is created through conventional signs of motion, the dashes and streaks familiar from comics. It is the outcome of vigorous drawing and broken outlines allied to a sure grasp of gesture and an understanding of how to suggest action. In contrast to Blake's swirling, jagged and jittery lines, Jonathan Heale's drawing in his foursquare prints for *Lady Muck* – each one framed in solid black – is bold and strong, creating thick, black outlines and shadows which impart a sense of stasis and timelessness. Not much happens, at least physically, in these images, but in the vignettes and scenes which face them, usually on the left-hand side of each page-opening, the paler, more delicate outlining allows for a greater degree of realism and a touch more animation.

Line can be used for purposes beyond separating figure from ground and suggesting animation. The lines, dashes and scorings of hatching and cross-hatching can be used to darken individual colours to suggest shadows and textures, and to model features. In *The Little Boat* Patrick Benson uses this device for a multitude of purposes. He shows us shadows cast by umbrellas on a sunny beach, the smooth roundness of children's legs, the rise and swell of waves at sea, the shimmering of the sea's surface in a flat calm and the glistening scales on the flanks of a giant fish. Anthony Browne uses hatching and cross-hatching too, but rather more sparingly and frequently in contrast with other effects. In *Gorilla*, as Hannah is swung through the trees away from her home and off to the zoo, the blue sky is darkened with cross-hatching in its upper two-thirds causing the moon and stars to shine out brightly. In the lower third the cross-hatching gives way to horizontal hatching strokes which allow for a lighter sky just above the rooftops. A frightened ginger cat leaps into the air from the top of a wall and beneath it the hatching changes direction appearing to propel the cat into the air. In *Voices in the Park*, the 'third voice' sequence begins with Charles peering out of a window in his home, the interior walls of which are densely hatched and cross-hatched, the directions of the hatching serving to clarify the succession of receding empty rooms and doorways. The plate on the facing page shows Charles in back view looking out across the green lawns of the park, most of which are an undifferentiated green except for the foreground where the vertical hatching darkens the tone and suggests the individual blades of grass. The cross-hatched shadow of Charles' mother leans in from the left and falls – both literally and metaphorically – across Charles' back.

Colour

Colour is perhaps the next most basic feature of picturebook pictures. This is not to suggest that picturebooks are always, or have to be, coloured. A number of successful books have relied upon monochrome drawing only, but the vast majority of picturebooks are now printed in colour. Line and colour together can be used to produce simple shapes that in the hands of an illustrator such as Dick Bruna can be transformed into the forms of everyday objects that infants can recognize and name. Modulation of colour and further variation of line produce more complex forms that can be placed in relation to one another, perhaps in an illusory space extending backwards from the picture plane. Thus, cartoon characters can walk down suburban streets, stuffed toys can play in the park and old-fashioned postmen can cycle down country lanes. Line and colour, then, are the two basic elements out of which the more complex features of pictures are built. In the next extract we see clearly how important colour can be in creating the world that the reader sees.

Nathan and I are looking at the fourth page-opening of *Time to Get Out of the Bath, Shirley*. The picture to the right shows some knights in armour galloping through a forest towards the figure of a girl, Shirley, who is hanging from a branch suspended above a waterfall. In keeping with Burningham's non-naturalistic approach, the colour scheme is rather odd, the forest floor being a purplish blue and the background – the space between and beyond the trees – a deep red. The reader is thus placed in a position not unlike that in the first extract. The picture is realistic up to a point but it possesses features that do not seem to fit.

DL: ... so what's going on over here?
N: (*snorts with laughter*) ... in the water ... but there's no splashes (*looking at the horses apparently galloping on the surface of some blue water*) there's two bunny rabbits
DL: that's right ... is that water, do you think?
N: No ... probably the blue path
DL: Hmm ... could be couldn't it?
N: They ... they've gone into the ... mm devils ... in the red thing
DL: Into the devils? What do you mean?
N: Yea ... mm hell
DL: Oh I see
N: 'Cos it's red (*the background to the riders*)

Nathan's mistakes are fairly obvious: he initially sees the horizontal blue band upon which the riders seem to be galloping as water, and then compounds the mistake by taking the red background to be a sign that Shirley, and the knights, are now in hell. Bizarre though these interpretations are, they are directly linked to colour cues. Unlike in the first extract, where the context is clear enough for Nathan not to genuinely mistake the towel for a fan, here the events in the picture sequence have become so strange that he is much more at risk of misunderstanding what is going on.

Colour thus plays an important role in building up the basic image but of course it possesses other functions too. The vibrant red of the baby's dungarees in *So Much* keeps him very much at the focus of our attention. He is easy to find even when he is surrounded by the much larger adults and is especially prominent in the pictures which depict, in tones of brown, grey and black, the other family members waiting for the next arrival. In fact, this muted palette acts as a clear signifier of the boredom depicted so clearly in these images. Colour can also connect or separate significant characters and objects, both within single pictures and across whole sequences. At the beginning of *Gorilla*, for example, the red of Hannah's jumper is contrasted with the blues associated with her father, signalling their lack of contact. By the end of the book the two characters are brought closer together, not only through the father's hands on Hannah's shoulders, but also through the matching reds of their clothing.

Action and movement

Since most picturebooks tell stories of one kind or another they must deal with commonplace features of narrative such as motion, action and the passing of time. Characters move through landscapes and interact with others, tasks are performed and events depicted, quests are followed and challenges met, and what the words tell of these things the pictures are frequently required to show. As a result, picture-book illustrators tend to be particularly adept at calling forth motion out of stillness and duration from instantaneity. For example, imagery that arrests motion immedi-ately prior to its completion can suggest the rapid or violent movement of objects, people and animals. In *All Join In* Quentin Blake's characters chase after a mouse, toss pots and pans about as they clear out a kitchen and are thrown off a sledge at the bottom of a particularly steep slope and in each case we are shown the moment just before events reach a climax. Similar moments can be found in *The Park in the Dark* where Barbara Firth chooses to depict the three friends on a swing at the high point of an upward arc, moments before the descent, and in *Drop Dead* where there are many pre-climactic images of jumping, flying and falling.

Less convulsive movement is often portrayed through what can appear at first glance to be simply a frozen gesture. Barbara Firth's toys walk, twist and turn convinc-ingly but more has gone into their animation than simple stopped motion. In fact, frozen gestures of the sort sometimes found in unposed snapshots can look distinctly awkward and not at all animated. Firth's skill enables her to use the dynamics of her designs to animate the still figures and she recruits our knowledge of facial expres-sion to help us interpret posture. Sometimes, however, it can be difficult to interpret the stilled gesture appropriately if an illustrator is unable to clarify the true nature of a movement.

Consider, for example, the following two extracts from a conversation with Jane about the wordless picturebook, *Where is Monkey?* by Dieter Schubert. *Where is Monkey?* is the tale of a stuffed toy, the monkey of the title, who is dropped by his young owner on a trip to a wood or park. The toy is found by a pack of rats who play with it and mistreat it for a while before it is passed on to various other groups of forest creatures. At one point it is carried off by a magpie who pulls out one of its glass eyes. In the second extract with Jane, she begins to tell her version of the story. The first plate shows the little boy reaching out with his left hand towards his toy monkey which is tucked up in bed in a box beneath a chair (see Figure 10). The figures and objects in the background make it clear that mother and son are about to go out for a cycle ride but Jane is momentarily unsure whether the reaching gesture is one of 'putting' or 'getting' as there is no unambiguous vector associated with the movement.

Figure 10 From *Where is Monkey?* by Dieter Schubert

J: (*quietly commenting on the first picture only*) Well first of all the little boy
        puts the monkey ... no he puts the monkey in a chair ... under the chair in
        a box and then after that he gets him out ...

Such misinterpretations are easy to make at the beginning of a book, particularly
one such as this where there are no words and no preceding sequence of pictures to
contextualize the actions. But later in the story, when the magpie has appropriated
the monkey, Jane has a similar problem, for a similar reason.

J: ... and it catches the monkey and it goes back to its nest ... (*laughs*) teeth!
DL: Hmm
J: ... and glasses and eyes ...
DL: Yes
J: glass eyes
DL: I think they must be glass eyes mustn't they?

Figure 11 From *Where is Monkey?* by Dieter Schubert

J: And he puts a pin in his eye 'cos he takes one of his eyes out
DL: Hmm
J: . . . 'cos it's shiny

The picture is intended to show the magpie trying to detach one of the toy's glass eyes but the arrangement of elements within the image is confusing, for although the bird seems to be leaning backwards and thus pulling, a clear vector formed by the bird's beak and the thread attaching the glass bead to the toy's head runs diagonally downwards from left to right, suggesting a pushing movement (see Figure 11). Jane therefore initially perceives the taut thread to be a pin being pushed into the toy's fabric ('he puts a pin in his eye') and then swiftly corrects herself without disturbing the flow of her narration ('he takes one of his eyes out').

Diagonals within pictures can create strong directional thrusts as the tendency to read from left to right interacts with our sense of gravity moving things downwards. Thus the diagonal from bottom left to top right always appears to ascend while the diagonal from top left to bottom right appears to descend. This opposition is clearly illustrated in a page-opening from *All Join In* where some typically Blakean children are caught in the act of sliding (see Figure 12). On the right a group of four on a sledge are depicted hurtling left to right down a snowy mountainside. On the left another group are taking turns to slide, right to left, down an elephant's trunk, but so powerful is the force of the vector that leads upwards from left to right that at least one of the children could easily be seen as shinning up the trunk rather than slipping down it.

Rudolph Arnheim points out in his book *Art and Visual Perception* that sometimes the postures in which artists freeze their subjects to gain the most animated effect are not even found in the real world (Arnheim, 1974). Galloping animals such as horses, for example, are still often shown with both fore and hind legs outstretched – as is the lion chasing the children in *Drop Dead* – although the serial photographs of Eadweard Muybridge revealed long ago that quadrupeds only adopt such a posture when leaping and never when running. The distortion comes about because 'Action pictures portray motion precisely to the degree displayed by the figure' (Arnheim, 1974: 424). Thus the depiction of rapid movement requires the full extension of the

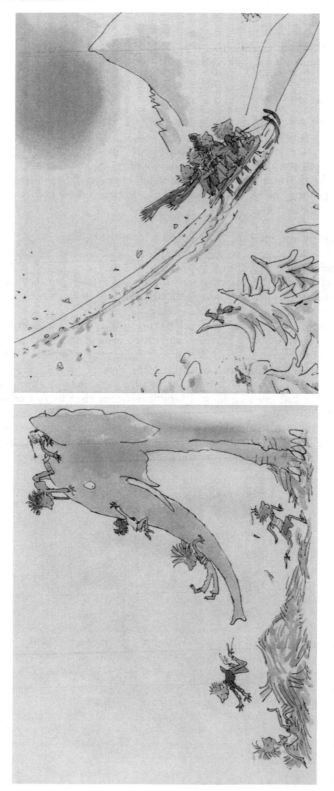

Figure 12 From *All Join In* by Quentin Blake

limbs even when such extension is 'unreal'. Slower, more sedate movement would require much less stretching and distortion.

Size and location

If we return for a moment to the misfortunes of Dieter Schubert's lost monkey we can examine how two more features of the visual image – the size and location of separate elements – affect our understanding. Having satisfied its craving for the bright shiny glass eye, the magpie drops the monkey and it falls past some bumble-bees into a lake or stream below. Jane, and another reader, Martin, on reaching this point in the picture sequence, both make the same error – they both see the bees as catching the monkey.

M: he drops it into the sea . . . he drops it from there
DL: Hmm
M: The bees grab it and drop it in the sea.
J: And . . . and then it falls and some bees try and catch it but they can't because it's too heavy and it goes into the water and goes down to the bottom . . .

The reasons why both children read the picture in this way are partly to do with the fact that the whole story has been structured around the serial abduction and mistreatment of the monkey so it makes sense to anticipate a further, similar episode. But their reading is also prompted by the way the elements of the picture are organized. The tiny bees are placed close to the picture plane making them much larger than is necessary and granting them a significance that they do not possess within the story. Moreover, one of the bees overlaps the figure of the monkey as it falls behind suggesting that the monkey is being borne on its back. A closer look at this image, however, reveals that the bees appear to be fleeing the falling object rather than trying to catch it. Size and location are therefore key factors in determining

Figure 13 From *Where is Monkey?* by Dieter Schubert

what we see, but it is not the absolute size that is important. Large objects in the background are not only diminished in size but also in significance, and small elements can be given prominence either by moving them closer to the picture plane or by bringing them closer than another larger, but more distant, object.

For example, in *The Little Boat* the tiny scrap of expanded polystyrene, no bigger than a child's hand, is brought forward towards the viewer and placed at eye level in the picture where it is becalmed in the middle of the ocean. This automatically makes it seem larger but on turning the page we find it brought even closer still as a giant fish rears up out of the depths and seizes it between its jaws. The fish, pressed up against the picture plane seems truly monstrous, but given the absolute size of the little boat, the fish can be no more than, say, one or two feet long. Another creature brought vividly to life, though only partly through its size and position, is the chimpanzee behind the bars of its cage in *Gorilla*. The poignancy of this image is brought about through the interanimation of many design features: the contrast in style with the relatively flat and non-realistic images around it; the severing of the creature's face into bands by the strips of white page which are also the cage bars; and the chimpanzee's level stare that meets our gaze and implicates us in its plight. But it is the fact that this is a life-size portrait, crammed up close to the reader's own face, and foreshortened so that the muzzle seems to push out through the bars that makes us pause.

There are a number of further ways that an object's or person's location within the picture might influence meaning. High and low, right and left are all locations that can have significance. William Moebius suggests that figures positioned up high may be interpreted as in ecstatic or dream-like states, or may be possessed of high social status or a positive self image. In contrast, a low position might suggest low status or low spirits. Important figures are usually centred but can, in another picture, be both literally and metaphorically marginalized. The left-hand side of a picture, Moebius claims, is a position of relative security while figures on the right are likely to be 'moving into a situation of risk or adventure' (Moebius, 1986: 140). Nodelman, following Arnheim, suggests that we are likely to identify with figures on the left, especially if they have their backs to us so that they appear to be seeing what we are seeing.

However, much clearly depends on the overall design of a particular book. High and low, left and right, can be readily identifiable locations within clearly framed or differentiated images. On pages where the pictures are mere vignettes or are only partially framed so that the words push in from the side, however, or where pictures are irregularly sequenced down or across the page in asymmetrical arrangements as they are in some parts of *The Man*, *All Join In* and *Drop Dead*, then high and low, left and right have no significant value. When we speak of such positions we make the assumption that the objects or figures concerned are located within a scene. Thus, Barbara Firth's three toys are positioned to the far right in front of a panorama of the park at the moment when terror strikes them and drives them home. Similarly, Anthony Browne's Hannah slumped on the ground, low down in front of the television set, is clearly miserable whereas Charles and Smudge excitedly at play in *Voices in the Park* are high up in trees, on slides and climbing frames. In fact, when we examine a range of different types of picturebook, and types of picturebook imagery, then we find that such positional codes are in fact used sparingly.

Rather more commonplace is the convention that places figures in motion facing left to right. Sometimes this is taken to be a feature unique to the picturebook but Arnheim makes it clear that pictorial representations have been read from left to right ever since the advent of 'sequential thought recorded in linear writing' (Arnheim,

1974: 33). This deeply ingrained habit creates a powerful vector, causing us to perceive movement from left to right across a picture as freer, easier and more natural than movement in the opposite direction. Thus Rosie the hen from *Rosie's Walk* plods steadfastly around the farmyard across each of the page-openings from left to right, dragging our eyes with her and inviting us to turn the page to see what happens next. Max from *Where the Wild Things Are* sails from left to right into the land of the Wild Things, only reversing the direction when he deems it time to return home. Further examples can readily be found in most narrative picturebooks. Thus Browne's dogs, Albert and Victoria, pursue each other around the park in the direction of the next page turn and the Jolly Postman's 'round' is in one direction only. Almost no one walks leftwards down the street in *Have You Seen Who's Just Moved in Next Door to Us?* and *The Little Boat* sails west to judge from the contrast between its point of departure and its point of arrival (from British seaside resort to Caribbean beach), but does it by sailing east, that is, to the right. So strong and all-pervasive is this bibliographic habit that its inversion almost always has a significance for the characters in the story. Anyone attempting to move from right to left can usually be seen to be deliberately interfering with the general movement of characters in the story, to be blocked in some way, to be returning from adventures or to possess a sinister purpose. A good example comes at the end of *The Park in the Dark* when the three toys, having had fun playing on the swings in the locked park, are frightened by a late commuter train rushing across the scene from the right-hand edge. The three friends turn tail and run towards the left-hand edge, back in the direction of home.

Symbolism

Each of the extracts taken from readings and discussions with children have so far in this chapter turned upon mis-readings of the illustrators' intentions. We could therefore be forgiven for believing that young children quite frequently make such mistakes and that learning to 'read pictures' is for them an arduous and slow process. In fact, the very opposite is true. Children are sometimes puzzled by what they see in pictures (see Maureen Crago on 'Incompletely Shown Objects in Picture Books' (Crago, 1979)) but mistakes such as the ones we have been examining here are actually quite rare and in every case have been caused by visual ambiguity or – sad to say – inept illustration. What is remarkable is not the fact that they make mistakes (in one sense they are not making mistakes at all) but rather the speed with which they recognize and interpret what happens in the pictures they look at. Nathan simply sees the fan-like stiffness of the towel just as Jane sees the magpie pushing a pin into the monkey's eye and Martin sees the monkey on the bee's back. There are, however, some features of visual images that are not so instantly recognizable.

Take, for example, the different ways in which Jane and Martin come to an understanding of the identity of the old man who finds and rescues the dilapidated toy in *Where is Monkey?* Immediately after the episode with the magpie and the bees, the toy is hooked out of the stream into which he fell by an elderly fisherman and taken home to be repaired. The next extract is Jane's response to this sequence of pictures.

J: ... it goes into the water and it goes down to the bottom where a big fish finds it (*turns page*) and the man is fishing and he catches some fish and it also catches the monkey.
DL: That's right
J: And luckily it's a toy-mender

How does she know that the old man is a 'toy-mender'? There is no written text to tells her that this is so. She does it by rapidly identifying the key features of the final plate of the page-opening (the man inserts a key into the lock of a cottage-like building which has rows of dolls and toys in the window and a sign above the door), recognizing the general significance of the sign (a red cross) and fine-tuning this understanding with the aid of supplementary information (the bits and pieces of dismembered doll stuck to the wall around the cross). This act of interpretation she carries out swiftly, and equally swiftly translates it into the phrase 'toy-mender'. She is probably unaware of these acts of judgement and interpretation but in narrating her story she reveals how her reading rests upon an implicit understanding of how elements within pictures are arranged and how pictures can exploit the symbols of a common culture.

Now contrast Jane's response to that of Martin.

M: Found the Monkey
DL: Hmm ... Hmm
M: (*quietly*) Takin' it back to his place (*turns page*) takin' it in his house ... stitchin' it up
DL: Hmm
M: Then he's in a bowl of water ... an' dryin' it
DL: Why do you think he's doing all that?
M: Don't know

At this point in our conversation, if Martin was aware of the symbolic significance of the red cross he was not letting on. Later, however, when the book was finished and we were discussing it, he revealed with some prompting that he did understand.

DL: ... when he gets caught by the man with the fishing rod ...
M: he gets repaired
DL: he takes him home
M: Look teddy ... ambulance ... toys
DL: Ah, right
M: He's an ambulance
DL: I wondered you see why the man repaired him ... do you know what that is?
M: It's an ambulance cross

The red cross symbol is almost universally recognized and understood so it would be strange if children, at least in the western world, were unaware of its significance. Nodelman is correct, however, to maintain that 'All symbols are inherently arcane' (Nodelman, 1988: 107) inasmuch as the meanings of symbols such as the red cross are hidden from those who do not possess the knowledge necessary to unlock their secrets. If you are born into a culture that neither uses nor recognizes the red cross – let us say, an Islamic society where the red crescent symbolizes medical assistance – then no amount of looking at the symbol alone will force it to reveal its significance (though I imagine you could work it out within the story from the surrounding textual information). On the other hand, authors and illustrators may well employ symbols that are not derived from the everyday-life-world of a specific culture and that only resonate within a particular book or within that author's or illustrator's oeuvre.

Take, for example, the following group of children discussing with their teacher some of the puzzling features of Libby Hathorn's and Gregory Rogers' picturebook story about the homeless child, *Way Home*. They pause to examine the *trompe l'oeuil* end papers which are designed to look like crumpled paper. At first, before they have read the story, they are concerned only with the surface features of the image. (Individual letters indicate different speakers. VB is the teacher.)

> T: and this is supposed to be creased-up paper
> P: it looks like tin foil

Later, having read and shared the book and having been primed to look for meanings beyond the superficial, they are prepared to suggest ways in which the endpapers may relate symbolically to the theme of the story.

> A: that's the newspaper he's lying on
> VB: yes it seems all scrunched up doesn't it?
> P: and crumpled
> VB: what is it?
> A&P: paper
> T: when I first saw it I thought it meant he'd have a lot to climb over
> C: I thought it meant his life was a bit crumpled
>
> (Burdon, 1996)

The key here is the expectation on the part of the children that images in a book of this kind may possess meanings over and above what is represented, allied to a willingness to use their understanding of the story to generate a plausible interpretation. An image of crumpled paper is what it is, but in the context of the picturebook *Way Home*, it carries a clear symbolic charge. Clearly there can be no appeal to a standard meaning as in the case of the red cross, but the interpretative processes at work are essentially the same.

Manipulation of line, colour, action conventions, object size and location, and symbolism are only a few of the ways in which pictures can be made to possess meaning. Illustrators also concern themselves with the way images are framed; how the preponderance of certain shapes can influence the reader's understanding; how facial expression and gesture can be translated from real life to the printed page and so on. Readers who are interested in researching the subject further could turn to Jane Doonan's detailed and accessible book, *Looking at Pictures in Picturebooks* or the first six chapters of Perry Nodelman's *Words About Pictures*. A slightly different approach is taken in D. A. Dondis' *A Primer of Visual Literacy*, but this book too is helpful (Doonan, 1993; Nodelman, 1988; Dondis, 1973).

A grammar of visual design

So far we have examined how some of the discrete features of an illustration – the lines, colours and symbols – might contribute to the meaning and effectiveness of the whole, but we have not as yet considered what kind of contribution might be made by any *structural organization* a picture may possess. In the Introduction to *Words About Pictures* Perry Nodelman hints at such pictorial structures when he writes, '[semiotics] suggests the possibility of a system underlying visual communication that is something like a grammar – something like the system of relationships and contexts that makes verbal communication possible' (Nodelman, 1988: ix). The idea of such a grammar of the image is not new. Indeed, artists themselves have sometimes sought for such an underlying structure. Many painters in the early

Figure 14 From *Gorilla* by Anthony Browne

years of the twentieth century, in particular those drawn towards abstraction, sought analogies from verbal language to support their efforts at uncovering a universal visual language. However, it is semioticians who have been the most persistent seekers after the grail of a visual grammar.

Roland Barthes' attempts in the 1960s to analyse the image syntactically foundered on his inability to identify both the discontinuous elements, the separate units, within the continuous field of the image that might be taken to correspond to the words, phrases and clauses of verbal language. Without such a 'vocabulary' it would seem that there could be no grammar. For these and similar reasons, there has been much scepticism over the possibility that pictorial representations will submit to anything like a grammatical analysis. Nevertheless, a further attempt has recently been made to outline a grammar that can be applied to the full range of visual images – paintings, cartoons, photographs, advertising layouts, diagrams, maps and so on – and a full account has been published under the title, *Reading Images: the Grammar of Visual Design*, by Gunther Kress and Theo van Leeuwen (Kress and van Leeuwen, 1996). I provide in this final section of the chapter a short introduction to this grammar, explaining some of the technical terms involved and supplying some simple examples, drawn from picturebooks, of the grammar in action. We will begin with one or two examples and then examine the underlying principles of the grammar, concluding with a further example of how the grammar might apply to picturebook images.

In *Gorilla*, Hannah and her friend spend some of their evening in the cinema. Sitting in the darkness they watch a 'Supergorilla' streaking across the screen from left to right (see Figure 14). For Kress and van Leeuwen this image would be typical of what they call an *action process*. In other words it is – rather obviously – an image of something happening. Somebody – an *actor* – is doing something. Picturebooks are full of action processes for they are primarily concerned to represent, in words and sequences of pictures, doings and happenings, most often in the form of narrative. We can tell that this is an action process rather than, say, a *conceptual process* like a diagram in a textbook because the image involves a *vector*, a strong directional thrust. In this case the body of Supergorilla himself forms the vector, pushing from left to right. He is therefore not only a *participant* in the action process (the character or object who is 'doing something') his torso and arms also direct our attention to what or where the action is directed. In this case, the action (flying, or streaking through the sky) is not directed at anything or anyone, so it is therefore a *non-transactional* action process. This fragment of an image structure, if put into words, might be represented as 'Supergorilla (actor) streaks (action process) through the sky'.

In *So Much*, on the other hand, the image of Aunt Bibba arriving at the house is organized in such a way that her left arm points towards the baby as she stoops down towards him (see Figure 15). This arm forms a vector, or directional thrust, linking Aunt to baby in a *transactional* process, unlike Supergorilla whose action is non-transactional. Aunt Bibba, who is the main actor within the image, reaches out to the baby who is *the goal*. Transcoded into words we might say that 'Aunt Bibba (actor) greets (action process) the baby (goal)'. Sometimes, of course, a picture will represent an *interaction* rather than an action, the process being bi-directional and the participants taking the roles of actor and goal either simultaneously

Figure 15 From *So Much* by Trish Cooke and Helen Oxenbury

or sequentially. Thus in Briggs' *The Man*, the boy and the Man threaten each other at the same time with, respectively, a mobile phone and a match, the aerial of the phone and the shaft of the match forming vectors that link Man to boy and boy to Man. Similarly, Uncle Didi from *So Much* makes to kiss his little nephew as the baby points with a delicate index finger. Here the baby's finger and his uncle's pouting lips form two tiny but distinct vectors linking the two figures together.

The terms *action process, conceptual process, vector, participant, transactional, non-transactional, actor* and *goal* have all been borrowed from the systemic functional grammar developed by M. A. K. Halliday (1985) and his associates and they tell us immediately that this is not like the traditional grammars taught in school. In this grammar, structure – whether of verbal language or visual imagery – is conceived in terms of meaning and function. In other words, the authors are not interested in dissecting the image into its separate features (line, colour, shape, etc.) and analysing them apart from each other, but are looking at the way the structure of an image contributes to what that image says to us. The participants in an image – the people and things that have roles to play – are organized upon the page, and are related to one another, in various ways. The principles of this organization, and the ways in which it contributes to how we understand the image, are what the grammar seeks to reveal.

The grammar is systemic because it involves the artist and/or illustrator (or writer when applied to verbal language) in making selections from different areas, or systems, of possibility. Thus, when language users speak, write, draw or paint they make choices – more or less unconsciously depending upon the circumstances and context – from the available resources in order to realize in sound, writing or pictures whatever it is they want to 'say'. Languages are therefore *systemic* in that they are composed of interlocking systems that require users to choose between options that the language makes available to them in order to realize their meanings. For example, if I want to tell my daughter to tidy her room I have to make vocabulary choices so I might refer to her by her first name, her full name or by her private, family pet name. I can also choose from a number of sentence forms: the imperative ('Go and tidy your room'); the interrogative ('Have you tidied your room yet?') or the declarative ('I'd like you to tidy your room'). Similarly, if I take a group photograph of my friends I might ask them to look straight into the camera lens or look away; to smile or not; to stand formally erect or to relax. Each choice made will affect the final meaning of the utterance or image. In the case of Supergorilla, Browne had the option of making the image transactional or non-transactional (the superhero could have been about to catch a falling victim); it could have been uni-directional or bi-directional (another figure could have attacked Supergorilla head on making both figures actors and goals). Of particular importance here is that the choices are about alternative structures rather than individual features such as line, colour, texture, etc. Structure is taken to be directly concerned with the construction of meaning and is not merely a formal skeleton holding the various parts together.

The functional aspect of the grammar is thus rooted in its concern with meaning. Kress and van Leeuwen maintain that, even today, most grammars tend to be formal, examining the separate parts of a language in isolation from its semantic aspects. In contrast, systemic functional grammar focuses upon the relationship between structure and meaning and is concerned with the uses to which images are put. The authors approach the task of analysis and description in this way because they begin from the assumption that visual imagery, like verbal language, is a form of *social semiotic* (Halliday, 1978). In other words, the signs from which images are composed have developed socially, in the interactions of image makers and their reader or viewers. What makes visual images intelligible is that makers and users alike share common understandings about how the world – real and imaginary, outer and inner – can be represented, and about how images can be and are used. The pictures in picturebooks, for example, possess certain functions that mark them out as being different from the pictures in art galleries, car maintenance manuals or photograph albums. Our images are part of the fabric of our shared culture and are put to use for various ends. Moreover, since visual languages, just as much as verbal ones, are concerned with encoding and communicating meaning, the developed system exists as a 'semantic pool' from which those inducted into the culture may draw.

Let us examine one more example of the grammar in action. Consider the picture in *Granpa* where the old man skips along his garden path watched by his grand-daughter (Figure 16). We could give a formal account of the image of Granpa emphasizing the fact that the figure of the old man is the most salient feature of the picture. He bears the most visual weight on account of his location, shape and size, but this would not tell us a great deal about how the organization of the image structures the meaning. If, however, we transpose the analysis into the terms of functional grammar we might say that Granpa is here a major participant who is an actor involved in a non-transactional action process: that is, he is doing something, but not doing it to, or aiming it at, anyone else. His depicted action has no goal and is thus analogous to the category of 'intransitive verb' in verbal language. In words we might say, 'Granpa is skipping'.

If we now look at the whole picture rather than just the image of Granpa we can identify a further participant, the granddaughter. Once again, in formal terms we could say that although she is a relatively small figure she gains weight and salience through her overlapping of the house in the background where the regular oval of her head stands out against the rectilinear shapes behind. Also, positioned

Figure 16 From *Granpa* by John Burningham

as she is to the far left of the picture she balances the larger figure of her Granpa just right of centre. In terms of the semantic relations within the picture, however, and employing the terms of functional grammar again, we might say that here there are two major participants, one a *reactor* (the girl) who through the eyeline of her gaze creates a vector that involves her in a *transactional* process (watching) directed towards a *phenomenon* (Granpa skipping). Transcoded into verbal language, we might say, 'the girl is watching Granpa skipping'.

Conclusions

Analyses of picturebooks which focus upon how the images work have been influential in the study of the picturebook since at least the 1980s and one can see perfectly well why this should be so. It seems fairly obvious that the more one knows about how pictures come to possess meaning seemingly cannot fail to be of value in our researches into how the picturebook works. Kress and van Leeuwen's grammar, for example, helps us to understand more clearly how the pictures in a book like *Gorilla* contribute to the story. Once we begin to notice reaction processes in pictures we soon realize that although the printed text tells us what Hannah, her father and the gorilla did, either by themselves or to and with one another, the pictures show more looking and watching than doing. There are scenes of action (Hannah's father works at his desk and walks to work, Hannah walks upstairs and rushes down again the following morning, and the gorilla swings through the trees and climbs the wall of the zoo) but many of these processes, such as the small scenes of walking to and from home, contribute little semantically to the unfolding story and function almost like the grammatical words in a sentence, a kind of connective tissue linking the parts of the story together.

In contrast, the scenes involving reaction processes seem highly significant. In its pictorial aspect, *Gorilla* is very much a book concerned with looking and being looked at. In the opening pages Hannah is shown reading a book, looking at television and watching her unresponsive father. He in turn reads the newspaper and ignores his daughter. All these images confirm the girl's isolation and alienation from her surroundings. To make matters worse, as I have already observed, Hannah's father never makes eye contact with his daughter, and this is true even at the end of the book when he stands behind Hannah to look at her birthday card, and despite the fact that the printed text says that she looked at him. In none of these scenes is there any 'bi-directionality' to the reaction processes. In contrast, once the toy gorilla has apparently come to life (watched, of course, by the horrified doll), Hannah and the gorilla do little else but gaze into each others' eyes, the vectors of their eyelines following the same path. They then look at the gorillas in the zoo, though here their looking is merely implied as they are positioned with their backs to the reader, and later we see them several more times face to face although again, in only one of these latter scenes are Hannah and the gorilla actually depicted with an eyeline connecting them. They have eyes closed as they kiss goodnight and are swivelled through ninety degrees so that Hannah has her back to the reader as they dance. This selective use of uni-directionality and bi-directionality in reaction processes makes a powerful contribution to the meaning of the story. The real father cannot be reached and the close social bond established and maintained through the primary sense of sight is transferred to a substitute father in the shape of the gorilla.

In cases such as this an increased sensitivity to pictorial structures seems to be extremely helpful. One might have spotted the 'looking and watching' theme without knowing about reaction processes but the systematic and organized nature of the grammar provides us with a way to focus our looking. Even so, when we come to analyse picturebooks we can only make use of our increased understanding of visual structures if we combine it with other kinds of knowledge. Our understanding of reaction processes in *Gorilla* would have been of limited use if we had not already known a good deal about Browne's story. Analyses of the pictures in picturebooks always need to be fed into an understanding of the book as a whole, and if our fine dissections of structure do not help us to understand more about the story to which they are contributing then they are of limited use to us.

References

Arnheim, R. (1974) *Art and Visual Perception: a Psychology of the Creative Eye*, London: University of California Press.

Crago, M. (1979) 'Incompletely shown objects in picture books: one child's response', *Children's Literature in Education*, 10(3): 151–7.

Dondis, D. A. (1973) *A Primer of Visual Literacy*, Cambridge, MA: MIT Press.

Kress, G. and van Leeuwen, T. (1996) *Reading Images: the Grammar of Visual Design*, London: Routledge.

Moebius, W. (1986) 'Introduction to picturebook codes', in P. Hunt (1990) *Children's Literature: the Development of Criticism*, London: Routledge.

Nodelman, P. (1988) *Words about Pictures: The Narrative Art of Children's Picture Books*, Athens, Georgia: University of Georgia Press.

Schwarcz, J. H. (1982) *Ways of the Illustrator: Visual Communication in Children's Literature*, Chicago: American Library Association.

Picturebook bibliography

All Join In by Quentin Blake, Jonathan Cape, 1990

The Man by Raymond Briggs, Julia MacRae, 1992

Gorilla by Anthony Browne, Walker Books, 1983

Voices in the Park by Anthony Browne, Doubleday, 1998

Come Away From the Water, Shirley by John Burningham, Jonathan Cape, 1977

Time to Get Out of the Bath, Shirley by John Burningham, Jonathan Cape, 1978

Drop Dead by Babette Cole, Jonathan Cape, 1996

So Much by Trish Cooke illustrated by Helen Oxenbury, Walker Books, 1994.

Way Home by Libby Hathorn illustrated by Gregory Rogers, Andersen Press, 1994.

The Little Boat by Kathy Henderson illustrated by Patrick Benson, Walker Books, 1995.

Rosie's Walk by Pat Hutchins, The Bodley Head, 1970

Lady Muck by William Mayne illustrated by Jonathan Heale, Heinemann,1997

Have you Seen Who's Just Moved in Next Door to Us? by Colin McNaughton, Walker Books, 1991

Where is Monkey? by Dieter Schubert, Hutchinson, 1987

Where the Wild Things Are by Maurice Sendak, The Bodley Head, 1967

The Park in the Dark by Martin Waddell illustrated by Barbara Firth, Walker Books, 1989

CHAPTER 13

TELEVISION AND FILM

Jackie Marsh and Elaine Millard

Literacy and Popular Culture: Using Children's Culture in the Classroom, London: Paul Chapman Publishing, 2000, pp. 138–62

It is television, more than any other medium, perhaps, that has attracted the fiercest criticism, with the tone of some critics becoming near hysterical:

> Perhaps the increase in the crime rate, the violence in society, the boredom suffered by children and teenagers, the lack of creativity in people's lives, the alarming suicide numbers, are connected to the thousands of not just wasted, but detrimental hours, young people have spent glued to the television.
>
> (Brooky, 1998: 3–4)

This chapter provides an overview of research on children and television in order to provide a more reasoned and measured response. In addition, it explores ways in which children's overwhelming attraction to the medium can be incorporated into the classroom in order to develop a range of literacy skills. First, however, we map out the full extent of children's engagement with television, video and film and discuss the implications of their fascination with the moving image.

Children's television consumption

The Livingstone and Bovill report (1999) found that 99 per cent of children and young people aged between 6 and 17 years watch television and that they watch it for, on average, two and a half hours per day. There was no significant difference in gender in terms of the amount of television consumption. The programmes they reported as their favourites contained no surprises: soap opera was the first choice, with cartoons second and sport third. However, when gender was brought into the equation, the picture changed. Girls liked soap operas best, followed by other serials (such as *Animal Hospital*) and then cartoons. Boys' first choice was sport, followed by cartoons and then soap operas. As with their computer games, girls appeared to be attracted primarily to narrative genres and boys to competitive sports (Millard, 1997). Livingstone and Bovill (1999) found that younger children enjoyed watching videos and generally children did not distinguish between videos and television.

One issue that has been of concern since the advent of television is that of displacement. The question for educationalists has been, if children spend more of their time watching television, what have they given up? The major worry, of course, is that children have stopped reading. However, it would appear that this fear is ill-founded. Neuman (1995) suggests that television-watching displaced listening to the radio, or going to the cinema, rather than reading and that as new media arrive they displace interaction with other media which offer equivalent experiences. In addition, she suggests that in some cases, the reading of books is *stimulated* by television-watching, a point we will return to later in the chapter. It would also appear that television viewing is seen by the children in the Livingstone and Bovill (1999) study as something to do when they are bored, thus suggesting that it displaces doing nothing. In addition, Neuman (1995) draws our attention to the fact that studies on the amount of reading children undertake each day have indicated that there has been no reduction in the amount of time spent reading. In the 1940s, 1950s and 1960s, children reported reading for 15 minutes each day (Lyness, 1952; Witty, 1967). This was also found to be the case in the 1980s (Neuman, 1988). Interestingly enough, Livingstone and Bovill (1999) reported that children in the 1990s also reported reading for 15 minutes each day. It appears that there is little evidence that watching television is displacing reading.

However, there have been other suggestions that television-watching does affect reading, in that children who watch more television are less fluent readers. Neuman (1995), in a thorough review of the literature, outlines many studies which found no significant relationship between the watching of television and cognitive development and some which found small but significant relationships. She suggests that, 'At the very minimum a negative, though modest, relationship exists between television and reading achievement' (Neuman, 1995: 42). However, it is clear that this evidence is not strong enough to warrant making any significant claims with regard to the relationship between television-viewing and reading. It may be that children who are less confident readers spend more time watching television because it is less demanding for them. This does not mean that television is a cause of their lack of skills and confidence in reading. In addition, Gunter and McAleer (1997) suggest that there is evidence that watching television can enhance children's cognitive skills. We would suggest that, as there is no strong evidence of a positive or negative effect on reading from the amount of television children watch, we should focus instead on ways it might be used to promote reading in the classroom. We will return to this issue later in the chapter.

Another fear voiced in relation to children's interaction with television is that of addiction. As with computer games, there have been many media scares that children are becoming 'TV zombies' (Storkey, 1999). Again, there is little concrete evidence to support this. Most children appear to watch television for about 18 hours a week on average (Livingstone and Bovill, 1999) and very few children report watching television as their sole pastime for hours on end. Rather, children appear to be mixing their use of media in that they watch television, read, play computer games and listen to music as leisure activities and are not particularly dependent upon any one of them. In addition, it is clear that children are not the passive viewers that many assume them to be. It has been noted that adults are far from being 'couch potatoes' when they watch television. Willis (1990) records studies in which adults have been watched as they sit in front of the screen. He notes that:

> when they are watching, they are far from passive. They shout back at the screen, make sarcastic comments about people's hair-styles and dress sense, sing along with the advertising jingles, talk about the programmes while they are still on. Far from being the passive watchers of political mythology, they actively collaborate with the screen to create and recreate a web of meanings that are relevant to them and anchored in their own lives.
>
> (Willis, 1990: 32)

It is no different with children. Palmer (1986), in an Australian study, found that children rarely sat for long periods of time watching television. Rather, they danced and sang in front of it, ate, slept, did their homework, played games and engaged in a range of other activities. When children do sit down to focus on a programme, like adults, they interact with the screen. Buckingham's (1993b) work has been central to the development of our understanding of how children make sense of the symbolic material with which they are presented and link their viewing with other aspects of experience. They are often, in fact, as active in their meaning-making in relation to television as they are when reading books or magazines.

However, there have been other criticisms related to violence and the conclusions reached are the same. For example, there is no strong evidence that violence on television and film has an effect on children (Barker and Petley, 1997). In fact, as Buckingham (1993b) points out in a study of 6–11-year-olds' television-viewing, it is very difficult to predict what children will find frightening, with some children reporting that sequences of *Mary Poppins* and Fairy Liquid advertisements had scared them.

From the evidence presented so far, it is clear that the moving image plays a central part in children's cultural lives, whether the medium in question is television, film or video. There are many differences between television and film which we do not have space to explore here. Throughout the chapter, we will refer to a focus on both as work on the 'moving image'. We now consider what similarities there may be in the processes involved in reading moving images and printed text.

Reading print and televisual narratives

It is important that the links between the reading processes used in decoding and understanding print and other forms of text are compared and contrasted in order to inform our understanding of the relationships between them. The work of Neuman (1995) and Robinson (1997) has been instrumental in illuminating the processes involved. Both have argued that children are active meaning-makers in relation to both print and televisual texts, rather than passive consumers of either. In a study of her son's responses to a book and television programme of the same narrative, Neuman concluded that:

> David's processing approach appears strikingly similar for both print and televised stories. In each, he is actively engaged in searching for meaning. As an experienced reader and viewer, he tends to be drawn to creating an interpretive framework for each story; individual symbolic elements of each medium are not mentioned. While the means of conveying information are different, the skills and knowledge needed to interpret each medium appear to be the same.
>
> (Neuman, 1995: 80)

In addition, Robinson (1997) asserts that it is in children's understanding of narrative where similarities are to be found. Television and print texts share a number of features. Narratives, whatever the medium used to construct them, draw on sets of conventions known and shared by their audiences. These conventions structure signs into chains of signification which are reinforced by repetition. A view of a row of wet slate roofs can signify a working-class district, or a close-up shot lit from below will signify menace, for instance. When children are encouraged to talk about television, they are learning to make sense of these storytelling conventions, some of which are shared with other forms of text. For example, character can be constructed through binary opposition. In Westerns, whether the medium is a comic-book cartoon or block-buster film, a white hat represents the goody and a black hat, stereotypically, the baddy. However, although televisual and print narratives share some of the same character-istics, they are also very different. For example, the moving image can provide details about character and setting which cannot be achieved without the interaction of sound and images. Similarly, written narratives can use intradiegetic and extradiegetic narrative techniques to reveal thoughts and feelings in a very different way from films and television. Children need to learn how the language of moving images and printed texts can both differ and offer the same ways of signifying meaning.

If we move from a consideration of the *forms* of the different media to the *pro-cesses* involved in reading each, we see that there is also overlap. We would suggest that the similarities between reading processes, needed in order to make sense of printed and televisual narratives, differ in the extent to which each medium draws upon aural or visual perception. In order to compare the processes involved in reading both print and televisual texts, we have drawn on a widely accepted model of the reading process produced by Marilyn Jager-Adams (Adams, 1990). Adams uses the diagram in Figure 17 to explain the relationship between phonic, syntactic and semantic cues.

We have added the italicized categories to Figure 18 in order to explain the different strands which can affect contextual understanding. We have learned from reader response criticism that the reader brings a set of prior expectations to any decoding of a new text (Iser, 1978; Fish, 1980). The socio-cultural context in which we read a text, as well as prior experience of that genre, affects the meanings we derive from it. A practising Moslem would derive much more meaning from a passage of the Koran, for example, than an atheist, having no knowledge of the Moslem reli-gion. As Robinson (1997) points out, children reading the Ahlbergs' popular book, *Each Peach Pear Plum*, need a familiarity with Western nursery rhymes in order to understand fully the text and its intertextual references. Figure 17 shows how these factors impinge on contextual processing. Adams (1990) suggests that the reading process demands the interplay of these different elements. The reader assigns meaning

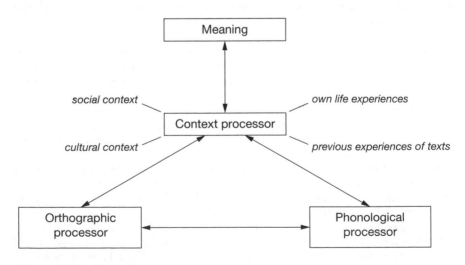

Figure 17 Reading print texts
Source: adapted from Adams (1990)

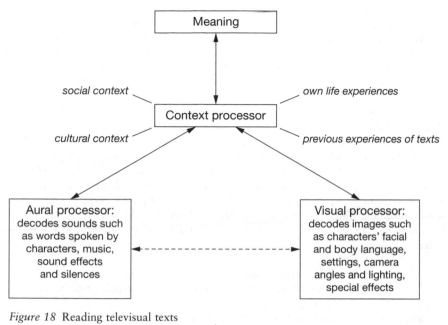

Figure 18 Reading televisual texts
Source: adapted from Adams (1990: 158)

to a printed text through decoding phoneme–grapheme relationships, while at the same time making sense of any intertextual relationships that exist. We would argue that this complex interplay between signifier and signified also enables the construction of meaning from televisual texts; it is only the nature of the decoding system which differs. Instead of depending on orthographic and phonological processing systems, the reader of televisual texts uses aural and visual processing skills to read the narrative (Figure 18).

The arrow between the visual and aural processors here is dotted. When reading printed text, there is a clear relationship between phonemes and graphemes. When reading televisual texts, some aural elements may relate to visual (as in characters' dialogue), others will not.

We know that children draw on semantic cues when reading both print and televisual texts. It has also been argued that they draw on syntactic cues and that both film and televisual texts have an underlying grammar, just as language does (Metz, 1974; Salomon, 1979; Turner, 1994; Messenger-Davies, 1997). Children absorb this grammar and use it when interpreting televisual texts. Messenger-Davies (1997) argues that parallels can even be seen in relation to active and passive sentences. As part of her doctoral research, Messenger-Davies showed people two versions of the same action on film. One was a medium-shot of a woman lifting a toy chair, which she suggested was analogous to the active sentence: 'The woman lifts the chair', as the most important aspect of the shot was the woman. The second shot included a close-up of the chair being lifted by the woman. This, the author argued, was equivalent to the passive sentence 'The chair is lifted by the woman'. Messenger-Davis commented:

Normally, people recall the agents of actions better than the objects they are acting upon. However, this is not the case with passive sentences, which put the object in the foreground and make it more memorable. As with recall of passive sentences, the people taking part in my research who saw the cut-to-close-up version were more likely to remember the chair than the woman. The opposite was the case with the uncut version ... The structure of the visual sequence thus seemed to parallel grammatical linguistic structures in viewers' minds.

(Messenger-Davies, 1995: 38)

Similarly, other theorists have created a grammar of film that analyses the framing of film narrative through camera angle, close-ups and long shots, camera movement and lighting (Turner, 1994). However, we feel that caution needs to be used here. The precise nature of grammar in relation to spoken and written language has been contested over the years (Halliday, 1973; Carter, 1990) and there are key differences between grammatical models used, for example, in relation to descriptive or prescriptive systems. Similarly, the grammatical systems created by the structural conventions of television and film are not fixed. As Buckingham (1993b) has argued in relation to Salomon's (1979) attempt to define the characteristics of television's symbolic system:

There is a danger here of defining this symbolic system as a kind of rigid 'grammar', in which discrete units are sent to possess a fixed, objective meaning. Yet a zoom, for example, may 'mean' very different things at different times; and it may on occasions 'mean' effectively the same thing as a tracking shot or an 'irising' movement or a cut to a close-up.

(Buckingham, 1993b: 30–1)

Interestingly, this may also be applied to the grammar of spoken and written language; a word can function as an adverb in one sentence and a noun in another. The complexity and instability of both systems means that comparison between different modes of communication is, at best, precarious. Nevertheless, it is clear that both televisual and printed texts are subject to structural systems which can be recognized and analysed and which help readers to make sense.

There are other ways in which the reading processes involved in both modes can be compared. Table 9 summarizes the key similarities and differences involved in reading printed and televisual texts. The two columns are not interrelated. As Table 9 demonstrates, we feel that children draw on some of the same skills when making sense of both print and televisual texts. Both involve a recognition of the nature of literacy as a set of practices which are embedded within our social and cultural lives (Street, 1984; Barton, 1994). It follows that teachers who are aware of the semiotic processes needed to decode both televisual and print texts are in a better position to draw attention to the parallels between them. In this way, each medium can be used to support the reading of the other.

Comparing book and film

Working with film and text versions of the same text is a valuable means of developing understanding of plot, setting, character and themes. The rich interplay possible between the media means that children can transfer their understanding from one form to the other. Browne (1999), in a study of her young daughter's juxtaposing of visual and printed versions of the same texts, reported that watching videos helped her daughter to gain confidence and enjoyment in the books. Children can become familiar with the language of books as they watch and re-watch videos. In addition,

Table 9 Similarities and differences in reading print and televisual texts

Similarities in reading print and televisual texts	Differences in reading print and televisual texts
Readers form 'interpretive communities' (Fish, 1980)	Printed texts make meaning through printed words and symbols, televisual texts use images, symbols, sounds, spoken and written words
Reading develops social, cognitive and emotional skills	Televisual texts can be more ephemeral if not taped and stored; printed texts can be revisited over time
Reading involves orchestration of a range of skills – either phonic, graphic, syntactic and semantic (print) or aural, visual and semantic (televisual)	Printed texts are more accessible to non-linear reading. Pages are easier to manage than screens for rereading (although the advent of new technology through digital versatile disc [DVD] is changing this)
Prediction is an important part of the reading process	Fictional printed texts are more likely to use a narrator; inference is not demanded in the same way as in some televisual texts
Readers are active meaning-makers, drawing from their own life experiences and encounters with texts	Printed texts can give more direct access to characters' thoughts and feelings and can develop more complex psychological frames
Readers are socially, historically, politically, economically and culturally situated	
Readers fill the gaps in the text	
Linear narratives occur in each medium (stories) as well as non-linear texts (some non-fiction, documentaries)	
Readers draw on their understanding of the particular genres they encounter	
Readers identify with or feel alienated from characters	
Readers willingly suspend disbelief	
Readers can reread texts	

film narratives can help children's oral and written responses to a text. David Parker, working with Key Stage 2 children on a film version of Roald Dahl's *Fantastic Mr Fox*, suggested that the children's implicit understanding of film narrative enhanced their comprehension skills and written responses to the text (Parker, 1999).

One junior class worked on the similarities and differences between the print and film versions of *The Lion, the Witch and the Wardrobe*. They were then asked to focus on a particular section of the book. The children read the section in shared reading sessions, then watched the film version of the same episode. The class were then asked to develop their own storyboard for that section of the book. Figure 19 is one girl's attempt at the task. From this, the children worked on a script for the characters in the scene (Figure 20). Finally, the children wrote a narrative version of the scene (Figure 21). The teacher felt that the children's writing had improved because of this work and that they had a greater insight into characters' actions, feelings and thoughts.

Children's work on characterization can be enhanced through opportunities to compare book and film. Films can provide us with a more concrete picture of characters and make visible characteristics which were implicit within the printed narrative, enabling the viewer to reach new insights. So, as one child said after watching the first few scenes of the film version of *Matilda*: 'I knew more about the mum after

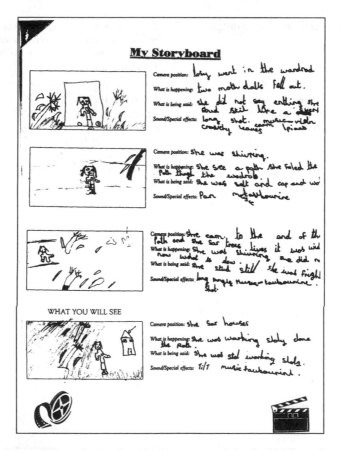

Figure 19 Storyboard

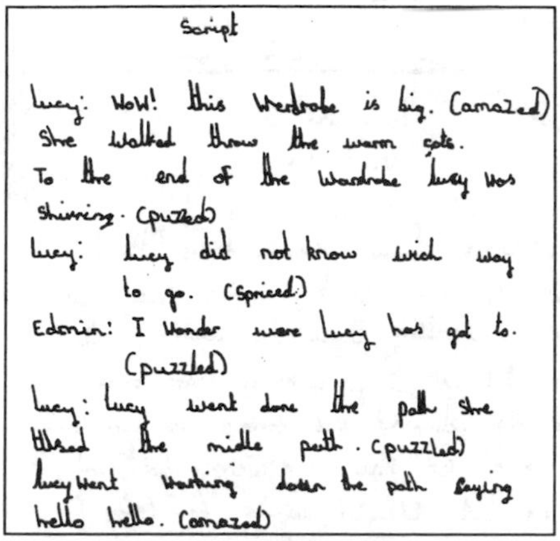

Figure 20 Script for characters in the scene

seeing the film and all she cared about was how she looked and she dropped the baby in the sink, going "Uh!Uh!". She only cared about herself.' On the other hand, some may feel that watching characters on film, when one has built up a private picture through reading, is too restrictive and channels interpretation into limited directions. Children could conduct a survey on people's reactions to this dilemma and explore how far expectations are met in relation to particular texts.

Genre is a theoretical construct which crosses many media and so can be drawn upon in any analysis of film and television. Generic conventions can be analysed, compared and contrasted across media. For example, detective stories in books and television share many features, e.g. setting, types of characters. However, there are certain features of the genre which appear in film and television that are obviously not contained in books, e.g. scary music, music which builds suspense, shot/reverse-shot cuts which show the reactions of suspects and so on. Such direct comparisons of the way in which genre is treated in each media are useful (Table 10).

Children's favourite genres can be identified and comparisons made with national surveys. Programmes which cross genres can be analysed, as they provide particularly rich sources of generic conventions and are usually popular with children. For example, a recent favourite is the American series *Buffy the Vampire Slayer* which mixes conventions from horror movies and mystery stories as well as incorporating humour and parody.

These are just a few suggestions for work which compares books with their filmed versions; there are many more valuable texts in the area which focus in much more depth on this topic (Craggs, 1992; Film Education, 1999a, 1999b). It would appear that this movement between media is essential, as televisual texts have a central place within the narrative system of children's cultural universe. Children are motivated to read those texts which relate to their television, film and video consumption. So Robinson (1997) notes that *Thomas the Tank Engine* books were around long before the television series appeared, but their popularity increased because of children's exposure to the narrative on television. Book sales increase whenever their narratives are released on film. Many children's shelves at home are filled with books and comics which relate to their television and film interests, whether that is cartoons, television series or Disney videos. Once again, we can see that intertextuality promotes,

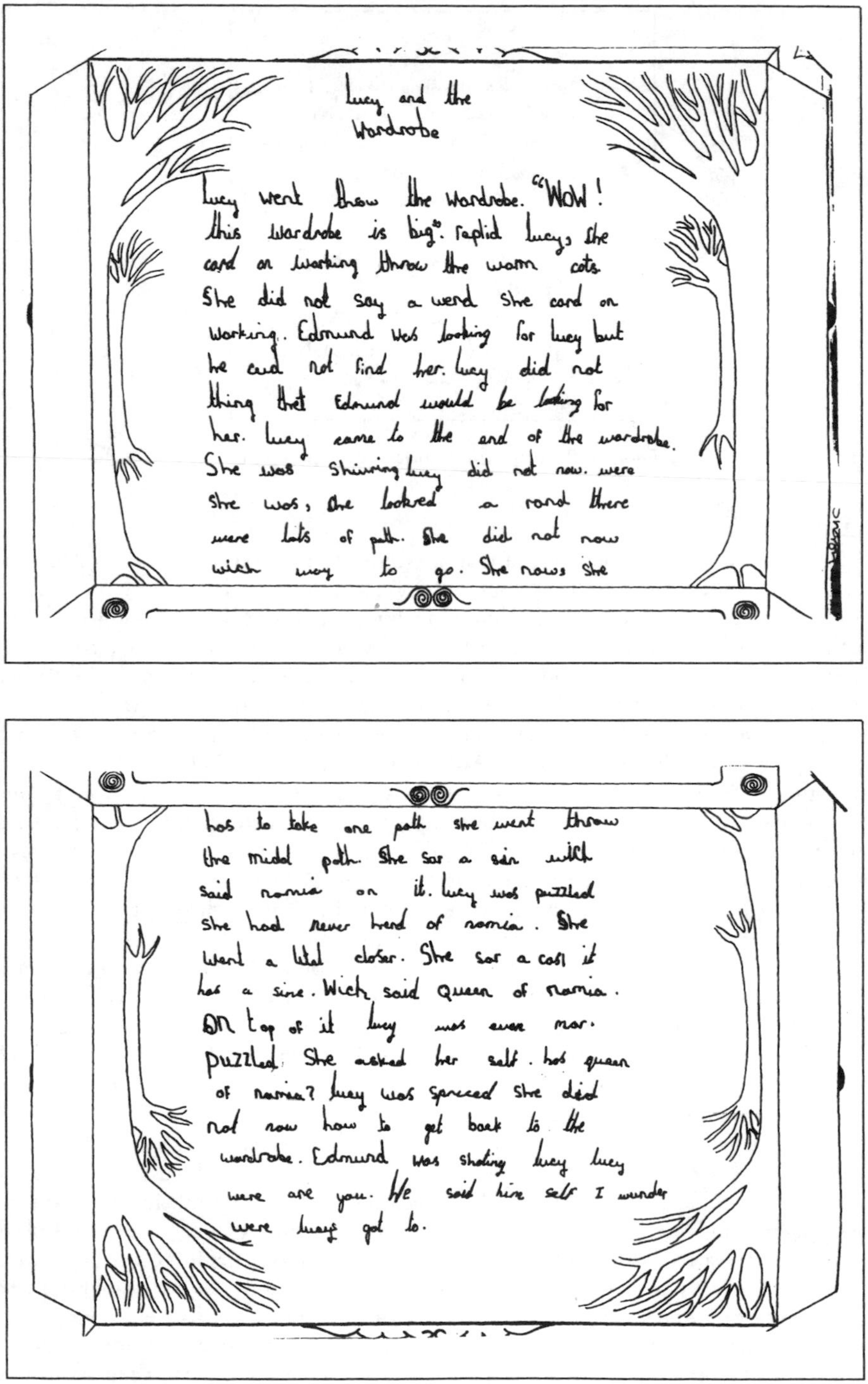

Figure 21 Narrative version of the scene

Table 10 Comparison of horror genre

Horror books	Horror films
Short sentences	Scary music
Cliffhangers at the end of each chapter	Dark lighting
Scary words, e.g. shriek, creep	Gruesome make-up

rather than inhibits, reading. This pattern emerges in a survey of the favourite books of a group of Reception children. The subjects of the books included:

- Pokémon
- Lion King
- Cinderella
- Little Mermaid
- Winnie the Pooh
- Pingu
- Toy Story
- Star Wars.

All these books relate to children's film, television and video consumption. This was a pattern found by Neuman (1995) in her study of three American families' literacy activities in the home. She reported that children moved from printed texts to television and back to printed texts again in their quest for pleasure and concluded that:

> Rather than displace one activity for another, the children often engaged in what appeared to be a spirited interplay between the media. As interests were established, children alternated between video-based and print-related experiences on the basis of its accessibility, and their capacity to make optimal uses of the particular medium. These activities seemed to be guided by children's rather consistent patterns of interest, instead of the specific medium presentation.
>
> (Neuman, 1995: 180)

This movement between media has become even more complex with the introduction of computer games, stickers, collectors' cards, toys and other artefacts which are all related to particular television programmes and/or films. The opportunities for reading are extensive and include the blurb on videos, as Bromley (1996) outlined in her description of a group of children who read the cover of a video and demonstrated a number of critical literacy skills. These included an ability to decode typographical features and to understand the marketing motives of the producers. However, we would not want to emphasize work in the classroom on comparison of printed text and film at the expense of a focus on the moving image itself. In the next section, we move on to examine the notion of 'media literacy'.

Media literacy

As with all labels, the term 'media literacy' has been open to debate and challenge. It is concerned primarily with literacy practices which enable children to access, analyse and produce media texts. Media education is the primary means by which children can develop skills in media literacy, but much work is also done through the subject of English. This does create difficulties, as Balzagette (2000) points out, in that the process of analysing the moving image is often made synonymous with that of analysing printed text, when in fact they are different kinds of texts and often (but, we would argue, not always) need different kinds of deconstructive and productive techniques. However, it is worth remembering that media education is much wider than the analysis of the moving image and the means of textual analysis for non-media printed material can easily be transferred to the analysis of newspapers, magazines, leaflets, advertisements and so on. Nevertheless, this chapter is concerned with film and television and so the focus will remain on developing children's ability to understand, analyse and produce moving images.

Reading of images

As we have argued, literacy should incorporate the ability to read visual images. This skill is essential when deconstructing films and television. Children need to be able to analyse camera angles and their uses, how lighting affects scenes, use of iconography, body language of characters and so on in order to become effective readers of the moving image. The Film Education Working Group (FEWG, 1999) outlined a broad curriculum framework for work on the moving image which consists of five stages. At Stage 1, they suggest that children should have the opportunity to watch a range of film, video and television (FVT) from across a range of cultures and be able to talk about particular sections of videos, as well as discuss their viewing outside of school. In addition, the group suggested that learners should be able to work in three main areas: film language (ways in which moving image texts are internally constructed), producers and audiences (ways in which the texts circulate) and messages and values (interpretations of the world offered by the texts). Here, we outline the learning outcomes identified for the first two stages as exemplars (Tables 11 and 12).

At Stage 2, it is suggested that children should have opportunities to watch and deconstruct a range of complex narratives and extend the range to include silent and subtitled films. The outcomes build on those outlined in Stage 1.

Again, there is not space within this chapter to examine in any depth the ideas suggested by the Film Education Working Group. Instead, we refer you to the full report produced by the group, *Making Movies Matter* (FEWG, 1999) and materials produced by both Film Education (1999a, 1999b) and the British Film Institute.

In addition to the study of the moving image, children need to be able to analyse how audiences are constructed in relation to films and television. Here, the concept of 'interpellation' has been used to describe this process. 'Interpellation' is a term introduced by the Marxist sociologist, Althusser, in order to demonstrate how ideology 'recruits' an audience:

> I shall then suggest that ideology 'acts' or 'functions' in such a way that it 'recruits' subjects (it transforms them all) by that very precise operation which I have called interpellation or hailing, and which can be imagined along the lines of the most commonplace everyday police (or other) hailing: 'Hey, you there!'.
>
> (Althusser, 1994: 162)

Thus, we can see how television programmes such as *Blind Date* interpellate the viewer when the host, Cilla Black, says to the camera about one of the contestants, 'Ooh, isn't he gorgeous?' The viewer is interpellated as a heterosexual female who would have an opinion as to the desirability of a young male. She certainly wouldn't be expecting a gay male viewer to reply, 'Oh, yes!' However, the concept of inter-

Table 11 Becoming cineliterate, Stage 1

Film language	Producers and audiences	Messages and values
• Identify and talk about structuring features such as music, changes in location, interior/exterior settings, actors and presenters	• Use credits, video covers and posters to identify titles and actors' names, likely audience category, and theme or genre	• Identify and talk about different levels of 'realism', e.g. naturalistic drama vs cartoon animation
• Use key words to refer to elements of film language when describing events in a story	• Identify broad categories of intended audience, e.g. 'this is for little children', and give reasons	• Use key words to refer to elements of film language when explaining personal responses and preferences
• Use key words in talking about character types, as well as referring to clues such as dress, casting, performance, etc.	• Identify common features between FVT, book and game versions of generic texts, e.g. myth, fairy tale, space adventure, etc	• Identify devices such as flashback, dream sequences, exaggeration – discuss why they are needed and how they are conveyed

Key words:

shot	zoom	pan	videotape	camcorder
cut	close-up	track	cinema	programme
fade	mid-shot	focus	film	animation
mix	long-shot	soundtrack	television	video-recorder special effects

Source: FEWG (1999: 74).

pellation has been criticized because of its rather abstract nature (O'Sullivan *et al.*, 1994) and the lack of attention to who is doing the hailing. A rather more useful concept might be that of Stuart Hall (1980) in which he proposes that media texts undergo an encoding and decoding process. Thus, the producers of a text *encode* certain ideological constructs into the text. These ideologies might be accepted by viewers when they *decode* the text according to their particular socio-cultural contexts and experiences, or they may be resisted to some degree. Whatever the processes involved in the construction of the viewer by the maker of media texts and the response of viewers to them, it is important that children are provided with opportunities to analyse critically these processes in order that the manipulation of the media is made transparent. Many people have underestimated children's skills in this area, believing them to be easily duped by media messages they receive. However, Messenger-Davies's work (1997) demonstrates how first-graders in American schools were able to understand how adverts worked by presenting a particularly rosy picture of the products. In addition, Tobin's research (2000), in which he analysed the responses of 6- to 12-year-old children to films, reveals the sophisticated understanding that many young children bring to the interpretation of media codes and conventions. It is essential that young children's skills in this area are not underestimated and that they are presented with relevant and challenging work.

Many proponents of media education stress the importance of children producing media texts as well as deconstructing them (Buckingham and Sefton-Green, 1994; FEWG, 1999). This is becoming much easier with the advent of digital technology, as digital video cameras are very light and portable in comparison with their older counterparts. Even if schools do not have access to editing facilities, much valuable work can

Table 12 Becoming cineliterate, Stage 2

Film language	Producers and audiences	Messages and values
• Describe how sound contributes to the overall meaning of a moving image sequence, using key words where appropriate	• Use key words to distinguish between different moving image delivery systems	• Use key words to identify ways in which FVT can show things that have not 'really' happened e.g. violence, magic
• Use key words to explain how a FVT sequence is constructed	• Identify and distinguish some production roles, using key words	• Explore reasons for and against censorship, age classification and the broadcasting 'watershed'
	• Suggest reasons why different people may have different responses to the same FVT text	
	• Explain why some FVT may cost a lot of money to make	

Key words:

angle	sound effects	composer	release	short	recorded	'watershed'
frame	projector	director	exhibitor	documentary	censorship	star
sequence	scriptwriter	broadcast	trailer	live action	classification	satellite
dialogue	script	channel	feature	live	budget	cable

Source: FEWG (1999: 75).

be done with a video camera such as video diaries, video narratives based on favourite pop songs, animated films. In one class of 6- and 7-year-olds, children watched and analysed weather reports before writing and filming their own. This project promoted valuable media literacy skills as well as developing their understanding of the weather. Work on animated films can be undertaken in a variety of media as children paint scenes, create plasticine figures or use the increasingly sophisticated software packages which are available. These activities can also provide rich opportunities for oracy and literacy work as children discuss plans, write scripts and read instructions. In the final part of the chapter, we consider other means of developing children's literacy skills in the context of work on television, video and film.

Television talk

In addition to reading, television and film can enhance children's oral skills. Carol Fox (1993) has demonstrated how children draw from their cultural repertoire in order to inform their oral storytelling. They take meaning from experiences with television, film and video as well as books in their play with language and their constructions of imaginary worlds. Because television is a medium which most children share, whatever their home culture, it can provide many opportunities for developing collaborative talk, either through play or more structured activities. We want to turn briefly here to the work of Bakhtin and Volosinov in order to explore this concept further.

Bakhtin and Volosinov were Russian literary theorists who were interested in the ways in which we create language communities. Bakhtin and Volosinov both suggested that language is a two-way process between speaker and listener in that our words only become meaningful in relation to others: 'there is no reason for saying that meaning belongs to a word as such. In essence, meaning belongs to a word in its position between speakers; that is, meaning is realized only in the process of active, responsive understanding' (Volosinov, 1994: 35).

The dialogic process is also subject to socio-cultural factors. Words take on meaning because of historical contexts and also our anticipation of what a particular word might mean in the future. Thus synchronic and diachronic contexts shape the meaning of our discourse and the significance of any particular utterance is open to negotiation. If the meaning of utterances is fluid and contestable, then Bakhtin and Volosinov's work also has implications for social discourse. The dialogic process means that children create shared meanings as they speak about common experiences together and become 'interpretative communities' (Fish, 1980) in relation to oral discourse:

> The living utterance, having taken meaning and shape at a particular historical moment in a socially specific environment, cannot fail to brush up against thousands of living dialogic threads, woven by socio-ideological consciousness around the given object of an utterance, it cannot fail to become an active participant in social dialogue.
>
> (Bakhtin, 1994: 76)

Children's talk about television and film is a primary site for such discourse as children construct shared meanings based on common interests. In a study of a nursery which incorporated work on the *Teletubbies*, Marsh (2000b) found that the discourse encouraged 3- and 4-year-old children to exchange information regarding the programme and build dialogic communities:

Lianne: I'm Po, that red Teletubby.
Nasia: I'm Po red.
Shaun: I got Teletubby video. I got lots of videos.
Peter: And I got Tinky Winky.
Nasia: I'm Tinky Winky.
Ansa: I watch Teletubbies. I got Teletubbies on my bed.

These 3- and 4-year-old children were in the early stages of acquiring English as an additional language and so these opportunities for building shared discourses were very important. These occasions provided spaces in which children could share their 'cultural capital' (Bourdieu, 1977) with each other and demonstrate that they had common interests. Television and popular culture provide key sites for such processes as most children have some access to the texts, no matter what their socio-economic, cultural or linguistic background. Teachers can use film, video and television to stimulate similar kinds of oral work in a number of ways. Children could be asked to watch a sequence of a soap opera which had had the sound removed and record on tape their version of the dialogue. Groups could deliver formal oral presentations to the class in which they present their findings on a particular project e.g. an investigation into the types of characters found on police drama shows. Older members of the family could be interviewed about their viewing preferences and history. Younger children could retell stories experienced in films, video and television as they play with puppets based on the characters. These are only a few of the opportunities that work on the moving image can provide for those classrooms in which children are steeped in the language and lore of film, television and video.

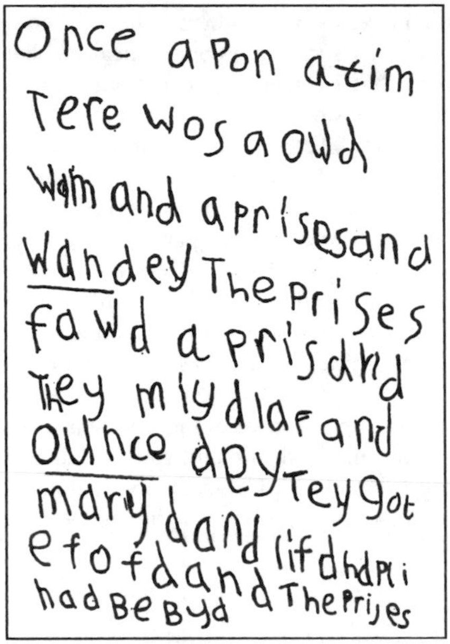

Figure 22 Kerry's story: *Text*: Once upon a time there was an old woman and a princess and one day the princess found a prince and they made love and one day they got married and lived happily ever after and the princess had a baby

Reading, writing and the moving image

Kerry, who was 4½-years-old, produced the story in Figure 22. Here, we can see that Kerry has been stimulated not only by a traditional world of fairy tales in which princesses marry princes, but also by the contemporary soap operas she watches in which couples indulge in pre-marital sex. In this world of 'Cinderella meets Coronation Street', children draw from a range of semiotic material in order to inform their writing. The work of Anne Haas Dyson (1996, 1997) has demonstrated how children use super-hero narratives drawn from television and film in their classroom. She argues that 'our texts are formed at the intersection of social relationship between ourselves as composers and our addressees and an ideological one between our own psyches (or inner meanings) and the words, the cultural signs, available to us' (Dyson, 1996: 4).

Dyson introduces Figure 23 to illustrate this dynamic interplay. This deceptively simple diagram is a powerful way of looking at the process of children's writing. Children draw from 'available signs or words' and, as the work of Kress (1997) and Pahl (1999) has demonstrated, these can include three-dimensional materials as well as signs, symbols, images and letters. This store of semiotic material also includes children's cultural texts used in order to demonstrate their own inner meanings. These meanings are then negotiated between author and receiver of the text. Thus children use television and film narratives in their writing, but these are not always immediately recognizable to others and the dialogic processes involved in meaning-making are open to multiple interpretations. It is also the case that teachers do not always approve of the store of 'available signs and words' upon which children draw. Some would rather the store used consisted of semiotic material which is more readily

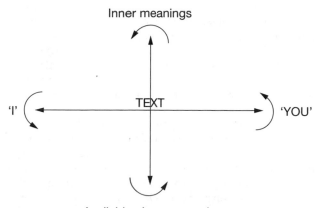

Figure 23 Composing as a dialogic process: its horizontal and vertical dimensions (from Dyson, 1996: 5)

recognized within the literary canon and discourage children from writing about their experiences with television and film. Yet, if children are allowed to mine the caverns of media material, their written compositions could be richer and more meaningful to them. Care has to be taken, however, in drawing children's attention to differences in the structure of film and print narratives, particularly in considering how setting and dialogue differ. Boys in particular draw heavily on film and television narrative in their own composition and this can be a disadvantage when conventional narratives are required for assessment (Millard, 1997).

Children's fascination with soap opera can be another source for writing in the classroom. A prime reason for the attraction of children to the genre is that soap operas are based in family life and so present real-life dilemmas to which they can relate. In addition, we would argue that the storylines of soap operas offer some of the attractions that fairy tales hold for children. Berger (1997) suggests five key reasons for children's love of fairy tales:

1   They generally begin with 'Once upon a time' and so situate the story away from the context of the child.
2   They often end with 'And they lived happily ever after', so offering satisfying closure.
3   They have a basic bipolar structure which children find attractive (good/evil; handsome/ugly; kind/cruel) – no ambiguity or ambivalence.
4   They centre on the actions of heroes and heroines who are typical, not specific and so children can relate to them.
5   Good and evil are omnipresent and the differences between them apparent.

(Berger, 1997: 86–7)

If these factors are applied to soap operas, then one can begin to understand their attraction for children. The theme tunes of soap operas are often much more distinct than other types of programmes and act as 'Once upon a time' does in written texts; it draws the viewer into the 'make-believe' world of the soap opera. The episodes do not always end happily; cliff-hangers are often used as a means of ensuring viewers tune in next time, but storylines are generally always resolved in one way or another.

In terms of the third point, it is clear that soap operas offer much potential for a paradigmatic analysis (Lévi-Strauss, 1967) as dualistic discourses are often apparent. There are usually heroic characters within soap operas with whom children like to identify and so they offer narrative satisfaction. Finally, the tension between good and evil is as central a part of soap operas as it is of fairy tales and children are drawn to both because of this. However, soap operas are especially attractive to children because these fundamental features of narratives are set within a 'real-life' context – contemporary, recognizable fairy tales.

Soap operas offer the same opportunities for analytical work on narrative structure and characterization as printed texts do. Children can be asked to compare and contrast different soap operas in terms of setting, character types, typical storylines and so on. Using Propp's (1968) analysis of the functions of characters in fairy tales, children could identify characters in soap operas who performed those functions. Children can devise their own soap operas. One class of 8-year-olds invented a street full of characters based on their experiences of living in an inner-city, multicultural neighbourhood and called it 'Soap Square'. The children then produced stories and plots which drew from these characters and which took their narrative cues from those soaps they watched regularly. Opportunities to film scripted sequences written as a result of such work can enable children to develop productive media skills in a meaningful context.

Quiz shows are another perennial children's favourite and can also be mined for opportunities to develop literacy skills. One class teacher exploited his children's interest in the programme *Who Wants to Be a Millionaire?* The phenomenal success of this programme is interesting and may be due to the fact that the questions are not situated within middle-class cultural domains as are the questions of other quiz shows such as *Mastermind* or *University Challenge*. Instead, the questions draw from a broad range of cultural knowledge which includes film, television and sport. The programme is also constructed within a more socially collaborative context than other quiz shows as contestants can 'ask the audience' a question or 'phone a friend'. In addition, the quiz master, Chris Tarrant, is a well-known presenter of other popular shows. Whatever the reasons, the class teacher realized that his class of children, who lived in a white working-class community which was hit by poverty and unemployment, could relate to this programme. He therefore asked the children to write three questions for their own class version of the quiz show as a homework task. The parents were as excited and committed to the task as the children, and they engaged in joint reading and writing activities as they researched and wrote the questions together. These questions were then sent back to school and placed in a class quiz booklet. The game was eventually played on the last day of the spring term, with Easter eggs as prizes. Each family was given a copy of the collectively-produced quiz booklet. This simple task engaged the interest of children and community alike, rooting the literacy experiences within their own cultural lives.

Media diaries are another valuable way of developing children's literacy skills. Children may be asked to keep a diary of their media consumption over a period of time, commenting on what they watched and their responses to it. These diaries can then be developed into interactive writing tasks with other adults. As children make comments on particular programmes or films watched, adults may insert a comment or question to promote further reflection by the child. Writing is, of course, inextricably linked to reading and so an activity such as this is useful in developing both skills. There are, however, specific activities which can be undertaken in order to promote reading.

Previously in the chapter, we examined how work which compares printed and film versions of the same text helps to develop children's literacy skills. There are many other opportunities for developing reading based on the moving image. Extracts from scripts of films and programmes can be used in shared reading sessions for work on aspects such as character, setting, genre, narrative and so on. Children can read schedules from magazines such as *Radio Times* and be asked to scan for particular information e.g. find all the programmes which relate to family life. Teachers may present children with descriptions of programmes which they need to place on a schedule (this would also provide a valuable means of working on concepts such as a 'watershed'). Texts related to favourite films, programmes or actors could be used to stimulate reading e.g. film reviews, magazines featuring television and film stars, related websites. Activities such as these promote an approach to literacy that involves children in a dynamic process in which they transform the texts around them and make them their own: 'Reading the word is not preceded merely by reading the world, but by a certain form of writing it or rewriting it, that is, transforming it by means of practical work. For me, this dynamic process is central to the literacy process' (Freire, 1972: 35).

This chapter has considered the use of video, television and film texts both as part of the intertextual frame in which the development of conventional reading is supported and as an important means of constructing meaning in their own right. We have argued that children need to be supported in developing their understanding of both processes. There are many more activities which could be undertaken in relation to children's experiences with film, television and video. This chapter can do no more than make a few suggestions that could be developed and adapted in relation to particular contexts and learning needs. Ultimately, there is an important role for educators in ensuring that children become competent and critical decoders, analysers and producers of televisual texts.

References

Benson, C. (1986) 'Art and language in middle childhood: a question of translation', *Word and Image*, 2: 123–40.

Davis, J. (1993) 'Why Sally can draw. An aesthetic perspective', Educational Horizons, 71: 86–93.

Gardner, H. (1980) *Artful Scribbles*, London: Jill Norman Limited.

Gilligan, C. (1982) *In a Different Voice*, Cambridge, MA: Harvard University Press.

Gombrich, E.H. (1960) *Art and Illusion*, London: Phaidon Press.

Hubbard, R. (1996) 'Visual response to literature: imagination through images', *The New Advocate*, 9: 309{en rule}23.

Kiefer, B. (1995) *The Potential of Picture Books: From Visual Literacy to Aesthetic Understanding*, Englewood Cliffs, NJ: Merrill.

Kress, G. and van Leeuwen, T. (1996) *Reading Images: The Grammar of Visual Design*, London: Routledge.

Lévi-Strauss, C. (1967) *Structural Anthropology*, New York: Doubleday.

Millard, E. (1997) *Differently Literate: Boys, Girls and the Schooling of Literacy*, London: Falmer Press.

Mines, H. (2000) 'The relationship between children's cultural literacies and their readings of literary texts', Ph.D. thesis, University of Brighton.

Nodelman, P. (1996) 'Illustration and picture books', in P. Hunt (ed.) *International Companion Encyclopedia of Children's Literature*, London: Routledge.

Perkins, D. (1994) *The Intelligent Eye: Learning to Think by Looking at Art*, Cambridge, MA: Harvard Graduate School of Education.

Sinatra, R. (1986) *Visual Literacy Connections to Thinking, Reading and Writing*, Springfield, IL: Ch. C. Thomas.

Vygotsky, L. (1986) *Thought and Language*, A. Kozulin (ed.) Cambridge, MA: MIT Press.

CHAPTER 14

PLAYING THE TEXT

Margaret Mackey

Literacies Across Media – Playing the text, London: RoutledgeFalmer, 2002, pp. 181–202

Literacy has never been a completely fixed set of skills. Kathleen Tyner's list of obsolete technologies ('Tallies, hieroglyphics, kinescopes, viewmasters, 78-rpm record players, and 8–8-track cassette players' (1998: 18)) is a reminder that literacy is always historically contingent. Literacies are grounded in a complex world of social custom and specific technologies, and change in literacy tools and equipment is not new.

The project, which analysed how a group of 10–14 year olds, made sense of narrative in a variety of formats, took place at a particular historical juncture, at a time when technological change was particularly rapid. In recording some of the behaviours of the young readers, I have captured not only the technologies of the late 1990s but also some glimpses of how readers respond to change, a topic that is not simply of local or historical interest. The challenge is to explore what useful general implications can be drawn from one specific and grounded set of examples. I want to begin that exploration in a roundabout way by looking at a possible description of text processing activities.

Playing the text

The word *ecology* is resolutely a noun; I can think of no verbal version of the word. Nevertheless, the concept of *ecology* is a shelter for verbs; it represents an idea whose very force is in dynamism. I am interested in exploring what verbs of text processing make the liveliest connections with our contemporary textual ecology.

I began this project with a bias towards stretching our use of the word *read* to include the interpretation of other kinds of texts as well, texts that are viewed or interacted with. As I worked with my large data set, the problems with this usage continued to bother me and I often lamented the absence in the English language of an all-purpose and unpretentious word that would cover how we understand and respond to texts in many media.

I have not solved the problem of a verb with the specific meaning of cross-media text processing. However, in the course of working on this project, I have come to recognize that there is, after all, a common word that will make room for a variety of activities, with multifaceted and multimedia connotations. That word is *play*. We use it as a verb to talk about music and games: we play the piano or play tag. As a noun, of course, it is a staged drama. But we can also have a play of light (on water, on a screen), or a play on words. The word has a valid function in many of the ways we talk about the arts; in that sense it is multimodal.

So how does the notion of 'playing the text' serve as a metaphor for some of the interpretive elements held in common across many media?

Playing as pretending or imagining

One of the most common and important meanings of the word 'play' involves some kind of make-believe, the shift to the world of 'as if'. We play house, we play doctors. We may talk about the shift into the *as if* world to distinguish between fiction and non-fiction. Alternatively, we may use the idea of this shift to distinguish between narrative and non-narrative or exposition. Time after time, the students in this project made the choice to consider the implications of the story *as if* they were stepping inside the fictional universe. The essential step into make-believe, the imaginative leap, took place over and over again, in all the media formats on offer.

Richard J. Gerrig (1993) and Jerome Bruner (1986, 1990) both discuss conditions of fiction, and both emphasize the importance of accepting a world where the future is not known within the world of the text, even though that text is always already concluded before the reader picks it up. Bruner speaks of moving into such a world where the future is still open as 'subjunctivizing reality' (1986: 26) and speaks of it as a way in which 'discourse keeps meaning open or "performable" by the reader' (1986: 26). Gerrig, describing anomalous suspense, suggests that at least some of our ability to suspend the fact that we know the outcome may be predicated on our assumption that every performance is unique (1993: 170). Either of these approaches leads to interesting questions about the *as if* switch. How do we learn about stepping into a world with an imaginary and still-open future? How do we learn to apply this switch to a new text, or a new format? How do we re-apply it to a text already known, so that we can participate in the subjunctive understandings of the characters inside that world?

Playing as performing

We not only pretend, we perform our pretending when we play. We play the fool or play the king. The issue of performance is one that is generally undervalued when it comes to many forms of text processing, particularly to reading. Though an oral, choral or dramatic reading may be acknowledged as a performance, silent and/or private reading is far less often viewed through this lens. It is useful in this context to compare and contrast the students' readings of *Shortcut* (Macauley, 1998) and of 'Tunnel' (Ellis, 1996). *Shortcut* evoked something much closer to our conventional idea of a 'performance', with voice, gesture, posture and attention all serving the cause of rendering the story coherent. The students were asked to read aloud, to attend to words and graphics, and to coordinate relevant information from both sources even when it appeared on different page openings; and to tie it all in with their general knowledge of the world. They produced a public manifestation of these processes that it is relatively easy to describe as performance. Yet the mental activities were not so very different when they turned to the short story and read it silently. They had to associate information from different parts of the text, and to assemble a useful working repertoire to make sense of the setting and context. They did not point for the benefit of another reader, but they did use their hands to mark places on the page with their pencils. They turned the paper to catch the light most usefully, they held a page in their right hand before flipping it over, and so forth. Small, habitual gestures, but all part of organizing their attention towards the text.

Performing involves some kind of bodily immersion in the activity. In many cases, the relationship between a text and a body is so subtle, so imperceptible and so taken for granted that we overlook it. Is it possible to think of a person sprawled on the sofa with a paperback thriller in hand, or hunched over a joystick making only tiny movements for hours at a stretch, or sagging in front of the television clutching a remote, as in any way *performing* the text under scrutiny? I think we must, even if much of the performance is interior and invisible and the self is the only audience. The body (hands, eyes, balance, breath) is engaged in directing and maintaining attention, often through a set of tiny, subliminal and habitual actions. The connection between body and text may be conventional and taken for granted, but it is real. The mind is hard at work, even if we call it play.

Playing as engaging with the rules of the game

'Play ball' says the umpire, and his words are performative: the time-out is over; the rules of the game are now in force. Actions now have legal consequences within the framework of the rulebook, though few in the 'real' world. Obviously, engagement with a text of any kind entails accepting and working with the rules and conventions in some way or other.

Humans appear to have a profound affinity for conventions of various kinds. Once, as an adult, I tried to remember a game I had played as a child, for the benefit of some neighbourhood children who were bored with all their own games. I could summon up only a fragment of the constituting rules that governed the game of my youth, but like paleontologists working with a scrap of bone, the local kids quickly fleshed out a set of living rules that reinvigorated the game in fully playable glory. I don't know if it matched my childhood game completely, but it worked, and it worked because of the children's intuitive respect for conventions and their ingenuity and speed in creating a set of meaningful rules.

And when their newly constituted framework failed them, they were adroit at stepping outside the game to discuss alternatives. Disengaging the rules temporarily in order to play the game better is an activity that comes easily to quite young children.

All these activities are visible in every one of the transcripts of the young readers. In their engagements with all the different media, the participants set up working conventions, open to change if they did not succeed in making the text operable. They renegotiated readily when it seemed appropriate, stepping outside the interior world of the story but not completely outside the textual world of engagement. They commented explicitly when they did not have enough information about the text to make working assumptions. Part of their judgement on fluency of access was based on whether they could provide or develop an adequate set of conventions to make progress readily.

Playing as strategizing

We talk about game play in strategic terms; we 'play deep', or 'play the line'. We 'play it cool'. The transcripts are simply full of talk about strategy, again across all the media. How to make progress through the set alternatives of the CD-ROM game, *My Teacher is an Alien*. How to use the hyperlinks to expand the very terse story of the CD-ROM *Anne of Green Gables*. How on earth to find the crucial stateroom in *Starship Titanic*. How to attend to the sudden and brief appearance of Johnny Depp in the opening scenes of *Benny and Joon*. How to 'read' the map and Pathé News tone of *Casablanca*. What balance to achieve between the diegesis of the film story and the DVD analysis of 'how we made this movie'. How to use the index in *The Way Things Work*. How to make connections between the untied rope and the subsequent adventures of the balloon-riding professor in *Shortcut*. What elements in the story 'Tunnel' to invoke in order to make sense of the strange girls in the culvert. Partly because the students were consistently asked to articulate their approaches to different texts and partly because the activity of strategizing is inherently important, their conversations were full of strategic evaluations.

It is important to remember that one major role of all this strategic analysis is to enable the performance of the story as an engageable if not necessarily believable world. Steven Poole, talking about video games, makes a useful distinction between 'imagining into' and 'imagining how'. Imagining how involves a strategic sense of how to make progress; imagining into enables us to 'understand the rules of the semiotic system presented, and act as if those rules and not the rules of the real world applied to oneself' (2000: 197). He says the game requires us to 'project the active (rather than just the spectating) consciousness into the semiotic realm' (2000: 197). The children who fleshed out the bare bones of my remembered game into a playable version for themselves almost certainly alternated between both activities – working out ways to imagine how so that they could get the game started, but then imagining into the game in order to find out how else to imagine how. It is a complex process to describe in such laborious terms but the activity itself was (there is no other precise word for it) playful.

The strategic necessity to be able to imagine how in order to be able to imagine into is perhaps another way of describing some of the issues of fluency and salience that students manifested in their assessment of the variety of text openings. Imagining how is a prerequisite for imagining into – except that sometimes we imagine into so successfully that imagining how follows without much need for attention. Often we call the narratives that overwhelm us in this way the texts that readers/viewers/players can 'grow' on. Witness Megan, ignoring the hard words on the first page of *The Golden Compass* because her attention was so thoroughly caught, despite her strategic caution about avoiding big words in other books. Most people have experienced something similar in playing a new game, reaching a point where the flow of activity mostly carries them past their inadequate understanding of the finer points of the strategy guide. Most of us know a child who reads way above his or her normal reading level when the topic is of passionate interest. Salience then governs fluency, not the other way around; 'imagining into' leads to 'imagining how'.

Playing as orchestrating

Sometimes we use the word *play* to indicate something more like orchestrating, as in, 'play percussion'. The percussion player must produce the drum roll, the cymbal clash and the triangle tinkle in appropriate combinations, a case of managing attention and automatic behaviours to maximize complexity. It is a rare usage for the word *play* perhaps, but it is a crucial connotation for the approach to texts of any kind. We orchestrate many activities for even the simplest form of text interpretation, and we must manage our affairs so that many of these activities can be conducted automatically. The more automatic the procedure, the more invisible; and so much of what we do when we read or watch a movie or play a computer game is unrecognized most of the time.

Some of the judgements made by the students on their way through the collection of texts, involved how readily they could move to a state of automaticity. The most visible example of such automatizing in all the tapes and transcripts probably involves the game of *Myst* played by Megan and Angela. Without necessarily gaining a much greater understanding of the game itself, they became more and more adept at moving around the island, retracing their steps, setting out purposefully for particular destinations. Their command of the local environment became automatic, even though their understanding of the nature and purpose of the game remained vague. With their control over negotiation of the local geography requiring less conscious attention, they freed attention to improve their understanding of other elements of the game. Their activity could become more complexly orchestrated, so to speak, because they no longer had to attend directly and consciously to every single element at once.

There are many examples of students realizing the need for orchestrating different kinds of information. Just about everyone, at some stage, consciously noted the necessity to pay attention to information carried in both the words and the pictures of *Shortcut*, rather than just in the words. The tapes show them adjusting their mental focus and also their bodily activities as a result. Students mentioned using cues from both the pictures and the accompanying music in *Casablanca* and *Benny and Joon*. At least some of them learned to use not only the information from the streets of *Virtual Springfield* but also that of the map and compass. Again and again, there is a palpable sense of activities and strands of attention being orchestrated in the cause of a more complete understanding.

Playing as interpreting

Implicit in some connotations of performance is the idea of interpretation; you play the sonata to present your own rendition of its complexities. Interpretation is a major element of all kinds of text processing except the most idle. (Just as a child may *play* idly with her hair, so it is tempting to posit a description, for example, of Madeleine sampling short snatches of movies she has seen before without any real attempt to engage any interpretive attention.) For the most part, however, these students were engaged in at least preliminary interpretive activities in all media. Much interpretation takes place after the encounter with the text is concluded and these students were given few opportunities to finish a text. Nevertheless, we can see their wits flexing, and in the two complete texts, *Shortcut* and 'Tunnel', there is considerable activity at the end of the reading to check any loose ends and sort out an interpretation that allows for balance and pattern as well as specific plot tidiness.

A different study would have evoked different forms of interpretive activity. By and large, either the texts encountered did not tap into any deep anxieties or interests or the students were not given the opportunity to pursue their personal emotional connections in any depth. The emphasis on sampling throughout this project means that we catch only glimpses in the transcripts of those kinds of interpretations that draw on deep personal concerns. But we do see a few examples: Colin tapping into fears about bullying in response to the book *My Teacher is an Alien*; Nasrin musing on the emotional perils of being an orphan as she looked at *Anne of Green Gables*; Jack pondering his own unknown future as he responded to 'Tunnel'. A different selection of texts and a different methodology might have evoked more of such deep connections. Even this very brief list gives some indication of how the individual's own private agenda may set up the warp of an interpretation so that the final texture can be woven using the specifics of the story as weft.

Playing as fooling around

We know what it is to play around with an idea or a suggestion. It is an exploration of possibilities without commitment. We try one option in our minds, mentally

extend our understanding of possible outcomes, weigh our views of potential consequences. Free of commitment, we then do exactly the same thing (or something a
little different) with an alternative – and maybe another.

Play in this incarnation is a set of trial experiments: what would happen if –?
For all its inconsequential appearance, it is also a form of rehearsal, and its application to the activities of text processing is obvious and important. Fluency requires
practice, and in many cases of textual interpretation, one goal is fluency to the point
of transparency in many elements of the task. Practice can be forced and laborious,
but in most of the cases I recorded, the text tinkering was easy and playful, only
turning into something more unpleasant when frustration superseded curiosity.

Providing an environment for safe fooling around does not sound like a grand
curricular initiative (or alternatively sounds like a recipe for Internet filters, V-chips
and witch-free libraries). Yet the capacity to experiment with texts, to fail sometimes, to try again without recrimination or penalty, and/or to abandon them, is an
important part of mastering new media. This is as true for small children learning
to decode print as it is for computer experts tackling a new piece of software.

Playing as not working

Playing demands a consequence-reduced zone. Unlike work, play does not have an
immediate practical outcome, nor do we expect any direct utility from our activity.
In play, we can try things out, work through our feelings about an idea in an arena
where the results are often unimportant. Naturally, this opens a zone where we can
contemplate very important ideas indeed, simply because the risk is lowered. To say
that it is not work does not imply that something is not difficult or that it is not
significant. Play can be extremely challenging (Papert's 'hard fun' (Johnston, 1999:
12) comes to mind), and its consequences can be profound and life-long.

I believe this element of not-work is highly important to the kind and quality of
attention that we pay to such texts. We live in an economy of attention that provides
many, many not-work calls on our time and energy, in a surplus of recreational
options. It is not surprising that even the youngest of these students could draw on
a sophisticated apparatus for marshalling forms of playful attention even in encounters with previously unfamiliar media.

Some implications of playfulness in the processing of texts

This chain of associations evoked by the verb *playing* is neither complete nor definitive. What it offers is a way of looking at the interpretive activities that cross a
number of media boundaries.

The prismatic, multi-faceted qualities of the concept of *playing* mean that we are
already familiar with the idea of this verb shifting meanings as it acquires new subjects
and objects and fits into new sentences. Such a protean verb meets the specialized needs
of a study that sets out to explore what is common and what is distinctive about the
ways in which we approach different kinds of text and media. In most cases, the word
has a common usage and we are not stretching things too far by using it in this way:
we regularly play music, play a video, play a game. Nevertheless, the phrase *playing
the text* is not in ordinary use, and there is no common precedent for speaking of playing a story or playing a reading. Playing makes room for the agency and energy of performers and calls for both internal and external accommodation to the activity: to play
involves a commitment of the mind as well as appropriate behaviour of the body, a
fruitful concept for considering the activities of text processing. Furthermore, the word

play makes room for a kind of mental and dispositional 'on-switch' – an active commitment to the engagement – whose importance is sometimes overlooked in ordinary language about different kinds of text-processing.

Theories of play and art

Many scholars, of course, have written about the subject of play, both in its free-form 'childish' incarnation and in the more deliberate forms of play that we describe as art. Two philosophers address issues that are particularly pertinent here.

Hans-Georg Gadamer draws an interesting common ingredient of the idea of *play* from such phrases as 'the play of light, the play of the waves, the play of gears or parts of machinery, the interplay of limbs, the play of forces, the play of gnats, even a play on words. In each case', says Gadamer, 'what is intended is to-and-fro movement that is not tied to any goal that would bring it to an end' (Gadamer, 1989: 103). The meaning of *play* thus described is a medial one; it happens *between*.

Gadamer, however, is not talking about play happening between players; his focus is on what happens between the player and the game, an intense form of imagining into that is internal rather than social. 'All playing', he says, 'is a being-played. The attraction of a game, the fascination it exerts, consists precisely in the fact that the game masters the players' (Gadamer, 1989: 106).

In terms of the medial qualities of play, it seems to me that Gadamer is referring, at least partially, to the elements I have described as present participles. The durational aspects of any narrative text processing involve what is *going on* as the reader/viewer/player moves through the story. The idea that the *going on* is the purpose of the activity is certainly one element of what we value as we process any kind of text; we do not do aesthetic (as opposed to efferent) text processing simply to be at the end (see Rosenblatt, 1970).

However, Gadamer's approach to the idea of playing is rather more monolithic than the behaviours I observed among the students in this project. Ironically, he does not seem to make much room for a more playful kind of playing, where the exercise involves medial movement within the playful activity and also movement in and out of the play itself. 'Play fulfills its purpose only if the player loses himself in play', he says, and, 'seriousness in playing is necessary to make the play wholly play. Someone who doesn't take the game seriously is a spoilsport' (Gadamer, 1989: 102). Yet the variety of engagements demonstrated and/or described by these students involved many variations of non-'serious' playing in Gadamer's terms. I observed many elements of tinkering and toggling that are outside his description. Indeed, often the capacity not to take the play seriously was actually part of the appeal of the kind of play on offer. Madeleine's many reiterations of, 'Oh, well, we'll just die and start again', are not exemplars of serious, all-consuming play. [. . .]

Gadamer, without specific examples and particular contexts, describes an idealized version of playing. Such an account is vitally useful, but it can perhaps be more useful if we recognize its schematic qualities. The quality and intensity of engagement during the play itself is important, but it is differently realized on particular occasions. Specific examples of situation and context will not only infill the background of what Gadamer is describing as pure and exclusive engagement, but may actually offer their own counter-examples of how real life behaviour is not necessarily so pure. Gadamer's iso-camera, so to speak, is fixed in ultra-close-up mode. What seems more useful is an idea that may perhaps be best described as an ecologically inflected present participle. Some conditions of engagement are contingent even as some are undoubtedly constant.

Gadamer is also interesting on the topic of the comparison between play as in children's make-believe and play as it manifests itself in a work of art: 'All play is potentially a representation for someone. That this possibility is intended is the characteristic feature of art as play. The closed world of play lets down one of its walls, as it were' (1989: 108). In a footnote, Gadamer adds, 'It is precisely the fourth wall of the audience that closes the play world of the *work of art*' (1989: 108). 'Openness toward the spectator', he continues, 'is part of the closedness of the play. The audience only completes what the play as such is' (1989: 109). The make-believer is essential to the make-belief, whether within the self-run world of a child's game or in the deliberately composed universe of a text-based make-believe where it is the audience who bring the essential make-believing agency to bear.

Mikhail Bakhtin also discusses the boundaries between make-believe and art, but takes a more plural perspective. Like Gadamer, he places the audience as spectator, part of the play but not inside it.

> While children are in the midst of a game, it is real experience for them, something innately experienced, imagined but not given as an image. But play may approach art when an 'actively contemplating' outside spectator begins to admire it. As long as such a spectator watches, we have the kernel of a dramatic aesthetic event. When the spectator leaves, or when he becomes so interested that he joins the game, what Bakhtin in later years would call 'footlights' disappears from the scenario and the aesthetic event returns to the status of play.
>
> (Morson and Emerson, 1990: 189)

Bakhtin and Gadamer both posit the spectator as essential to play becoming art, but Bakhtin's spectator is livelier, moving in and out of different relationships with the text, an account that accords more closely with the behaviour of the students in this study, and an account that makes more theoretical room for oscillating behaviours.

A comparable (and highly important) distinction could operate between our regular understanding of *playing a game* (from the inside, with wholehearted commitment to the internal premises of the narrative) and my newer idea of *playing the text*. In this latter case, the element of spectatorship provides the crucial ingredient of outsidership, where not only the premises but also the form and shape of the text are part of what is played. Oscillation between surface and interior is an essential element of such a spectator role. *Receiving* a text, on the other hand, is confined to the outside.

Re-workings and re-playings

One striking phenomenon of our contemporary cultural ecology is the way that many texts are produced in simultaneous cross-media incarnations. Indeed, Frank Zingrone argues that the 'one-medium user is the new illiterate' (2001: 237). The implications for the reading/viewing/playing public are substantial.

In a postmodern ecology of attention, originality may not always be regarded as highly prized. Yet the students in this study were not oblivious to issues of 'which came first', and did not automatically find any reworking of interest simply because it opened a space between one version of a story and another. Many who thoroughly enjoyed the movie of *Men in Black* rejected the computer game. It was clear that the general enthusiasm for the video of *Anne of Green Gables* was based on its merits as a text in its own right; otherwise the students would have been equally enthusiastic about the CD-ROM of the same story, and they were not. At the same time, it is clear that they were open to the charms of the space between texts when the space itself was of interest. The dynamic between the television program of *The Simpsons* and the CD-ROM of *Virtual Springfield* intrigued some (though not all) of the students and was clearly a factor in their judgement of the computer text. But the opening of such a space, all by itself, was not interesting enough to please them without any further qualification; they had to value the second text on its own terms to take an interest in the space between.

The word *replay* as it is commonly used today involves an identical reproduction of a recorded moment. But I think there is room for a secondary meaning, perhaps signified by a hyphen. To treat an adaptation as a re-*play* of a story can be a useful antidote to a more earnest approach that values slavish fidelity to the original as the main criterion of judgement. Many of the young people I have spoken to in this and other studies treat adaptations in this more playful way, speaking of textual variations and discrepancies as interesting rather than annoying. But, to succeed, the re-played text has to offer its own play value (a common enough phrase but one whose literal meaning is useful in this context).

The production of a new version of a previously published text is commonplace in our culture, and it raises other interesting aesthetic and cultural questions. Some theorists argue that adaptations should be evaluated:

> not in terms of their fidelity, or even . . . in terms of how the cinematic adaptation functions as an autonomous work of art, but rather in terms of how the encounter with a literary source creates a commentary on the narrative process itself.
>
> (Mayne, 1988: 6)

The students in this study, moving easily between versions, are quite sophisticated in terms of the 'narrative process itself', not a surprising turn of events if Mayne is right in her analysis. Peter Lunenfeld offers a different perspective on the plurality of versions which these students clearly take for granted. Talking about the potential of hypertext to create a story that is never finished, he goes on to address the issue of changes in the publishing industry and their impact on multiple versions:

> French literary theorist Gerard Genette refers to the 'paratext': the materials and discourses that surround the narrative object. Genette generated his theories from a study of literature and considers the paratext in terms of the publishing industry: cover design, book packaging, publicity materials, and so on. I would say, however, that the transformation of the publishing industry in the past two decades – the melding of publishers with movie makers, television producers, and comic book companies, and the development of media conglomerates like Time Warner, Disney/ABC, and Sony – has bloated the paratext to such a point that it is impossible to distinguish between it and the text.
>
> (Lunenfeld, 2000: 14)

Using the example of the 1995 film *Johnny Mnemonic*, Lunenfeld talks about the numerous incarnations of this single story (movie, soundtrack, CD-ROM game, merchandise, websites, etc.) that were released simultaneously. He addresses the implications for our cultural life in a world of unfinished works:

> The result of such dubious corporate synergy is the blending of the text and the paratext, the pumping out of undifferentiated and unfinished product into the

electronically interlinked mediasphere. Final closure of narrative can not occur in such an environment because there is an economic imperative to develop narrative brands: product that can be sold and resold.

(Lunenfeld, 2000: 15)

Living in a world of such narrative flux and flexibility, it is not surprising that students played with narrative form in many ways, not simply in dealing with the adaptations. They crossed many kinds of diegetic boundaries with skill and ease. The media formats most unfamiliar to them (the e-book, the CD-ROM picture book, the DVD) caused them to articulate most explicitly how they alternated attention between looking through and looking at the surface presentation of the text, but such shifts (swift and reversible) happened in all of the texts. The narrative of 'Tunnel' became opaque as they failed to find their initial predictions fulfilled, and they paid more attention to the verbal surface in the latter stages of their reading. Their developing perception of *Shortcut* as a kind of game led them to adjust their seating and posture and to attend differently to details of information in print and graphic forms. Their confusion in the initial stages of the computer games led them to scan in an open-ended way for unspecified possibilities, but their demeanour shifted when they perceived a detail that could be processed purposefully within the parameters of a story. The movement back and forth between surface and depth was constant, and seemingly independent of medium.

These students moved back and forth between media, drawing on different experiences to support their text-processing activities. Not surprisingly, it is possible to observe that even 'old' media are changing to take account of such an increase in sophistication. Eliza Dresang, in her book *Radical Change: Books for Youth in a Digital Age* (1999), discusses ways in which texts addressed to young people and produced in print on paper are altering. She supplies an enormous list of examples to support her argument that texts are changing as reading changes, and vice versa, the very epitome of an active ecology. The plasticity of attention which the students in this study brought to bear on the different texts supplied to them is a feature of a contemporary ecology where an alert flexibility is a hallmark of successful literacies.

An ecology of attention

Reading and viewing and playing are socially framed practices and these social frames are layered. At one level, all the students in this project met each text within the social framework of the project itself. This framing existed as a very specialized and distinctive subset of another set of social frames, those that marked and bounded their daily life in school over the two years of the study. The participants also engaged with the texts within the context of their own social, cultural, economic and political histories, and their own roles as late twentieth-century Western consumers. At another level, their encounters with the texts varied according to the nature of the engagement established by the nature of the text itself. The ways in which the participants' attention was attracted, directed and sustained were affected by these elements, and undoubtedly by many others. [. . .]

The agency of the participants is necessary but not sufficient when it comes to reading or other forms of text processing; the text must, in some way, attract the attention of the reader. Psychologists speak of attention being captured, a word that has an involuntary ring to it, even if subjects subsequently choose to reject or resist the object that has, as we say, caught their eye. The word *stimulus* makes many people uneasy, for good historic reasons, but no matter how much the response to a text is created by a reader, there is still an essential element of any text being *outside* the reader and having to draw the reader in. As Gadamer says, the playing is a being-played (1989: 106).

There are consequences to this inevitable 'outsideness' of a text. When you look at the mysterious empty dock of *Myst*, for example, there are some conclusions you may not draw: you are not looking at a simulation of a crowded football game, for example. And you may choose not to take an interest in the opening scene, but you probably cannot refuse to hear the waves lapping on the dock. You may (you probably must) set up the warp of your own interpretive concerns, priorities and expectations, but some of the weft you incorporate into your textual fabric comes from the conditions of the text – not simply the content but also the nature of its invitation to your participation.

Other readers or players are also 'outside', and their contributions to the playing of the text come in many ways. Obviously, all text processing is socially governed in the large sense in which conventions are worked out by a kind of implied collective. On a more local and detailed level in this project, it was possible to see social influences at work in more contingent ways. Furthermore, there were examples of social impact at many different stages: before engagement (Jack's friends pressing him to read *The Golden Compass*), during engagement (Angela and Megan instantly picking up the graduate students' references to time travel and applying them at once to their game of *Myst*), and after engagement as part of the process of establishing coherence (Kyle's quick exchanges with his friends, on the day after programme aired, to establish the point of obscure *Simpsons* jokes).

The close-up conditions of this study mean that it provides examples of that point of encounter between a specific individual and a particular text. The singularity of any one of these encounters is irrefutable and irreducible. Yet there are generic elements also at work. [. . .]

Does the idea of playing the text alter how we view this complex ecology? I believe it may affect certain implicit assumptions.

For example, in terms of play as not-work, one obvious place to consider the idea of playing the text is the English classroom. 'Now we're going to play this new book', is a small change in vocabulary, yet, taken seriously, one with radical potential for altering the framework of many classroom discussions. There are plenty of teachers who already think of reading as a form of deep play ('hard fun', perhaps), yet the notion of reading only as work often triumphs, and many students are the losers as a consequence.

Emphasizing the performance elements of silent reading or movie viewing is another useful bonus of this approach. It is too easy to think of such activity as routine and invisible, with one instance simply reproducing another. A performance involves a singular incarnation that is never identical to a predecessor.

Making allowance for the bodily requirements of playing the text is another helpful fall-out from this discussion. It is possible for people – students seated at their classroom desks, for example – to do a variety of text processing activities all in a condition of identical posture. You can read a printed text, watch a video, check items on a graph, all while stationary in a hard and probably uncomfortable chair with your desk a fixed distance from your eyes. The idea of play, however, does raise serious questions about posture and attention. The concept of *playing* does imply a certain autonomy for the player, even in physical details. In play, conditions of attention are determined by the requirements of whatever is being played and by the decisions of the player. I think we can usefully ask about conditions of attention in many classrooms. Real attention also involves at least a minimal amount of autonomy and cannot be commanded simply through an enforcement of certain postures and physical attitudes.

Perhaps even more importantly, the idea of playing offers a connotation of relative freedom, of not being confined to the tramlines, of negotiating at least some of the terms of engagement. With regard to how we approach texts, this implication has particular importance for teachers who often imply, whether they mean to or not, that there is a single meaning to a text that is more correct than all the others. Robert Morgan, talking about media education, refers to it as 'a kind of disciplinary unconscious, which posits meanings as simply *there*, immanent in the object of attention, waiting to be "discovered"' (1996: 16). If we say that a text has a certain amount of *play* in how it is interpreted, we are describing exactly the kind of flexibility (constrained but real) that Morgan says is all too often missing in the 'disciplinary unconscious'.

Conditions and constraints of the study

Although the students explored texts in a variety of media, there was one element that all the titles had in common: in the final analysis, they were all texts that had already been crafted and closed. Students experienced them differently but in all cases they were aware that somebody else had organized the potentialities and possibilities of their encounters long before they had begun. I stress this point because it is important to recognize that not all the texts these students will be meeting, either today or in the future, fall into this category of being completed by somebody else before the engagement begins. The development of more interactive and open-ended forms of text may represent a major ecological change of our era (for example, see Murray, 1997).

Be that as it may, this study did not explore the kinds of open-ended texts where readers are contributors to the ongoing development of the text itself. The students in this project were using their understandings of conventions and protocols to explore texts that were essentially closed before the readers came anywhere near them. All the students were exceedingly familiar with the nature of this kind of text, and clearly drew on a broad range of understandings in order to make sense of new materials and formats as they were presented to them.

Similarly, it is worth noting that I made no attempt to engage the students with texts outside the Western, the familiar, or the contemporary. It was a deliberately applied constraint; I was trying to work within the students' likely comfort zone of experience and expertise.

Yet even with this deliberate restriction of the study to materials likely to be similar to texts already known to the students, there were moments when the intuitive leap had to happen for interpretive progress to be made – and sometimes that leap was missing. The role of that *zap* moment when the strands come together and the text begins to take shape is often overlooked, but its absence is crippling. And more readers and players than we may sometimes acknowledge are wary of being unable to make some necessary connection and of 'failing' in understanding and even in enjoyment.

A Ph.D. student once highlighted this concern to me:

> I know I have, before I start reading a book, in any context . . . some anxiety about being interested in this book. And I always think about that when I start. Okay, when's it going to be that I get it, that I catch on to what's going on? When's it going to be?

(Mackey, 1995: 216)

Willingness to take on a new text, familiarity with conventional approaches, an inclination to experiment and/or wait for the text to make itself clearer: all of these textual approaches are necessary but in the final count not sufficient. The reader or viewer or player has to 'get it' – to make the text work as a whole. And I suspect that no amount of outside observation and analysis is ever going to completely disentangle the mystery of that moment.

Conclusions

A recapitulation of the strands that have woven through the study lead to a description of some general patterns of text processing behaviour. In meeting a text for the first time, the students appeared to apply a measure that explored the balance between issues of personal salience and questions of fluency of access. In all of their engagements with different texts, they oscillated readily between 'looking through' the text to get into the meat of the story and 'looking at' the text to explore the way it worked. Furthermore, they moved easily among diegetic levels, including an extra-diegetic zone where they could discuss questions of strategy, or investigate elements involved in the making of the story. They drew on conventions of one medium to make sense of another, and where they could not find an easy way to do so, they fell back on a default position of being maximally observant of details in the text while seeking possible categories with some narrative potential. They responded to puzzles and enigmas with as full a strategic arsenal as they could readily muster, yet they also maintained a certain attitude which I can best describe as a necessary readerly passivity in the face of the givens of the text.

Perhaps it is appropriate that the clearest way of summarizing how such activities fit into the broader textual ecology is by means of a metaphor. If we think of a camera focused in close-up on an activity and then gradually panning backwards, it becomes relatively straightforward to picture a complex encounter. In the case of this study, we have the added ingredient that there literally was a camera focused in close-up on at least some of the textual activities, and the question of what that camera did and did not see is a fascinating one.

In extreme close-up then, we are perhaps closest to Gadamer's pure present participle of playing, though elements of that engagement are beyond the purview of any external camera. Extrapolating from the students' words and actions concerning the text in hand, we may consider their decisions about salience and fluency. Salience is in many ways at the heart of any textual encounter; it is probably a deeply personal sense of salience that activates the on-switch of the performance, so to speak.

What the real camera does record in this close-up perspective is an associated materiality of the text. Students engage with the text, in whatever medium, with hands and bodies as well as minds.

Still in the close-up perspective, we can observe many elements of oscillation between 'looking through' and 'looking at' the surface of the text. As we pan our metaphorical camera back to a mid-shot, we can see this oscillation working both between diegetic layers of the text on hand and also between alternative forms of the text in different media. In addition, the boundary crossing at work in many of the encounters recorded in this study sometimes operated between the story world and an outer but associated 'zone of influence', often involving strategic considerations or ways of thinking of the text as a construction. On other occasions, the boundary crossing drew in external but related texts. The set-up of the study itself did not make a lot of room for more generic intertextual connections, but these were undoubtedly part of the picture as well.

Panning our camera further back again, we can see that such connections among layers of text and among assorted related texts are a strong feature of the contemporary popular culture in which these young people were learning about texts and interpretation. The students developed expertise in particular elements of this culture and shared their knowledge with their friends as part of their normal daily conversations. Yet, as Victor Watson reminds us, this environment is not neutral. He says we:

> need to accept the fact that all meetings between texts and children – whether they take place in quiet libraries, in crowded classrooms, in drama studios, or at screens of one kind or another – in a very real sense take place in a marketplace, within the apparently implacable realities of publishing and marketing economics.
>
> (Watson, 2000: 5)

The camera metaphor implies that it is possible to enlarge our perspectives steadily and in a rather linear fashion. But in fact, the market factor feeds back into some of the close-up perspective: part of how the text is addressed to the readers, part of the deictic connection, is often related to the economics of the production of the text itself. Cross-references between different versions of the same story, for example, have an aesthetic impact within the textual encounter itself but they are also driven by a particular market imperative, and many of the conversations recorded in this study demonstrate that the students are aware of both layers.

The cultural and financial materiality of textual engagements is as important an issue as the tactile materiality. It is perhaps easier to see this element at work in those texts we conventionally see as emanating from a commercially motivated apparatus: *Friends, The Phantom Menace, The Young and the Restless*. But the fact that these students could read a contemporary Canadian short story is also the consequence of a history of deliberate commercial decisions; thirty years ago there was virtually no Canadian publishing for young people.

Aesthetic, commercial and technological issues intertwine in many ways. *Shortcut* is a genuinely successful exploitation of the technological qualities of the bound picture book on paper: the quality of printed images, the aesthetic and intellectual implications of the limits of the page and the binding, the conventions that ensure readers will assume connections between disparate plot elements, a long history that makes many such texts affordably available thus enabling readers to learn how to read them: all these ingredients mesh together. By contrast, *Lulu's Enchanted Book* suffers in some respects by its sheer novelty. The technology of the still and moving image in this particular CD-ROM is cumbersome and clumsy. Commercial distribution of CD-ROMs has never been completely successful, so the texts are more expensive than they should be and correspondingly rarer; thus readers' comfort with their conventions is lower. Such difficulties also ensure that there are fewer examples of success, as even breaking into the market is difficult.

Another vital issue, and one addressed in this study only through the interviews, is the question of agency. These young people make use of texts to foster and present an idea of themselves. They were willing to cooperate with me, and in many cases they genuinely enjoyed the texts, but the elements of selection and self-presentation, which are heavily implicated in our private and independent text choices, were severely constrained for them in the context of this study. Their conversation about their own choices of movie, television programme, book and computer game occupied a different psychological and social framework, one where they are involved in creating a sense of self along with an understanding of genre, skill with convention and so forth.

Tia DeNora talks about the importance of such self-definition in terms of music:

> music is an active ingredient in the organization of self, the shifting of mood, energy level, conduct style, mode of attention and engagement with the world. In none of these examples, however, does music simply *act upon* individuals, like a stimulus. Rather, music's 'effects' come from the ways in which individuals orient to it, how they interpret it and how they place it within their personal musical maps, within the semiotic web of music and extra-musical associations.
>
> (DeNora, 2000: 61)

Particularly in the interviews that concluded this study, it is possible to see the Grade 9 students working on terms of orientation, interpretation and personal agency in connection with particular texts; thus we see the *Star Wars* expert or the bashful viewer of a daily soap opera drawing on their understanding of particular texts to create elements of their social identity.

All these issues do not fit comfortably into the image of our camera steadily panning backwards. Nevertheless, if we can return to that metaphor for a moment, I think it still has a few insights to offer. As our camera takes in an ever-widening angle on the encounters with these texts, we can see other elements at work. Students' domestic lives impinged in many ways on how they processed the texts I offered. What kinds of texts and technologies they had domestic opportunities to master certainly affected how they dealt with my selections. What they could do at home, at their friends' houses, at school, all mattered. What other kinds of support were on offer at home was also an issue of great significance. Leonard's mother faithfully taping *The Young and the Restless*, Jack's parents in two different cities turning up Jeffrey Archer books for him to read, Janice's family making regular outings to National Hockey League games and Angela's family tracking their hockey-playing cousin on the Internet, Madeleine's little brother sharing his ten-year-old perspective on computer games, the Grade 5 girls all being knowledgeable about *Where in the World is Carmen Sandiego?* because just one of them owned it – this list could go on indefinitely. The conversations emphasized the degree to which Gadamer's pure present participle can actually be observed *only* in extreme close-up, at least when it comes to text. Undiluted make-believe is possible in what we normally understand as children's play; it is possible to play a game with no props apart from the imagination of the participants. Textual play, however, involves the materiality of the text (whether that be book, Internet site, stage play or ballet, television programme, whatever) and therefore some elements of outside agency necessarily impinge on the purity of the engagement. In the case of these young people, many of the material conditions of access to texts depended on their families and friends.

Other background scenarios impinge on textual encounters, depending on where we direct the focus of the camera. The local Alberta curriculum undoubtedly had an impact on these young people and what they understood about the world; so did the textual practices of their school environments (the Young Readers' Choice Award promotion in the elementary school, the daily reading break in the junior high, for example). Friends offered crucial access to alternative tastes as well as particular technologies and texts.

The domestic, economic and ethnic backgrounds of these students are not identical. Nevertheless, they are all accustomed to moving fluently through standard Western texts. I do not think I am stretching things to say that they regard themselves as the implied audience for many of the kinds of texts I gave them, a self-image that incorporates a variety of political and commercial assumptions. Whatever the local details, in general terms they are all part of a North American mainstream audience and regard themselves as full participants in that particular culture, with repertoires that strike them as appropriate to the kinds of tasks I offered. Yet despite this generic 'goodness of fit' between the items of contemporary culture that I offered and these young readers, the details of each individual case also remain singular.

In short, the ecology revealed by the recorded encounters with texts, the diaries and the conversations of the young people that combined to form this study, is complex, mobile and determined by innumerable interacting factors. Yet despite its complexity, these students move through it with ease and assurance. They know how to process some kinds of text and they fully understand that literacy in their lifetime also involves developing strategies to deal with completely new forms of text, as well as strategies for directing the scarce resource of their attention.

I said goodbye to these students with great regret. Returning to the transcripts meant reactivating the present participles of our encounters, a fascinating and satisfying activity with its own potential for surprises. Yet even as I work through the records of our meetings, I know these students have already moved on, learned more, enjoyed more, been frustrated by more. The textual ecology within which they function is fluid; so are they.

References

Bruner, J. (1986) *Actual Minds, Possible Worlds*, Cambridge, MA: Harvard University Press.
—— (1990) *Acts of Meaning*, Cambridge, MA: Harvard University Press.
Collins, C. (1991) *The Poetics of the Mind's Eye: Literature and the Psychology of Imagination*, Philadelphia: University of Pennsylvania Press.
DeNora, T. (2000) *Music in Everyday Life*, Cambridge: Cambridge University Press.
Dresang, E.T. (1999) *Radical Change: Books for Youth in a Digital Age*, New York: H.W. Wilson.
Ellis, J. (1996) 'Tunnel' in *Back of Beyond*, Toronto: Groundword-Douglas & McIntyre.
Gadamer, H.-G. (1989) *Truth and Method*, 2nd edn, trans. J. Weinsheimer and D. Marshall, London: Sheed & Ward.
Gerrig, R.J. (1993) *Experiencing Narrative Worlds: On the Psychological Activities of Reading*, New Haven, CT: Westview Press.
Johnston, C. (1999) 'Children Need to Have Hard Fun', *Times Educational Supplement*, 3 September, 12.
Lanham, R.A. (1994) *The Electronic World: Democracy, Technology, and the Arts*, Chicago: University of Chicago Press.
Lunenfeld, P. (2000) 'Unfinished Business', in P. Lunenfeld (ed.), *The Digital Dialectic: New Essays on New Media*, Cambridge, MA: MIT Press.
Mackey, M. (1995) 'Imagining With Words: The Temporal Processes of Reading Fiction', unpublished dissertation, University of Alberta.
Mayne, J. (1988) *Private Novels, Public Films*, Athens, GA: University of Georgia Press.
Morgan, R. (1996) 'PanTextualism, Everyday Life and Media Education', *Continuum* 9: 14–34.
Morson, G.S. and Emerson, C. (1990) *Mikhail Bakhtin: Creation of a Prosaics*, Stanford: Stanford University Press.
Murray, J.H. (1997) *Hamlet on the Holodeck: The Future of Narrative in Cyberspace*, New York: Free Press.
Poole, S. (2000) *Trigger Happy: The Inner Life of Videogames*, London: Fourth Estate.
Rosenblatt, L. (1970) *Literature as Exploration*, London: Heinemann, 1938.
Tyner, K. (1998) *Literacy in a Digital World: Teaching and Learning in the Age of Information*, Mahwah, NJ: Lawrence Erlbaum Associates.

Watson, V. (2000) 'Introduction: Children's Literature is Dead: Long Live Children's Reading', in E. Bearne and V. Watson (eds), *Where Texts and Children Meet*, London: Routledge.

Yanal, R.J. (1999) Paradoxes of Emotion and Fiction, University Park, PA: Pennsylvania State University Press.

Zingrone, F. (2001) *The Media Symplex: At the Edge of Meaning in the Age of Chaos*, Toronto: Stoddart.

PART V

EXPLORING WRITTEN TEXTS

CHAPTER 15

READING RIGHTS AND RESPONSIBILITIES

Eve Bearne and Gabrielle Cliff Hodges

Issues in English Teaching, Jon Davison and John Moss (eds), London: Routledge, 2000, pp. 8–22

What rights and whose responsibilities?

> Controversy about the teaching of reading has a long history, and throughout it there has been the assumption, at least the hope, that a panacea can be found that will make everything right. . . . there is no one method, medium, approach, device or philosophy that holds the key to the process of reading. We believe that the knowledge does exist to improve the teaching of reading, but that it does not lie in the triumphant discovery, or re-discovery, of a particular formula . . . A glance at the past reveals the truth of this.
>
> (DES, 1975: 77)

The informed words of the Bullock Report, written a quarter of a century ago, are a reminder that current concerns about reading are part of a long history of debate. What is it about reading that so fires an emotional response in educators and politicians? Just as there is no easy answer to the teaching of reading, there is equally no slick summary of why debates rage so fiercely – in every generation it seems. Part of the answer may lie in the fact that satisfying or satisfactory reading does not just depend on the range of texts available to a particular age group, but on readers, contexts and communities. Since contexts for reading, the experience of readers and the communities they inhabit are not static, it is no wonder that the issues have to be regularly revisited. The fact that every age invents new types of text (see, for example, Alberto Manguel's splendidly wide-ranging *A History of Reading*) is another consideration, and it becomes clear that teaching reading is still a hot issue because the precise nature of reading changes with time (Manguel, 1996).

This chapter explores what reading means for young people and their teachers, in particular their rights and responsibilities. Using examples from students in Key Stages 2 and 3, it asks some key questions such as what do teachers know and what can they find out about readers? How can teachers use what they know to develop fruitful ways of teaching reading?

However, there are some important matters of principle to get into the open before trying to deal with all the complex factors involved in teaching reading. In his wry and incisive book, *Reads Like A Novel*, Daniel Pennac (1994: 145–6) offers the following as 'rights':

1 The right not to read
2 The right to skip pages

3   The right not to finish a book
4   The right to re-read
5   The right to read anything
6   The right to 'bovarysme' (that is, reading for the instant satisfaction of nothing but our feelings)
7   The right to read anywhere
8   The right to browse
9   The right to read out loud
10 The right to remain silent.

What emerges strongly is the right to be a committed reader, an individual making choices according to inclination as well as need. It would be good if we could make this our target for children in the UK rather than 'reaching Level 4 by the age of 11'! The cool prose of government documents cannot, of course, capture such fervent determination. However, it is not so much the wording of National Literacy Strategy or National Curriculum documents which deserves attention; the new text element that needs scrutiny is the format (with its attendant implications for teaching approaches). For example, the National Literacy Strategy presents a framework for teaching, which, together with its multiplicity of training materials, begins to look very like the kind of 'triumphant discovery' of one particular formula, precisely the approach against which the Bullock Report cautions us. Teachers are having to make space within the framework to meet the needs of individual students' development, interests and preferences. Is space also available for students to exercise their right to choose?

The principle of fostering avid, committed and critical readers can only be realised in practice if students are motivated. If students are not motivated to read, then they will not engage in the breadth and depth of reading necessary for that development to take place. Jerome Bruner's analysis of what he calls 'the will to learn', although written over thirty years ago (Bruner, 1966), provides some valuable pointers to anyone teaching reading. Motivation, says Bruner, is fuelled by the satisfaction of curiosity. Experienced readers learn not just to decode text but also to satisfy curiosity through reading and to sustain their curiosity 'beyond the moment's vividness'. They learn, if given the opportunity, how to channel their curiosity actively to accomplish their own ends, not just passively to meet the demands of others. Bruner goes on to explore another intrinsic element of motivation, namely 'the drive to achieve competence'. Most people know, if given the chance to experience it, the pleasures that can be derived from a sense of achievement. Furthermore, 'we get interested in what we get good at'. However, for pleasure and interest to be sustained we need ultimately to master things for their own sake rather than for extrinsic rewards. A third point about motivation, crucial for teachers of reading, is the power of role models, in reading as in so much else. What Bruner means by 'role model' is 'a day-to-day working model with *whom to interact*' (our italics). Teachers are very well placed to interact with less-experienced readers, not so much because they offer behaviours for students to imitate, but because they are more experienced readers with whom students can engage in dialogues about reading: dialogues which they later learn to internalise.

Bruner's analysis is predominantly sociocultural. It reminds us how important reading is to our concept of what it means to be human. Reading is therefore inevitably political. Being political implies enfranchisement and the right to vote; it also means that the voter carries responsibilities to the community. It follows, then, that if reading is politically situated and a political act, then readers – teachers and students – have both rights and responsibilities. A report by an Advisory Group on Citizenship, entitled *Education for Citizenship and the Teaching of Democracy in Schools* (QCA, 1998b), reinforces this view, linking the twinned concepts of rights and responsibilities with skills and aptitudes such as the 'ability to use modern media and technology critically to gather information' and the 'ability to recognise forms of manipulation and persuasion'. The more experienced members of a community are those who carry the responsibilities until the younger ones can take full status, so this chapter will give weight to teachers' responsibilities and younger readers' rights, suggesting ways in which these gradually move towards a more equal distribution of each. Since this is a chapter about *teaching* reading, and about what it is to become a reader, it will also be important to look at how success as a reader can be measured. Just what kinds of assessments are most likely to provide useful information for all members of the 'voting' community – for readers, families, educators and employers – about standards of reading?

Reading experience and experiences

One of the most significant shifts in thinking about reading over recent years has been not just the acknowledgement, but the value, given to reading and pre-reading experiences in homes and communities. The greatest emphasis in this area, however, has been given to the early stages of reading. The later years of Key Stage 2 and the early secondary years do not figure as much in discussion of how to teach reading, or in this case of how to build on the experience and experiences of young, already fairly fluent, readers. This lack of attention to older readers reflects a view of reading which measures successful reading according to how well young readers can decode the words on the page and demonstrate this by reading aloud. In its worst manifestation, the idea is that once children can decode and read aloud fluently, then we don't need to teach them any more about reading. Nothing could be further from the truth. Surface-skating the text is potentially more harmful to a young reader than still having problems in articulating complicated text. If you are struggling with a text, you have to be engaged with it in some sense. But if you glide over its surface you never have to get to grips with it at all. Margaret Meek describes her unease about those who 'decontextualise reading in order to describe it':

> The reading experts, for all their understanding about 'the reading process' treat all text as the neutral substance on which the process works as if the reader did the same things with a poem, a timetable, a warning notice.
>
> (Meek, 1988: 7)

A full reading curriculum goes beyond this basic assumption, and considers the range of texts which a reader needs to tackle, alongside the range of reading processes and strategies which might help. It also takes into account the development of reading preferences and reading experience drawn from homes and communities.

There are many assumptions and prejudices about young people's reading at home. Difficulties lie in how reading is being defined – both by students and by those who question them – and in methods of gathering information. For example, pupils are often reluctant to admit to certain types of reading – newspapers, comics, magazines, computer texts, television – because they think that these are not the kinds of things teachers want to hear about and don't count as reading. If reading is much more broadly defined to include everything that students read within and outside the school, then the reality is usually complex and quite a shock.

For example, the responses of one Year 5/6 class in a Cambridge primary school to a questionnaire about home and school reading showed both boys and girls reading twice as much at home as they did in school. Another example involved information gathered from interviews carried out for a small-scale research project with six Year 7 students from a Cambridge secondary school (whose Ofsted report noted that 'pupils do not usually read for pleasure or elect to tackle challenging texts'). The group was mixed ability and included three boys and three girls, for one of whom English was an additional language. For pleasure and interest they read Roald Dahl novels, film and TV tie-ins, e.g. *The X-Files* and *Jurassic Park*, series books such as *Point Horror*, *Famous Five* and *Sweet Valley High*, *Horrible Histories*, humorous poetry, joke books, wildlife books, comics, special interest magazines, local and national newspapers, novels, picture books (with younger siblings), encyclopaedias, books about computer programming, information and letters received from charities and clubs they belong to, CD-ROMs, the Internet, catalogues, and more besides. The EAL student also read letters, forms, and so on, for her mother who knew too little English to be able to do so for herself. Judging by this evidence, if we do not find out about, or pay attention to, the whole picture of young people's reading, then our conclusions about their reading experiences, capabilities and the curriculum we provide for them are going to be simplistic and lacking in precision.

Information from a very large-scale survey directed by Christine Hall and Martin Coles adds to the complexity of the picture. Their *Children's Reading Choices* project sought to replicate Frank Whitehead's earlier study for the Schools Council, *Children's Reading Habits 10–16* (Whitehead *et al.*, 1977). The survey's findings not only support the view that young people, both boys and girls, read a wider variety of texts than we might suppose, but also that within those texts, especially magazines, they encounter an extensive range of genres: fiction, non-fiction and 'faction' (Hall and Coles, 1999).

When students note the television, video and computer reading they do, the range is equally diverse. Teachers, analysing the results of a survey carried out in their Essex secondary school, comment:

> Over and over again pupils made comments like *I watch TV for fiction* and while no-one would want to advocate that this should mean we do not encourage reading of fiction we do need to expand our concept of reading so that we can teach pupils to be critical readers of all sorts of text – fiction, fact and the communications media.
>
> (Spratt and Sturdy, 1998: 104)

Forms of 'cineliteracy' play an increasingly important part in students' reading and have significance not just for the content of the programmes, but particularly for the structures of the verbal and visual texts involved. While soaps depend on dialogue, news coverage combines commentary with analysis. Sitcoms use more visual and verbal humour and are often concise in their plot structures, while film plots cover wide ranges of space and time. The verbal and visual language of advertising and exquisite 30-second narratives offer yet more text experiences, which feed into other kinds of reading. The huge popularity of Baz Luhrmann's film of *Romeo and Juliet* (even taking into account the Leonardo DiCaprio factor), which involves a sophisticated multiplicity of verbal and visual texts, provides evidence of the highly developed cineliteracy of most young people today. Building on the success of the film, as so many did, teachers acknowledged the value of linking the pleasures and interests of voluntary reading with the possibilities of studying Shakespeare's plays in the classroom. Such a wide range of home experience of reading serves as a very strong platform for the reading demands of a varied curriculum.

Several questions for teachers arise from even the limited findings of the small-scale classroom research referred to above. How can teachers find out as precisely as possible what students read beyond the classroom, and how does this relate to their reading at school? How can teachers build on aspects of reading with which students already feel confident, and help them to learn more about the kinds of reading and texts with which they are not already familiar or confident? There are many possible answers to these questions, but one thing is absolutely clear, namely the need to find out about students' home reading in the first place.

Gender and reading

Another issue that is likewise much more complex than some would have us believe, and that needs to be treated as such, is the whole business of boys' and girls' reading. Elaine Millard, in her book *Differently Literate*, points out that: 'it is tempting, when arguing from the kinds of reading undertaken by the majority of pupils, to distribute the subsets of reading genre along gender lines' (Millard, 1997: 97). Elaine Millard researched secondary schools, but gender difference is an aspect of reading practice that can provide cause for concern at a much earlier stage in children's education. Hazel Davies, a primary-school teacher in Essex, wanted to investigate why some of her Year 6 boys had lost interest in reading. After a very carefully observed study, she concluded:

> The reasons are many and complex, but three main issues stand out. Firstly cultural attitudes: *it's not cool to read* and *Dad's only reading is the Evening Gazette, backwards* Oliver told me. Secondly, the reading materials we provide. This has been the main focus of my project, and the very positive response from Chris and Jamie, and all the boys involved in the project, has shown that we can provide a range of books that is interesting and stimulating to boys of any age throughout the school. Thirdly, the way in which reading is offered in school. Yes, as teachers, we all appreciate the peace of silent reading, but the part of the reading project which gave the boys the most pleasure was sharing the books: looking at the pictures together, working out the puzzles together and talking together.
>
> (Davies, 1997: 9)

In secondary school, the matter becomes even more complicated. Caroline Daly (1999) observed Year 9 boys using literacy in different subject areas. Their reading behaviours raised for her the question:

> What significance lies in the agreements, acquiescences and resistances that fluctuate in the course of a school day across a range of subjects?
>
> (Daly, 1999: 8)

She concludes that 'boys as well as girls know well how to act like a "reader"'. But there is a problem in using the undifferentiated term 'boys':

> The critical question 'which boys' seems an obvious one. Current initiatives to raise boys' achievement often fail to acknowledge that class and race might have a complicating impact on such an all-embracing objective.
>
> (*ibid.*)

In another study, Judith Solsken points out further complexities:

> The learning biographies of the children in this study show that the gender dynamics around literacy in each family involved a highly specific interaction of many factors, including in addition to the mother's predominant role, the participation of fathers in children's literacy activities, the gender and relative age of siblings and their role in each other's literacy, and the treatment by family members of literacy as work or play.
>
> (Solsken, 1993: 56)

A recent Ofsted report on gender and performance also confirms these views, namely that, although there is evidence that boys lag behind girls in literacy performance, 'there are no simple explanations for the gender gap in performance, nor any simple solutions' (Arnot *et al.*, 1998). There *are* solutions nevertheless, drawn together, for example, in publications like the thought-provoking *Boys and Reading* (Barrs and Pidgeon, 1998), the outcome of a working party set up to explore this issue precisely. These include: more focused monitoring of boys' and girls' reading; using different groupings: mixed and single sex; extending the range of texts available; greater involvement of adult role models, especially males, taking account of class and ethnicity; discussions about individual progress with students; planned and thoughtful teacher intervention. As members of that group remind us, however, the solutions are more likely to be plural than singular, given the many-faceted experiences brought by readers – both boys and girls – into classrooms.

Mindful of the relative rights of all students to become satisfied and committed readers, it is important to discover the complexity of what makes a reader like he or she is, not to neglect our responsibility to include a variety of types of text, and to teach as wide a range of approaches to texts as possible. Here, as elsewhere, though, one principle which can guide us in the search for multiple solutions is that of *action research*. This can lead teachers to link their own research findings with planning, teaching and assessment in informed and reflective ways, finely tuned to the nuances of their own classrooms and students. Undertaking such research might be a daunting prospect if it weren't for the knowledge that help is at hand. This help comes not from outside agencies, but from the readers themselves, as they give us access to their responses to reading.

Responsibility and response

Students given the chance to talk or write about their reading in conversations conducted face to face, or through reading journals and reading autobiographies, will often communicate not only huge enthusiasm but also insights of startling perception and clarity. Once again, there is much to learn from these dialogues, not just about what students read or what motivates them to read, but about the very act of reading itself. They provide us with rich material from which to construct different 'frameworks for teaching' rather than leaving us to attempt to fit everything into a single model.

Consider, for example, how the following students' comments provide guidance for their teachers to build on. A Year 5 teacher in an Inner London school established group reading and reading journals as an attempt to raise motivation for reading. Students were asked to give advice to teachers who wanted to help children to improve their reading. Leigh comments:

One of the best things to make someone a better reader must be confidence from whomever they are reading to and self confidence pulls a lot of people through. Here is a bit of advice for the person who is listening to whomever is reading:

1   Remain calm at all times
2   Try and give the reader help with a word by splitting it up
3   Do not rush the reader on any word
4   Have confidence in the reader at all times.

(Bearne, 1994: 18)

This ten-year-old recognises the affective elements of reading, which do not appear in the official documentation. Elizabeth sums it up succinctly:

What I think you need to encourage reading are: a patient teacher, a book that suits you and a good imagination.

(*ibid*.: 19)

Spencer gives a complete explanation of the reading curriculum:

I like to do things like reading books. Every morning my class do reading. We fill in a little book called our Reading Record. I have not always liked reading. I do not like reading books without pictures, and books that are sometimes easy. I like to read books that are challenging. I read a lot of the time when I don't even know I'm reading. I like a lot of adventure and funny storys. In our class we have group reading. I like this and I like following storys when other people are reading them. I like all Judy Blume storys. My teacher reads us first chapters of books where we write down notes and then what we think of the story. In assembly my teacher reads books. After she reads them she asks us questions about the story she has read to us. I like it when our teacher asks the questions. I like reading through my rough drafts of work.

(*ibid*.: 19)

He makes it very clear that he, for one, doesn't see reading pictorial text as 'easy' but that he welcomes the challenges picture books offer. He also recognises the range of reading experiences on offer in his classroom, including explicit attention to environmental print, and reading drafts of his own writing. All of the children in this class, regardless of their fluency in reading, were keen to talk and write about their reading, knew a range of strategies for getting meaning out of print and clearly saw themselves as readers who could offer constructive advice on reading to others.

A primary school in Essex operated a system of reading partners where Year 5 pupils teamed up with Year 3 pupils. The students' comments reveal not only an awareness of the processes of reading, but a gradual development of a language through which to talk about reading. The younger children comment:

I have made a new friend. It helps me and it's fun. I've never had a reading partner before. It's better than reading to the teacher because he's a boy like me. It means we can laugh about it at the end and teachers wouldn't have had time to. As he's older than me he knows more words than me and he can correct me. He sometimes tells me to split words up. Sometimes he tells me to look at the picture.

> She is a good reading partner. I knew her before. If I miss out a word by acci-
> dent she tells me to go back. She says, 'sound words out', or she finds a little
> word inside a big word. She lives right near to me so it's nice to have her as
> my partner. With a friend you can look at the pictures afterwards – teachers
> can't do that because they have other children to listen to. You get more reading
> time. You can get more clues to what is going to happen in the story, before
> you read it all at once. With the teacher you only read a bit at a time.

The confident use of meta-language to talk about reading reminds us forcefully
of Bruner's argument for interactivity in role-modelling. Furthermore, a look at
secondary-school students reflecting on their reading in reading-journals shows that
they gradually develop the use of internal and therefore independent dialogue, as we
shall see below.

Reading-journals have many benefits, not least that they can provide an opportunity for students and teachers to reflect jointly on the students' reading. Their value
lies in students recording in some detail their initial encounters with texts, rather
than simply their final ideas and opinions. The accumulated record of reading processes
and developments, reflection and response, can form the basis for more carefully
shaped course-work at a later stage. What it provides in the meantime, though, is a
continuous record of reading, both the texts *and* the processes of reading them.
Using journals for responding to whole-class texts as well as independent reading,
helps students to learn that similar approaches may be adopted with any text, regardless of who has chosen it or what kind of text it is. By writing about texts
studied by the whole class, students learn what kinds of questions or observations
it is interesting to ask or record. These can then be applied to their personal reading
as well. To list only a few of the important points: students can be encouraged to
predict; to reconsider earlier journal entries; to write down questions that they want
the text to answer for them at a later stage; and to be explicit about how they are
drawing on their own social, cultural or intertextual experiences in order to make
sense of what they are reading.

Here a Year 9 reader (aged 13 years) studying Susan Hinton's *The Outsiders*
notes, for example, that reading narrative is not always a straightforward linear
process:

> I like the way the book goes backwards and forwards so we are always learning
> more of the gang ... I said earlier that the book keeps going 'backwards and
> forwards'. This did happen like Johnny saying 'Stay gold'. That didn't make
> sense when we first heard it but it did at the end.

Another student from the same group demonstrates an understanding of the potential unreliability of a narrator:

> I dislike Ponyboy's part. To me he seems too sure of himself, maybe that's the
> way they are. He judges other people's character too closely. I quote 'Dally only
> thinks of himself' but we found out today that it wasn't true.

Not all students like using journals. Why? For some it is because they interfere
with the pleasures of reading:

> I don't like journals but they're better than reviews. I'd rather do without jour-
> nals or reviews and just get on with the book.

Others prefer to talk rather than write:

> I don't like putting books into writing. I just like to say about it instead of writing.

So what would be a better way for teachers to find out about students' reading?

Ask them!

> Use tapes instead of reading logs because it would be a lot quicker, you'd get more in and save rainforests.

However, others express very different views:

> I like to write a review because when I read a book I like to tell people or write it down so I can read it in the future.

> I find that if I don't tell someone about a book that I'm really enjoying I feel as if I'm going to burst. This is another reason why I like reading journals.

> It helps you to find how your views have changed by looking back on earlier entries and if your predictions were right.

> It gives you more freedom to write your thoughts.

> There are not any set answers in a reading journal.

The kinds of insight that emerge from students' written and spoken dialogue with teachers and each other can be used – by the teacher who is looking out for them – not just to summarise or comment on the stage of reading development that students have already achieved, but more importantly to identify what they might achieve next. Journal dialogues make an ideal site for Vygotsky's 'zone of proximal development', the place where the teacher's instruction is 'that which marches ahead of development and leads it' (Vygotsky, 1986).

While heeding the points made by students who like to talk rather than write about their reading, and ensuring that they have plenty of opportunity to utilise their preferred learning styles, there are equally important arguments for keeping journals, precisely because they *are* written, not spoken. Because there are not any set answers in a reading journal, students can begin to understand that their reading may be as valid as the next person's, without the anxieties that may arise from having to present their suggestions in front of a large group of people. This understanding can increase confidence and develop a more sharply defined awareness of what it means to be a reader. The permanence of the writing enables the subtle and shifting nuances of the reading process to be made visible and can lead students to see more clearly the nature and power of written text.

It must be remembered that the kinds of activities being referred to here will be of only limited use if they are not seen as part of a whole-school approach to reading. This point is made very clearly by Alastair West in 'The production of readers', a summary of research he conducted in the 1980s. Of the three secondary schools included in the study, he writes that all of them:

placed a high valuation upon reading in their rhetoric, but only one had discovered ways of giving that high valuation any structural form within the working practices and social relations of the institution.

(West, 1986: 7)

For some schools and teachers the National Literacy Strategy offers a structure to help them realise their aims and implement their reading policies. For others, however, it will not be enough. For them the framework is too rigid, the rationale too thin. They are seeking altogether richer and more varied approaches, woven out of a fabric which represents more fully the developing thoughts and feelings of the students that they teach.

Insights, planning and assessment

Comments by students, such as those quoted above, show just how important it is for teachers to have a vocabulary through which to describe what 'getting better at reading' involves in order to model reflective comments for developing readers. Reflecting on reading doesn't just contribute to personal development, but to progress in reading. Most importantly, it contributes to the development of independence and discrimination, making choices about when, what, and how to read. Having an insight into the mind of the reader also allows the teacher to plan for future development. Judging by the teaching objectives (not 'learning' objectives) in the National Literacy framework, criteria for progress would be firmly tied to knowledge about text structures, knowledge about language (at sentence and word level), comprehension and composition. There is nothing wrong with that except for the yawning gap it leaves. What is missing is the essential element of developing preferences and choices, in other words, becoming a reflective, responsive and critical reader.

In an attack on summative forms of testing, based on a wide-ranging study of all the recent research on assessment, Paul Black and Dylan Wiliam argue that standards are only raised by changes that are put into direct effect by teachers and pupils in classrooms:

There is a body of firm evidence that formative assessment is an essential feature of classroom work and that development of it can raise standards. ... Our education system has been subjected to many far-reaching initiatives which, whilst taken in reaction to concerns about existing practices, have been based on little evidence about their potential to meet those concerns.

(Black and Wiliam, 1998: 19)

This raises some questions about Standard Assessment Tests (SATs) and terminal examinations as helpful forms of assessment, especially given the extent to which they are privileged in league tables and media coverage of reading standards. For example, the results for the Key Stage 2 Reading SAT (1998), taken by the Year 5/6 class whose reading habits at home were reported earlier, showed some significant disparities. About a third of the class did not finish the paper, and so about six or seven children were awarded Level 3 when their classroom performance showed that they were much more accomplished readers than this. If the main assessment tools – SATs – are summative, looking largely at the 'comprehension' elements of reading, not at the readers' abilities in making critical choices (in spite of teachers' attention to the structure of texts), then we do not end up with a description of genuine progress, let alone achievement, in reading.

Useful assessment, according to Black and William, should be related to:

> the quality of teacher–pupil interactions, the stimulus and help for pupils to take active responsibility for their own learning, the particular help needed to move pupils out of the 'low-attainment' trap, and the development thereby of the habits needed by all if they are to become capable of life-long learning. Improvements in formative assessment which are within reach can contribute substantially to raising standards in all of those aspects.
>
> (*ibid*.: 15)

The writers go on to emphasise that improvements in formative assessment will depend on a properly funded and managed in-service programme, on acceptance of slow development and low-key (at first) dissemination; the removal of teachers' feelings of 'insecurity, guilt, frustration and anger' about assessment; continuing research in 'active development work' about teachers' perceptions and experience, and continuing evaluation of such a programme.

Conclusions

The teachers described in this chapter, and many more whose work is detailed in other texts to which we have referred, are continually discovering for themselves the value and efficacy of reflecting on, discussing and theorising their own classroom approaches to the teaching of reading. They are, to borrow Margaret Meek's words, 'researchers in their own classrooms rather than simply those who carry out instructions' (Meek, 1997). If the teaching of reading is to lead to communities of avid and attentive readers, who read with pleasure and passion, who question and interpret, listen and respond, criticise and initiate discussion, then what is needed is space, time and positive encouragement for teachers to take intellectual as well as practical responsibility for the development of the reading curriculum, and for students to enjoy more of the reading rights to which they are entitled. Reading is a delicate business and requires finely tuned instruments to record and assess progress and development. Pennac concludes *Reads Like A Novel* with a reminder that a sensitive rather than a heavy-handed touch may be the most productive.

> Reading offers [man] no definitive explanation of his fate, but weaves a tight network of correspondences between life and him. These correspondences, tiny and secretive, speak of the paradoxical good fortune of being alive, even while they're illuminating the tragic absurdity of life. The result is that our reasons for reading are quite as strange as are our reasons for living. And no one is charged to have us render an account of that intimate strangeness.
>
> The few adults who have really given me something to read have always effaced themselves before the books, and they've always been careful not to ask me what I had *understood* in these books. To them, of course, I'd talk about what I'd read.
>
> (Pennac, 1994: 177–8)

What is needed, above all, is that we keep thinking about reading and noting our emerging understanding of the processes and texts that make up reading experience and experiences. For, as Robert Scholes avows:

> Reading is not just a means to other ends. It is one of the great rewards for the use of our capacities, a reason for living, an end in itself.
>
> (Scholes, 1989: 18)

References

Arnot, M. *et al.* (1998) *Recent Research on Gender and Educational Performance*, London: HMSO.

Barrs, M. and Pidgeon, S. (1998) *Boys and Reading*, London: Centre for Language in Primary Education.

Bearne, E. (1994) *Raising Reading Standards: Course Evaluation*, London: Southwark Council.

Black, P. and William, D. (1998) *Inside the Black Box: Raising Reading Standards Through Classroom Assessment*, London: Kings College School of Education.

Bruner, J. (1966) *Towards a Theory of Instruction*, Cambridge, MA: Harvard University Press.

Daly, C. (1999) 'Reading boys', *Changing English: Domains of Literacy*, vol. 6, no. 1, University of London Institute of Education.

Davies, H. (1997) unpublished assignment for the Essex Reading Project.

Department of Education and Science (1975) *A Language for Life. Report of the Committee of Inquiry appointed by the Secretary of State for Education and Science* [The Bullock Report], London: HMSO.

Hall, C. and Coles, M. (1999) *Children's Reading Choices*, London: Routledge.

Manguel, A. (1996) *A History of Reading*, London: HarperCollins.

Meek, M. (1988) *How Texts Teach What Readers Learn*, Stroud: Thimble Press.

Meek, M. (1997) 'Rhetorics about reading', in *Changing English: Domains of Literacy*, vol. 4, no. 2, University of London Institute of Education.

Millard, E. (1997) *Differently Literate*, London: Falmer Press.

Pennac, D. (1994) *Reads Like a Novel*, London: Quartet Books.

Qualifications and Curriculum Authority (on behalf of the Advisory Group on Citizenship) (1998b) *Education for Citizenship and the Teaching of Democracy in Schools*, London: QCA [Crick Report].

Scholes, R. (1989) *Protocols of Reading*, New Haven and London: Yale University Press.

Solsken, J. (1993) *Literacy, Gender and Work in Families and in School*, New Jersey: Ablex.

Spratt, N. and Sturdy, R. (1998) 'Reading and gender', in E. Bearne (ed.) (1998) *Use of Language Across the Secondary Curriculum*, London: Routledge.

West, A. (1986) 'The Production of Readers', *The English Magazine*, 17 (Autumn): 4–9, London: ILEA English Centre.

Whitehead, F. *et al.* (1977) *Children and their Books: The Final Report of the Schools Council Project on Children's Reading Habits, 10–16*, Basingstoke: Evans/Methuen Educational.

CHAPTER 16

THE READER IN THE WRITER

Myra Barrs

Reading Literacy and Language, 2000, 34(2): 54–60

Introduction

The first time I attended a conference in the USA for teachers of English, one of the teachers I met asked me 'Are you a reading teacher or a writing teacher?'. This was the thing that made me realise why America needed the 'whole language' movement. Although in the UK we often do talk about reading and writing as if they were separate, we have never divided reading from writing to the extent that they are taught separately on primary school timetables by different teachers, as has happened sometimes in the USA.

Most teachers of English and literacy in UK primary or secondary schools, would agree that reading and writing are, as Vygotsky suggested, two halves of the same process: mastering written language (Britton, 1982). Now, with the National Literacy Strategy (NLS), official policy also seems to put these two halves together. But in this relationship, writing has been, at primary school level at least, the poor relation. For many years a child's 'reading age' was a crude shorthand measure of their competence in English, even at age 11. The coming of the National Curriculum (NC) and the assessment of writing as well as reading, has at any rate changed all that.

The new emphasis on writing (and current concerns about targets at KS2) has raised urgent questions about how children do learn about written language beyond the early stages, and what it is that marks progress in writing. The NC writing attainment target now makes this progress largely a matter of increasing technical accuracy, widening vocabulary, and increasing control over structure and organisation. However, the writing programme of study does also suggest that 'pupils should be taught (to draw) on their reading'. This may be the way in which teachers and pupils can go beyond the stripped-down agenda embodied in the new NC (DfEE, 1999) and engage with the complexities of creating satisfying texts, both in fiction and non-fiction.

The relationship between the writer and the reader

The work of skilful and experienced children's authors, who know how to make worlds and engage readers, is one of the main resources we have for showing children what words can do. The critical fashion which highlights the role of the reader often ignores the role of the writer, referring us instead to the *text*. Yet writers are never as completely absent from their texts as reader-response theories imply; reading is always an act of relationship between reader and writer with the text as a meeting place, and this relationship may be particularly important for young reader/writers.

The critic Bakhtin (1981) describes how the different space-times that the writer and the reader inhabit touch in the act of reading. In *The Dialogic Imagination*, he writes:

> We are presented with a text occupying a certain specific place in space, that is, it is localised; our creation of it, our acquaintance with it occurs through time. The text as such never appears as a dead thing, beginning with any text ... we always arrive, in the final analysis, at the human voice, which is to say we come up against the human being. ...
>
> (Bakhtin, 1981: 88)

Bakhtin insists on the *voice* of the writer, which he maintains that we hear even when we read silently to ourselves. In order to understand the closeness of the relationship between reader and writer, it's important to realise that it is the writer's *inner speech* that we hear in our minds or ourselves give voice to, in our own inner speech. It's the very personal nature of this communication, direct from mind to mind, that makes reading such an act of intimacy.

Daniel Pennac (1994), a French teacher of literature, describes how he went about reawakening one class's enjoyment of reading, deeply buried under years of French secondary education, by reading aloud to them. The book he chose was Patrick Susskind's *Perfume*. When Pennac took the thick book out of his bag and announced his intention of reading it aloud, the class were horrified. ('You're going to read us that whole book, out loud?') They were also offended ('We're past the age for that'). But within ten minutes the students were hooked on the narrative, and on the author's way of telling it.

Pennac reflects on what was going on. These were students who had forgotten that reading could give pleasure. Reading in school had been for them a constant series of tests; they were obsessed by a fear of not understanding what was read. Pennac suggests that one of the things that happened for them during the reading aloud was that they formed a relationship with Susskind, a relationship that began in their sense of the author's *voice*.

> With the public reading of *Perfume*, they found themselves in front of Susskind: a story, of course, a fine narrative, amusing and baroque, but a voice as well, the author's (later, in their essays, this will be called his 'style'). A story, yes, but a story told by someone. ... The final page turned, it's the echo of that voice which keeps us company.

So these students learned to read again in a way that their academic French education had fundamentally inhibited – for the pleasure of narrative, of listening to a storytelling voice. They developed a growing appreciation of how the writer was working on them. They became fans, admirers of the skills of Marquez, Susskind, Calvino, Salinger, Stevenson and began to look about for more books by the writers they liked; they wanted to immerse themselves in these books.

Children respond to the work of particular authors from a much earlier age, perhaps from babyhood, from the moment when they begin to have a favourite book. When they start to be aware of writers and to become fans, they begin to read and listen, in a different way. Older children who have enjoyed a story often want to write one like it. As Margaret Meek Spencer suggests, 'If we want to see what lessons have been learned from the texts that children read, we have to look for them in what they write' (Meek, 1988: 38). Our favourite texts are where, as readers, we apprentice ourselves to writers.

A six year old girl began a story like this:

> The circus was coming, and the animals had babies. But one animal did not have a baby. She looked high and low for a baby to suit her. But no, she could not find one.
>
> (Barrs *et al.*, 1990: 83)

Here we recognise the signs of a writer learning to mark the tune of a story for her readers, drawing on her own experience of literary styles and rhythms. The rhythms are so strongly marked that we may be confident of this writer's familiarity with the language of books. We can sometimes track these influences in children's work more precisely, finding stories which seem to directly echo Enid Blyton or Jacqueline Wilson. But although children do often model their writing directly on known texts, when I asked one prolific nine year old writer where he got the ideas for his stories, – whether he ever directly imitated the style of his favourite authors – he replied succinctly: 'I sort of get the feeling from reading lots of books' (Barrs, 1983).

When we come to know books well, through rereading, we absorb their characteristic tunes and patterns, which find a place inside us. If we return in later life to a book that we knew in childhood, we immediately recognise those same familiar tunes. James Britton, in one of his last essays, discussed the experiences of recalling a poem through what he called its 'powerfully remembered cadences', and suggested that poetry and literary language are remembered and stored partly as rhythms and partly as grammatical structures (Britton, 1993). Writers who are also readers are people with a large number of tunes and structures in their heads.

Shaping writing

The question of how children learn to shape their writing and what role reading plays in this learning is raised in a particularly acute fashion by a recent publication from the QCA (1999) called *Improving Writing at Key Stages 3 and 4*. Because of its title, primary teachers might be inclined to pass this report by, but it is an interesting document both in itself and for the insights it offers into currently fashionable views on what good writing is and how we learn written language.

The pamphlet is primarily a report from a QCA project called the Technical Accuracy Project, which undertook a study of the linguistic features of different grade levels of writing in GCSE English. The project team investigated 'large numbers' (no details given) of examples of GCSE pupils' writing in an attempt to analyse the linguistic characteristics of A, C and F grade writing. The findings are presented as a way of making explicit what it is about writing at a particular grade that makes it fit that grade. Thus, for instance, we learn that 'A class' writing tends to make greater use of abstract nouns, parenthetical commas, subordinate clauses and place adverbials (rather than time adverbials) to link paragraphs. 'F grade' candidates, on the other hand, characteristically link clauses by 'and', make little use of adjectives, largely omit paragraphs and make sparse use of commas. This kind of information is of moderate interest, but of course it begs many questions. After all, as David Olson (1994) points out:

> Children of bookish parents may learn to speak with subordinate clauses, paren-
> theticals and the like, marking structure lexically by means of subordinating
> conjunctions, relative pronouns and speech act verbs. Such bookish parents can
> do so because writing can and does provide a model for their speech.
>
> (Olson, 1994: 253)

What we need to know more about is how those 'A' class candidates came to be
able to manipulate these features of written language so confidently.

The QCA project was confined to a study of technical accuracy only; issues of
meaning and content were not under discussion. Unfortunately, there is a tendency
within the pamphlet to present this way of looking at writing as a more reliable way
of assessing effectiveness *in general* than that provided by more holistic approaches.
'The process of quantifying linguistic features' claim the writers 'has enabled us to
put flesh onto the qualitative judgements many English teachers habitually make'.

The real problem, though, comes in the section of the pamphlet called 'Implications
for Teachers'. In this follow-up to the project, a group of English departments were
invited to come up with plans for integrating the teaching of grammatical features
into their existing teaching of reading and writing. Here is the usual trap and those
involved in producing this pamphlet have fallen headlong into it. It is this: we may
have discovered, or think we have discovered, that skilful writers at GCSE use more
abstract nouns – but that does not mean that teaching children to sprinkle abstract
nouns through their texts will necessarily improve their writing.

The kind of pedagogy that is described in the second half of this pamphlet is
fraught with weaknesses. In one unit that was developed, pupils looking at paragraph linking were 'given a "quota" in their own writing and encouraged to use two
place adverbial links for every time link'. In another, pupils were asked to calculate
the proportion of abstract and concrete nouns. We must hope that the experiences
of these pupils were more meaningful than these summaries suggest. Did they justify,
in terms of quality of writing, the tactics adopted by the teachers? Did they justify
the time taken away from actual experience of reading and writing? Because no
examples of pupils' writing are given, we are not permitted to judge for ourselves
whether this kind of coaching actually achieved anything. It seems unlikely, for two
reasons.

Firstly, good writing usually involves a closer relationship between meaning and
form than is assumed in this pamphlet. The focus on form rather than content in
these experiments seems unlikely to generate writing which is purposeful, focused,
strongly felt, or strongly expressed. The pedagogical approaches adopted are the
opposite of those described in the important recent report on *Effective Teachers of
Literacy* (Medwell *et al.*, 1998). One of that project's key findings about the
teachers identified as particularly effective was that they believed that 'the *creation
of meaning in literacy was fundamental', and focused attention first of all on the
content* of texts *and on composition. In Improving Writing at KS3 and 4* (QCA,
1999), content and meaning come a poor second to the overriding preoccupation
with linguistic features.

Secondly, it seems inherently unlikely that these short-cuts to linguistic sophistication would actually work. Pupils who write skilfully and use language in striking
and varied ways are likely to be linguistically experienced, especially in relation to
written language. Direct teaching of particular linguistic features is no substitute for
substantial experience of reading and writing. The role of reading, in particular, in
teaching writing, is something that contemporary discussions of teaching writing need
to take more account of.

The research project

A recent piece of research planned and conducted by the staff of the Centre for Language in Primary Education took a different approach to the improvement of children's writing from that adopted in the QCA pamphlet. We set out to explore a common supposition: that the quality of what children read is likely to affect how they write. We wanted to look particularly at the influence of children's reading of challenging literary texts on their writing development at KS2.

Although our basic assumption could have been thought of as a truism, and is a central premise of the NLS, hardly any relevant research was identified in our initial search of research literature. Among the few studies which seemed to have a direct bearing on our topic was Carol Fox's (1993) *At the Very Edge of the Forest*, a study of young children's oral storytelling. Like Fox, we wanted to trace the relationship between children's narrative and literary competences and their experiences of books.

The project involved six Y5 teachers and classes in five primary schools in Greater London. The fact that all of the participating teachers were teaching Year 5 was not a planned aspect of the study, but a fortunate coincidence. It enabled us to compare children's work across the project schools more easily and also meant that, because of the introduction of the NLS, all of the participating teachers were working to the same general objectives.

It was clear that the classes being visited were already involving children with high quality literature, but we nevertheless wanted to introduce an element of commonality across all six classes. We selected two 'standard texts' to be studied, one in the Spring term: *The Green Children* by Kevin Crossley Holland (1994) and one in the Summer Term: *Fire, Bed and Bone* by Henrietta Branford (1997). These texts fitted well into the NLS Framework for Y5, which suggests that children should study legends and 'explore the differences between oral and written story-telling' in the Spring Term and should look at the 'viewpoint from which stories are told' in the Summer Term. The language and style of the books were powerful; we hoped that their influence would be detectable.

Throughout the school year 1998–99 the project coordinator, Val Cork, visited the classes involved in the project, observing classroom activities, interviewing selected case study children and discussing the project with teachers. We collected all the writing by eighteen children across the six classes, and carried out in-depth case studies of six children, samples of whose writing across the year were analysed. Our aims were to examine any developments that took place in children's writing when they studied challenging literature, to investigate whether any kinds of teaching were particularly effective in teaching writing, and to observe whether any texts had a particular impact on children's learning of writing.

The effect of writing in role

One of the project's main findings concerns the effect on children's writing of writing in role. All the children were involved in working and writing in role during the project: in all the participating classes *The Green Children* was introduced with the help of a drama workshop, conducted by a drama consultant. This drama session, which occupied only one literacy hour, was an important intervention for children and teachers alike. One of its important features was that the introduction of the text itself was delayed until the fictional world and the themes of the story had been prefigured through drama. This had a big impact on the children, who seemed to relate much more closely and personally to this text because they had already 'lived through' some of its events and situations.

Following the drama work and the reading of the text, most children wrote in role as a character within the story. Their writing in role was almost universally well done and sometimes led to an observable shift in the case study children's writing. For instance, children filled in more imagined detail around the narrative, in a way that had obviously been suggested by the drama:

> It was a normal day when everybody would go to the fair, buy something, or go on terrifying rides. Bargains going on and children breaking things and messing about ... I even remember what kind of day it was. The blazing sun shone down on us. The ground was hot like fire, it burnt my feet, until everything went quiet, there was a big crowd of people all staring at one thing.

Writing in role seems to be a real aid to children's progress as writers because it moves them out of their personal language register and into other areas of language. It involves them in writing in first person – in a way that they are accustomed to and that is an extension of their speech. But it also involves them in taking on a different persona – in a way that enables them to get inside other experiences and other ways of talking, thinking and feeling. As in any well-conducted drama session, children are enabled to access language that is beyond their normal range.

The influence of quality literature

As part of our data analysis of children's writing samples we took T-unit length, a measure of syntactic complexity, as one index of change in their writing. A T-unit is defined as 'one main clause with all the subordinate clauses attaching to it' (Hunt, 1964). T-unit length is sometimes used as a measure of increasing maturity in children's writing. Any discussion of T-unit length, however, has to be preceded by an acknowledgement of the limitations of this measure; as Carol Fox (1993) points out: 'it is pointless to value syntactic complexity for its own sake'. We certainly did not find that the length of children's T-units increased in any uniform way over the project year. What was interesting about the use of the measure, however, was the way in which it revealed the influence on children's writing of the texts that they were reading.

For instance, S. was a writer who habitually wrote in relatively long T-units but analysis of her samples revealed marked changes in the length of her T-units in the course of the year. In her earliest sample, the average T-unit length was 11.1, and in her last sample it was 10.5. But in her middle sample, a piece of writing in role based on *The Green Children*, T-unit length fell dramatically, to 6.1. This was a striking change, but when we came to look more closely at the text she was writing in response to, the change became more explicable. Kevin Crossley-Holland's style in this book is plain and speech-based. The average T-unit length of a sample page from *The Green Children*, when analysed, proved to be 6.6, not very different from the average we found in the analysis of S.'s writing. It was apparent that S., in responding to Crossley-Holland's text, was mirroring these very short T-units.

Not all of the children in the sample studied our second standard text, *Fire, Bed and Bone*, but those who did wrote very impressively in response to this book. Branford's novel is a historial novel based on the Peasant's Revolt; the narrator is an old hunting dog belonging to a family that, early in the book, is imprisoned because of their suspected complicity in the Revolt. The first chapter of the book is however a picture of peace; the whole household is asleep at night, in the same big room, with a fire burning. The hunting dog is awake; she is about to have puppies and expects them to be born next day. Her musings build up a picture of the world around the house.

The following examples are not taken from the case study children's samples but are drawn from two particular classes, in order to show how high the general standard of writing was in response to this text:

A child writing as Humble the cat:

> I am a creature of very different worlds.
> I know where the dormice nest in the oat fields. I know valleys that have deep blue rivers with the silver fish.
> I know the house and the warmest place in front of the fire. I know where the rats play at the back of the house. I know the tops of the tall pine trees. I know where the plumpest birds nest. I know the comfiest branch.

Two children writing as the hunting dog, living in the wild with Fleabane her puppy:

> 1. That night was a cold one.
> Fleabane was asleep as soon as we got in from hunting. I soon dozed off but not for long. I sensed danger and my hackles rose. I got up and sniffed the air. I looked over at Fleabane, he was asleep. I was worried I didn't want to lose Fleabane as I did Parsnip and Squill. I strolled over to him and bent closer just to hear him breathe, and I rested my paw on his paw. I knew he was safe now but my hackles were still aroused.

> 2. I caught two wild hare. The glorious scent tickled my snout.
> I hurried back to Fleabane. I ran into the den. He was playing with some hay. He lifted his droopy eyes, I knew he was hungry.
> I gave him the small hare and kept my careful eye on him. I felt a sunbeam from the early horizon. I tucked into my hare. It was tasty.
> I could hear Rufus and Comfort, I turned to the doorway. I saw nothing. It didn't feel right being free as the wild wind while Comfort and Rufus were locked up. I wanted to be at home.

Two children writing as Fleabane in captivity:

> 1. I lie fretting in an empty barrel.
> I run out the barrel forgetting the chain.
> I run so fast the chain pulls me back into the barrel, my ear catches on a nail and I yelp in pain. I can feel the hot sweaty blood dribbling down my face.
> The wolves barked last night as they spoke to me of freedom but I didn't want to think of freedom all I wanted was my mother.
> My mother used to tell me that humans were good, that they gave you a bed and a nice warm fire to sleep next to. I do not believe that.

> 2. The hole at the top of the barrel lets in a howling draught, a draught that sends frightening shivers down my back. Blood dribbles down the side of my face. I know I shouldn't try to escape, it's just so tempting. I don't want to move I only want to dream, dream of far, far away where I could forget my terrible memories of being beaten with the metal whips leaving cuts long and large, sharp and sore.

Two children writing poems based on the first chapter of the book:

1. Rats playing in the kitchen
    munching and making noise.
    Fire sparkling brighter
    than the glowing sun.
    Ticking stars reflecting
    into a diminutive puddle.
    The tumbling of horses
    and a moon so bright
    it is beaming into my eyes.

    Foxes cry and run about
    on the crackly, mist green
    and copper brown ground.
    Bats fly through the smoke
    and smell of the ashes
    of the dying fire.

    My belly is aching with pain,
    it is torture.

2. Lying there ashes spitting on my fur
    as they die down slowly.
    Crackling from the windows
    as a small draft comes in
    and sways in my fur.

    Humble curling up towards me
    stroking her luxurious tail against my aching back.

    Chickens scuttling about
    rats tapping their tiny feet in the pantry.

    The calling of the owls as 'tis just coming morning.
    The bright moon shining shining on me
    as the crystal snow falls . . .

What was apparent in all the children's writing that was done in response to this text was the strong sense of empathy with the characters, especially the animal characters in the text. Children wrote with real feeling about the predicament of the scattered 'family' and in writing as the hunting dog, especially, they seemed to 'live through' and feel acutely some of the pains and anxieties of being a parent ('I didn't want to lose Fleabane . . . I bent closer just to hear him breathe and rested my paw on his paw'). The writing was finely imagined in a detailed way that suggested that children were absorbed in the world of the text.

Dorothy Heathcote says that drama touches on areas that are in the main avoided in school: 'understanding of the place and importance of emotion, and language with which to express emotion' (Heathcote, 1984). *Fire, Bed and Bone* is an emotionally powerful text and it spoke to children strongly. Texts with emotionally powerful themes communicated immediately with children in the project classes. They seemed to help children to adopt other points of view and to explore the inner states of characters, taking on the language with which to express emotion.

Children also responded to the poetic language of this text and to its music. Henrietta Branford's writing in this book, especially in the first chapter, exemplifies David Olson's (1994) description of literary language as 'poeticised speech', yet is simple enough to be accessible to the whole ability range and to children learning English. Children's poems, in particular, echoed the incantatory rhythms of the first chapter.

Transforming classroom practice

Although the main aim of the project was to consider the effects of the study of challenging literature on children's development as writers, we also wanted to look at the kinds of teaching that seemed to be making a difference to children's progress in writing. But our project coincided with the introduction of the NLS and was therefore taking place in a far from typical year. We tried to turn this coincidence to good account by documenting as far as possible the impact of the NLS on the project teachers' practice.

Although the teachers felt that NLS *Framework for Teaching* (DfEE, 1998) had helped them in planning a literature curriculum for each term, and raised their awareness of particular authors and genres, during the first term of implementing the literacy hour, they all began to voice the same major concern. They found that children did not have enough time to work on longer narratives and that many pieces of writing were being left unfinished at the first draft stage. The whole practice of a writers' workshop, where attention could be given to the development of children's texts, was being eroded, and the work in writing was becoming 'bitty'. Some children complained because they had too little time to write. A number of the project teachers, with extensive experience of teaching writing, felt that the standard of children's writing was suffering. As a result of these concerns, five of the teachers decided to extend the time for literacy to one and a half hours a day and one teacher began to use two sessions a week for extended writing. By the end of the project year, all of the participating teachers had effected 'positive transformations' in the literacy hour in some way, most especially to allow time for extended writing.

Two practices which stood out as being particularly influential in these classrooms were the use of response partners to help children develop their texts and the use of reading aloud in the teaching of literature and writing. Most of the teachers we observed put a great deal of emphasis on encouraging children to work on their writing together, through the use of response partners or writing partners. Lessons were structured in such a way as to allow time for children to read their texts aloud to a partner, and to respond to each other's writing. The use of pairs was more common, and appeared more effective, than the use of small groups for this kind of collaborative work on writing. The consistent use of response partners was popular with children. It helped to develop children's sense of the impact of their writing on a reader.

The teachers in these classrooms, just like Daniel Pennac, believed strongly in the value of continuing to read aloud to older children and regarded this as an important way in which they could bring texts alive for them and engage them with literature. In some classrooms where children were inexperienced readers and writers, a particularly strong emphasis was put on rereading. Although children sometimes had copies of the text being read aloud, quite often they did not. Reading aloud seemed to be a particularly helpful way of foregrounding the tunes and rhythms of a text in a way that subsequently influenced children's writing. It was also a powerful prelude to the subsequent discussion of texts.

Conclusions

The new didacticism that characterises so much official discussion of the teaching of literacy and writing wants to short-cut some of the learning that goes on as children listen to, reread and reflect on texts that they have become familiar with. There is an impatience around, and this impatience is partly with learning itself, the time it takes, its idiosyncracies. It seems so much more efficient and time-saving to analyse the linguistic features that characterise successful texts and teach these features directly to children. But this 'common-sense' approach needs to be set against another kind of common-sense, that of experienced teachers such as those included in our study, whose experience – both generally and within the project – had convinced them of the value of dwelling on texts in more depth and detail, of rereading, of reading whole texts rather than extracts, and of taking time with children's writing.

Although our project was predominantly a study of writing development, over the project year children also began to read more demanding texts. They had been introduced to books that they might not normally have chosen and been taken in directions they might not normally go. In addition, they brought to their reading a growing consciousness of how writers work – readers who are aware of what is involved in structuring a narrative experience for others are likely to read more critically and responsively. It seems unlikely that there can be any fundamental writing development without reading development, and vice versa. Once we fully recognise that progress in one mode is intimately related to and dependent on progress in the other, we should be better able to draw out the implications for teaching written language in a way which is both more unified and more effective.

Acknowledgements

I should like to thank the project co-ordinator, Val Cork, the staff and children of the project schools and all others involved in the project, including Susanna Steele, Fiona Collins, Margaret Meek Spencer and the staff of CLPE.

References

Bakhtin, M.M. (1981) *The Dialogic Imagination*. Austin: University of Texas Press.
Barrs, M. (1983) Making Stories: Young Children's Fictional Narratives. Unpublished M.A. Dissertation, University of London.
Barrs, M., Ellis, S., Hester, H. and Thomas, A. (1990) Patterns of Learning: The Primary Language Record and the National Curriculum. London: CLPE.
Barrs, M. and Cork, V. (2001) *The Reading in the Writer: The Links between the Study of Literature and Writing Development at KS2*, London: CLPE.
Branford, H. (1997) *Fire, Bed and Bone*. London: Walker Books.
Britton, J. (1982) *Prospect and Retrospect*. London: Heinemann.
Britton, J. (1993) *Literature in its Place*. London: Cassell.
Crossley-Holland, K. (1994) *The Green Children*. Oxford: Oxford University Press.
Department for Education and Employment/Qualifications and Curriculum Authority (1999) *The National Curriculum: English*. London: DfEE/QCA.
Fox, C. (1993) *At the Very Edge of the Forest*. London: Cassell.
Johnson, L. and O'Neill, C. (eds) (1984) *Dorothy Heathcote: collected writings on education and drama*. London: Hutchinson.
Medwell, J. *et al.* (1998) *Effective Teachers of Literacy*. Exeter: University of Exeter.
Meek, M. (1988) *How Texts Teach What Readers Learn*. Stroud, Glos.: Thimble Press.
The National Literacy Strategy Framework for Teaching. DfEE, 1998.
Olson, D. (1994) *The World on Paper*. Cambridge: Cambridge University Press.
Pennac, D. (1994) *Reads Like a Novel*. London: Quartet.
Qualifications and Curriculum Authority (1999) *Improving Writing at Key Stages 3 and 4*. London: QCA.

CHAPTER 17

WHAT DOES RESEARCH TELL US ABOUT HOW WE SHOULD BE DEVELOPING WRITTEN COMPOSITION?

Mary Bailey

Raising Standards in Literacy, Ros Fisher, Greg Brooks and Maureen Lewis (eds), London: RoutledgeFalmer, 2002, pp. 23–37

Introduction

What does research say about how we should be developing written composition? It is worth considering why this question is asked and who is, or perhaps should be, interested in its answer. In the context of a drive to raise standards in literacy, and when standards of achievement in writing are of particular concern – national test results in writing lag behind those in reading for eleven year olds in the United Kingdom – there is an awareness that we need to be more informed about the implications of research for practice. Where there is a national policy for the teaching of literacy, including unprecedented attention to the teaching of writing, one might reasonably expect that policy to exemplify, if not to explicate, the link between research and practice. However, this chapter will argue that there are two areas in which this link is fragile: first, that there is a gap (in the United Kingdom, at least) between what writing research suggests should be done and what national policy advocates; and, second, that there is a gap between what policy advocates, and how this is being interpreted in the classroom. There are also areas of debate in the connections between research, policy and practice in the teaching of reading, and, of course, there is an intrinsic relationship between reading and writing, but it is arguable that both policy makers and classroom teachers tend to be less clear about the research basis for developing writing than they are for developing reading.

This is not to imply that there should be a simple, unidirectional link from research to policy to practice. There are different influences at play: the best research takes into account real contexts and practical implications; policy should be determined by both good quality research and good practice (which, if properly evaluated, is also research); policy affects what research findings are promoted and what research is conducted, in that policy makers – at national government level – influence the allocation of some sources of research funding.

This chapter argues that for standards of achievement in writing to be raised we need to make the research basis for national literacy initiatives more explicit, and to question policy where it is not supported by research. We need to ensure that more teachers are confident in their understanding of children's writing development and the rationale for effective pedagogy.

The National Literacy Strategy in England: policy and practice

The implementation of the National Literacy Strategy in England can be used as an illustration of how the research–policy–practice link can be disrupted, despite the best intentions of those who drafted it. There have been significant changes in policy and practice in the teaching of literacy in the United Kingdom: more structured approaches to the teaching of writing and grammar are being introduced, including more direct teaching of whole classes. The aim of this critique is not to discredit the National Literacy Strategy, which is focusing much-needed attention on the development of writing, but to argue that some of the problems encountered with its implementation might be alleviated by making more explicit links to research.

Let us take a brief look, first, at the fragile link between research and policy. The two latest versions of *English in the National Curriculum* (DfE, 1995; DfEE, 1999) have specified the content of writing teaching – what should be taught – and, to some extent, how it should be taught, particularly with respect to the model of drafting and the key genres to be taught. Recent publications supplementing the National Curriculum have included further guidance, aimed at the secondary-aged sector, on improving writing (QCA, 1999a) and on the teaching of grammar in context (QCA, 1999b), both of which were informed by research, as well as the report of the Qualifications and Curriculum Agency Technical Accuracy Project (QCA, 1999c), which analysed the linguistic features of writing for GCSE examinations. With respect to writing, the current National Curriculum represents an example of policy refined through practice and relatively well grounded in research, albeit implicitly. However, the National Curriculum has not been charged with providing a detailed specification for the teaching of writing.

The introduction of *The National Literacy Strategy* (DfEE, 1998), for primary schools, and the *KS3 Strategy Framework for English* (DfEE, 2001a), for secondary schools, signifies a new political agenda in specifying exactly how writing should be taught. In these 'frameworks for teaching', learning objectives are presented at word, sentence and text level, allocated to different school years (and school terms, in the primary framework). This creates clearly delineated stages of progression out of the more general programmes of study in the National Curriculum, which were originally intended to guide teaching over a two to four-year period (depending on the Key Stage). The other strand to the National Literacy Strategy is the promotion of particular pedagogies, which move from demonstration and supported work into independent work within a daily structure. In the primary sector, this daily structure is known as the Literacy Hour. In the standards debate, the main area in which there seem to be anxieties is that of language structure and there has thus been more focus on the word and sentence levels recently, most notably in the National Literacy Strategy publication *Grammar for Writing* (DfEE, 2000). The National Literacy Strategy was under-theorised in its original form, although much of it draws implicitly on research. The NLS model of writing composition is influenced by the EXEL teaching model (Wray and Lewis, 1997), which is derived from the authors' own extensive research and clearly informed by the Australian genre school (for example, see Cope and Kalantzis, 1993) and by the neo-Vygotskian concept of scaffolding (Bruner, 1985; Maybin, Mercer and Stierer, 1992). One can also trace the influences of composition studies (notably Bereiter and Scardamalia, 1987) in the modelling and interventions of shared and guided writing.

There are other areas of the National Literacy Strategy which, in my view, are not so strongly supported by research and which are potentially confusing. For example, a 'searchlights model', which has little connection to research on reading, is proposed as a metaphor for the reading process (DfEE, 1998: 4). There is not space in this chapter for a full critique, but the main problem is that the 'model' is not a model: it provides a useful list of some of the factors that influence understanding (phonic, grammatical, contextual and visual) but it does not show how these are interrelated; it could be taken as suggesting an atomistic sub-skill view of reading; it does not indicate the nature of the relationship between visual representation and meaning; and it makes no reference to the social or intentional environment within which any act of reading occurs. More worryingly, it is also suggested that, by simply reversing the searchlights model, we have a useful metaphor for the writing process. The searchlights model is still referred to in recent publications such as *The National Literacy Strategy: Developing Early Writing* (DfEE, 2001b), which is otherwise full of sensible advice and suggestions for classroom activities.

Hilton (2001) challenges Beard's (2000a) claims that the approach to teaching writing in the National Literacy Strategy is supported by research, particularly for primary-school-age pupils. She argues that there are a number of flaws in the proposition that the teaching of 'basics', through direct instruction in discrete elements of grammar, and decontextualised shared and guided writing, will lead to a rise in the standard of children's writing. It should be clear from these examples that it might be difficult for teachers to discriminate between those areas of the National Literacy Strategy that are supported by research and those that are not.

The need for more explicit identification of supporting research has been recognised by the architects of the National Literacy Strategy who have commissioned post-hoc research reviews to make public the research basis of the strategies (Beard, 2000a, for primary; Harrison, in preparation, for Key Stage 3). However, these have been criticised. Hilton (2001) points out that Beard (2000a) devalues the National Curriculum model of teaching writing by interpreting this as a 'simple process' model when it is (rightly, in my view) described by Hilton as representing 'a hard-won victory for educationists who had maintained steadily over several years that children, like all writers, learn to write most effectively through deploying a series of complex recursive stages as the work progresses'. This 'recursive stages' model was substantially supported by composition research carried out with secondary level and undergraduate level writers, as well as 'expert' adult writers (Flower and Hayes, 1981, 1984; Hayes and Flower, 1980; Bereiter and Scardamalia, 1987). It is arguable that the National Literacy Strategy model is the more 'simple' model of writing pedagogy. To interpret the recursive stages model as a 'simple process' is to make the same mistake that teachers do if they teach drafting in an ineffective way. Teachers are just as, if not more, likely to teach the National Literacy Strategy simplistically, as a 'simple toolkit' model. Teachers will only teach writing effectively within the National Literacy Strategy if this is informed by, and orientated within, an understanding of the complexities of composition processes. It is also important not to elide 'process pedagogy' with 'process models' of composition – there are important differences. Hilton also disputes Beard's categorisation of 'shared writing' as an 'environmental' approach claiming that it is really more like Hillocks' (1995) less successful category of 'presentational' writing.

Turning to the link between policy and practice and how this can become fragile in certain circumstances, we can see how the interpretation of the National Literacy Strategy in schools and classrooms can, in some cases, lead to a further breakdown between policy and practice, and thus make the link between research and practice even more tenuous. Frater (2000) found, as a result of survey work in 32 primary schools in 1999/2000, that there was a tendency for teachers under pressure to interpret the National Literacy Strategy at a literal level, as a set of discrete and arbitrary activities. This 'anxious literalism' means that the National Literacy Strategy has had the unintended effect of leading to 'the discrete teaching of language skills and concepts' and 'the diminution, by such discrete work, of written composition'. This echoes the current widespread concern among classroom teachers that there is not enough time for extended and creative composition within the National Literacy Strategy. Frater found that in the less effective of the 32 schools, where achievement in writing had made least progress:

> the practice of written composition has been given such time as remains after concepts and skills, handled discretely, have been delivered. It can be added that the more discretely skills and knowledge about language are handled, the more abstract, harder and less relevant they will seem to pupils, the longer the time required to reach them is likely to be, and the less likely it is that pupils will apply them effectively in practice. And boys in particular, are all too likely to switch off altogether.
>
> (Frater, 2000: 110)

By contrast, in the schools with effective literacy policies, Frater found that 'teachers were professionally self-confident in approaching the National Literacy Strategy'. These teachers were able to draw upon the National Literacy Strategy Framework much more flexibly, constantly making 'connections between text-level work, and word and sentence-level study. And with them, *using language always carried the highest priority*' (*ibid.*, original emphasis). These findings are consistent with other evaluations of the National Literacy Strategy carried out by the government (Ofsted, 1999, 2000) and independently (Fisher, Lewis and Davis, 2000), which have found variability in the teaching of writing. Nor are those who drafted the NLS 'likely to have intended that any primary teachers might feel de-skilled or de-motivated' (Frater, 2000). Thus we see the model of literacy in the National Literacy Strategy being translated, by unconfident teachers, into an even more 'limited literacy' (Flower, 1994) than intended, particularly with respect to the teaching of writing. Frater argues for the need for teachers' opinions to be valued more highly by the community generally and by policy makers in particular. I would say that it is equally important that teachers have access to professional development that fosters understanding and confidence with educational principles that are supported by research. Without this there is little chance of standards being raised.

The implementation of the NLS, admittedly still at a relatively early stage, illustrates how a simplified pedagogy can emerge in the translation of policy into practice. This is, arguably, more likely to occur when the policy lacks explicit links to research evidence that would allow teachers to reconstruct the theoretical background necessary for an informed interpretation of the National Literacy Strategy: an interpretation that goes beyond the literal. The practice of simplified pedagogy is more likely to occur when teachers lack confidence due to low motivation and/or inadequate understanding of literacy development. It is also understandable that the content of training in a new policy initiative becomes simplified, due to the rush to implement policy and to the constraints of the training provision. However, there are clearly, here, a set of forces that might lead to a reductionist and oversimplified approach to the teaching of writing. Research evidence on the importance of teachers needing to connect up theory and practice in order to be effective comes from the Teacher Training Agency funded 'Effective Teachers of Literacy' project (Medwell *et al.*, 1998). The effective teachers identified in this project were well theorised, were able to verbalise strong connections between their theory and practice, and integrated skills teaching smoothly in meaningful contexts. By contrast, the less effective validation group teachers placed great emphasis on the teaching of skills, but were less well-theorised, and tended to teach the skills in a decontextualised manner (*ibid.*: 43).

Competing discourses in writing research

This chapter does not present a full review of research on effective teaching methods for developing children's writing. It is not going to say that particular teaching methods lead directly to measurable improvements in children's writing. What it attempts instead is to review key developments in writing research and composition studies, in order to find a way through the 'competing discourses' (Fairclough, 1989) in this area, and to establish some key principles that are supported by theory. Some of this research has not been widely disseminated at the level of primary and secondary education. I would also argue that it is useful to look to the broader field of composition research to complement empirical studies that focus on effective writing behaviour, by providing a more complex picture of composition. As Coe (1994: 167) stresses, 'the process is best understood by describing not a writer's behaviour, but the system within which that behaviour makes sense'. In attempting to make sense of a range of research perspectives on writing it is hoped that some key principles will emerge that will help more teachers to have a grasp of the nature of the 'system' of composition.

Empirical studies of pedagogical effectiveness are important, and we need to have more of them. However, such studies need to be seen through the lens of an understanding of the fundamental processes of composition. Otherwise they will inevitably emphasise discrete skills, the 'basics' where accuracy can be easily measured, in the search for definitive answers: the much-demanded evidence for foolproof strategies for raising standards. There can be a tendency to privilege a quantitative, empirical approach that devalues other sources of evidence, such as messier, qualitative approaches, or the consensus that emerges from a range of perspectives.

At this point it is appropriate to raise the issue of the generalisability of composition research to school contexts. Hilton (2001) criticises Beard (2000a) for applying Hillock's (1986) conclusions to primary pupils when they are intended for secondary age pupils. Clearly a distinction needs to be made between research on pedagogy, which must take account of pupils' prior experience of and relative familiarity with, for example, particular grammatical structures or genres, and research on fairly fundamental cognitive, social and cultural processes involved in composition. It is this latter area that is the focus of composition studies.

There have been several attempts, at various times, and in different ways, to map the field of writing research (for example, Hillocks, 1986, 1995; Bereiter and Scardamalia, 1987; Nystrand, Greene and Wiemelt, 1993; Smith and Elley, 1999; Applebee, 2000; Beard, 2000b). The rest of this section focuses on what we can learn about writing from different research discourses within the field of composition studies, presenting an overview, necessarily very selective and concise, of three major theoretical perspectives: cognitive, genre theory and sociocognitive. For each of these perspectives key concepts will be identified, as well as implications for the development of writing. Discussion of sociocognitive perspectives leads into a consideration of the work of Flower (1994) who, in the context of the broader standards debate, proposes a compelling theoretical framework for understanding composition. (For a fuller discussion of the 'intellectual history' of the field of composition studies up to the early 1990s, see Nystrand, Greene and Wiemelt, 1993. It is also worth pointing out that, although there are connections, composition studies is a distinct field from that of academic literacy or English for specific purposes.)

Cognitive models of composition

Writing fifteen years ago Wilkinson (1986: 35) stated that 'writing as a cognitive act has not had the attention it deserves' from United Kingdom researchers and educators, but that 'what we neglected was being developed in the United States', by which he means North America, as he makes significant reference to the early work of Bereiter and Scardamalia in Toronto. It seems that we in the United Kingdom have only begun to recognise the importance of this work in the last five years or so – and the work of Bereiter and Scardamalia (see 1987) is now getting the attention it deserves.

The cognitive perspective was dominant in the field of composition studies in the 1970s and 1980s, and typically focused on the behaviour and cognitive processes of individual writers. From a cognitive perspective, writing is seen as a problem-solving process. In fact, one of the main attractions for cognitive researchers was that it was an example of complex human problem-solving, and a major early focus, as in other areas of problem-solving research, was that of expert–novice differences. A dominant methodology is the use of concurrent 'think aloud' protocols, which, despite their limitations, proved a valuable means of gaining insight into the decision-making processes and metacognition of experts and novices while writing. There was acknowledgement of the intended audience and the context in which these individuals were writing, insofar as they were part of the writer's cognitive representation of the task. However, there was generally little or no attention to the wider social or cultural context of writing.

Cognitive perspectives on writing have been very valuable in clarifying the organisation of writing processes (planning, organising, translating and reviewing), and how these vary between individuals. These differences have been explored most notably in the seminal work of Hayes and Flower, a cognitive psychologist and a rhetorician, respectively (Hayes and Flower, 1981, 1984; Flower and Hayes, 1980). Most of the cognitive research on writing at this time was done with undergraduate students, although some was done with high school students, and Bereiter and Scardamalia (1987) developed a cognitive model of writing alongside research on pedagogy in schools. Another important contribution of the work of Hayes and Flower and Bereiter and Scardamalia was that they provided a model for knowledge about the content of writing – meaning – and about writing itself – rhetorical knowledge – and, crucially, about the interaction between the two in the composition process. A significant concept was that of 'knowledge-transforming' writing (Bereiter and Scardamalia, 1987) through which writers change their understanding of the content area as a result of solving rhetorical problems.

It is important to note the distinction between cognitive process models of writing at a theoretical level, and the 'process approach' to teaching writing in the classroom (Graves, 1983) at a pedagogical level. The two approaches have developed somewhat independent parallel paths. Teachers in the United Kingdom have been more likely to be aware of the 'process approach' of Graves, but cognitive models of writing have had an impact on our understanding of teaching and learning in writing, and thus on pedagogy. This impact lies in two areas: a useable model of the writing process and support for particular kinds of interventions. A focus on task representation and constraints, planning, reviewing, and learning through writing, through the interaction between content knowledge and genre knowledge, supports an informed use of drafting, rather than what can at worst be meaningless redrafting at whole text level – which can occur in writers who do not have such understanding. To support writing development, this cognitive perspective implies the use of worked examples and supported constraint reduction (essentially removing some of the demands by providing scaffolds or deferring checking for grammatical correctness, for example). Bereiter and Scardamalia (1987) developed effective classroom interventions based on their model, designing activities to encourage reflective writing – again a means of scaffolding children's learning. (See Levy and Ransdell (1996) for more recent research within a cognitive perspective.)

Genre theory

In Australia, genre theory (see Cope and Kalantzis, 1993) grew out of systemic linguistics (Halliday, 1985), and has had a significant impact on the pedagogy of writing in Australia and, largely through the work of Wray and Lewis (1997) and the National Literacy Strategy, in the United Kingdom as well. By contrast, the version of genre theory that originated largely in North America (Swales, 1990; Freedman and Medway 1994), which is different in some important ways, has not had as much impact in United Kingdom schools – not least because it emphasises the fluidity of genres and consequently limited possibilities of analysis, thus making it appear difficult to apply in classrooms. As well as having a strong theoretical and research base in applied linguistics, the Australian genre researchers worked with local teachers to develop a robust pedagogy for teaching children text genres important to school literacy, particularly in relation to six key examples: report, explanation, procedure, discussion, recount and narrative. The motivation of this work was the empowerment of disadvantaged groups by providing access to the genres of the dominant culture. Whilst teaching focused on the linguistic features of texts within the six genres, it was intended that this was always within a view of genres as social processes. Because of this attention to teaching genres through example texts, the Australian genre school has been characterised as static and prescriptive by North American genre researchers (Freedman and Medway, 1994), but this is an exaggerated dichotomisation of two perspectives that have a considerable amount of overlap, despite their differences in emphasis and level of linguistic analysis. However, the Australian genre school does have a structured model for explicit instruction, where the teacher takes on the role as expert in leading pupils through the stages of modelling (investigating the features of the genre model), joint negotiation (similar to shared writing in National Literacy Strategy terms) and independent writing. Thus the pupil is led through a scaffolded cycle from reading to independent writing within a critical, analytical framework.

The development of genre theory represented a shift in emphasis to seeing writing as social communication within particular cultural contexts: 'Whereas meaning in the 1970s was mainly a cognitive issue, by the 1980s, it had become "socialized" [partly in] direct reaction to the hegemony of cognitive research in the early 1980s' (Nystrand, Greene and Wiemelt, 1993). In the last decade, there has been a resurgence of interest in the cognitive aspects of writing. Sociocognitive, or social cognitive, perspectives on writing (for example, Berkenkotter and Huckin, 1993; Flower; 1994) have emerged in recognition that early cognitive models effectively partitioned off the 'social', as a set of external contextual factors. They have also built on recent developments in neo-Vygotskian theory, in situated cognition (Brown, Collins and Duguid, 1989) and in genre research. However, cognitive models that take into account social factors are not necessarily truly sociocognitive. Hayes (1996) has developed the original Hayes and Flower model of writing to produce 'a new framework for understanding cognition and affect in writing', which might be seen as belonging to this perspective, although he rejects the term 'social-cognitive', describing his model as 'individual-environmental'. It is thus more accurate to see this as a relatively unre-constructed cognitive model.

Sociocognitive models

Sociocognitive models of composition are concerned with 'how individual intention and agency insert themselves within culturally and socially organised practices' (Nystrand, Greene and Wiemelt, 1993). They emphasise the dynamic relationship between meaning, form, social context and culture, but see the act of composing as essentially cognitive, as Flower (1994) explains:

> The strong case for cognition lies, I believe, in the fact that the agent in even a socially extended process of making meaning is not society, community or a discourse; that is, meanings are not made by an abstract, theoretical construct but by individual writers, readers, speakers, and listeners who are interpreting inferred meanings around them, constructing their own, and attempting to share those meanings with or impose them on other members of their social or cultural collective. Individual meaning is not *sui generis*, but it is nonetheless a cognitive construction, created out of prior knowledge in response to the multiple layers of a writer's social, rhetorical, and cultural context.
>
> (Flower, 1994: 89)

Within a sociocognitive perspective, becoming literate depends on both knowledge of social conventions and individual problem-solving. We need to teach pupils strategic skills, rather than what Flower terms 'a pedagogy of correctness'. She suggests that in order to be literate pupils need the skills:

- to read a situation;
- to plan, organise, and revise;
- to build and negotiate meaning;
- to use and adapt conventions;
- to figure out what new discourses expect and how to enter them.

(adapted from Flower, 1994: 7)

An effective means of developing composition is thus through the use of collabora-tive writing to model these strategic skills when writing in an authentic context. We also need to investigate 'how children's understandings of the genres and functions within and across particular kinds of reading or writing activities affect the approaches used, the meanings conveyed and the learnings that ensue' (Langer, 1986: 143).

Although the sociocognitive perspective on writing can be seen as a synthesis of the cognitive and genre approaches, these do remain three distinct research discourses. These research perspectives cannot be fully reconciled at a theoretical level, but there is a considerable degree of overlap in their pedagogical implications. If we go beyond the characteristic discourses of the different perspectives, we can see that two key themes for developing writing receive particular support from across the range of research:

- scaffolding understanding of written communication – through activities that model strategic writing skills and analysing genres in context

- scaffolding the writing process – through reducing constraints, providing structural support and collaborative writing.

The professional development of teachers

The importance of teachers' professional knowledge in developing pupils' writing, as in other areas of education, is widely accepted (Coe, 1994; Wray and Lewis, 1997; Smith and Elley, 1999; Beard, 2000b). Generally one would expect that teachers who are well-theorised – who have an informed and sophisticated understanding of the complexity of the writing process – will be able to teach 'the basics' of literacy in more meaningful contexts and thus more effectively than those who do not.

There has been a tendency to overlook composition studies and theoretical models of writing, especially when some of the supporting research has been carried out in non-school contexts, such as in the field of composition studies. The fact that it can be easier to find 'hard' evidence for teaching technical skills, which lend themselves to more empirical approaches, than more complex compositional skills, means that discrete technical skills are sometimes over-emphasised, leading to a reductionist, componential approach. However, the previous section has attempted to show how the integrated models and theoretical perspectives of composition can improve our broader understanding of the writing process. As a result of this, it should be possible both to readjust our ideas about the fundamental skills of writing and to have the professional confidence to teach technical skills in a more integrated way.

Interestingly, there is an analogy here between the teaching of writing in schools and the training of teachers of writing. The teaching of writing is a similarly complex process, in social and cognitive terms, to writing itself. It is inadequate for pupils to be taught a model of writing which simply reproduces the behaviour of good writers, or indeed the behaviour of 'novice' writers, as is sometimes the case, whether this is through an oversimplified drafting approach or an oversimplified genre approach. Similarly, teachers don't just need training to reproduce the behaviour – the moves or stages – of effective literacy teachers. They also need to understand the teaching of literacy at a strategic level – just as we need to teach writing strategically (Bereiter and Scardamalia, 1987; Flower, 1994). Teachers need principles, rather than routines, in order to be (or to become) confident teachers of writing.

Conclusions: some principles for developing writing – and teachers of writing

It is not surprising that the research–policy–practice link is fragile. There is a tension between forces for simplification at the levels of policy and practice, and forces for complication at the level of research, where specialised and competing academic discourses can make it difficult to draw out implications for practice. Researchers and policy makers may be too tempted to try to find, or indeed fund, research to support elements of writing pedagogy in a piecemeal and retrospective way, and risk misapplying this through not having a sufficiently complex picture of writing. Teachers need to avoid the mechanical implementation of structured teaching, particularly at the word and sentence level. In order to discourage these trends we need to do two other things. First, we need to identify some fundamental principles about composition, which we can then use in teacher education and as criteria by which to both evaluate and orientate current initiatives in the teaching of writing. Second, we need to develop pedagogy by supporting more extensive research into the teaching of writing in meaningful classroom contexts.

I would like to suggest that we already have such a set of principles. Flower presents a set of 'strong claims' for 'a social cognitive alternative to the public story of literacy' (1994: 19–30; summarised below), which can serve as a powerful set of fundamental principles for understanding writing, and which reinstate thinking and learning in the writing process, as well as confirming the primary role of meaning-making in writing, at every stage.

1   *Literacy is an action.* Literacy is not a generalised ability a person possesses (or does not possess). Literacy is a set of actions and transactions in which people use reading and writing for personal and social purposes.
2   *Literacy is a move within a discourse practice.* When people engage in literate action, they are doing more than decoding or producing text. Like any social practice, it has a history with a set of expectations and conventions. A discourse practice cannot be reduced to a genre or a kind of text; it is a social and rhetorical situation in which texts play a specialised role.
3   *Becoming literate depends on knowledge of social conventions and on individual problem solving.*
4   *The new 'basics' should start with expressive and rhetorical practices.* From this perspective, what is basic is the how-to knowledge [that] goes by various names – heuristics, process plans, rhetorical or problem-solving strategies, critical thinking skills – but in essence, they are action plans for carrying out a literate act. In this rhetorical tradition, the basic, foundational skills in learning to be literate are the skills one needs to read a situation; to plan, organize, and revise; to build and negotiate meaning; to use and adapt conventions; and to figure out what new discourses expect and how to enter them (Flower 1994: 27).
5   *Literate action opens the door to metacognitive and social awareness.* In other words, literacy as a social cognitive act creates some opportunities for strategic thinking and reflection that are absent in the pedagogy of textual conventions and correctness.

I will conclude by stressing that the most important way of developing pupils' writing is by developing teachers' understanding of writing. In the United Kingdom we have a mixed history of dissemination of theory and practice in the area of literacy. We can see that much of the National Literacy Strategy, particularly shared and guided writing at its best, is supported by the research on writing reviewed in this chapter, even if this is not always explicit in the framework itself. However, there is a danger that without a principled understanding of writing such as that offered by Flower (1994) we will, perhaps implicitly, disseminate a 'simple view' of writing, in the same way as Purcell-Gates criticises the 'simple view of reading' in the United States. Teachers need the 'whole picture': a more integrated and fully developed model of writing rather than a set of activities, however well devised. I would like to argue that the importance of embracing complexity is what research tells us about how we should be developing writing:

> Under the pressures of outside evaluation and the exigencies of instruction, many administrators and teachers may opt for limited literacies, designating some feature (whether it be correctness, self-expression, or a disciplinary practice like literary analysis) as basic and turning it into the signifier and test of literacy. Complexity and dialectic are hard to sell.
>
> (Flower, 1994: 32)

References

Applebee, A. (2000) 'Alternative models of writing development', in R. Indriasano and J.R. Squire (eds) *Perspectives on Writing: Research, Theory and Practice*, Newark, DE: International Reading Association.

Beard, R. (2000a) 'Clarion call for another century', *Times Educational Supplement*, 6 October, Curriculum Special (p. 7).

—— (2000b) *Developing Writing 3–13*, London: Hodder & Stoughton.

Bereiter, C. and Scardamalia, M. (1987) *The Psychology of Written Communication*, Hillsdale, NJ: Lawrence Erlbaum.

Berkenkotter, C. and Huckin, T.N. (1993) 'Rethinking genre from a sociocognitive perspective', *Written Communication* 10(4): 475–509.

Brown, J.S., Collins, A. and Duguid, P. (1989) 'Situated cognition and the culture of learning', *Educational Researcher* 18: 32–42.

Bruner, J. (1985) 'Vvgotsky: a historical and conceptual perspective', in A. Sinclair, R. Jarvella and W.J.M. Levelt (eds) (1987) *Making Sense: The Child's Construction of the World*, London: Methuen.

Coe, R.M. (1994) 'Teaching genre as process', in A. Freedman and P. Medway (eds) *Learning and Teaching Genre*, Portsmouth, NH: Boynton/Cook.

Cope, B. and Kalantzis, M. (1993) 'Introduction: how a genre approach to literacy can transform the way writing is taught', in B. Cope and M. Kalantzis (eds) *The Powers of Literacy: A Genre Approach to Teaching Writing*, London: Falmer.

Department for Education (DfE) (1995) *English in the National Curriculum*, London: DfE.

Department for Education and Employment (DfEE) (1998) *The National Literacy Strategy: Framework for Teaching*, London: DfEE.

—— (1999) *English in the National Curriculum*, London: DfEE.

—— (2000) *The National Literacy Strategy: Grammar for Writing*, London: DfEE.

—— (2001a) *KS3 Strategy Framework for Teaching English*, London: DfEE.

—— (2001b) *The National Literacy Strategy: Developing Early Writing*, London: DfEE.

Fairclough, N. (1989) *Language and Power*, Harlow: Longman.

Fisher, R., Lewis, M. and Davis, B. (2000) 'Progress and performance in National Literacy Strategy classrooms in England', *Journal of Research in Reading* 23(3): 256–66.

Flower, L. (1994) *The Construction of Negotiated Meaning: A Social Cognitive Theory of Writing*, Carbondale: Southern Illinois University Press.

Flower, L. and Hayes, J.R. (1981) 'A cognitive process theory of writing', *College Composition and Communication* 32: 365–86.

—— (1984) 'Images, plans and prose: the representation of meaning in writing', *Written Communication* 1(1): 120–60.

Frater, G. (2000) 'Observed in practice. English in the National Literacy Strategy: some reflections', *Reading* 34(3): 107–12.

Freedman, A. and Medway, P. (eds) (1994) *Learning and Teaching Genre*, Portsmouth, NH: Boyton/Cook.

Graves, D. (1983) *Writing: Teachers and Children at Work*, Portsmouth, NH: Heinemann.

Halliday, M.A.K. (1985) *An Introduction to Functional Grammar*, London: Edward Arnold.

Harrison, C. (2004, forthcoming) *Understanding Reading Development*, London: Sage.

Hayes, J.R. (1996) 'A new framework for understanding cognition and affect in writing', in C.M. Levy and S. Ransdell (eds) *The Science of Writing: Theories, Methods, Individual Differences and Applications*, Mahwah, NJ: Lawrence Erlbaum.

Hayes, J.R. and Flower, L. (1980) 'Identifying the organization of writing processes', in L. Gregg and E. Steinberg (eds) *Cognitive Processes in Writing*, Hillsdale, NJ: Lawrence Erlbaum.

Hillocks, G. (1986) *Research on Written Composition*, Urbana, IL: National Conference on Research in English/ERIC Clearinghouse on Reading and Communication Skills.

—— (1995) *Teaching Writing as Reflective Practice*, New York: Teachers College Press.

Hilton, M. (2001) 'Writing process and progress: where do we go from here?', *English in Education* 35(1): 4–11.

Langer, J.A. (1986) *Children Reading and Writing*, Norwood, NJ: Ablex.

Levy, C.M. and Ransdell, S. (1996) *The Science of Writing: Theories, Methods, Individual Differences and Applications*, Mahwah, NJ: Lawrence Erlbaum.

Lewis, M. and Wray, D. (2000) *Literacy in the Secondary School*, London: David Fulton.

Maybin, J., Mercer, N. and Stierer, B. (1992) 'Scaffolding learning in the classroom', in K. Norman (ed.) *Thinking Voices: The Work of the National Oracy Project*, London: Hodder & Stoughton for the National Curriculum Council.

Medwell, J., Wray, D., Poulson, L. and Fox, R. (1998) *Effective Teachers of Literacy*, Exeter: University of Exeter, for Teacher Training Agency.

Myhill, D. (1999) 'Writing matters: linguistic characteristics of writing in GCSE examinations', *English in Education* 33(3): 70–81.

Nystrand, M., Greene, S. and Wiemelt, J. (1993) 'Where does composition studies come from? An intellectual history', *Written Communication* 10(3): 267–333.

Office for Standards in Education (Ofsted) (1999) *The National Literacy Strategy: An Evaluation of the First Year of the National Literacy Strategy*, London: OFSTED.

—— (2000) *The National Literacy Strategy: The Second Year*, London: OFSTED.

Qualifications and Curriculum Agency (QCA) (1999a) *Improving Writing at Key Stages 3 and 4*, London: QCA.

—— (1999b) *Not Whether But How*, London: QCA.

—— (1999c) *Technical Accuracy in Writing in GCSE English Examinations: Research Findings*, London: QCA.

Smith, J. and Elley, W. (1999) *How Children Learn to Write*, London: Paul Chapman.

Swales, J.M. (1990) *Genre Analysis*, Cambridge: Cambridge University Press.

Wilkinson, A. (1986) *The Quality of Writing*, Milton Keynes: Open University Press.

Wray, D. and Lewis, M. (1997) *Extending Literacy: Children Reading and Writing Non Fiction*, London: Routledge.

CHAPTER 18

CAN TEACHERS EMPOWER PUPILS AS WRITERS?

Carole King

Issues in English Teaching, J. Davidson and J. Moss (eds), London: Routledge, 2000, pp. 23–41

If pupils are to be empowered as writers, then they need to understand the potential of writing: to recognise and appreciate it as an active social process within their own lives. Robinson suggests:

> What is basic to the development of literacy, I would argue, is the same as what is basic to its full exercise: the empowerment of individuals to speak freely in such voices as they have about matters that concern them, matters of importance, so that conversations may be nourished. The most debilitating suggestion in our dominant metaphors for literacy is this one: that a language must be learned, a voice acquired, before conversation can begin.
>
> (Robinson, 1990: 264)

This chapter argues that from pre-school onwards, pupils need to be able to talk about themselves as writers, and value writing as a way of 'constructing' as well as 'conveying meaning' (DES, 1989). It suggests that prescriptive training and teaching curricula will not necessarily enable this to happen unless teachers recognise that progress in writing cannot be measured simply by a growing command of its code and conventions.

The chapter exemplifies approaches to teaching writing which do empower pupils as writers who are able both to explore and share themselves as individuals, through the process of writing within the expressive and poetic modes (Britton *et al.*, 1975). The chapter draws on work within Key Stages 1 and 2 and has implications for secondary English teaching, since the principles which underpin the practices described are valid for all age groups.

Home literacy: why do pupils choose to write?

Five-year-old Hannah, drawing on home-literacy experiences, covers scraps of paper with notes, lists, letters to friends, thoughts and statements about herself, all of which are concerned with sorting out personal relationships and expressing preferences (Figure 24). Six-year-old Ann is able to fictionalise herself as the main protagonist in a book full of stories based on family happenings real or imagined (Figure 25). Unable to articulate the reason why she writes she says, 'I don't know really what happens. Don't know how the ideas pop in.' But she feels 'good when its finished. I want to get it done quickly so I can do another one.' Her ten-year-old brother,

Amy
you
ur
im
be sttr t
frend x Hannah
x x x x x xx x

Figure 24 Hannah's work

who initially provided the model for her own independent story-writing, is able to
be explicit about his enjoyment, relating it to playing with Lego(tm) figures, where
the toys speak to each other. 'It's like writing a story because you're thinking about
what to say, playing it out.' Eleven-year-old Gary, in a class discussion on home
writing explains:

> I just write on paper at home. If I've been naughty, about being sorry and it
> lets me off. I make a paper aeroplane and fly it down with words. Or just
> because you want to and then read it yourself.

These children have an implicit understanding of the genres they use and have
discovered for themselves the power of writing to act in and on their lives. Essentially
they write to satisfy personal needs, but their writing has different functions.

Britton's functional writing categories were developed in the 1970s from the work
of D. W. Harding (1960), and still provide an illuminating way of looking at what
writers are actually doing with their writing and at the roles they take as they write.
These are aspects of writing that are easily overlooked in classrooms. Covering the
curriculum and achieving good public test results seem often to be the most important
reasons for the teaching and learning of writing. Britton summarised his functional
categories as follows:

language in the role of the participant designates any use of language to get things done, to pursue the world's affairs, while *language in the spectator role* covers verbal artefacts, the use of language *to make something* rather than *to get something done*.

(Britton, 1993: 28, his emphasis)

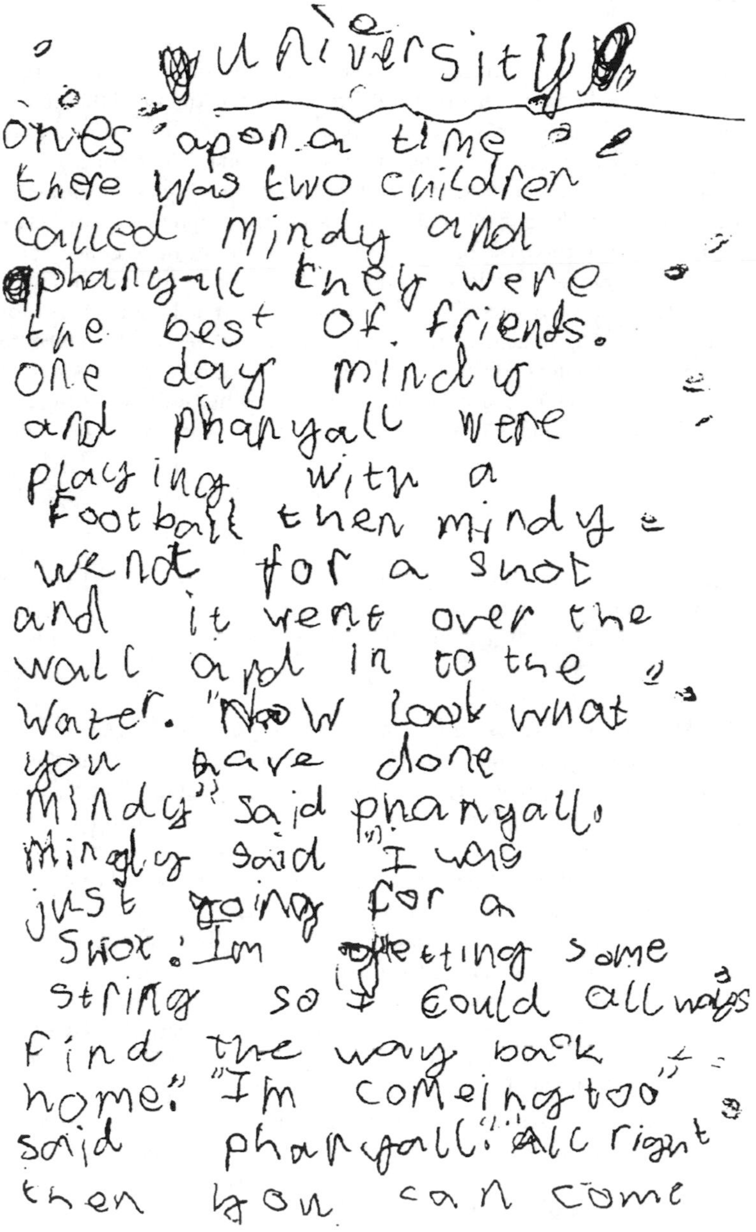

University

Ones apon a time
there was two children
called mindy and
phangall they were
the best of friends.
One day mindy
and phangall were
playing with a
Football then mindy
wendt for a shot
and it went over the
wall and in to the
water. "Now look what
you have done
mindy" said phangall.
mindy said "I was
just going for a
shot. Im getting some
string so I could allways
find the way back
home." "Im comeing too"
said phangall. "All right
then you can come

Figure 25 Ann's work

Language in the role of		Language in the role of
Participant ————————————————————		Spectator
Transactional ——————— Expressive ———————		Poetic

Figure 26 Britton's continuum of language development

The participant/spectator distinction has been a central, though controversial, tenet of Britton's functional linguistic theory, yet Britton always maintained that these should not be seen as mutually exclusive categories. Figure 26 shows the relationship between the language functions and the suggested modes of writing. These form a continuum of development, where the 'transactional' and 'poetic' modes typify the participant and spectator roles respectively, and where a third mode, the 'expressive', sits between the two and may well form the basis for more explicit development of either (*ibid.*).

Writing in the expressive mode shares many similarities with spoken language. It is loosely structured, close to the self, and dependent upon a shared context for interpretation. Its audience is limited to the writer him/herself or one 'assumed to share much of the writer's context' (Britton *et al.*, 1975: 89). Often the reader is the only intended audience; as one Year 6 pupil remarked about her journal writing, 'It's like my face on the page.' Hannah's notes and Gary's aeroplane apologies fall within this expressive mode, and are transactional in purpose.

Ann and Paul, as spectators of real or imagined experiences, craft their ideas into stories. They write in the poetic mode, using:

> language as an art medium. A piece of poetic writing is a verbal construct, an object made out of language. The words themselves, and all they refer to, are selected to make an arrangement, a formal pattern.
>
> (*ibid.*: 90)

Applebee (1984) has refined Britton's classification system and argued that the spectator and participant roles are terms that help us to recognise and value the different ways that we represent the world to ourselves through language. They provide vital foci for research (Applebee, 1978). Indeed, Britton's category system has been extensively used for empirical studies of the way that writing for different functions and disciplines may result in different kinds of learning (Durst and Newell, 1989). However, these studies generally focus on the way that transactional writing requires the analysis and synthesis necessary for the reformulation of ideas. They neglect the way that writing in the poetic mode is equally concerned with such cognitive activities.

This chapter recognises the importance of expressive journal writing, but focuses mainly on writing within the poetic mode. Adopting a constructivist view of learning, it advocates that writing poetry and stories need to be recognised and appreciated as learning processes. Writing within the spectator role can enable pupils to review, reflect upon and make sense of conflicting experiences. Existing knowledge can be modified in the light of the new, so that the act of writing becomes another 'way of knowing' (Baker *et al.*, 1996). Genre theory itself highlights the significance of Britton's functional categories as ways of valuing writing. However, its concentration on the transactional forms leads to the neglect of the expressive and poetic as ways of making meanings, which are also dependent on 'a cultural process rather than the solitary invention of the individual' (Willinsky, 1990: 206).

Current models of school literacy: why do pupils write?

Bruner advises that 'the curriculum of a subject should be determined by the most fundamental understanding that can be achieved of the underlying principles that give structure to that subject' (1960: 31). The original National Curriculum (DES, 1989) was generally underpinned by such principles, but this did not necessarily lead to an improvement in the teaching of writing; some teachers misinterpreted the content because they did not understand the principles. It stressed the meaning-making potential of writing and recognised that 'written language serves many purposes both for individuals and for society as a whole, and is not limited to the communication of information' (DES, 1989: 33).

The 1995 revision of the curriculum, while recognising 'the value of writing as a means of remembering, communicating, organising and developing ideas and information, and as a source of enjoyment' (DfE, 1995a: 9) has a greater stress on communicative competence. The 'Initial Teacher Training National Curriculum for English' (DfEE, 1997b), listing the standards to be achieved for qualified teacher status (QTS), has a similar emphasis. The half page given to the teaching of compositional skills makes no mention of children writing for their own purposes, neither is any explicit connection made between writing and learning. The main focus is on teaching technical aspects. This focus is further emphasised by the reports on national curriculum assessments for seven- and eleven-year-olds, where the critical summaries of the strengths and weaknesses of these developing writers foreground technical aspects at the expense of meaning making (Qualifications and Curriculum Authority, 1998d, e).

This concentration on the surface, rather than the deep structures of writing, negates the power of writing, for it implies that the stories and poems that pupils write have no function other than to prove their ability to use structural and stylistic features. Unless teachers themselves understand that writing is about developing meaning, they are likely to view it as a list of skills to be learnt in the practice of a range of 'forms', rather than as a complex social, cultural and historical activity, involving both affective and cognitive processes, some of which are evident in the comments and writing of the pupils quoted within this chapter.

A recent study designed to 'help the Teacher Training Agency and teachers in England to understand more clearly how effective teachers help pupils become literate' found that 'the effective teachers tend to place a high value upon communication and composition in their views about the teaching of reading and writing: that is, they believed that the creation of meaning in literacy was fundamental' (Medwell *et al.*, 1998: 3). This did not mean that technical aspects were neglected, rather that 'they were trying very hard to ensure such skills were developed in pupils with a clear eye to the pupil's awareness of their importance and function' (*ibid.*: 31).

Although it was designed to improve literacy teaching, the National Literacy Strategy (DfEE, 1998) may well have the reverse effect if teachers fail to understand the need to teach skills in meaningful contexts. Yet this can be difficult for teachers, for though they are all able to write, this does not imply that they understand fully the nature and purpose of written language.

The student teachers who take a writing module as part of their course at the University of Brighton admit that they had not previously given much thought to writing itself. Though well used to writing assignments, most have little recent experience of writing stories or poems and plays. They are expected to be able to help pupils to do so without fully appreciating either the pleasures or problems such writing involves. By participating in writing workshops run on the lines suggested by Elbow (1973), where they are encouraged to respond to each others' writing in structured, supportive but non-threatening ways, all students gain greater understanding of writing and awareness of themselves as writers. In an assignment where she had explored the way that writing itself can develop the relationship between language and thought, one student, Amy, wrote 'To some extent the act of writing the assignment made explicit things that I implicitly knew'.

This is a pertinent comment, since it relates to an observation made in the Medwell study: 'although all primary teachers are effective readers and writers ... they have learned these skills without necessarily having become explicitly aware of them' (Medwell *et al.*, 1998). This comment would seem to suggest that such knowledge is likely to produce more effective teachers of writing. Drawing on Britton's work, Amy wrote:

> Having done almost no writing in the poetic mode in the last ten years, I am now aware of the way in which it can convey thought. Expressive writing is the closest mode of writing to speech and most direct link to thought. However, poetic writing can be more powerful because the writer can manipulate the language and writing conventions available to her to enable her thought to become clearer to the reader.

How does explicit knowledge about writing inform practice at Key Stage 1?

First, it enables teachers to help pupils discover what writing is for, as Beryl, a reception teacher and primary-school language co-ordinator, demonstrates. As a keen writer and an avid journal keeper, she is able to draw from her own writing experiences when teaching pupils. She 'tries to provide opportunities for pupils in the nursery to hold on to their experience, to go over it and to evaluate it through writing so that they are encouraged to make sense of the world through writing'. This is evident also in her work with Reception pupils. Valuing the role of expressive journal writing as a way of connecting with one's thinking, she introduces her pupils to think books. At the beginning of the autumn term, she models how to use them by writing her own thoughts about a teacher who is ill: 'I am thinking about Miss Bryant who is in hospital.'

The pupils are then given A4 plain paper books, told to write their names on the front, and then write what they are thinking. They all complete the first in their own way, and then, selecting a variety of writing equipment and their own place to write, settle down to transfer thought to paper. Charlie fills the page with linked 'm's (Figure 27) and, when asked what she is thinking about, replies: 'I'm thinking about my mummy waiting for me at the school gate.' Throughout the year, these journal entries reveal the pupils' concerns and interests as they record friendships, visits, pets and school events. From the beginning, writing is seen as a powerful way to access thinking, which, as is evidenced later in this chapter, can then be worked on for publication.

Observing Beryl working with a group of Reception pupils at the end of the year, it is clear that they have no hesitation in writing their own thoughts. The pupils have been studying texture and shape as a topic. Having drawn a pineapple, Beryl now wants them to 'respond in words'. Her learning intentions are thus concerned with meaning rather than technical skills. The writing does naturally involve the pupils in using handwriting or keyboard skills, working out spellings and ordering their ideas, but in pursuit of meaning rather than as a way of ticking off teaching

Figure 27 Charlie's work

objectives. The session begins with pupils responding critically to each other's pictures before re-examining the pineapple, and suggesting relevant adjectives and phrases which are written, with their help, on a flip chart. These are then removed and the pupils begin to write their poems. There is sustained silent writing for fifteen minutes, the teacher intervening only occasionally to encourage an early finisher to be more reflective or suggest ways of tackling an unknown spelling. At the end of the time the pupils share what they have written and this is scribed on the flip chart for discussion. Amy reads her poem (Figure 28):

It's juicy
It's spiky
It's green
It's nice

Beryl's response, 'There's something about that,' encourages others to begin to be critically appreciative and Fiona suggests, 'It's good words.'

Beryl writes it on the board, correcting spellings and putting in the apostrophe as she does so. She then asks them to read it together and clap the rhythm, praising the writer and saying, 'I like the rhythm.' Later she admits that, 'This is not a teacherly response – a genuine one. This is fun – almost my naive understanding of form.' Thus, in every sharing, the pupils' attention is drawn to the form as well as the words as they bring together their knowledge about, and feelings for, the pineapple. Their language is close to the expressive, but, as they 'shape at the point of utterance' (Britton, 1982: 110), so they show the beginnings of writing in the poetic mode. In spectator role they write their way between home and school learning, drawing on their past experiences of pineapples and their school discussion and observation.

Although the content is prescribed, in all other ways these pupils have ownership of their work, even to the point of one child refusing to share it until it has been reworked with a friend's help. Beryl accepts this for 'I value the chance when writing to opt out but on the other hand I sometimes need deadlines. It's a question of knowing your pupils.'

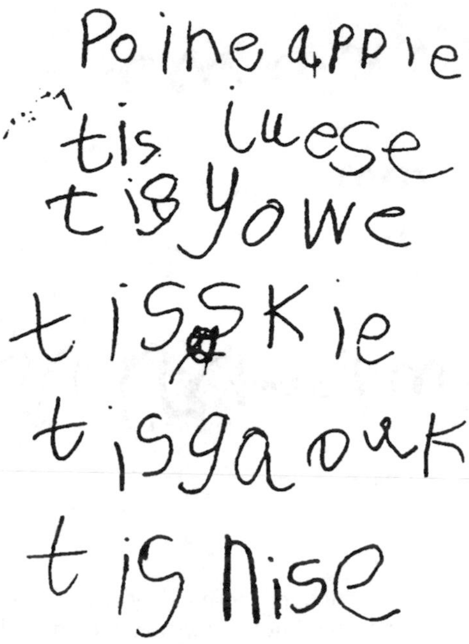

Po ine aPPie
tis luese
t is yowe
t isskie
t isga ouk
t is nise

Figure 28 Amy's work

This guided writing session exemplifies much that is needed if pupils are to be empowered as writers. As members of this writing workshop they learn about:

- generating and shaping ideas;
- supporting and responding to each other;
- developing critical appreciation;
- writing poetry;
- developing transcription skills as they compose.

The act of literacy here is an empowering one because it enables pupils to use their writing as a way of looking anew at their subject. It also nourishes their self-esteem and respect for each other as writers with something to say.

How does explicit knowledge about writing inform practice at Key Stage 2?

When teachers have little personal understanding of the writing process and of writing as an active meaning-making strategy, then becoming members of a writing work-shop is one powerful way of helping them to develop and extend their understanding. Kate, a primary-school teacher, attended a series of writing workshops run over one year in her school as a form of continuing professional development. The teachers were invited to keep journals using the expressive mode to reflect upon both them-selves as writers and their practice as teachers of writing. They also experimented with collaborative and individual writing in the poetic mode, learning how to share and respond in the same way as the students at university had done, and as the Reception pupils were learning to do.

From the workshop writing, Kate recognised the value both of explicating her own ideas about writing and of the need to write from real knowledge and experience. She changed her practice. Ceasing to 'pluck a title out of the air', she encouraged her pupils to use topic work as a starting point, maintaining that it was important for them to make connections between school and home knowledge. The value of this approach was demonstrated by the following poem written by Simon, a Year 3 pupil, after completing a unit of work on batteries and magnets (Figure 29):

Temper Temper
I'm losing my temper
It's making me mad
I feel I'm going to do
Something bad.
Like a magnet my brother is
Pulling me
But I repel him easily.

Cognitive and affective processes and formal and informal knowledge come together in the writing of this simple poem, which itself becomes an extended metaphor, symbolising the relationship between himself and his twin brother. As spectator of his own experiences, Simon is able to forge new understanding and see himself anew. This poem enabled Kate to see that 'When we were talking about writing – we write best when we need to say something, some emotion – obviously the same here.' In her next class she wanted her Year 5/6 pupils to feel this need to write, for 'If they haven't felt that, that's what's missing. That's what gives them the power to write what they want and how.' Her pupils had become more fully engaged in their writing, but she was still the instigator, invariably setting both subject and genre.

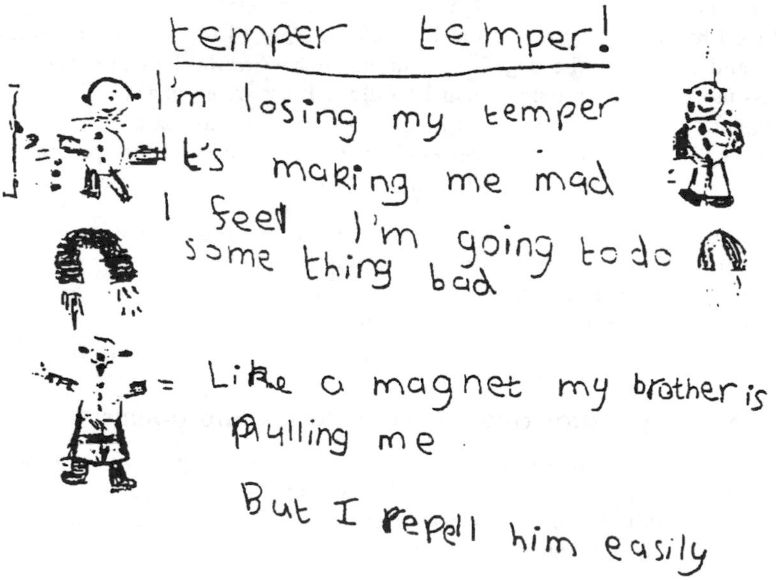

Figure 29 Simon's work

Writing in the expressive mode: using think books

As part of the workshops, Kate had benefited from keeping a reflective journal. Like Beryl, Kate therefore introduced think books, where the pupils could write freely, linking home and school concerns, because: 'What's going on in their minds is mostly to do with out of school'.

Through constant discussion, the pupils had become able to articulate their ideas about writing, and could explain how they used their think books for a range of reasons, writing about 'feelings', 'happenings', 'worries' and 'secrets'. While such writing could be 'fun', the comfort of being able to communicate with the page was valued. 'I kind of like, think it talks back. It makes me happy when I'm lonely, just someone to talk to.' Such replies do reveal how much outside life can interfere with what the pupils should be doing in school, as Kate had recognised. Quarrels with parents and friends, the death of pets, and worries about school work obviously affected the extent to which these pupils were able to give full concentration to the demands of school tasks that must often seem irrelevant to their immediate concerns and needs. The fact that their journals were rarely shared, stressed the personal value of this expressive writing as a way both of coping with present problems and remembering past experiences.

Sally, who struggled both to articulate and transcribe her ideas, not only enjoyed the freedom to write what she liked in her journal, but also the fact that her think book allowed her to write without the need to be correct. She had quarrelled with her cousin and 'can't think straight because I'm thinking about what to say to her next time.' This bears out Kate's comment on pupils' thoughts being mainly concerned with their outside lives. Sally expected that writing about her feelings of anger would help her put them aside and get on with other things, just as writing a poem about her dead budgerigar had helped her to cope with the loss: 'It did make me feel a bit happy but then at lunch time I was sad as I read it.' She also used her journal writing to overcome problems with her mother, for it was 'easier to write to her then talk to her.'

Mark used his journal more cautiously, preferring not to reveal 'his dark feelings like anger and hatred on the page.' As a home storywriter he had discovered that 'I'd express more feeling in a story than I would if I just wrote it down.' Like Sally, he was implicitly aware of the spectator role, but he chose to craft his experiences and feelings into a story or poem. Britton claimed 'that activity in the spectator role represents above all a mode of handling the data of experience' and said:

> If the world we operate in is shaped by the way we represent it to ourselves, then it must follow that the means we employ to maintain the unity, coherence, and harmony of that representation – its truth to experience as we have felt it – must be of lasting concern to each of us.
>
> (1993: 29)

Writing in the spectator role: sharing stories and poems

Based on her workshop experiences, Kate determined that her pupils should be free to write a story or poem, about anything they wanted, for class publication, using their journals for ideas (an approach to which the National Literacy Strategy gives little importance). She modelled how to do this and:

> Not one of them came to me and said, 'What shall I write about?' When they write because it's personal to them they don't seem to need me so much, apart

from editing so they can now sustain different kinds of writing and choose how and what to write with few problems.

Drawing on their autobiographical journal material, some wrote fantasy stories, enjoying inventing and peopling their own worlds, where they were almost always predominant players. Others based their work very much within their own lives. Topsy's confident explanation of her choice epitomises the way in which many of the pupils in this class had by now developed their understanding. She chose to write a poem about her past experiences of being bullied. Writing 'to get it fresh out of my mind,' she explains 'in a story you can fictionalise it or change the time but in a poem you can express more feelings.'

These writers had clearly discovered that when they shaped their raw material into a story or poem, the cognitive processes involved have their own intrinsic value. The writing allows them to review and to make something of their experiences, thus illustrating the power of writing within the spectator role. The chosen genre is a forming influence, for not only does it determine the work's structure, but as the writer struggles to bring his/her material under the direction of that structure and its anticipated demands, then the thinking develops. These writers realised the need to redraft and revise as an inherent part of their writing.

Mark was the most articulate here, being very aware of his own composing processes: 'No. I didn't choose it. It just came'. It is not, however, an easy task, but the enjoyment comes from 'what goes into it. Lots of concentration, very realistic if it's like horror' and the satisfaction from 'just enjoying myself, using imagination wisely.' Joanne's explanation for revising work echoes many of their concerns:

> Sometimes I judge my work on if it expresses . . . or if I thought I got what I meant over. Sometimes you write poems and they don't get the point over you wanted. It's the words, they could mean two things at the same time.

Creating a writing community: Emma and Rosie in conversation

Unknown to each other, both writers chose to write about their relationship. Emma chose 'one of the bits with most feeling in' from her journal but, conscious of her audience, changed it 'to make it more like a story.' During the writing, 'all I could think about was her, all the time' and the detailed events of the story illustrate the way that strong feelings raise vivid memories, especially her references to the way Rosie looked at her.

Emma's story is shown below:

> It was just an ordinary day. I pulled up the shutters and the sun shone in my eyes. I crept down stairs to find my mum sitting on the sofa.
> She said, 'Don't forget you're going to Sarah's and the pictures.'
> When I got to school, Sarah was already in class. She is a quiet girl and quite a laugh. She has brown hair, a big smile and a bad temper too! The day passed quite fast. On the way home, I couldn't wait to get to Sarah's house. I got home and changed and was ready to go.
> When I got to Sarah's house she started being fussy. She didn't really like what I was wearing. I could tell she wasn't in a good mood with me. Her mum was a good cook and made a lovely meal. In the car, Sarah and the rest of us were excited. Her mum left us having made sure we were in our seats. She had some shopping to do.

It didn't feel right or like being Sarah's friend. For once in my life I felt not wanted. I could see the hatred in her eyes. She kept looking at me, giving me evil looks. It was nearly time for the film to start. Sarah looked over every few seconds so I pulled faces back at her and she turned away. I went to the toilet to get away from her but I could still picture her in my mind. I was going to my seat when I saw Sarah in my seat. I gave her an evil look as she often did to me. She moved, whispering to Claire and I could tell it was about me.

After the film, she continued to be horrible. In the car she was trying to ignore me. That's how it seemed anyway. I was never going to talk to her again. I went home and cried. I thought she was a friend I would never lose.

Writing as spectator of her own experiences encouraged reflective revisiting and evaluation of the events and enabled her to begin to deal with her sadness. Knowing that this work would be publicly shared was also a factor in the writing.

Ironically, Rosie too was concerned with their friendship, but her poems bear little relationship to the events described in her journal (Figure 30). She chose to write in a more generalised way, crafting her concerns into a first poem where addressing the audience for help and advice seems to be parallel with Emma's tacit plea for reconciliation. Both girls wrote from very strong feelings. Both were unable

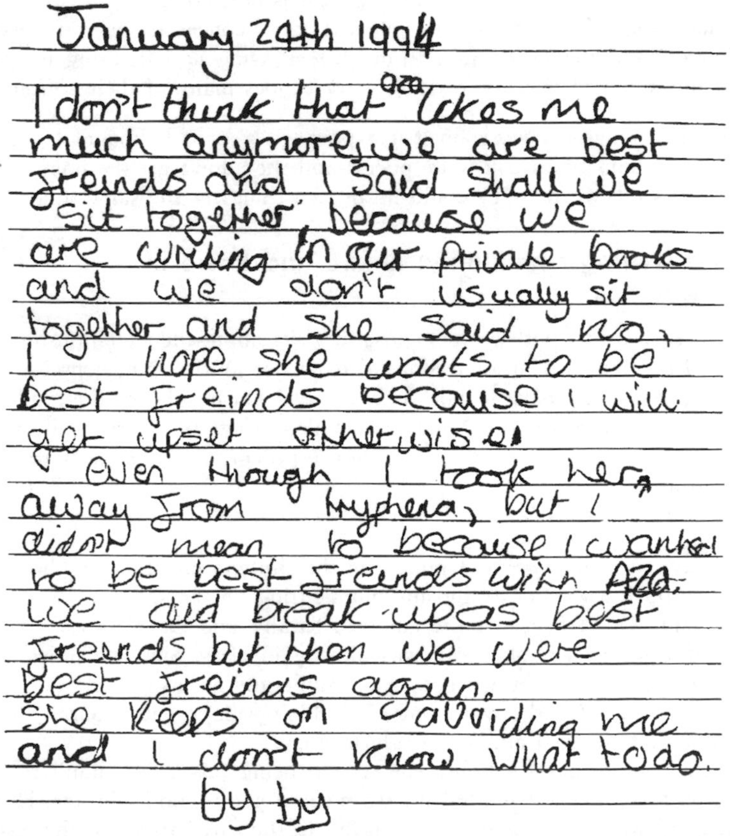
January 24th 1994
I don't think that Aza likes me
much anymore, we are best
freinds and I said shall we
sit together, because we
are writing in our private books
and we don't usually sit
together and she said no,
I hope she wants to be
best freinds because I will
get upset otherwise.
Even though I took her
away from Tryphena, but I
didn't mean to because I wanted
to be best freinds with Aza.
We did break up as best
freinds but then we were
best freinds again.
She keeps on avoiding me
and I don't know what to do.
by by

Figure 30 Rosie's journal

to understand their situation. Both expected that writing about it might help. Here is Rosie's first poem:

> Why is she, so horrible to me?
> Why is she so mean?
> I wonder if you know because I honestly don't.
> Why do we constantly argue?
> Why do I sometimes feel such hate?
> I wonder if you know because I honestly don't.
> Why is there such envy between us?
> Why are we such enemies?
> I wonder if you know because I honestly don't.

Rosie insisted that no spite was intended:

> Me and Emma are always arguing. It wasn't to get back at her. Emma's story isn't all true. I can't remember. She was arguing with me as well and I was getting really angry and we were allowed to fictionalise it. She was nice enough to change my name.

Once the two girls had read each other's work, Rosie wrote a second poem that suggested some reconciliation, and both agreed that sharing their writing had enabled them to 'know how each other feel and stops us arguing. We know both sides.'

> *Arguments with Emma*
>
> Emma always slaps me,
> And I slap her back.
> Emma called me stupid,
> So I called her fat.
> Emma pulled my hair,
> And I pulled her's back.
> Emma said, 'Sorry',
> And I said it back.

These are examples of the writer crafting an artefact in words where the affective is the dynamic force. Emma's narrative account is very simply told but the feelings are strongly expressed. Rosie's confident and competent handling of two different genres of poetry shows how the form moulds the material, for the first one, with its repetitive refrain, suggests a sense of something to be resolved, which the tight rhyming structure of her second poem clearly defines. The rhyming pattern expresses the balance in this relationship and countermands the power conflict implicit in Emma's story. They are friends again, although Emma is still seen as the protagonist.

Articulating themselves as writers

The pupils selected their own work for a class anthology, while giving reasons for their choices. It was obvious that they valued their work, not just for its technical merits, but because it speaks to them from the page. 'It makes me feel good', and 'This is about my sister leaving home and how I felt when it was happening.' Many comments were related directly to the spectator role in their writing. The observation that 'it made me feel as though I was really there' illustrates the way in which these young writers recognised their power to create and recreate worlds that interest, amuse or concern them.

Eleven-year-old Josh demonstrates this when writing and talking about his poem. Not only was he able to reconcile form and feeling in its creation, but he could also explain how this had been achieved. He also recognised his position in the community of writers within his class; however serious the subject, he knew that his audience would expect some humour.

> *Leaving*
> At the end of next month,
> I will be leaving,
> A new web of school,
> I will be weaving.
> Six weeks of worrying,
> I will be fretting,
> And loads more homework,
> I will be getting.

Teacher: Where did the idea come from?

Josh: I got a brain wave and wrote it in two minutes. I started with 'leaving' and 'weaving' and I thought 'basket', but it wasn't right.

Teacher: This is where the rhyme sent you . . .?

Josh: To other things. I thought of web and spider. I had a picture of weaving – classes, whole new web as if I've already weaved a web here and know everything about it, so I'd quite like to do a new one.

Teacher: What kind of things make the web?

Josh: All my friends, teachers, way round school, dinners. I'll be on the inside spinning towards the outside from year one to the end. And as I weave I'll know it from the inside to the outside.

Teacher: Where did the word 'fretting' come from?

Josh: 'Fretting' – from my mum. She lost her purse and said that she'd been fretting for ages. It was a different word for me; another kind of worry. I was rhyming alternate lines, so 'fretting' and 'getting' came together. The ending is funny because, as I'm serious first, I usually like to have some humour.

In Vygotskian tradition, Josh was perceptive enough to recognise that it is the rhyming pattern that leads him to new ideas (Vygotsky, 1962). He is thus able to create an extended metaphor, which gives him a new perspective on himself. He has shaped his thinking into a genre for publication, and so other pupils are able to share and learn from his insights.

Kate had felt 'that their writing, like their play ought to satisfy both their private and social needs'. Certainly private needs were met, but the pedagogy that had developed in this class had also enabled the pupils to use their writing to meet social needs. Like Anna, the student teacher quoted earlier, they discovered the potential of story and poetry for 'showing the meaning of a person's thought to others'. The forming influence of their chosen genre enabled them to share themselves with their peers by a process of 'metaphorical enactment' (Britton, 1993: 60).

New directions in the teaching of literacy brought about by the introduction of the Literacy Hour and the NLS require that pupils should be much more articulate about the processes of reading and writing. In whole-class and group reading and writing sessions they are actively encouraged to discuss, for example, the way they tackle new words, structure stories and write letters. However, pupils need to appreciate how the discrete elements of writing they daily practise can combine to satisfy 'both personal and social needs'. They must know why they write. This can happen only if teachers themselves realise the nature and function of writing. To achieve this, teachers need to move from tacit to conscious reflexive awareness, so that they, like their pupils, may learn not as objects of a prescribed curriculum, but as subjects of their own.

Conclusions

This chapter began by reaffirming the potential of writing to empower children to find and share their own voices. It advocated a writing pedagogy that would enable children to articulate themselves as writers, so that they could recognise writing as a means of both constructing and conveying meaning in their lives.

Britton's functional linguistic categories were introduced as a way of foregrounding the importance of recognising that writers do adopt different roles when they write. Appreciating the participant/spectator division can enable teachers to realise the learning potential for writing, especially within the expressive and poetic modes. The chapter then considered the way that current curricula for both schools and ITT, together with national testing of writing, are likely to restrict classroom practice, unless teachers become more effective practitioners. To achieve this, they need to develop their own knowledge and understanding about writing.

Using examples of classroom practice at Key Stages 1 and 2, the chapter demonstrated how two teachers were able to draw upon their explicit understanding of writing and the writing process to enable children to:

- use expressive writing in the form of think books;
- adopt the spectator role within the poetic mode to both 'construct and convey' their own voices.

Throughout the chapter, a central theme has been emphasised: namely that children need to be able to become writers who can choose their own subjects and genres, discuss their own composing processes and recognise the learning that can take place through revision and redrafting. In this way, they can be writers whose work does, indeed, empower them to take part in conversations both with themselves and others from the very beginning of their literacy development.

References

Applebee, A. N. (1978) *The Child's Conception of Story,* Chicago: University of Chicago Press.
Applebee, A. N. (1984) *Contexts for Learning to Write,* Norwood: N. J. Ablex.
Baker, D., Clay, J. and Fox, C. (eds) (1996) *Challenging Ways of Knowing: in English, Maths and Science,* London: Falmer Press.
Britton, J. (1982) *Prospect and Retrospect: Selected Essays of James Britton,* Montclair: Boynton/Cook.
Britton, J. (1993) *Literature in Its Place,* Portsmouth, NY: Boynton and Cook/Heinemann.
Britton, J., Burgess, A., Martin, N., Macleod, A. and Rosen, H. (1975) *The Development of Writing Abilities, 11–000,* London: Macmillan.
Bruner, J. (1960) *The Process of Education,* New York: Vintage.
Department for Education (1995a) *English in the National Curriculum,* London: HMSO; Cardiff: Welsh Office Education Department.

Department for Education and Employment (1997b) 'Annex B: Initial Teacher Training National Curriculum for English Teaching', in *High Status, High Standards of the Teacher Training Agency*, London: DfEE.

Department for Education and Employment (1998) *The National Literacy Strategy: Framework for Teaching*, Sudbury: DfEE Publications.

Department of Education and Science (1989) *English for Ages 5–16* [The Cox Report], London: HMSO.

Durst, R. K. and Newell, G. E. (1989) 'The Uses of Function: James Britton's Category System and Research on Writing', *Review of Educational Research*, 59(4): 75–94.

Elbow, P. (1973) *Writing without Teachers*, New York: Oxford University Press.

Harding, D. W. (1960) 'Psychological Processes on the Reading of Fiction', in *British Journal of Aesthetics*, 2(2).

Medwell, J., Wray, D., Poulson, L. and Fox, R. (1998) *Effective Teachers of Literacy: A Report of a Research Project Commissioned by the Teacher Training Agency*, Exeter: University of Exeter.

Qualifications and Curriculum Authority (1998d) *Standards at Key Stage 1 English and Mathematics: Report on the 1998 National Curriculum Assessments for 7 Year Olds*, London: QCA.

Robinson, J. (1990) *Conversations on the Written Word: Essays on Language and Literacy*, Portsmouth, New Hampshire: Boynton and Cook/Heinemann.

Vygotsky, L. S. (1962) *Thought and Language*, Cambridge, MA: MIT Press.

Willinsky, J. (1990) *The New Literacy: Redefining Reading and Writing in the Schools*, New York: Routledge.

POSTSCRIPT
The journey continues

Teresa Grainger

Although the knowledge and understanding demonstrated by all our guides about the world of language and literacy has deep roots in the soil, their ongoing research and reflection will continue to yield new insights and literacy will continue to change. The challenge for the traveller is not only to grapple with the theoretical perspectives and underpinning principles offered, but also to consider the consequences for our practice in whatever sphere. A response is demanded from each one of us, as individuals and as educationalists. The contributors to this Reader, guides on our expedition, deserve at least that and the children of tomorrow deserve even more. Like Lyra and Will, the fictional heroines, from Philip Pullman's trilogy, they deserve informed guidance and imaginative support as they travel through challenging territory into new worlds.

The consequences of the research evidence and discussions offered here suggest at the very least there are ramifications in relation to curriculum design and the curriculum in action. However, in order to adapt and transform the curriculum effectively, the reflective and investigative nature of education professionals, who explore their understanding and research their practice, needs to be both more widely recognised and genuinely valued by parents, policy makers and politicians. With a wider vision and a clearer sense of direction, pathways into the future can be mapped, informed by the multiplicity of personal and textual experiences, interests and expertise of the learners. The recognition that literacy can be liberating, dominating or exploitative is central to finding a way forward and to developing a fuller understanding of what it means to be critically literate in the twenty-first century. In questioning taken-for-granted representations of the world, and in learning what literacy is good for and whose perspective it represents, as well as whose purposes it serves, young people can learn how texts work in the world.

Playing our way forward, we need to create environments of possibility, which offer opportunities for such critical text analysis and encompass choice and the chance to experiment with ideas, with forms of language and different modes of communication. In an increasingly uncertain world, both teachers and children need to develop the ability to adapt to conditions of enduring unpredictability and contestability and learn to tolerate the ambiguity of living. In the classroom, we should be supporting children in handling the challenge of change, and enabling them to appreciate multiple viewpoints through interrogating and inhabiting texts in ways that challenge their understanding, transform their perspectives and develop their critical literacy.

Teachers too, need to feel sufficiently secure in their subject knowledge and pedagogical understanding to take risks, raise questions, explore different stances and live with the emotional discomfort of operating under uncertainty. Adopting a broader conception of literacy, teachers need to recognise the varied literacy practices which children engage in at home and in their communities, and offer rich textual encounters that bridge between the children's own cultural capital (Bordieu, 1977) and the culture of school. In this way children can learn through language and about language in ways that capture their imagination, link to their popular cultural world and engage them cognitively, affectively and aesthetically. The official curriculum cannot be ignored, but it can and must be reshaped and transformed in response to the changing face of communication, the shifting landscape of literacy and the complexity of children's meaning-making practices. The challenge is ours, the journey continues.

ANNOTATED BOOKLIST

Mapping the landscape of literacy

Barton, D., Hamilton, M. and Ivanic, R. (2000) *Situated Literacies: Reading and Writing in Context* London: Routledge

This scholarly yet accessible book offers a varied collection of writings from international authors on emergent literacy practices in specific situations. It makes a real contribution to understanding the ways in which such practices are part of wider social processes, and explores the functions of literacies in shaping and sustaining identities in communities of practice. Building upon an earlier text by Barton and Hamilton, (1998) *Local Literacies: Reading and Writing in One Community* (London: Routledge) many of the authors make use of detailed ethnographies to demonstrate the argument about the existence of multiple situated literacies. David Barton, in his chapter, also makes a powerful case about the need for teachers to research their own literacy practices as well the everyday practices around them, as he observes both the researcher and the researched can learn more about literacy through this process. The New Literacy Studies are valuably examined by Paul Gee and Janet Maybin in separate chapters which both contextualise this movement, and explore the distinctive nature of its research insights into the exploration and theorisation of the social and cultural aspects of people's literacy activities.

Lankshear, C. (1997) *Changing Literacies* Buckingham: Open University Press

This book seeks to establish and interpret the nature and scope of ongoing educational change. Through a critical and socio-cultural perspective, Lankshear explores the debates and discourses around literacy, drawing on diverse settings. He examines how language and literacy are framed within different social practices and how these in turn shape and frame language and literacy. He argues about the importance of critical language awareness and, through classroom snapshots of students' social practices with new technologies in home and community settings, reveals massive differences in teachers' understandings of new technologies and their interrelatedness. Acutely aware of issues of social justice, and the complexity of the forces which bear upon culture creation in the classroom, Lankshear raises many questions and sets the agenda for future research.

Exploring literacy and learning

Wray, D., Medwell, J., Poulson, L. and Fox, R. (2002) *Teaching Literacy Effectively in the Primary School* London: Routledge/Falmer

This book emerged from a TTA commissioned project into effective teachers of literacy undertaken by David Wray and his team in the late 1990s, which aimed to identify the key factors in what such teachers know, understand and do in the classroom context. It was clear these professionals saw the creation of meaning as the purpose of teaching literacy and used high quality shared texts to contextualise their teaching of knowledge about language. They also emphasised the function and purpose of such learning and had strong and coherent belief systems which guided their approaches and their selection of materials. A key issue raised by this work concerns the professional development opportunities offered to teachers and the significance of researching their own practice as part of personal/professional growth and curriculum development.

David, T., Raban, B., Ure, C., Goouch, K., Jago, M., Barriere, I. and Lambirth, A. (2000) *Making Sense of Early Literacy: A Practitioner's Perspective* Staffs: Trentham

This book draws on research and development projects based in four different countries: Australia, England, France and Singapore and examines early literacy learning in these post-industrial societies. The work was cross cultural rather than comparative and sought to make sense of the understandings held by early childhood educators in the different pre-school settings. Examples of children engaged in literate play with the encouragement of their teachers enrich the text, which examines conceptions of childhood, playful approaches to early learning, and the concept of teachable moments. In particular, Ticia David and her colleagues high-light the importance of local learning communities in providing support and interaction between practitioners. Through such networks, knowledge and understanding, ideas and practices can be shared and developed. The book itself is a good example of such networks operating at both local and international levels.

Exploring oral texts

Wells, G. (1999) *Dialogic Enquiry: Towards a Sociocultural Practice and Theory of Education* Cambridge: Cambridge University Press

In this book, Gordon Wells focuses on how children learn and draws upon Vygotsky's seminal ideas on learning and development, as well as Halliday's functional approach to language as a social semiotic. He seeks to exploit their complementarity in order to investi-gate the discourse of teaching and learning in school. Examples from the classroom are used to explore the forms of oral discourse that mediate educational activities, and the genre of discussion he calls 'progressive discourse'. The zone of proximal development is revisited, re-examined and widened, to encompass a multiplicity of forms of assistance and to consider the complex transformations in learning.

Taylor, P. *The Drama Classroom: Action, Reflection, Transformation* (2000) London: Routledge Falmer

In this text, Philip Taylor examines the drama praxis of two influential drama educators, Cecily O'Neill and David Booth and explores how particular tenets of their work, such as pre-text and the nature of storydrama, can be understood in the classroom. In using exam-ples from a wide range of age groups, Taylor demonstrates the role of engagement, reflection and transformation in the context of a changing conceptualisation of the drama curriculum. He explores how drama praxis can create satisfying partnerships that value the individual, profile reflective insights and transform those involved. Such partnerships, Taylor argues, can liberate educators to examine their curriculum and themselves in new ways.

Exploring visual texts

Anderson, A. and Styles, M. (2000) *Teaching through Texts* London: Routledge

This edited collection profiles pictorial texts and examines strategies for the informed explora-tion of a wider than normal range of genres with an emphasis on popular culture. In the dozen, short but accessible chapters, rich descriptions of imaginative practice are shared examining for example the use of the *Beano*, the book and the film of *James and the Giant*

Peach, environmental print, catalogues and travel brochures, rhythm and rhyme and the use of playscripts and improvised drama. Opportunities for flexible and responsive teaching and learning are made manifest in contexts which encourage and study the transformative nature of text exploration. Its partner text, *Where Texts and Children Meet* edited by Eve Bearne and Victor Watson (2000, London: Routledge) also grew out of a significant Homerton College Conference on the subject and is well worth reading too. *Teaching through Texts* shows how an understanding of visual and other texts can enrich classroom endeavour, build upon the world of popular culture and make connections between literacies old and new.

Cliff Hodges, G., Drummond, M.J. and Styles, M. (2000) *Tales, Tellers and Texts* London: Cassell

This edited collection examines oral, visual and historical new narratives and highlights the range of ways in which stories are currently encountered in traditional and popular forms. It celebrates the diversity of children's experiences and argues that learners need to hear different narrative voices in order to make them sound for themselves in both reading and writing. The writers draw on the work of Bruner (1986) to show that narrators 'traffick in human possibilities rather than in settled certainties' and are therefore involved in boundary crossing and potentially empowering engagements with texts. Professional storytellers, authors and a museum education officer share their perspectives alongside academics, widening the views and voices offered. Some explore the potential for creative play in investigating and studying narratives in the classroom, others closely examine the nature and construction of particular types of narrative. Eve Bearne closes the book with a consideration of the challenge of new texts and highlights how the grammars of texts offer signposts to guide the reader through visual, verbal, multimedia or multi-modal texts.

Exploring written texts

Hall, K. (2003) *Listening to Stephen Read: Multiple Perspectives on Literacy* Buckingham: Open University Press

This imaginatively constructed text takes as its focus one child as a reader, and examines the responses of eight academics to a video and transcript of Stephen reading and retelling *Bear* by Mick Inkpen. A miscue analysis was also made. Hall divides the text into four parts, and uses the scholars' views to illuminate particular perspectives on reading. A pyscho-linguistic perspective, cognitive–psychological perspective, a socio-cultural perspective and a socio-political stance are all examined in order to demonstrate the complex and multi-dimensional nature of reading and literacy. Areas of commonality are drawn out, alongside evident differences of emphasis, which help to shape the argument that teachers must begin with the learners, not methods, frameworks or programmes and use their knowledge of literacy and learning to design appropriate teaching and learning environments that respond to learners' needs.

Sharples, M. (1999) *How We Write: Writing as Creative Design* London: Routledge

This text seeks to combine new insights into writing as design with an understanding of creativity and offers an account of the mental, physical and social aspects of writing. Using a range of examples from writers, both successful and unsuccessful, Mike Sharples examines the habits and strategies employed by them as he explores how children learn to write, cultural influences, the writing process and in particular creativity and the generation of ideas. He also explores the visual design of text and considers the future of writing in our technological age, noting that while linear writing is in decline, new forms of multimedia authoring demand not only the new skills of media integration, interactive design and web production, but also the key skills of imagination and creative design.

Changing English:
studies in reading and culture

EDITOR
Jane Miller, *Institute of Education, University of London, UK*

ASSOCIATE EDITOR
Susan A. Fischer, *Medgar Evers College, CUNY, USA*

Supported by an International Editorial Board

Changing English: studies in reading and culture is an established journal for English teachers at every level. The journal aims to encourage international dialogue between teachers and researchers and support teachers and schools on issues surrounding literacy and language. In particular, the journal considers the future of English as a subject in the context of its history and the scope for development and change.

Recent years have seen new arguments and new contents offered for English in many countries, at a time when governments have given issue in English teaching a new prominence. *Changing English* provides a forum for necessary debate and for evaluation of new perspectives.

The editors encourage articles and reviews from writers concerned with English teaching worldwide. Contributions are welcome which discuss development in aspects of language, literacy and literature teaching in a areas of the curriculum.

This journal is also available online. Please connect to www.tandf.co.uk/online.html for further information.

To request a sample copy please visit: **www.tandf.co.uk/journals**

SUBSCRIPTION RATES
2003 – Volume 10 (2 issues)
Print ISSN 1358-684X
Online ISSN 1469-3585
Institutional rate: US$244; £148
(includes free online access)
Personal rate: US$81; £47 (print only)
NATE members rate: £12 (print only)

 Carfax Publishing
Taylor & Francis Group

For further information, please contact Customer Services at either:
Taylor & Francis Ltd, Rankine Road, Basingstoke, Hants RG24 8PR, UK
Tel: +44 (0)1256 813002   Fax: +44 (0)1256 330245 Email: enquiry@tandf.co.u
Website: www.tandf.co.uk
Taylor & Francis Inc, 325 Chestnut Street, 8th Floor, Philadelphia, PA 19106, U
Tel: +1 215 6258900 Fax: +1 215 6258914 Email: info@taylorandfrancis.cor
Website: www.taylorandfrancis.com

ccen